Power and the Presidency in Kenya

In December 1963, Kenya formally declared its independence yet it would take a year of intense negotiations for it to transform into a presidential republic, with Jomo Kenyatta as its first president. Archival records of the independence negotiations, however, reveal that neither the British colonial authorities nor the Kenyan political elite foresaw the formation of a presidential regime that granted one man almost limitless executive powers. Even fewer expected Jomo Kenyatta to remain president until his death in 1978. *Power and the Presidency in Kenya* reconstructs Kenyatta's political biography, exploring the links between his ability to emerge as an uncontested leader and the deeper colonial and postcolonial history of the country. In describing Kenyatta's presidential style as discreet and distant, Anaïs Angelo shows how the burning issues of land decolonization, the increasing centralization of executive powers, and the repression of political oppositions shaped Kenyatta's politics. Telling the story of state-building through political biography, Angelo reveals how historical contingency and structural developments shaped both a man and an institution – the president and the presidency.

ANAÏS ANGELO is a postdoctoral researcher at the University of Vienna, where her research focuses on the history of presidentialism, political biographies, and women in politics in postcolonial Africa. She holds a Ph.D. in history from the European University Institute and has conducted extensive archival research in Kenya.

African Studies Series

The African Studies series, founded in 1968, is a prestigious series of monographs, general surveys, and textbooks on Africa covering history, political science, anthropology, economics, and ecological and environmental issues. The series seeks to publish work by senior scholars as well as the best new research.

Editorial Board
David Anderson, *The University of Warwick*
Catherine Boone, *The London School of Economics and Political Science*
Carolyn Brown, *Rutgers University, New Jersey*
Christopher Clapham, *University of Cambridge*
Michael Gomez, *New York University*
Richard Roberts, *Stanford University, California*
David Robinson, *Michigan State University*
Leonardo A. Villalón, *University of Florida*

Other titles in the series are listed at the back of the book.

Power and the Presidency in Kenya

The Jomo Kenyatta Years

ANAÏS ANGELO
University of Vienna

CAMBRIDGE
UNIVERSITY PRESS

University Printing House, Cambridge CB2 8BS, United Kingdom

One Liberty Plaza, 20th Floor, New York, NY 10006, USA

477 Williamstown Road, Port Melbourne, VIC 3207, Australia

314–321, 3rd Floor, Plot 3, Splendor Forum, Jasola District Centre, New Delhi – 110025, India

79 Anson Road, #06–04/06, Singapore 079906

Cambridge University Press is part of the University of Cambridge.

It furthers the University's mission by disseminating knowledge in the pursuit of education, learning, and research at the highest international levels of excellence.

www.cambridge.org
Information on this title: www.cambridge.org/9781108494045
DOI: 10.1017/9781108625166

© Anaïs Angelo 2020

This publication is in copyright. Subject to statutory exception and to the provisions of relevant collective licensing agreements, no reproduction of any part may take place without the written permission of Cambridge University Press.

First published 2020

Printed in the United Kingdom by TJ International Ltd, Padstow Cornwall

A catalogue record for this publication is available from the British Library.

Library of Congress Cataloging-in-Publication Data
Names: Angelo, Anaïs, 1987– author.
Title: Power and the Presidency in Kenya : The Jomo Kenyatta Years / Anaïs Angelo.
Description: Cambridge, United Kingdom ; New York, NY : Cambridge University Press, 2020. | Series: African studies | Includes bibliographical references and index.
Identifiers: LCCN 2019037029 (print) | LCCN 2019037030 (ebook) |
  ISBN 9781108494045 (hardback) | ISBN 9781108713832 (paperback) |
  ISBN 9781108625166 (epub)
Subjects: LCSH: Kenyatta, Jomo. | Kenya–Politics and government–1963-1978. |
  Kenya–History–1963– | BISAC: HISTORY / Africa / General
Classification: LCC DT433.583.A64 2020 (print) | LCC DT433.583 (ebook) |
  DDC 967.6204–dc23
LC record available at https://lccn.loc.gov/2019037029
LC ebook record available at https://lccn.loc.gov/2019037030

ISBN 978-1-108-49404-5 Hardback

Cambridge University Press has no responsibility for the persistence or accuracy of URLs for external or third-party internet websites referred to in this publication and does not guarantee that any content on such websites is, or will remain, accurate or appropriate.

To my parents, Annik and Vladimir.

To my parents, Anita and Vladimir

Contents

Acknowledgments		*page* viii
	Introduction	1
1	Kenyatta's Stateless Political Imagination	38
2	From Prison to Party Leader, an Ambiguous Ascension (1958–1961)	66
3	Kenyatta, Land, and Decolonization (1961–1963)	95
4	Independence and the Making of a President (1963–1964)	115
5	Kenyatta, Meru Politics, and the Last Mau Mau (1961/3–1965)	141
6	Taming Oppositions: Kenyatta's "Secluded" Politics (1964–1966)	179
7	Ruling over a Divided Political Family (1965–1969)	219
8	"Kenyatta Simply Will Not Contemplate His Own Death" (1970–1978)	250
	Conclusion	266
Sources		276
Bibliography		280
Index		304

Acknowledgments

First and foremost, I thank Dirk Moses for the trust and constant support he put in this project from the early drafts of my dissertation, on which this book is based, to the publication stage. His comments and corrections not only greatly improved my work, but also broadened my intellectual horizon. Daniel Branch and Federico Romero, who acted as co-supervisor and second reader, provided generous encouragements and insightful suggestions throughout the writing of my thesis. John Lonsdale was an equally great source of intellectual support and I would especially like to thank him for his detailed reading of the final draft, which helped me to improve it further.

My research greatly benefited from the support of the French Institute for Research in Africa (IFRA), and in particular that of its directors, Christian Thibon and Marie-Emmanuelle Pommerolle who warmly welcomed me into their teams. The British Institute of Eastern Africa (BIEA) also provided great support. I thank its director Joost Fontein, who introduced me to join his team and its assistant director Freda Nkirote, whose help was precious to organize my research trip to Meru. This trip would not have been so productive without the help of Njuguna Gĩchere of the Nairobi National Museum and of Reverend Stephan Mûgambî, who literally opened their doors and address books to me. I am also indebted to John Kirugia of the National Museum in Meru, who acted as much more than an assistant, and without whom the long trips within the district would not have been half as informative and entertaining. I must also thank Caroline Elkins, who without knowing me personally, kindly provided contacts and recommendations for my research trips. The Kenyan National Commission for Science, Technology & Innovation has made my research in Kenya possible by issuing me with a research permit, for which I am grateful. The Department of African Studies at the University of Vienna provided the ideal framework to turn this dissertation into a book. I thank more particularly Kirsten Rüther for her support, her advice, and unceasing enthusiasm for my work.

The European Union Institute (EUI), IFRA and BIEA administrative teams were of incredible help. I thank in particular Anna Coda, Marion Asego, John Arum, Humphrey Mathenge, Janet Njoroge, and Fabian. Furthermore, my research in the Kenyan archives was facilitated by the incredible work of Richard Ambani and Peterson Kithuka, who dug out so many "lost" files for me.

Research for this book was made possible by the financial support provided by my employment through the Ecole des Hautes Etudes en Sciences Sociales (School for Advance Studies in the Social Sciences) and the generous support of the EUI, which included several travel grants.

Throughout my academic training, I had the chance to meet professors and researchers who took time to discuss my ideas and whose helpful suggestions greatly improved my work, and whom I would like to thank: David Anderson, Bertrand Badie, Jean-François Bayart, Anna Bruzzone, Nic Cheeseman, Hélène Charton, Ariel Colonomos, Dominique Connan, Frederick Cooper, the late Jan-Georg Deutsch, Yvan Droz, Marie-Aude Fouéré, Yves Gounin, Musambayi Katumanga, Gabrielle Lynch, Hervé Maupeu, Robert Maxon, Godfrey Muriuki, Anne-Marie Péatrik, Ellen Spence Poteet, and Tom Wolf. Finally, I would like to thank the two anonymous reviewers, for their thoughtful comments and suggestions that improved this project further.

I thank my corrector Julie Northey for her diligent and continuous support. I thank my friends for their long-term support despite the many kilometers and months that often separated us. My family has been a unique source of support, and treated me to becoming fully engaged with Kenyan history to better understand my project. I want to thank them for their unceasing and loving encouragements, which strengthened me through these years. This book would certainly not exist without my husband, Jakob Lehne, who took the time to read and discuss every part of it. His unfailing support, patience, and love for endless discussions have been immensely helpful throughout this project.

Introduction

October 20, Mashujaa Day (Heroes' Day), celebrates Kenya's heroes who contributed to the struggle for independence. It commemorates the declaration of the Emergency by the British colonial government in 1952, in the midst of the Mau Mau violent uprising, and the arrest of Mzee Jomo Kenyatta, who was accused of leading the Mau Mau movement. Some sixty years later, on October 20, 2015, as I sat in a local canteen in Makutano town, Meru district, an old television high up on the wall was showing the British documentary "End of Empire. Chapter 12: Kenya."[1] One could hear the late politicians Bildad Kaggia and Fred Kubai, who were arrested by the British government alongside Kenyatta on October 20, 1952, affirming in an interview that Jomo Kenyatta was no Mau Mau, and knew nothing about the movement. Due perhaps to the poor quality of sound and image, the program did not arouse much curiosity in the restaurant. No one seemed to care about the documentary: a disinterest that tempered this surprising choice of film to be broadcast on Mashujaa Day.

Less than thirty kilometers away from Makutano is the Mau Mau Veteran Centre of Muthara, still in Meru district. There, the well-known photograph of President Mzee Jomo Kenyatta embracing the Mau Mau leader Field Marshal Mwariama (when the two met immediately after Kenya became a republic in 1964) is proudly exhibited on the picture wall of this humble museum. It has been placed prominently in between pictures of M'Iminuki Linyiru, Meru's first paramount chief, and of Mwariama himself shortly before his death in 1989, his hair cut short and wearing a Western-style beige suit with a black tie. Below is a series of pictures of aged Mau Mau veterans, facing the camera with expressionless faces. This famous picture of Kenyatta can be found displayed in various publications, on Internet

---

[1] "End of Empire," Granada Television.

websites, and in museums.[2] To historians, the ambiguity that defined Kenyatta's relationship to Mau Mau fighters is no longer doubted. Research has shown how Kenyatta failed to acknowledge the painful sacrifices the Mau Mau war brought to those involved, willingly or not, in the movement.[3] Even so, many veterans continue to affirm that Kenyatta was "the owner of Mau Mau."

The photograph of Kenyatta and Mwariama confirmed the endurance of Kenyatta's ambiguity to this day. It showed, once again, that asking after his "true" relationship to the Mau Mau war continues to produce very different answers in very different settings. The odd combination of photographs, that of a paramount colonial chief, of Kenyatta embracing Mwariama during the crucial meeting that brought together the president and the Mau Mau fighters, and of Mwariama's polished appearance twenty-five years later, far away from any Mau Mau symbolism, seeks to portray a different narrative. It suggests of course a clear continuity between the Mau Mau war and independence. Most importantly, the Mau Mau narrative seems to have overshadowed that of the transition from colony to post-colony. The president is not pictured as a nationalist fighter: he is pictured as a friend of the Mau Mau.

This picture is unique. No other nationalist leader is shown, at least in public Kenyan institutions, embracing Mau Mau leaders. Does this singularity explain how Kenyatta became the first president of independent Kenya? This question goes beyond the findings of historical studies that showed how a new independent state was built to tame the Mau Mau movement, emphasizing in particular the creation of a loyalist government and administration in the wake of the Mau Mau war. It asks, instead, why such a political system functioned with Mzee Jomo Kenyatta as its "sole spokesman."[4] In other words, why Kenyatta?

---

[2] For further insights on visual construction of these national narratives, see Chloé Josse-Durand, "Le 'Temps des Musées': Bâtir les Mémoires Locales, Donner Corps au Récit National. L'Hybridation de l'Institution Muséale au Prisme des Appropriations Contemporaines du Passé au Kenya et en Ethiopie" (Ph.D. diss., University of Bordeaux, 2016), chapter 4.

[3] See, for example, the work of Caroline Elkins, *Britain's Gulag: The Brutal End of Empire in Kenya* (London: The Bodley Head, 2014).

[4] I borrow the idea of the "sole spokesman" from Ayesha Jalal's *The Sole Spokesman: Jinnah, the Muslim League and the Demand for Pakistan* (Cambridge: Cambridge University Press, 1994).

Jomo Kenyatta: Biographical Background

Jomo Kenyatta was born around 1895, shortly before the East Africa protectorate formalized the process of colonization initiated in 1888 under the auspices of the (private) Imperial British East African Company.[5] This was a time when British colonization was still at its early stages in Kenya. At the heart of the development of the protectorate was the construction of a railway that was to link today's Kenyan coast with Uganda, facilitating colonial expansion, European settlement, and commerce.[6] From 1902, European settlement was encouraged to boost the export of the British colony.[7] In 1903 and 1904, ever more Europeans arrived, acquiring and claiming ever more land for agricultural and ranching purposes in what became known as the "White Highlands," the central uplands that encompassed the most fertile lands stretching over Kalenjin, Kikuyu, and Maasai territory. Nevertheless, Kenya never officially became a settlers' colony, where colonial immigration implies the displacement and even elimination of natives, in contrast to exploitation colonies that focused on the extraction of production surplus. White settlers and British administrators differed strongly about the politics of immigration and of land alienation to be adopted. White settlers aspired to turn Kenya into a "white man's country," following the South African model. Yet, British government officials were undecided about the type of colonization they wanted to promote in Kenya, seeking also to protect the indigenous rights over land.[8]

British indecisiveness regarding the colony's legal status became an urgent issue as land alienation progressed rapidly. The situation was particularly tense in Kikuyu country, where Kenyatta was from – he

---

[5] His exact birthday is unknown, Jeremy Murray-Brown, *Kenyatta* (London: George Allen & Unwin Ltd., 1972), 33.
[6] See John Lonsdale, "The Conquest of the Kenya State, 1895–1905" and Bruce Berman, "Coping with Contradictions: The Development of the Colonial State, 1895–1914," in *Unhappy Valley: Conflict in Kenya & Africa*, eds. Bruce J. Berman and John M. Lonsdale (London: James Currey, 1992), 13–44, 77–100.
[7] Robert M. Maxon, *East Africa: An Introductory History* (Morgantown: West Virginia University Press, 2009), 164.
[8] Maurice P. K. Sorrenson, *Origins of European Settlement in Kenya* (London: Oxford University Press, 1968), 1–5; Robert L. Tignor, *Colonial Transformation of Kenya: The Kamba, Kikuyu, and Maasai from 1900–1939* (Princeton, NJ: Princeton University Press, 2015), 155–156.

was born in Ngenda, in a district later known as Kiambu – and which quickly became a stronghold of colonial occupation. Legal conflicts multiplied over the definition and regulation of land tenure, opposing European formal laws to Kikuyu tribal practices. In 1902, the Crown Land Ordinance was passed: where land was occupied, indigenous rights should be protected, whereas unoccupied land would become the property of the Crown. The ordinance allowed Europeans to own land previously occupied by the Kikuyu, themselves reduced to the status of workers. A year later, the first Kikuyu reserves were created, confining the "natives" and forcing them sell their labor to cultivate land.[9] In 1905, the Colonial Office took over the administration of the protectorate. By then, land alienation had halted in Kikuyu country, but new socioeconomic problems were emerging in the reserves.

The political and economic confusion of the early years of colonization and land alienation produced a fragile status quo. Settler agriculture was developing rapidly (coffee and sisal were particularly successful exports) and as ever more land was alienated, European colonizers found it more profitable to force Africans to sell their labor, imposing taxes, low wages, coercion, and bans on cash-crop growing.[10] At first, they allowed Africans to "squat" – that is, to reside on their land in exchange for cultivation. Yet, the squatters' rights to land became restricted too, as the need for forced labor increased. Already in the early 1910s, the dramatic increase in the number of squatters showed the limits of this compromise. The opportunities within the squatter economy (rapid improvement of their living conditions and a subsequent demographic increase) could not, in an imperial economy, be boundless. The next decade of European economic expansion was accompanied by even more restrictive economic policies limiting their rights to own land, to accumulate livestock, and to grow food crops. A stronger state control was established too. More importantly, as land shortage increased, so did conflicts about land and labor rights.[11] This was a particularly disruptive situation for Kikuyu political, economic, and social organization.

---

[9] Ibid., 53, 176–186.
[10] Maxon, *East Africa*, 166; Charles Hornsby, *Kenya: A History since Independence* (London: IB Tauris, 2013), 32.
[11] See Tabitha Kanogo, *Squatters and the Roots of Mau Mau (1905–1963)* (London: James Currey, 1987), chapters 1 and 2.

The Kikuyu were the largest ethnic group in Kenya, followed by the Luo (second largest ethnic group), Luhya, Kamba, Kalenjin, the Maasai people, and number of smaller ethnic minorities.[12] They were also the most affected by colonial land alienation.[13] Land played a central role in defining the Kikuyu people: land tenure and labor forged and structured Kikuyu social relationships. As John Lonsdale noted, precolonial Kikuyu were not "politically – or in any other sense – a tribe."[14] They constituted, instead, a complex hierarchical society brought together by a common ethnic identity as well as strong lawmaking institutions.[15] They were a self-regulated group in which authority and power were civic virtues acquired through wealth, itself interpreted as a moral virtue.[16] Power and authority were the result of individual achievement and private accumulation that knew no institutional limitations other than those determined by social interaction.[17] With colonization and land alienation, more was at stake than mere economic or even geographical change: the very social organization of the Kikuyu people was disrupted.

---

[12] The geography of these ethnic groups corresponds roughly with the Kenya provinces after independence: Kikuyu: Central province; Luo, Luyha and Kamba: Western province; Kalenjin and Maasai: Rift Valley; Arab, Somali, and other minorities: Coast and Eastern provinces. Hornsby recalls that, in 1962, the Kikuyu represented 19 percent of the Kenyan population. See Hornsby, *Kenya*, 21–24. For an in-depth discussion of the notion of "tribe," its history and the distinction with that of "ethnicity," see John M. Lonsdale, "The Moral Economy of Mau Mau, Wealth, Poverty and Civic Virtue in Kikuyu Political Thought," in *Unhappy Valley*, 315–504.

[13] John Overton, "The Origins of the Kikuyu Land Problem: Land Alienation and Land Use in Kiambu, 1895–1920," *African Studies Review* 31, no. 2 (1988): 112–122. For a history of the development of colonial administration and economy, see Bruce Berman, *Control and Crisis in Colonial Kenya: The Dialectic of Domination* (Nairobi: East African Publishers, 1990).

[14] Lonsdale, "The Moral Economy of Mau Mau, Wealth, Poverty and Civic Virtue in Kikuyu Political Thought," 341.

[15] Ibid.   [16] Ibid., 334.

[17] Anne-Marie Peatrik, "Un Système Composite: L'Organisation d'Age et de Génération Des Kikuyu Précoloniaux," *Journal des Africanistes* 64, no. 1 (1994): 3–36; Greet Kershaw, *Mau Mau from Below* (Oxford: James Currey, 1997); Yvan Droz, "L'Ethos du Mûramati Kikuyu: Schème Migratoire, Différenciation Sociale et Individualisation au Kenya," *Anthropos* 95, no. 1 (2000): 87–98.

Kenyatta's concern for land issues came rather late. Born under the name of "Kamau wa Ngengi" ("*Kamau, son of Ngengi*") to ordinary peasants, he enjoyed a peaceful childhood in a traditional village. Kamau was still a young boy when his parents died. He went to live with his grandfather, a traditional witch doctor. In 1909, he encountered a white man for the first time, and, according to his biographer Jeremy Murray-Brown, was so fascinated by the stranger's act of writing that he decided to join the Togotho mission, where Scottish missionaries would educate him for the next five years. There, he converted to Christianity and was baptised Johnstone Kamau. He was also circumcised, purportedly according to Kikuyu tribal customs, yet, the circumcision was performed by a mission-trained nurse, Samuel Njoroge.[18]

Kenyatta had just completed his primary education with the Scottish missionaries and was about to leave village life to work in the colonial capital, Nairobi (to the despair of his missionary mentors), when the outbreak of World War I delayed his plans. To avoid forced enrolment, Kenyatta found refuge in Maasailand from 1916 to 1919. This is where he would have earned the nickname of *Kinyatta*, the Maasai word for the beaded belt he would wear.[19] A few years later, in the early 1920s, he was recruited by the Nairobi Municipal Council as store clerk and water reader. With the good salary he earned, he was now "one of the recognised figures of Nairobi," and led the life of a dandy, a privilege few natives enjoyed.[20] He did not show any particular interest in the nascent nationalist politics. Meanwhile, dissent was growing among the colonized population: living conditions worsened, land alienation expanded, and landless people were squeezed into the reserves. Because of the pressing issue of land alienation, the Kikuyu were the first to organize politically. The early 1920s saw the birth of a Kikuyu nationalist association. In 1922, the Kikuyu Central Association (KCA) was established to defend historical Kikuyu rights over land; it was to become the most influential political party.

Chance and opportunism led Kenyatta to join the KCA. Because of his good knowledge of English, he first helped the party as a translator in 1925–1926. When, in 1927, the KCA had the opportunity to send a representative overseas, Kenyatta's language skills and urbane

---

[18] Murray-Brown, *Kenyatta*, chapter 3. I thank John Lonsdale for this useful piece of information.
[19] Murray-Brown, *Kenyatta*, 53, 75, chapter 6.   [20] Ibid., 95.

manners tipped the scales in his favor. He might have seen an opportunity to further upgrade his lifestyle and to pursue education, for which he had been longing.[21] In 1929, he left behind his first wife and child and sailed for London. There, he struggled to meet Colonial Office officials, and had only few contacts within the small political and intellectual circles interested in African affairs. In 1930, he returned to Kenya, yet only briefly, for the KCA decided to send him again to press for the Kikuyu cause at the Colonial Office a year later.[22] Some KCA leaders doubted his ability to fully represent the Kikuyu (perhaps because his rebellious life had become seen as decadent), so he was accompanied by another Kikuyu, an Anglican from Murang'a (then Fort Hall) district, Parmenas Githendu Mukiri.[23] Once in England, Kenyatta realised, again, that the British authorities showed neither interest in him nor in the grievances of the Kikuyu, and he was quick to understand that he needed to build an authoritative voice, together with a stronger intellectual project before taking on the role of nationalist politician.[24]

Kenyatta's years abroad were that of a solitary figure navigating between political and intellectual mentors. He polished his political ideas through interaction with his few Labour friends, and sharpened his political language with the Pan-Africanist George Padmore, whom he met during his first stay in London and with whom he travelled to Moscow. Their trip eventually gained the attention of British intelligence, which suspected Kenyatta had communist sympathies – although Kenyatta had little liking for the ideology, affirming himself instead as a nationalist and a "big bourgeois."[25] The high point of

---

[21] Murray-Brown, *Kenyatta*, 106.
[22] Murray-Brown, *Kenyatta*, chapters 10–12.
[23] This is an important detail, for it highlights the nascent competition between two Kikuyu districts: Murang'a and Kiambu. See John M. Lonsdale, "Henry Muoria, Public Moralist," in *Writing for Kenya: The Life and Works of Henry Muoria*, eds. Wangari Muoria-Sal, Bodil F. Frederiksen, John M. Lonsdale, and Derek R. Peterson (Leiden: Brill, 2009), 36 and endnote 56.
[24] Bruce J. Berman and John M. Lonsdale, "The Labors of *Muigwuithania*: Jomo Kenyatta as Author, 1928–45," *Research in African Literatures* 29, no. 1 (1998): 16–17.
[25] Woodford McClellan, "Africans and Black Americans in the Comintern Schools, 1925–1934," *The International Journal of African Historical Studies* 26, no. 2 (1993): 380; Murray-Brown, *Kenyatta*, chapters 10–18. On British intelligence reports on Kenyatta, see Calder Walton, *Empire of Secrets: British Intelligence, the Cold War and the Twilight of Empire* (London: Harper Press,

Kenyatta's intellectual journey was reached in the form of a fortuitous encounter in 1934 with the well-known London School of Economics (LSE) professor of anthropology, Bronisław Malinowski.[26] Kenyatta realised that anthropology could become a "miraculous weapon" to defend Kikuyu land.[27] Under Malinowski's supervision, he completed a history of Kikuyu tribal culture, later published as *Facing Mount Kenya*, for which he was awarded a non-degree diploma in anthropological studies. It gave him the expert knowledge with which to advance his political arguments in colonial institutions, and to claim to represent his people as a traditional African leader. With the publication of his thesis in 1938, Kenyatta swapped his dandy outfit for a monkey fur and a hunting spear he found in a London costume shop. He signed himself for the first time under the name Jomo Kenyatta.[28]

2013), 258–273, chapter 6 more generally. Two other biographies were dedicated to Kenyatta as the latter was still alive, but lack the thoroughness of Murray-Brown's, see George Delf, *Jomo Kenyatta: Towards Truth about the Light of Kenya* (London: Gollancz, 1961); Guy Arnold, *Kenyatta and the Politics of Kenya* (Nairobi: Transafrican Publishers, 1974).

[26] See Berman's and Lonsdale's exhaustive research articles on Kenyatta's encounter and writing of anthropology: Bruce J. Berman and John M. Lonsdale, "Louis Leakey's Mau Mau: A Study in the Politics of Knowledge," *History and Anthropology* 5, no. 2 (1991): 143–204; "The Labors of Muigwuithania"; "Custom, Modernity, and the Search for Kihooto: Kenyatta, Malinowski, and the Making of *Facing Mount Kenya*," in *Anthropology, European Imperialism and the Ordering of Africa*, eds. Robert J. Gordon and Helen Tilley (Manchester: Manchester University Press, 2007), 176. See also Bruce Berman, "Ethnography as Politics, Politics as Ethnography: Kenyatta, Malinowski, and the Making of *Facing Mount Kenya*," *Canadian Journal of African Studies* 30, no. 3 (1996): 313–344; John M. Lonsdale, "The Prayers of Waiyaki; Political Uses of the Kikuyu Past," in *Revealing Prophets: Prophecy in Eastern African History*, eds. David M. Anderson and Douglas Hamilton Johnson (London: James Currey, 1995): 240–291; "'Listen While I Read': The Orality of Christian Literacy in the Young Kenyatta's Making of the Kikuyu," in *Ethnicity in Africa: Roots, Meanings & Implications*, eds. Louise de la Gorgendiere, Kenneth King, and Sarah Vaughan (Edinburgh: University of Edinburgh Centre of African Studies, 1996), 17–53.

[27] "The Miraculous Weapons" is the title of a collection of poems by Aimé Césaire, *Les Armes Miraculeuses* (Paris: NRF Gallimard, 1946).

[28] On the cover of the book, Kenyatta is wearing a fur one of his friends found in a shop selling carnival costumes in London. He grew a beard in solidarity with Haïlé Sélassié, who, at the time, had to flee from an invaded Ethiopia. He has long hair, another difference from the shaved head typical of the traditional Kikuyu chief. Yet, as the anthropologist Anne-Marie Peatrik noted, no elder would wear such a spear, reserved for warriors. Far from the dandy that he was in the 1930s (see the photographs in Murray-Brown's biography), this

As his friend and brother-in-law-to-be Mbiyu Koinange recalled, Jomo Kenyatta's public persona was both a literary and political invention:

> Jomo wore my Hyrax and blue monkey cloak for a photograph to be used in the author's preface to his book "Facing Mount Kenya". We sharpened a piece of wooden plank for a spear. Our main object was to give the book on Agikuyu by an elderly Mugikuyu - an elderly tone in contrast to books written by non-Africans about us ... This was followed by the cross-word puzzle to retain "J" in Johnston and the coining of an African name to go with Kenyatta. "Why all this trouble, man, don't you have a name?", I asked. He hesitated for a while still with his pen on the paper. I repeated my question, but his thoughts were still centred on the puzzle before us. "My name is Kamau" - and your father's name? I interrupted. "Ngengi" he replied. "Then why on earth are we taking all this trouble to find names while you have 'Kamau wa Ngengi'? You see, I am known by the name Kenyatta, I want to retain it." We proceeded to make a combination of vowels and consonants until we agreed on "Jomo".[29]

With the publication of *Facing Mount Kenya*, Jomo Kenyatta was no longer just a nationalist: he was a "man of science" *and* a "Kikuyu."[30] When he returned to Kenya in 1946, he was welcomed by a joyful crowd. Few people had read his book, but he was seen as a writer who possessed the "White man's magic."[31] Although he had achieved very little concretely, he was full of political hope. Little is known on Kenyatta's political activity once he arrived back in Kenya after eighteen years of voluntary exile in Great Britain. He married the daughter of the well-respected Kikuyu chief, Chief Koinange, and became "very deliberately, a senior elder."[32] He bought land, and built himself a

---

construction of authority has no ethnographic foundations. Anne-Marie Peatrik, "Le Singulier Destin de *Facing Mount Kenya. The Tribal Life of the Gikuyu* (1938) de Jomo Kenyatta. Une Contribution à l'Anthropologie des Savoirs," *L'Homme* 4, no. 212 (2014): 71–108.

[29] Mbiyu Koinange, "Jomo Colleague in the Struggle for Freedom and Independence" in *Struggle to Release Jomo and His Colleagues*, ed. Ambu H. Patel (Nairobi: New Kenya Publishers, 1963), 21–22.

[30] John M. Lonsdale, "Jomo Kenyatta, God & the Modern World," in *African Modernities: Entangled Meanings in Current Debate*, eds. Peter Probst, Heike Schmidt, and Jan-Georg Deutsch (Oxford: James Currey, 2002), 33.

[31] Lonsdale, "Henry Muoria, Public Moralist," 271.

[32] John M. Lonsdale, "KAU's Cultures: Imaginations of Community and Constructions of Leadership in Kenya after the Second World War," *Journal of African Cultural Studies* 13, no. 1 (2000): 114.

small farm.[33] He was positioning himself on the side of the "landed," and, what is more, on the side of the Kiambu he had represented when he left for England in 1928.[34] He wanted power. By now, he was a middle-aged man, educated in England, but he still needed local political recognition and support.[35] The prospect of working for the colonial institutions quickly faded away, and Kenyatta focused his energies on the African Teacher's Training College, a Kikuyu independent school his brother-in-law Peter Mbiyu Koinange had set up in Githunguri, Kiambu.[36] He was elected president of the Kenya African Union (KAU) in 1947, as James Gichuru (one of the KAU's founding fathers and soon-to-be Kenyatta's brother-in-law) stepped down for him. The KAU provided him with a useful political platform, but he knew the nationwide party could not overtake tribal loyalties. He needed a rural, traditional base just like Githunguri. Yet, in order to breathe political life into the Githunguri school, he needed money.[37] Accounts of his leadership are rather shady. The colonial authorities would later blame him for his corrupt management of the money raised for the sake of the school.[38]

The pace of political change in the aftermath of World War II seems to have left him with limited capacity to control events.[39] The

---

[33] Murray-Brown, *Kenyatta*, 230.   [34] Kershaw, *Mau Mau from Below*, 199.
[35] Delf, *Jomo Kenyatta*, 134.
[36] The Kikuyu Independence School Association emerged in the aftermath of the female circumcision controversy, which opposed the missionaries against the Kikuyu leaders. To defend a practice they considered inherent to their identity, the Kikuyu established their own schools. Kenyatta supported the movement initiated by his brother-in-law and close political comrade, Mbiyu Koinange. See Bodil F. Frederiksen, "Jomo Kenyatta, Marie Bonaparte and Bronislaw Malinowski on Clitoridectomy and Female Sexuality," *History Workshop Journal* 65, no. 1 (2008): 23–48; Theodore Natsoulas, "The Politicisation of the Ban on Female Circumcision and the Rise of the Independent School Movement in Kenya, the KCA, the Missions and Government, 1929–1932," *Journal of Asian and African Studies* 33, no. 2 (1998): 137–158. According to Murray-Brown, Kenyatta did not want to join a local council because its political scope was too restricted. He nonetheless became a member of the African Land Settlement Board from 1947 to 1949. See Murray-Brown, *Kenyatta*, 233.
[37] Murray-Brown, *Kenyatta*, 233–234.
[38] Frank D. Corfield, *The Origins and Growth of Mau Mau: An Historical Survey* (London: Her Majesty's Stationery Office, 1960), 182–189. See also Kershaw, *Mau Mau from Below*, 199–200.
[39] See Spencer's critical study of Kenyatta's leadership over the KAU in John Spencer, *KAU: The Kenya African Union*, first edition (London: Kegan Paul International, 1985).

economic boom triggered by the demands of the war economy boosted both settlers and indigenous farmers. But the British colonial government and the white settlers tighten their control over the lucrative colony. African representation in the colonial institutions increased extremely slowly. In 1947, the British colonial government agreed to increase the African representation in the Legislative Council (LegCo) to four seats, a very small concession for an educated elite committed to reformist changes. In 1950, Kenyatta wrote to the minister of state for the colonies, John Dugdale, to express his dissatisfaction and reminded him that at least half the seats should be reserved for Africans.[40] Although some constitutional reforms were promised, the British colonial government was ignorant of the rising dissatisfaction in the Highlands, where a desire for revolt was slowly growing.

The outbreak of the Mau Mau war embodied the frustration over the lack of development of African political representation and brutally halted Kenyatta's political ambitions. In contrast to the constitutionalist and nonviolent politics adopted by the KAU, Mau Mau freedom fighters claimed a radical version of Kikuyu nationalism for themselves. It was a revolt against land alienation, economic inequalities, and political oppression. Mau Mau fighters were convinced that the land British colonizers had acquired could only be retaken by force – a stance from which Kenyatta always disassociated himself.[41] Although agitation had been latent since the 1930s, the killing of the prominent Christian and anti-Mau Mau Senior Chief Waruhiu wa Kungu on October 7, 1952 convinced the British that the situation was serious

---

[40] Keith Kyle, *The Politics of the Independence of Kenya* (New York: Palgrave Macmillan, 1999), 43.
[41] Lonsdale, "KAU's Cultures." On interpretations of the outbreak of the Mau Mau war, see in particular Carl G. Rosberg and John C. Nottingham, *The Myth of 'Mau Mau': Nationalism in Kenya* (New York: Praeger, 1966); Don Barnett and Karari Njama, *Mau Mau from Within: Autobiography and Analysis of Kenya's Peasant Revolt* (New York: Monthly Review Press, 1966); Kanogo, *Squatters and the Roots of Mau Mau (1905–1963)*; David W. Throup, *Economic and Social Origins of Mau Mau 1945–1953* (London: James Currey, 1987); Frank Furedi, *The Mau Mau War in Perspective* (London: James Currey, 1989); Marshal S. Clough, *Mau Mau Memoirs: History, Memory, and Politics* (Boulder, CO: L. Rienner Publishers, 1998); Wunyabari O. Maloba, *Mau Mau and Kenya: An Analysis of a Peasant Revolt* (Bloomington: Indiana University Press, 1998); Kershaw, *Mau Mau from Below*; Elisha S. Atieno-Odhiambo and John Lonsdale, *Mau Mau & Nationhood: Arms, Authority & Narration* (Oxford: James Currey, 2003).

enough to declare a State of Emergency on October 20. It was a reaction not only against the Mau Mau movement, but also against all forms of African nationalism.[42] Kenyatta's relationship to the Mau Mau movement and more particularly its central committee was unclear. He attempted to distance himself from the movement and condemned it in speeches, asserting that: "He who has ears should now hear that KAU claims this land as its own gift from God ... He who calls us the MAU MAU is not truthful. We do now know this thing MAU MAU."[43] Yet, Kenyatta's idiosyncratic phrasing fell on deaf ears, as the extreme fear of Mau Mau violence quickly developed into a generalized paranoia.

The British colonial authorities believed not only that he was a Mau Mau leader, but also that the Githunguri college had been turned into headquarters for Mau Mau oath-taking. On the day the State of Emergency was declared, more than 180 leaders were arrested, among them Jomo Kenyatta and five other leaders of the Mau Mau central committee and the KAU: Bildad Kaggia, Paul Ngei, Kungu Karumba, Fred Kubai, and "Ramogi" Achieng-Oneko. Their trial was held at Kapenguria, a town in western Kenya. Despite a clear lack of evidence and Kenyatta's repeated assertion that he had always denounced the Mau Mau movement, he was found guilty of oathing and leading an illegal organization.[44] On April 8, 1953, after four months of what appeared to be a rigged trial, he was condemned to seven years of hard labor and indefinite restriction.[45] Together with Kaggia, Kubai, and Kungu Karumba, he was imprisoned in the remote Lokitaung, in the desert northern region, where British colonizers hoped they would be forgotten.

Because of his age (he was about sixty years old), Kenyatta was released from hard labor and served as a cook for his fellow prisoners. The detention conditions remained harsh nonetheless. The poor diet, chafing, and the desert climate caused him great skin torments. His

---

[42] Hornsby, *Kenya,* 40–43.
[43] Kenyatta's speech at a meeting at Nyeri on July 26, 1952 is quoted by Murray-Brown, *Kenyatta,* 244.
[44] Horsnby, *Kenya,* 48.
[45] See the records of his trial in Montagu Slater, *The Trial of Jomo Kenyatta* (London: Secker & Warburg, 1955); John M. Lonsdale, "Les Procès de Jomo Kenyatta. Destruction et Construction d'un Nationaliste Africain," *Politix* 17, no. 66 (2004): 190.

guards even expected him to die. His relations with the other prisoners were tense. Kaggia, Kubai, and Kungu Karumba were accusing Kenyatta of not being a true supporter of the Mau Mau movement or teasing him for not being the real author of his anthropological dissertation, *Facing Mount Kenya*. Kenyatta later found a friend in a new detainee, General China, a former Mau Mau leader captured in 1954 and detained in 1955. Thanks to China, who was acting as his bodyguard, Kenyatta escaped two assassination attempts.[46] As this book will show, his release in 1961 was mainly a political operation stage-managed by his fellow politicians in search of a political symbol. Most of his political contemporaries belonged to a much younger generation, carefully promoted by the British. They hoped that Kenyatta would be their pawn, and did not expect that a mere political symbol could turn into a powerful politician.

The outbreak of the Mau Mau war has been interpreted as a sign of Kenyatta's failure to assert his authority on the political scene.[47] This certainly holds true, but the exact explanations are still debated. John Lonsdale criticized the views that the KAU was unable to fulfill the demands of the impoverished Kenyan peasantry and the squatters. According to him, such views rely on an "all-inclusive, all-mobilizing view of nationalism" that disregard the political as well as the moral complexity of nationalist dynamics.[48] He insisted on the moral arguments that the (moderate) branch of the KAU defended. For Kenyatta, individual commitment to mutual respect was necessary to build authority. Without reciprocal moral values, Africans would be neither morally nor politically empowered. So, Kenyatta preferred the role of the Kikuyu elder to that of the doctrinaire, even if this caused him isolation and frustration.

Kenyatta was not out of touch with the political realities of his time. According to his biographer Murray-Brown, he "knew the crisis could not long be delayed."[49] Nevertheless, his relation to the Mau Mau movement remains enigmatic. As he recalled during his trial (and later upon his release), he denounced it on several occasions.[50] He always disassociated himself from them, claiming that the word did not

---

[46] Murray-Brown, *Kenyatta*, 291–295.
[47] Kershaw, *Mau Mau from Below*, chapter 7.
[48] Lonsdale, "KAU's Cultures," 111. [49] Murray-Brown, *Kenyatta*, 246.
[50] In April 1952, the KAU, Kenyatta's party, launched a campaign to dissociate themselves from the Mau Mau movement.

"belong to any of the languages that I do know" and emphasized that he "could not have been his (Mau Mau) friend if I did not know him ... it is an emphatic way of denying connection with something, but not just a mere 'I do not know'."[51] During the anti-Mau Mau campaign led by the KAU in 1952, Kenyatta insisted that he "told the people that the best thing to get rid of Mau Mau would be to look for it, put a rope round its neck; then find an axe handle, hit it on the head and finish with it for good."[52] His opposition did not alter after his imprisonment. In a meeting in Githunguri in September 1962, he described the Mau Mau as "hooligans" and "a disease which had been eradicated."[53]

The brutal Mau Mau war, combined with the destructive effects of colonization, had left an open wound on the country. Upon independence, President Kenyatta inherited a scarred Kikuyu community. The estimated number of 30,000 Mau Mau fighters or supporters stands in sharp contrast with the estimated statistics on the numbers of detainees in British camps: John Blacker's demographic study argues, however, that 50,000 Kikuyu died during the Emergency; David Anderson further added that close to 10,000 Mau Mau died in conflict.[54] During colonization, 7.5 million of acres had been alienated in the White Highlands (mostly in the Rift Valley and Central provinces), with 20 percent of the best lands declared Crown property, without proper compensation (or no compensation at all) provided to the dispossessed African families.[55]

Kenyatta also inherited an economically, socially, and politically divided country torn apart by the land issue. In the last decades of colonization, the European elite had favored a small, landed African bourgeoisie, tying economic favors and support to political interests, a critical step to conclude an independence deal favorable to the Europeans themselves.[56] As the independence negotiations established that land properties would not be redistributed for free, the squatters and

---

[51] Slater, *The Trial of Jomo Kenyatta*, 153–155.   [52] Ibid., 154.

[53] Jomo Kenyatta, *Suffering without Bitterness: The Founding of the Kenya Nation* (Nairobi: East African Publishing House, 1968), 189.

[54] John Blacker, "The Demography of Mau Mau: Fertility and Mortality in Kenya in the 1950s: A Demographer's Viewpoint," *African Affairs* 106, no. 423 (2007): 205–227; David Anderson, "Burying the Bones of the Past," *History Today* 55, no. 2 (2005).

[55] Hornsby, *Kenya*, 26.

[56] Colin Leys, *Underdevelopment in Kenya* (London: Heinemann, 1975), chapter 2.

landless Africans, those who had neither land rights, means to recover or acquire land, nor access to plots of land through traditional land sharing practice, were fundamentally excluded from Kenya's agricultural economy. The number of squatters rose at an alarming rate.[57] In 1948, they were estimated to be 220,000, roughly one quarter of the Kikuyu population, and this number continued to grow under the Emergency.[58] At independence, 92 percent of the Kenyan population still lived in rural areas, and land ownership was mostly familial, communal, or collective.[59] Statistical studies nonetheless leave us only with either incompatible or incomplete data that prevent us from having a comprehensive understanding of how many squatters remained throughout Kenya after independence: although an official government document estimated the remaining squatters at 75,000 families in 1965, these numbers were often underestimated.[60]

Understanding the President and the Presidency in Kenya

Kenyatta was a complex and multifaceted character, and his personal reinvention reflected the intricacies of both colonization and decolonization. Studying his leadership, biographers and historians have been confronted with a central contradiction. He seemingly lacked control over crucial political events, yet had a formidable ability to survive political crises, even though without achieving anything at all.[61] Furthermore, none of his political comrades or competitors was able to challenge his presidential seat during his fourteen years of rule. Rather vague descriptions of his leadership saw Kenyatta as an "enigmatic" leader, an oligarchic "prince," going so far as to stating that "as both

---

[57] On the making of a landed bourgeoisie, see Christopher Leo, "Who Benefited from the Million-Acre Scheme? Toward a Class Analysis of Kenya's Transition to Independence," *Canadian Journal of African Studies* 15, no. 2 (1981): 210–212, and, for a more general interpretation on a landed bourgeoisie and the rise of neocolonialism, see Leys, *Underdevelopment in Kenya*, chapter 3.
[58] Hornsby, *Kenya*, 37; Leys, *Underdevelopment in Kenya*, 47.
[59] Hornsby, *Kenya*, 21.
[60] See the 1965 "Precis of the Report on the Squatter Problem by the Special Commissioner for Squatters," Kenya National Archives (KNA), BN/97/3. See also Leys, *Underdevelopment in Kenya*, 63, footnote 1.
[61] Kershaw, *Mau Mau from Below*.

charismatic leader and founding father, [he] needed no philosophy to rule."[62] Nevertheless, the assumption of tribal politics and sporadic use of repression do not explain how he managed to maintain stability in an ethnically, regionally, and ideologically divided political class.

In contrast to other leaders of his generation, Kenyatta did not seek to distinguish himself through monumental national or ideological achievement. Unlike the leaders who built their names with well-defined ideological theories, like the Ghanaian Kwame Nkrumah (and his plea for Pan-Africanism), the Tanzanian Julius Nyerere (who theorized the idea of *ujamaa*, or the African family), the Senegalese Léopold Sédar Senghor (who formulated the concepts of negritude and the civilization of the universal), or even the Guinean Sékou Touré (who defended a strict vision of African socialism), Jomo Kenyatta remained estranged from any of the grand ideologies of the 1960s.[63] He had little interest in international politics, disliked travel, and hence delegated foreign affairs to his most trusted ministers, in particular to Joseph Murumbi (who alternately served as Kenya's representative at the United Nations, as second vice president, and as minister of foreign

---

[62] Mordechai Tamarkin, "The Roots of Political Stability in Kenya," *African Affairs* 77, no. 308 (1978): 298; Robert H. Jackson Jr. and Carl G. Rosberg, *Personal Rule in Black Africa: Prince, Autocrat, Prophet, Tyrant* (Berkley: University of California Press, 1982), 98–112; Hornsby, *Kenya*, 107. John Lonsdale made a clear plea against such clichés, dedicating large parts of his work to unveiling Kenyatta's political imagination. See Lonsdale, "Jomo Kenyatta, God & the Modern World." Despite such prominent attention, Kenyatta's postcolonial politics have remained understudied.

[63] During his London years, Kenyatta became close to Pan-Africanist intellectuals, in particular George Padmore with whom he travelled to the USSR. He also participated in the organization of the fifth Pan-African Congress in Manchester in 1945. His contribution remained fairly noncommittal, however, in contrast to Kenneth O. Nyangena, who stretches Kenyatta's Kikuyu ethics to some vague Pan-African horizon, see "Jomo Kenyatta: An Epitome of Indigenous Pan-Africanism, Nationalism and Intellectual Production in Kenya," *African Journal of International Affairs* 6, nos. 1–2 (2003): 1–18. For a more thorough discussion of Kenyatta's Pan-African ideas, see Simon Gikandi, "Pan-Africanism and Cosmopolitanism: The Case of Jomo Kenyatta," *English Studies in Africa* 43, no. 1 (2000): 3–27. The biographies of C. L. R. James and George Padmore offer useful insight to the minor role Kenyatta played in the Pan-Africanist movement, see Kent Worcester, *C. L. R. James: A Political Biography* (Albany: State University of New York Press, 1996); Leslie James, *George Padmore and Decolonisation from Below: Pan-Africanism, the Cold War, and the End of Empire* (New York: Palgrave Macmillan, 2014).

affairs) and his brother-in-law and close cabinet minister, Mbiyu Koinange.[64] Kenyatta's ideology as president was, in fact, the complete antithesis of a nationalizing campaign: he revived the long African tradition of self-help, "*harambee*" in Swahili, and this became his rallying cry, concluding each of his public speeches.

Literally meaning "let's pull together," *harambee* could be defined as communal self-help organizations set up on an ad hoc basis to provide social services and infrastructures locally.[65] Along with the public assemblies known as *baraza*, *harambee* is part of Kenya's "culture of politics."[66] Upon independence in 1963, *harambee* projects provided Kenyatta with a pragmatic tool with which to shape and impose his authority on the country, while more modern institutions like his party or the national assembly remained profoundly divided.[67] More importantly, *harambee* politics allowed Kenyatta to act as a unique arbitrator, supreme yet close to the people, a quality and image he cultivated throughout his rule.[68] Although the government would sponsor certain projects, at no point did *harambee* suggest a transfer of power from the state down to the local level, even if the political instrumentalization of *harambee* ceremonies, as well as the political

---

[64] Joseph Murumbi and Anne Thurston, *A Path Not Taken: The Story of Joseph Murumbi* (Nairobi: The Murumbi Trust, 2015). On Kenya's foreign policy, see John J. Okumu, "Some Thoughts on Kenya's Foreign Policy," *The African Review* 3, no. 2 (1973): 263–290; Samuel M. Makinda, "From Quiet Diplomacy to Cold War Politics: Kenya's Foreign Policy," *Third World Quarterly* 5, no. 2 (1983): 300–319; John Howell, "An Analysis of Kenyan Foreign Policy," *The Journal of Modern African Studies* 6, no. 1 (1968): 29–48; Harry Ododa, "Continuity and Change in Kenya's Foreign Policy from the Kenyatta to the Moi Government," *Journal of African Studies* 13, no. 2 (1986): 47–57; Asher Naim, "Perspectives – Jomo Kenyatta and Israel," *Jewish Political Studies Review* 17, nos. 3–4 (2005): 75–80.

[65] Joel D. Barkan and Frank W. Holmquist, "Peasant–State Relations and the Social Base of Self-Help in Kenya," *World Politics* 41, no. 3 (1989): 359–380.

[66] Haugerud provided an insightful analysis of the practice of *barazas* in Kenya, but did not study systematically Kenyatta's use of these public assemblies. See Angelique Haugerud, *The Culture of Politics in Modern Kenya* (Cambridge: Cambridge University Press, 1997).

[67] Njuguna Ng'ethe, *Harambee and Development Participation in Kenya* (Ottawa: Carleton University, 1979).

[68] Frank Holmquist, "Self-Help: The State and Peasant Leverage in Kenya," *Africa* 54, no. 3 (1984): 72–91.

use of the economic resources it fostered, stirred local political competition.[69] Nevertheless, Kenyatta's *harambee* philosophy should not overshadow specific concerns about his leadership.

The last thirty years have seen the development of a wide-ranging and fascinating historiography of postcolonial Kenya, with the more recent work of Keith Kyle, Charles Hornsby, and Daniel Branch helping to map the ever-growing field.[70] Nevertheless, none of this work provides an extensive analysis of the construction of the institution of the presidency upon the independence negotiations. It is this that is the main focus of this book. The question of the historical origins of presidentialism has all too often been ignored in the historiography dedicated to the formation of the African state.[71] An enquiry into the origin of the idea, its constitutional negotiation, and the historic actors who established it as a political system can provide answers to many questions that have long tormented political analysts. These include the authoritarian tendency of African presidents, the personalization of power, or the "synonymity" between the founding fathers of independence and their countries.[72] As this book shows, the birth of the presidency deserves thorough investigation – it cannot be

---

[69] E. Martin Godfrey and Gideon-Cyrus Makau Mutiso, "The Political Economy of Self-Help: Kenya's '*Harambee*' Institutes of Technology," *Canadian Journal of African Studies* 8, no. 1 (1974): 109–133; Philip M. Mbithi and Rasmus Rasmusson, *Self Reliance in Kenya: The Case of* Harambee (Uppsala: The Scandinavian Institute of African Studies, 1977); Peter M. Ngau, "Tensions in Empowerment: The Experience of the '*Harambee*' (Self-Help) Movement in Kenya," *Economic Development and Cultural Change* 35, no. 3 (1987): 523–538; Barbara P. Thomas, "Development through *Harambee*: Who Wins and Who Loses? Rural Self-Help Projects in Kenya," *World Development* 15, no. 4 (1987): 463–481.

[70] Hornsby, *Kenya*; Daniel Branch, *Kenya: Between Hope and Despair, 1963–2011* (New Haven, CT: Yale University Press, 2011).

[71] See, for example, Mahmood Mamdani, *Citizen and Subject: Contemporary Africa and the Legacy of Late Colonialism* (Princeton, NJ: Princeton University Press, 1996); Paul Nugent, *Africa since Independence: A Comparative History* (Basingstoke: Palgrave Macmillan, 2004); Crawford Young, *The African Colonial State in Comparative Perspective* (New Haven, CT: Yale University Press, 1994) and *The Post-Colonial State in Africa: Fifty Years of Independence, 1960–2010* (Madison: The University of Wisconsin Press, 2012).

[72] See in particular the literature that emerged after Jackson's and Rosberg's publication *Personal Rule in Black Africa*. For a review of the historiography of the time see Anthony H. Kirk-Green, "His Eternity, His Eccentricity, or His Exemplarity? A Further Contribution to the Study of HE the African Head of State," *African Affairs* 90, no. 359 (1991): 163–187.

reduced to a colonial legacy – and calls for more than a mythical history of the father of the nation. This book proposes to examine the historicity of state-building by reconstructing the political trajectory of both the man and the institution, and, in doing so, exploring the ties that eventually bound the president to the presidency.

This book is primarily concerned with the events that helped simultaneously establish Kenyatta as potential president of Kenya and the genesis of the presidency itself. Surprisingly, the connection between these two historical contingencies has hardly been researched in much detail. The persisting arguments stating the predominance of the colonial legacy over the Kenyan postcolonial state does not explain how the presidency was established upon independence, despite the novelty of the institution at the time.[73] The reevaluation of the importance of the colonial legacy for Kenya distinguishes this book from Wunyabari O. Maloba's biography of Jomo Kenyatta and Nicholas K. Githuku's long history of the Kenyan Mau Mau war.[74] Both are extremely informative historical works based on extensive archival research – and, as such, they provide a unique historical analysis on Kenya and Kenyatta's politics.

Maloba's two-volume biography stands, together with that of Jeremy Murray-Brown, as one of the most detailed accounts of Kenyatta's life and politics.[75] It shows, con brio, the formidable political transformation of the former "leader to death and darkness," put painstakingly under surveillance by British colonial and postcolonial governments throughout most of his career, while at the same time taking care to systematically fit Kenyatta's political trajectory into the larger political spectrum of his time. Maloba argues that Kenyatta's political figure was shaped by the British colonial legacy, just as it was later under the yoke of neocolonialism (as the title of the second volume covering the postindependence years, *The Anatomy of Neocolonialism*, plainly suggests). He underlines that neither Kenyatta nor his government sought any "major revision in the structure of the

---

[73] Wunyabari O. Maloba, *The Anatomy of Neocolonialism in Kenya: British Imperialism and Kenyatta (1963–1978)* (Cham: Palgrave Macmillan, 2017); *Kenyatta and Britain: An Account of Political Transformation, 1929–1963* (Cham: Palgrave Macmillan, 2018).
[74] Nicholas K. Githuku, *Mau Mau Crucible of War: Statehood, National Identity, and Politics of Postcolonial Kenya* (London: Lexington Books, 2015).
[75] Murray-Brown, *Kenyatta*.

inherited state"; nor did they challenge the domination of imperial capitalism, for the sake of Kenyan development.[76]

Nicholas K. Githuku paints a similar portrait of Jomo Kenyatta and his regime. Githuku plainly states that there is a clear continuum between the colonial and postcolonial Kenyan state, and that independence was but a "pyrrhic victory" that barely masked the colonial character of the new state and its politics. The novelty of his analysis lies in the way he identifies the grievances and survival struggles of everyday Kenyan citizens since independence and gives them political and historical significance. Speaking of the "Mau Mau war crucible of state formation," he posits that the Kenyan postcolonial state was born out of colonial counterinsurgency politics, and actively recreated them as an official state ideology after independence. Githuku explains: "the war continues to affect or shape postcolonial politics, national identity and the evolution of the contemporary Kenyan state."[77] At no point did the Mau Mau's anticolonial ideology completely fade away: the "mentality of struggle" has remained a defining feature of contemporary Kenyan society: after independence, "discontent continued to simmer in the unassailable realm of the mind."[78]

Historians and political scientists have reflected at length on the genesis of the African postcolonial state. As Paul Nugent notes, the question "how far back should we go?" has haunted historians and political analysts: a question that stems from the difficulty in disentangling actual and "invented traditions" in precolonial, colonial, and postcolonial Africa.[79] The notion that a colonial legacy pervaded all African postcolonial states is a relevant, if sometimes rather too convenient, analytical tool. References to colonial legacy can be found in the grand narratives on African governance, arguing that territories were too large to be controlled by a central state, that the "colonial rationality" pervaded African "commandement," or that elites were caught in patrimonial networks of power. Very little, however, is said

---

[76] Maloba, *The Anatomy of Neocolonialism in Kenya*, 4 and chapter 3.
[77] Githuku, *Mau Mau Crucible of War*, 7.   [78] Ibid., 219, 480.
[79] Nugent, *Africa since Independence*, 3–4. Eric Hobsbawm and Terance O. Ranger, *The Invention of Tradition* (Cambridge: Cambridge University Press, 1992). On the idea of postcolonial blurred temporal frontiers, see Achille Mbembe, *On the Postcolony* (Berkley: University of California Press, 2001), xviii; Frederick Cooper, "Conflict and Connection: Rethinking Colonial African History," *The American Historical Review* 99, no. 5 (1994): 1518, 1545.

Understanding the President and the Presidency in Kenya 21

about the complex history of presidential power.[80] A study of the origins of presidential power may be the missing link for a refined conceptualization of the postcolonial African state, in that it encourages an emancipation from models of state authority solely taken from the colonial past.[81]

This book argues, therefore, for an analysis of the making of the presidency as a historical moment *sui generis*. By studying the making of a presidential state from the perspective of the president himself, the traditional dichotomy established between the British colonial government and the Kenyan African elite fades away, to reveal a more complex web of interactions. At the same time, a prioritization of the role of individuals in this political game calls for a different focus than that of a traditional biography. The complexity of the negotiations over the presidency has often been overshadowed by the myth of the "father of the nation," popularized in biographies of African leaders.[82] This book distances itself from this historiographical perspective because it seeks to weave together the historical contingency and structural developments of both the president and the presidency: the man and the institution. Turning away from individuality as the sole explanation, it explores how a personality is shaped by a contingent historical context, and vice versa. It seeks to shows how the man himself must be situated within a more complex political machinery. In other words, it seeks to show how Kenyatta forged the presidency.

Retracing the history of presidential power, this book contributes to different aspects of Kenya's postcolonial historiography. First, it adds

---

[80] Jeffrey Herbst, *States and Power in Africa: Comparative Lessons in Authority and Control* (Princeton, NJ: Princeton University Press, 2000); Mamdani, *Citizen and Subject*; Jean-François Bayart and Romain Bertrand, "De Quel 'Legs Colonial' Parle-T-On?" *Esprit* 12 (2006): 134–160; René Lemarchand, "Political Clientelism and Ethnicity in Tropical Africa: Competing Solidarities in Nation-Building," *The American Political Science Review* 66, no.1 (1972): 68–90; Jean-François Médard, *États d'Afrique Noire. Formations, Mécanismes et Crises* (Paris: Karthala, 1991).

[81] For a critique of "the shaping influence of colonial rule on forms of governance that evolved after independence," see Andrew Burton and Michael Jennings, "The Emperor's New Clothes? Continuities in Governance in Late Colonial and Early Colonial Postcolonial East Africa," *International Journal of East African Histories* 40, no. 1 (2007): 1–26.

[82] On the development and political uses of the concept of "father of the nation," see "Héros Nationaux et Pères de la Nation en Afrique," special issue edited by Marie-Aude Fouéré and Hélène Charton, *Vingtième Siècle. Revue d'Histoire* 118, no. 2 (2013).

to the history of the debate over centralization versus regionalization (better known as "*majimboism*") of state powers, showing that it was essentially over by 1962. The negotiations between the British colonial government and the moderate elements of the Kenyan African elite (read Kenyatta) over land settlements had led to the creation of a Central Land Board that de facto secured centralized access to state resources. Although Kenyatta and his Kenya African National Union (KANU) fellow politicians were viscerally opposed to *majimboism*, they never called into question the regional, and much less the ethnic equilibrium inherited from colonization.[83] As such, they never questioned the backbone of *majimboism*: the tribal spheres of influence. What they opposed, however, was a federal distribution of executive powers. *Majimboism* was not to be replaced by, but subsumed under, a centralized state, with highly concentrated executive powers.[84] A closer focus on the independence negotiations and the formation of presidential rule thus shows that, to the British, KANU was not as politically dangerous as they had thought – and that the change of British favor from the Kenya African Democratic Union (KADU) to the KANU appeared slightly earlier than historians had thought.[85]

Shortly after a presidential republic was established, the question of the stability of the presidency arose, and with it the renewed debate on the fate of the (still unfinished) Mau Mau war.[86] As mentioned earlier, Kenyatta's ambiguous and fairly negative relationship to the Mau Mau

---

[83] Anderson noted in his seminal article on the issue that *majimboist* debates survived the achievement of independence, see David M. Anderson, "'Yours in Struggle for *Majimbo*': Nationalism and the Party Politics of Decolonisation in Kenya, 1955–64," *Journal of Contemporary History* 40, no. 3 (2005): 548.
[84] Ibid.
[85] See in particular Anderson, "Yours in Struggle for *Majimbo*"; Robert M. Maxon, *Kenya's Independence Constitution: Constitution-Making and End of Empire* (Madison, NJ: Fairleigh Dickinson University Press, 2011).
[86] See George Bennett and Carl G. Rosberg, *The Kenyatta Election: Kenya 1960–61* (Oxford: Oxford University Press, 1961); Carey Jones, *The Anatomy of Uhuru: An Essay on Kenya's Independence* (Manchester: Manchester University Press, 1966); Gary Wasserman, *Politics of Decolonisation: Kenya Europeans and the Land Issue* (Cambridge: Cambridge University Press, 1976); Bethwell Allan Ogot and William Robert Ochieng', *Decolonisation & Independence in Kenya: 1940–93* (Athens: Ohio University Press, 1995); Kyle, *The Politics of the Independence of Kenya*; David A. Percox, *Britain, Kenya and the Cold War: Imperial Defence, Colonial Security and Decolonisation* (London: I. B. Tauris, 2004); Maxon, *Kenya's Independence Constitution*; Hornsby, *Kenya*.

movement is acknowledged by most historians. Given the traumatic history of the movement, and its dramatic consequences, one is bound to ask: How did the president succeed in maintaining this ambiguity after independence? This is all the more intriguing as Kenyatta retained a loyalist administration and persistently refused to redistribute land for free to the landless – the key demand of the Mau Mau movement.[87] In his recently reedited autobiography, Duncan Ndegwa, former governor of the Central Bank of Kenya and former head of the civil service, noted that Kenyatta always disliked Mau Mau supporters, yet used many of them as personal bodyguards, suggesting that there was more than meets the eye behind Kenyatta's public calls to "forgive and forget" the past, and the general collective amnesia that such discourses fostered.[88] The constant opposition between the landless and the governmental elite has tended to reduce Kenyatta's status to that of a (neo)colonial stooge, a bias that obscured the agency of the government itself.

The historiography has focused extensively on the Mau Mau resisistance and local politics – much less so on the posterity of the movement – with the exepction of Githuku's book, although this focuses on the persistency of Mau Mau grievances among the people and not on the "top down" decisions made by the government after independence. The historians Frank Furedi, Tabitha Kanogo, and Maina wa Kinyatti, in particular, regard the post-Mau Mau period as the tortuous defeat of resistance "from below." Focusing on the local battlefields where resilient fighters who had formed the Kenya Land Freedom Army (KLFA) opposed KANU local elites, they documented the fierce quest to take over the party branches and to build

---

[87] Daniel Branch, *Defeating Mau Mau, Creating Kenya: Counterinsurgency, Civil War, and Decolonisation* (Cambridge: Cambridge University Press, 2009), chapter 6.
[88] Duncan Ndgewa, *Walking in Kenyatta Struggles: My Story* (Nairobi: Kenya Leadership Institute, 2011), 275. Ndegwa's account is quite outstanding given the fact that other leaders use their autobiographies to prove at all costs that they too were Mau Mau fighters, in spite of their prominent functions in a loyalist government and administration. See in particular the autobiography of Jeremiah Gitau Kiereini, *A Daunting Journey* (Nairobi: Kenway Publications, 2014). Kiereini took specific care to deny, not necessarily convincingly, Caroline Elkins' allegations in her book *Britain's Gulag* that he was a ruthless participant in torture in a Mau Mau detainees' camp, see *Britain's Gulag*, 97, 105, 109. On Kenyatta's call to forget and forgive the past, see Atieno-Odhiambo and Lonsdale, *Mau Mau & Nationhood*.

strong organizational bases.[89] Their studies emphasize that the postcolonial government's war to crush remaining Mau Mau fighters was a mix of avoidance strategy, manipulation, repression, and, even, as in the case of the most vocal defenders of the landless, assassination: Mau Mau "Field Marshal" Baimungi in 1965, the KANU politician and journalist Pio da Gama Pinto in the same year, the Luo KANU leader Tom Mboya in 1969, and the Kikuyu leader J. M. Kariuki in 1975.[90] Overall, the post-Mau Mau period was depicted as a failure of decolonization.[91]

A more fundamental question has not been addressed, however. Why did the resilient freedom fighters or the millions of landless fail to maintain revolutionary action? The military defeat of the Mau Mau movement does not suffice to explain why the landless and the remaining Mau Mau's land claims – those Githuku successfully retrieved – never seriously endangered the government. Neither does it explain how Kenyatta succeeded in maintaining the ambiguity surrounding his relationship to the Mau Mau. This book further demonstrates how the repression of Mau Mau resilience is intimately linked to state-building after independence, to the changes in Kenyatta's governement's attitude to Mau Mau resilience after independence, and, more particularly, to the killing of one of the last Mau Mau leaders, Field Marshal Baimungi in 1965. Baimungi's death was not a collateral effect of the British counterinsurgency strategies. His killing resulted, rather, from the Kenyan government's strategy to stifle the military resilience of Mau Mau fighters, to disrupt Mau Mau agitation, and muzzle the grievances of the landless. The triangular connection between the repression of Mau Mau resilience, land decolonization,

---

[89] On the local politics and the use of the KLFA, see in particular Furedi, *The Mau Mau War in Perspective*, 172–182; Kanogo, *Squatters and the Roots of Mau Mau (1905–1963)*, 163–175.

[90] Tom Mboya was also assassinated in 1969. Daniel Bourmaud also signaled other "accidental disappearances," that of Argwings-Kodhek in 1969 and Ronald Ngala in 1972, see Daniel Bourmaud, "Élections et Autoritarisme. La Crise de la Régulation Politique au Kenya," *Revue Française de Science Politique* 35, no. 2 (1985): 215.

[91] Furedi, *The Mau Mau War in Perspective*, 213–214; Kanogo, *Squatters and the Roots of Mau Mau (1905–1963)*, chapter 6; Maina wa Kinyatti, *Mau Mau: A Revolution Betrayed* (Jamaica, NY: Mau Mau Research Center, 1991).

and the increasing centralization of executive power forms the core of this book.[92]

The historiography dedicated to the land issue in Kenya can be split into three distinct categories. The first one is a general history of the technicalities surrounding institutional negotiations and grassroots implementation. Written in the mid-1970s and early 1980s, this branch of historiography displays an evident economic bias that reflects the growing pessimism of the time. It saw economic development in African countries burdened by "neo-colonial" political structures and tended to ignore the agency of African elites.[93] The second category is politicized history, focusing on what seems like land grabbing rather than land politics.[94] Finally, a small number of studies

---

[92] The necessity to conceptualize state-building within a larger political history was emphasized by the social scientist Gavin Kitching in 1985, who underlined that the Kenyan state, because it is the site of constant and fluctuating struggles for power involving multiple forms of capital and multifaceted social, economic, and geographical relationships, is all the more difficult to define with a single concept. Kitching's critique should not inexorably lead to the conclusion that any conceptualization of the state is doomed to fail. This point is emphasized by Michael Chege, "Introducing Race as a Variable into the Political Economy of Kenya Debate: An Incendiary Idea," *African Affairs* 97, no. 387 (1998): 210.

[93] See the "Kenyan debate" during the 1970s and 1980s: Leys, *Underdevelopment in Kenya*; Colin Leys, "Capital Accumulation, Class Formation and Dependency. The Significance of the Kenyan Case," *Socialist Register* 15, no. 15 (1978): 241–266; Nicola Swainson, *The Development of Corporate Capitalism in Kenya, 1918–77* (London: Heinemann, 1980); Rafael Kaplinsky, "Capitalist Accumulation in the Periphery: The Kenyan Case Re-Examined," *Review of African Political Economy* 7, no. 17 (1980): 83–105; Steven W. Langdon, *Multinational Corporations in the Political Economy of Kenya* (London: Macmillan, 1981); Björn Beckman, "Imperialism and Capitalist Transformation: Critique of a Kenyan Debate," *Review of African Political Economy* 7, no. 19 (1980): 48–62; Gavin Kitching, "Politics, Method and Evidence in the 'Kenya Debate'," in *Contradictions of Accumulation in Africa*, eds. Henry Bernstein and Bonnie K. Campbell (Beverly Hills, CA: Sage Publications, 1984), 115–151.

[94] David Himbara, *Kenyan Capitalists, the State, and Development* (London: L. Rienner Publishers, 1994); Ato Kwamena Onoma, *The Politics of Property Rights Institution in Africa* (Cambridge: Cambridge University Press, 2010). See also the *Report of the Commission of Inquiry into the Illegal/Irregular Allocation of Public Land* (Kenya: Commission of Inquiry into the Illegal/Irregular Allocation of Public Land, 2004); Otsieno Namwaya, "Who Owns Kenya?" *East African Standard*, October 1, 2004; Dauti Kahura, "Who Is Who in the Exclusive Big Land Owners' Register," *East African Standard*, October 3, 2004.

point out different paradigms, nuancing, for example, the role of ethnicity in land politics.[95] They emphasized the continuity between colonial and postcolonial land politics, showing that, although land settlements in the early 1960s were officially intended to alleviate land hunger in the White Highlands, the policies were designed by colonial civil servants unwilling to change the structure of the Kenyan economy (and virtually uninterested in the fate of the landless masses). Land settlement contributed to the preserving of the white settler's political and economic influence after independence.[96] In-depth studies have revealed the failure of the politics of settlement and the collateral rise of a gentrified class of landowners and farmers.[97] A two-tier system emerged, with two types of settlement schemes: the Million Acres Scheme, with "high density settlement schemes" designed for small and poorer farmers, and which were largely inefficient, versus the "low density settlement schemes," transferring European mixed farms to a new class of Kenyan capitalists, rich, and, many of them, loyalist "big men," endowed with significant economic assets.[98] In fact, rather

[95] Nicholas Nyangira looked into the complex relationship between ethnic alliance and land politics, emphasizing how ethnic alliance can be instrumental – rather than predetermining, see "Ethnicity, Class and Politics in Kenya," in *The Political Economy of Kenya*, ed. Michael G. Schatzberg (New York: Praeger Publishers, 1987), 27–29. See also Chege, "Introducing Race as a Variable into the Political Economy of Kenya Debate"; John O. Oucho, *Undercurrents of Ethnic Conflict in Kenya* (Leiden: Brill, 2002), chapter 7; Ngeta Kabiri, "Ethnic Diversity and Development in Kenya: Limitations of Ethnicity as a Category of Analysis," *Commonwealth & Comparative Politics* 52, no. 4 (2014): 513–534.

[96] Gerald Holtham and Arthur Hazlewood, *Aid and Inequality in Kenya: British Development Assistance to Kenya* (London: Routledge, 1976), 76–101.

[97] John W. Harbeson, "Land Reforms and Politics in Kenya, 1954–70," *The Journal of Modern African Studies* 9, no. 2 (1971): 231–251; Gary Wasserman, "Continuity and Counter-Insurgency: The Role of Land Reform in Decolonizing Kenya, 1962–70," *Canadian Journal of African Studies* 7, no. 1 (1973): 133–148; Christopher Leo, "The Failure of the 'Progressive Farmer' in Kenya's Million-Acre Settlement Scheme," *The Journal of Modern African Studies* 16, no. 4 (1978): 619–638 and "Who Benefited from the Million-Acre Scheme?"; Simon Coldham, "Land Control in Kenya," *Journal of African Law* 22, no. 1 (1978): 63–77 and "Land-Tenure Reform in Kenya: The Limits of Law," *The Journal of Modern African Studies* 17, no. 4 (1979): 615–627.

[98] On Kenyan "big men," see Gene Dauch, "Kenya: J. M. Kariuki ou L'Éthique Nationale du Capitalisme," *Politique Africaine* 2, no. 8 (1982): 21–43; Jean-François Médard, "Charles Njonjo: Portrait d'un 'Big Man' au Kenya," in *L'État Contemporain En Afrique*, ed. Emmanuel Terray (Paris: L'Harmattan, 1987), 49–87; Gabrielle Lynch, "Moi: The Making of an African 'Big-Man'," *Journal of Eastern African Studies* 2, no. 1 (2008): 18–43. For a recent

than a profound land reform entailing substantial changes in the land tenure system and the size of land plots (the divisions of small plots would have enabled the poorest people to own land), land settlement programs simply transferred land ownership from a European to a new loyalist and moderate African elite.[99] The historiography of land politics has been predominantly centered on the arguments about patterns of colonial continuity and dependency, as well as the study of land as a resource for political patronage, to the detriment of more refined political narratives. Although passive colonial continuity is undeniable in the structure and development of land politics in Kenya, this book is concerned with recognizing the active agency and interests of the Kenyan government in reappropriating colonial-style land politics.

The connections between the ongoing land decolonization, the increasing centralization of executive power, and the repression of any political opposition are still missing from the narratives of state formation. Recent research has shown a more complex picture of the layers of decision-making involved in land politics. Kara Moskowitz demonstrated, for example, how Kenyatta took decisions that were at odds with the required administrative procedure, eventually fueling fierce ministerial infighting.[100] This new evidence opens the way for a more complex understanding of the balance of state institutions under Kenyatta's regime. So far, the emphasis has been laid on the often disproportionate distribution of powers emanating from the "top" (Kenyatta's ministerial cabinet), favoring the provincial administration at the expense of party organization and civil society.[101] Kenyatta's

anthropological study of Kikuyu ethics of capitalism, see Dominique Connan, "La Décolonisation des Clubs Kényans: Sociabilité Exclusive et Constitution Morale des Elites Africaines dans le Kenya Contemporain" (Ph.D. diss., Paris 1, 2014).

[99] Holtham and Hazlewood, *Aid and Inequality in Kenya*, 87.

[100] Kara Moskowitz, "'Are You Planting Trees or Are You Planting People?' Squatter Resistance and International Development in the Making of a Kenyan Postcolonial Political Order (c. 1963–78)," *Journal of African History* 56, no. 1 (2015): 99–118.

[101] Cherry J. Gertzel, *The Politics of Independent Kenya, 1963–8* (London: Heinemann, 1970); David K. Leonard, *African Successes: Four Public Managers of Kenyan Rural Development* (Berkeley: University of California Press, 1991); Tamarkin, "The Roots of Political Stability in Kenya," 297–320; David W. Throup, "The Construction and Deconstruction of the Kenyatta State," in *The Political Economy of Kenya*, ed. Michael G. Schatzberg (Portsmouth: Praeger, 1987), 33–75; Peter Anyang' Nyong'o, "Succession et Héritage Politiques: Le Président, l'État et le Capital après la Mort de Jomo

rule is deemed "personal," but the boundaries of his actions have been little studied, overlooking in particular the issues or conflicts, which Kenyatta simply ignored, preferring passivity to direct control. The insistence on patronage as the main source of political loyalty offers only partial explanation of a much wider question: that of how Kenyatta's purportedly clannish or tribal thinking – his favored relationship to his Kikuyu ministers, his Kikuyu ethos of capitalism, and his neglect of the poor and landless – coexisted with his ability to maintain loyalty among his opponents, strengthen a multiethnic government, and secure popularity and stability of power for more fifteen years of rule.

This book attempts to situate land politics within a larger narrative of state-building, reflecting on how presidential decisions on land policies not only affected the functioning of state institutions, but also enabled the president to neutralize popular discontent. Political scientists and historians all agree that, after independence, Kenyatta used the provincial administration, and the provincial commissioners (PCs) in particular, to assert his authority throughout the territory.[102] The fact that virtually all PCs were prominent Kikuyus is testament to Kenyatta's heavy reliance on this section of the administration.[103]

Kenyatta," *Politique Africaine* 1, no. 3 (1981): 7–25; Joel D. Barkan and Michael Chege, "Decentralising the State: District Focus and the Politics of Reallocation in Kenya," *The Journal of Modern African Studies* 27, no. 3 (1989): 431–453; Jennifer A. Widner, *The Rise of a Party-State in Kenya: From "Harambee" to "Nyayo!"* (Berkeley: University of California Press, 1992); Daniel Branch and Nicholas Cheeseman, "The Politics of Control in Kenya: Understanding the Bureaucratic-Executive State, 1952–78," *Review of African Political Economy* 33, no. 107 (2006): 11–31.

[102] Gertzel, *The Politics of Independent Kenya, 1963–8*; Henry Bienen, *Kenya: The Politics of Participation and Control* (Princeton, NJ: Princeton University Press, 1974).

[103] On the provincial administration and its Kikuyu predominance, see Stanley Meisler, "Tribal Politics Harass Kenya," *Foreign Affairs* 49, no. 1 (1970): 111–112; Throup, "The Construction and Deconstruction of the Kenyatta State"; Tamarkin, "The Roots of Political Stability in Kenya"; Susanne D. Mueller, "Government and Opposition in Kenya, 1966–9," *The Journal of Modern African Studies* 22, no. 3 (1984): 399–427; Barkan and Chege, "Decentralising the State." For the portraits and profiles of some of these PCs, see Leonard, *African Successes*. For a discussion on ethnic or tribal politics, see Kenneth Omolo, "Political Ethnicity in the Democratisation Process in Kenya," *African Studies* 61, no. 2 (2002): 209–221; Elisha S. Atieno-Odhiambo, "Hegemonic Enterprises and Instrumentalities of Survival: Ethnicity and Democracy in Kenya," *African Studies* 61, no. 2 (2002): 223–249; Rok Ajulu, "Politicised Ethnicity, Competitive Politics and Conflict in Kenya: A Historical

The strategies by which he combined and balanced the powers of the provincial administration with that of his inner circle of cabinet ministers has gone unobserved, however. Duncan Ndgewa's autobiography, again, hints at the competition between the civil service and cabinet ministers, targeting Kenyatta's general attorney, Charles Njonjo.[104] These tensions suggest that more thorough exploration is needed to understand how Kenyatta ruled over, and perhaps even used the disputes between these two state organs, to his own benefit.

Archival evidence points to the necessity for a reexamination of Kenyatta's use of the provincial administration. While the historiography has emphasized Kenyatta's far-reaching executive powers and informal control over state institutions, relying either on loyal (Kikuyu) civil servants or settling issues through personal interventions, it has not accounted for Kenyatta's ever greater isolation as president.[105] Kenyatta did not like to work with groups, parties, or institutions, just as he did not care about the potential disorder his actions, decisions, or promises might stir within state institutions.[106] As this book shows, Kenyatta established a system of rule in which he, as president, would not be held accountable for the effectiveness – or failings – of its

---

Perspective," *African Studies* 61, no. 2 (2002): 251–268; Bruce Berman, Dickson Eyoh, and Will Kymlicka, *Ethnicity & Democracy in Africa* (Oxford: James Currey, 2004); Michaela Wrong, *It's Our Turn to Eat: The Story of a Kenyan Whistle Blower* (London: Fourth Estate, 2009); Daniel Branch and Nicholas Cheeseman, "Democratisation, Sequencing, and State Failure in Africa: Lessons from Kenya," *African Affairs* 108, no. 430 (2009): 1–26; Gabrielle Lynch, "Negotiating Ethnicity: Identity Politics in Contemporary Kenya," *Review of African Political Economy* 33, no. 107 (2006): 49–65; "Electing the 'Alliance of the Accused': The Success of the Jubilee Alliance in Kenya's Rift Valley," *Journal of Eastern African Studies* 8, no. 1 (2014): 93–114.

[104] Ndgewa, *Walking in Kenyatta Struggles*, 300, 311–317.

[105] See in particular Bienen, *Kenya*; Gertzel, *The Politics of Independent Kenya, 1963–8*; Richard Stren, "Factional Politics and Central Control in Mombasa, 1960–1969," *Canadian Journal of African Studies* 4, no. 1 (1970): 33–56.

[106] On the squatter issue in particular, see the article by Moskowitz, "Are You Planting Trees or Are You Planting People?" This is an element Duncan Ndegwa himself confirmed in his autobiography: "[Kenyatta] also did not seem to consider direct contact between the Permanent Secretary to the Office of the President and Provincial Commissioners always necessary. However, whenever he visited the provinces, PCs had his ear, some even finding an organic connection with the center, a practice that at times cause considerable confusion within the Civil Service," in Ndegwa, *Walking in Kenyatta Struggles*, 300.

politics. Cherry Gertzel described the provincial administration as a "rubber stamp" used by the government to contain local grievances and agitation. From this analysis, I have drawn the concept of "disempowered regionalism" to explain the shaping of a provincial administration powerful enough to impose government's politics onto local communities and absorb popular discontent, yet too much cut off from the Office of the President to challenge the government's authority.

Last, but not least, this book is a necessarily modest attempt to fill some of the gaps left in the scholarship dedicated to Kenyatta's leadership. Kenyatta's decision-making was an inherently secret and informal process, rarely transcribed into written correspondence. Once president, he would receive privately various delegations set up by local citizens, politicians, or members of parliament (MPs).[107] When it came to making a decision, the influence of his inner circle of advisers – the cabinet ministers Mbiyu Koinange, James Gichuru, Njoroge Mungai, and the attorney general Charles Njonjo – has been widely acknowledged. As Charles Njonjo expressed in a press interview in May 2015, power under Kenyatta's regime was literally that of a "rungu (club)."[108] To what extent this influence meant power to make decisions for Kenyatta is still unclear.[109] Furthermore, large chronological gaps remain. Historians have noted that Kenyatta's reinvention from convicted Mau Mau fighter to father of the nation was not his own, but very little is known about the political negotiations that reinvented Kenyatta as this national symbol.[110] On top of

---

[107] Branch, *Kenya*, 73.
[108] Njonjo continued: "but at least we were united. I could go to North Eastern and come back. You try and do that today, you'll be back a corpse," in Jackson Biko, "I Miss the Power to Do Good, Former AG Njonjo Says," *Daily Nation*, May 22, 2015.
[109] For insightful research on Kenyatta's regime, see in particular Joseph Karimi and Philip Ochieng, *The Kenyatta Succession* (Nairobi: Transafrica Press, 1980); Gene Dauch and Denis Martin, *L'Héritage de Kenyatta: La Transition Politique au Kenya, 1975–1982* (Paris: L'Harmattan, 1985); Throup, "The Construction and Deconstruction of the Kenyatta State"; Anyang' Nyong'o, "Succession et Héritage Politiques"; Hornsby, *Kenya*, chapters 2–6; Branch, *Kenya*, chapters 1–3.
[110] Kyle mentions that the Luo politician Oginga Odinga started the so-called Kenyatta campaign in 1958, but the political negotiations among the divided Kenyan nationalist elite and with the British government have not been explored. See Kyle, *The Politics of the Independence of Kenya*, chapter 6. The

that, Kenyatta's political thinking and actions after his release from jail and throughout the independence conferences from 1961 to 1963 remain virtually unknown.[111] Finally, analyses of Kenyatta's decision-making after independence are at best sporadic, at worst anecdotal, and reveal a much wider gap in the analysis. The three core issues of Kenyan postcolonial history – the aftermath of the Mau Mau movement, land politics, and the distribution of political and economic resources to state institutions – are generally treated as separate political issues, and hence studied as distinct histories. They can, however, be used to form a common narrative: that of the disregard for the landless masses, the political accumulation of land by the governmental elite, and the excessive centralization of power within the Office of the President. The history of Jomo Kenyatta's path to the presidency is the key to understanding the connections between these issues.

Reconfiguring Institutions, Individuals, and Power

Kenyatta was a distant and discreet president. This suited his idea of leadership, which he at no point imagined as an exemplary authority for all. As Chapter 1 shows, Kenyatta considered the state as an instrument of law and order, not of political change and certainly not of redistribution. For him, leadership was a matter of individuals; at no point did he imagine the state as an authority for all. Being discreet and distant was also a political necessity. Chapter 2 captures the politics that underpinned the campaign to release Kenyatta from jail, and turned him into a nationalist figure. Although Kenyatta's liberation was stage-managed by his political comrades, none of them seriously imagined that the "Old Man" would come back to Kenyan politics. If the so-called Kenyatta campaign eventually provided the latter with a nationalist audience, Kenyatta quickly realized that he could not rely on any formal institutions to promote his own agenda. He had

---

recently released migrated archives provide useful information to examine the period in a fresh ways, see chapter 2.

[111] And so, in spite of a very rich historiography that has shown the political and constitutional complexities of the independence negotiations, see in particular H. W. O. Okoth-Ogendo, "The Politics of Constitutional Change in Kenya since Independence, 1963–69," *African Affairs* 71, no. 282 (1972): 9–34; Kyle, *The Politics of the Independence of Kenya*; Anderson, "Yours in Struggle for Majimbo"; Maxon, *Kenya's Independence Constitution*.

virtually no control over the nationalist party, KANU, and always felt at a loss with the formal codes and institutional order of the new state, which he consequently disregarded.

To overcome these weaknesses, he concentrated his efforts on maintaining a personal character that was different from every other politician. His Kikuyu people believed he was a Mau Mau, and being able to control the Kikuyu vote was a significant political asset for which many politicians competed. Yet, this singularity alone cannot explain how Kenyatta strengthened his presidency, nor does it explain how he remained aloof from political divisions that gnawed the party, the state institutions, and sometimes even his own circle of cabinet ministers. Jomo Kenyatta's political biography here serves as a point of entry by which to examine a structural phenomenon: the roots of presidentialism in postcolonial Kenya. Chapter 3 traces the making of presidential rule in Kenya. It draws attention to the ways in which the decolonization and reinvention of land institutions laid the groundwork for Kenyatta's presidential powers, as the principle of centralized institutions was settled on, and the British government realized that backing up Kenyatta was the safest political bet. Upon independence, Kenyatta lacked any reliable political base, but the cursory negotiations for the presidential seat opened the door for totalizing executive powers. Exploring how Kenyatta negotiated and institutionalized these so far uncertain, blurred, and contingent presidential prerogatives, Chapter 4 shows how the making of Kenyatta's career merged with the making of presidentialism, outgrowing weaker state institutions.

The negotiations of presidential power were an inherently contingent process, built less on the political strength and assets of one actor (Kenyatta had virtually none, besides the fame of his name) than on the shared weaknesses of an elite divided by its personal ambitions, interests, and resources. Kenyatta was certainly aware of this contingency, and consequently refrained from revealing his hand – hence the distant and discreet president. At the same time, he understood that he could strengthen his already significant powers and even use presidential favors, as long as the multiple divisions were maintained and tamed within a subtle political, tribal, and administrative (im)balance.

Kenyatta's subtle personal political style is best shown in the way that he dealt with the remaining Mau Mau freedom fighters, whom he saw as a threat to his rule and popularity. Chapter 5 unravels the complex relationship between the government's repression against the resilient Mau Mau fighters, the land issue, and the necessity to control local politics. Focusing on Meru district, it shows how the hunt for the last Mau Mau leaders, Field Marshal Baimungi and General Chui, must be read in parallel to the making of one of Kenyatta's most powerful ministers, Jackson Harvester Angaine, minister for lands and settlement.

Chapter 6 then provides a deeper insight into Kenyatta and his politics of land and shows that Kenyatta preferred to delegate the negotiations of land politics to his most trusted ministers, and was, to a certain extent, even ignorant of the details involved. Whether it concerned local political disputes or institutional infighting between the provincial administration and his cabinet ministers, Kenyatta always avoided committing himself, and confined his public appearances to sporadic interventions. Behind this lack of commitment, however, was a clear strategy of deregulating and bypassing state institutions by distributing his personal favors. Kenyatta's presidential power amounted neither to centralization nor to regionalization. Instead, it created a form of disempowered regionalism: secluding the powerful regional administration from the Office of the President, thus ensuring Kenyatta's isolation from popular discontent. The concept of disempowered regionalism is meant to illustrate the vertical ties that bound the administration to the president and to give a sense of the lack of horizontal cohesion that prevented regional solidarities.[112] At the same time, Kenyatta's lack of commitment was in tune with his political imagination, which was built on the clear absence of any responsive duty, whether to state institutions, personal promises, or people's hopes.

After 1965, however, as Kenyatta's health showed the first signs of decline, Kenyatta retreated into an arbitrary role, gradually transforming into a more "tribal" Kikuyu conception of leadership. Chapter 7 (1965–1969) explores a period characterized not only by greater repression against dissident politicians, but also by the governing elites' attempts to buy more land throughout the country and secure their land titles. The debates over the Africanization of land ownership in Kenya show that the early politicization of the land resources reached a new level with continuous attempts to either alter or

---

[112] I thank Frederick Cooper for his excellent suggestion to express the power dynamics of disempowered regionalism along vertical and horizontal axes.

circumvent the existing legal framework governing the land market. Kenyatta played a role of a "reconciler" among an inherently divided political elite, abusing his political and economic powers to increase his personal wealth or to strengthen loyalties.

In 1969, the assassination of the prominent minister and nationalist politician Tom Mboya, marked the beginning of a new phase of political activity. As Kenyatta's health kept deteriorating, the struggle to succeed the president intensified. Throughout the 1970s, Kenyatta's death would be the overarching theme of discussion among his supporters, opponents, and British officials, who observed the evolution of the political scene closely. Yet, no one dared challenging the president openly and so Kenyatta continued to strengthen his control over the state and its political institutions. As Chapter 8 shows, the president's untouchable status, combined with the effects of the succession struggle led to a political standstill. This inertia was used by Kenyatta (and his family) for increasingly authoritarian politics, while they became ever more detached from the everyday reality of the Kenyan masses.

Presentation of Sources

The greatest difficulty with writing this book was to overcome dislike for protocol and formal correspondence.[113] Kenyatta rarely signed a document.[114] Even the most "Top Secret" documents transmitting his orders to PCs were generally issued by one of his top ministers. The absence of first-hand archives prevented me from producing an exhaustive account of his political doings. Just as the trail of decision-making implied various intermediaries, each confined to a specific range of tasks, potential archives were similarly scattered between various institutional bodies. Reviewing each of them would have been practically difficult, probably ineffective, and would have

---

[113] According to the British high commissioner and friend Malcolm MacDonald, Kenyatta disliked protocol. See Malcolm MacDonald to Mrs. David Hardy for the Ford Foundation, August 16, 1963, Durham University Special Collections, MacDonald Papers, 47/2/50. Reproduced by kind permission of the trustees of the Malcolm MacDonald Papers, and Durham University.
[114] During the independence conference, for example, Kenyatta delegated his correspondence and party affairs to Joseph Murumbi, see Murumbi and Thurston, *A Path Not Taken*, 85.

led to what we already know: that Kenyatta held private meetings, gave secret orders, or made personal promises. Rather than retracing day-do-day decision-making, I reflected on why Kenyatta did not (and perhaps did not want to) leave any trace of his actions. This eventually helped me to unmask him as a distant and discreet president: a recurrent theme throughout this book. This also explains the necessary detours through selected institutions, ministers, and localities in the following chapters. The political biography that thereby took shape attempted to make sense of the political system that Kenyatta designed, and to expose both his well-calculated passivity and the institutional palliatives that compensated for it.

Kenyatta's private papers have disappeared.[115] To trace his ascension to power from his release from jail to his appointment as the president of KANU, I relied on two types of archives. First, I used the administrative reports written by the district commissioners from the various locations where Kenyatta was jailed. These very descriptive and factual documents revealed the colonial authorities' relative sympathy for Kenyatta, whom they considered a model detainee. However, once Kenyatta was released in 1961, no report (whether from the district commissioner or intelligence services) was found. I therefore relied on the recently released files from the British "migrated archives."[116] Issued by the Colonial Office, these files were, of course, infused with British interests. Nevertheless, the British government made contacts with nationalist leaders (mostly former KAU members) supposedly better fit to foresee Kenyatta's ideas and acts. Their account of discussions led to the realization of something previously overlooked by the historiography: Kenyatta's return was very much unexpected, and perhaps even undesired by his political comrades.

---

[115] John M. Lonsdale, "Ornamental Constitutionalism in Africa: Kenyatta and the Two Queens," *The Journal of Imperial and Commonwealth History* 34, no. 1 (2006), endnote 37.

[116] These were recently released by the Foreign Commonwealth Office, in the wake of the appeal by Mau Mau veterans against the British government. See Ian Cobain and Richard Norton-Taylor, "Sins of Colonialists Lay Concealed for Decades in Secret Archive," *The Guardian,* April 18, 2012.

Postcolonial archives, as Caroline Elkins rightfully observed, are biased relics of a past, left behind by political elites who skillfully reviewed and rewrote their historic roles.[117] The blatant incompleteness of so many inventories in the Kenya National Archives perfectly illustrates this point. The "Office of the President" files contain only Kenyatta's speeches (and much irrelevant information). Yet, many of these speeches are missing dates and signatures, which raises the question whether they were always drafted by Kenyatta himself. The Murumbi Africana Collection, perhaps the most complete collection, provided useful files on party politics, but, overall, contained very little information on Kenyatta's postcolonial rule, perhaps because the former minister and vice president Joseph Murumbi distanced himself from Kenyatta after 1966. I had to compromise between browsing all ministerial and regional archives, or selecting the most influential institutions and political actors to which Kenyatta granted his trust. I focused on the Eastern region archives and on the files of the Ministry of Land, because they are the most complete archival collections. The Eastern region files disclosed important and useful information on how Kenyatta's regime dealt with one of the main political threats after independence: Mau Mau resilience. They were also a rich source of information concerning Kenyatta's relationships with provincial and district commissioners. The land files, from the Ministry of Lands and Settlement, enabled me to further place these politics in perspective. These files ranged from governmental meetings, land purchase accounts by the government, loan repayments, politics of the landless, and reports on the land in the districts to the complaints about land sent either by politicians or civil servants to the Office of the President. They were a useful source with which to map the political dynamics involving various actors in the land negotiations, while probing the potential gap between the government's private doings and publicized intentions.

Despite an evident political bias, British archives also provided a substantial source of information, all the more important since Kenyatta, as well as his most influential ministers, were regularly in touch with the representatives of the British High Commission in Kenya, and of the Commonwealth Relations Office in London. Most importantly,

---

[117] C. Elkins, "Looking Beyond Mau Mau: Archiving Violence in the Era of Decolonisation," *The American Historical Review* 120, no. 3 (2015): 865.

these two bodies maintained a dense correspondence with the British officers who remained in Kenya as part of the post-independence technical assistance. Reports of discussions circulating between these three institutional bodies proved very helpful in giving a sense of Kenyatta's main concerns, while guiding his logics of action. Most importantly perhaps, the British account of the negotiations over land politics with the Kenyan government not only showed the diverging strategies of British and Kenyan land administrators, but also pointed to infighting within Kenyan ministries and administration, further helping to situate Kenyatta within the convoluted process of political negotiations.

Finally, a note on the missing voices and numbers of the landless masses, squatters, and resilient Mau Mau fighters is needed. Their absence highlights that the government took very little interest in their welfare. As this book shows, Kenyatta did not understand the complexity of the technicalities involved when settling landless masses, and, what is more, only cared about the issue when he considered that the landless were a potential threat to his authority. This lack of interest was palpable in the archive material I used: the landless are invisible. The hundreds of letters of complaint sent to the president remained, for the most part, unanswered and my intuition is that Kenyatta did not even know about them – since he would meet delegations of landless people only privately. Alternative sources such as the newspapers also proved inconclusive, as they only offered biased or partial accounts of the government's politics. A study of Kenyatta's public meetings, for example, would have amounted to a list of public donations to various local projects, with very few other sources to put it into perspective. Similarly, popular tales of Jomo Kenyatta are often nothing more than rumors, at best banal, at worst highly improbable.[118] Even those who visited Kenyatta at his Gatundu house recalled that he either stayed silent or replied with a vague "yes" to every request. Less than a myth that no one dared to criticise, however, Kenyatta's political aura remains tantalizingly mysterious. This book thus attempts to explain why the president had to keep political distance from the landless.

---

[118] For an example of an analysis of rumors and politics in Kenya, see Grace A. Musila, *Death Retold in Truth and Rumour: Kenya, Britain and the Julie Ward Murder* (Woddbridge: James Currey, 2015).

1 | Kenyatta's Stateless Political Imagination*

In 1928, just two years after he joined the Kenya Central Association, Kenyatta started a career as a journalist, as founder editor and writer for the Kikuyu vernacular journal *Muigwithania* (*The Reconciler*). During his years in London, from 1929 to 1930 and from 1931 to 1946, Kenyatta wrote in English to get the British attention and support for the Kikuyu cause he was defending. The highlight of his literary production was certainly the historical anthropology of the Kikuyu he wrote under the supervision of the LSE professor of anthropology, Bronisław Malinowski, and published in 1938 under the title of *Facing Mount Kenya*. Later, Kenyatta further explored Kikuyu history in two other pamphlets, *My People of Kikuyu and the Life of Chief Wangombe* (1942) and *Kenya: The Land of Conflicts* (1945). After 1945, however, that is to say, just a year before his return to Kenya, he no longer published anything, except, much later, a collection of speeches.[1]

His vision was born out of a disrupted colonial world, at a time when indigenous political organizations were still nascent and when educated elites were searching for a new political authority. The Kikuyu had a long tradition of debate over moral and social values (i.e., the exchange of ideas about social and cultural relationships, not to be confused with arguments about what constitutes morally good or evil),

---

* This chapter is derived, in part, from a book chapter published as Anaïs Angelo, "Virtues for All, State for No One?: Jomo Kenyatta's Postcolonial Political Imagination," in *African Thoughts on Colonial and Neo-Colonial Worlds: Facets of an Intellectual History of Africa*, ed. Arno Sonderegger (Berlin: Neofelis, 2015), 67–86.
[1] Jomo Kenyatta, *Facing Mount Kenya* (New York: Vintage Books, 1965), *My People of Gikuyu and the Life of Chief Wangombe* (London: Luttersworth Press, 1942), *Kenya: The Land of Conflict* (London: Panaf Service Limited, 1945), and *Suffering without Bitterness*.

which defined the attributes of political authority.[2] Political participation was reserved to adult men, manhood and adulthood depending on socioeconomic capital, and more precisely on the access to property and labor. With colonization, the introduction of the chieftaincy as the representative institution of the "tribe," and the strengthening of colonial rural capitalism, the internal structure of Kikuyu political and social relations was radically altered.[3] Land alienation prevented men from acquiring property and fulfilling social duties. Deprivation of territory was breaking the virtuous circle of the moral economy: "being a Kikuyu" was meaningless and political order was impossible. The struggle was, however, less about reinventing a political organization than to defend a political territory jeopardized by colonization. The competition for rightful narratives of land ownership that set white settlers against the Kikuyu further contributed to politicize historical narratives. It was, therefore, a moral struggle that engaged the redefinition of legitimate authority over both a community and a territory.[4]

Kenyatta belonged to a generation of Kikuyu elites who emancipated themselves through (colonial) literacy: the mission educated, or "readers," or *athomi*, as those converted to Christianism were called, saw in their new education a way to push forward a new political project empowering their young generation.[5] In colonial Kiambu, just a few years before Kenyatta become politically active, competition for authority split the educated Kikuyu and their animist elders.[6]

---

[2] See Lonsdale, "The Moral Economy of Mau Mau, Wealth, Poverty and Civic Virtue in Kikuyu Political Thought," 315–504; John M. Lonsdale, "Moral Ethnicity, Ethnic Nationalism and Political Tribalism: The Case of the Kikuyu," in *Staat und Gesellschaft in Afrika*, ed. Peter Meyns (Hamburg: Lit, 1996), 93–106; Dominique Connan and Johanna Siméant, "John Lonsdale, le Nationalisme, l'Ethnicité et l'Economie Morale: Parcours d'un Pionnier de l'Histoire Africaine," *Genèses* 2, no. 83 (2001): 133–154.
[3] Lonsdale, "The Moral Economy of Mau Mau, Wealth, Poverty and Civic Virtue in Kikuyu Political Thought," 330.
[4] Ibid., 347–348.
[5] John M. Lonsdale, "Contest of Time: Kikuyu Historiography, Old and New," in *A Place in the World: New Local Historiographies from Africa and South Asia*, ed. Axel Harneit-Sievers (Leiden: Brill, 2002), 205. On power and generation from colonization to independence in Kenya, see Paul Ocobock, *An Uncertain Age: The Politics of Manhood in Kenya* (Athens: Ohio University Press, 2017).
[6] Marshal S. Clough, *Fighting Two Sides: Kenyan Chiefs and Politicians, 1918–1940* (Niwot: University Press of Colorado, 1990), 26.

This new generation of elites was looking to redefine the notion of authority that would match the emancipation from tribal customs that they were advocating. They defended a cyclical past that entitled them to claim an authority that had been, so far, reserved to their "dynastic" elders.[7] Most importantly, "readers" were the first generation of writers who broke away with a tradition of oral history and used literacy to justify their claim to authority to communicate over their political agenda. Readers politicized Kikuyu history, as they wrote about an "ordered" past that entitled them to debunk the traditional attributes of power – age, social relations, and land – in favor of a generational renewal.

These two struggles, generational and territorial, directly inspired Kenyatta's writings.[8] Kenyatta was an "organic" intellectual or a professional Kikuyu historian, as Lonsdale and Muriuki (respectively) described him, who used the Kikuyu language of moral virtues to tell the story of a selected past to support his own political aspirations.[9] His writings were as much influenced by the generational split over the definition of authority as by the contest over whom were the first "civilizers" of land that the colonizers had set up.[10] In a context of extremely politicized historical and ethnographic knowledge, his writings appeared filled of intellectual compromises and, at times, contradictions. These have been extensively studied, and it is not the place here to summarize long and complex debates.[11] Yet, it is worth recalling that, through writing, Kenyatta was less looking for authenticity than to reshape moral rules as *condition sine qua non* for political

---

[7] Lonsdale, "Contest of Time," 206–216. For more insights on the language of politics and "creative writing," see Derek R. Peterson, *Creative Writing: Translation, Bookkeeping, and the Work of Imagination in Colonial Kenya* (Portsmouth, NH: Heinemann, 2004).

[8] Lonsdale, "Contest of Time," 409.   [9] Ibid., 205.   [10] Ibid., 231.

[11] See in particular Bernardo Bernardi, "Old Kikuyu Religion Igongona and Mambura: Sacrifice and Sex: Re-Reading Kenyatta's Ethnography," *Africa: Rivista Trimestrale Di Studi E Documentazione dell'Istituto Italiano per l'Africa E l'Oriente* 48, no. 2 (1993): 167–183; Berman, "Ethnography as Politics, Politics as Ethnography"; Lonsdale, "Listen While I Read"; Berman and Lonsdale, "The Labors of *Muigwuithania*"; Gikandi, "Pan-Africanism and Cosmopolitanism"; Lonsdale, "Jomo Kenyatta, God & the Modern World"; Nyangena, "Jomo Kenyatta"; Lonsdale, "Les Procès de Jomo Kenyatta"; Lonsdale, "Ornamental Constitutionalism in Africa"; Frederiksen, "Jomo Kenyatta, Marie Bonaparte and Bronislaw Malinowski on Clitoridectomy and Female Sexuality"; Peatrik, "Le Singulier Destin de *Facing Mount Kenya*."

unity in a disrupted world.[12] His vision of political authority was intimately linked to his understanding of a political community and would later influence his presidential rule.

Analyzing Kenyatta's writings and speeches, this chapter attempts to unveil the rich and complex interaction of his imagination of what we now call postcolonial society, with his understanding of the constraints of the realpolitik. Building on Lonsdale's article "Jomo Kenyatta, God & the Modern World," dedicated to Kenyatta's political imagination, I argue that Kenyatta's conception of authority (infused with conservative moral values) and of leadership (which he considered less important than moral autonomy), led him to erect the "family" as the ultimate base and limit of his politics of state-building. This chapter first attempts to situate the "family" in his early writings. Then, it explores the intellectual legacy of his writings *after* independence, and show how Kenyatta was at pains to enlarge and adapt his moral discourse to the new Kenyan nation. After examining how the discourse of moral virtues eventually taints the logics of state-building, it locates the transfer of the "family" into the politics of state-building.[13]

The Family between Social Relations and Authority

The moral guidance Kenyatta was looking for was not about immovable maxims of life. It was made of practical solutions meant to overcome the social and moral disruptions caused by colonization and to legitimate his aspiration to eldership and authority.[14] During his London years, Kenyatta was as impressed by the British art of parliamentary debate, as much as he was appalled by the British government readiness to break commitments.[15] Just a few months after he had landed in London, in 1929, he reported in *Muigwithania* his amazement at the opening of the British parliament and urged his

---

[12] Kenyatta wrote: "try hard to seek out (trace) the Kikuyu customs that are good and hold on to them firmly, so that you may be able to take your stand alongside the customs of the other nation" in *Muigwithania*, July–August 1929. Vol. 2. no. 2, KNA, DC/MKS/10B/13/1, Machakos district. I relied on the English translation by A. R. Barlow, missionary from the Church of Scotland, and kept Barlow's own hesitations regarding the translation, which explains the words in parenthesis (as for the subsequent references).
[13] I thank Yvan Droz for his helpful insights on this question.
[14] Lonsdale, "Jomo Kenyatta, God & the Modern World," 37.
[15] Lonsdale, "Ornamental Constitutionalism in Africa."

readers to "learn well to trust or rely upon one another among your own selves, so that you may be trusted and respected ('feared') by other nations."[16] Calling for trust, Kenyatta was not simply pushing for moral and political unity, he was establishing trust as the precondition for a community to exist. Trust could not bear the weight of institutions, nor was it given or negotiated: it could only be achieved through self-reliance. For a stateless society like the Kikuyus, Kenyatta considered trust as key to surviving and maintaining dignity.[17] It was not just a functional ornament of social relationships, it drew the boundaries of inclusion and exclusion in a community. Kenyatta had to define social cohesion and authority in ways that mutual trust would not be impaired. This was a tricky task, for the Kikuyu moral economy rested, primarily, on the supremacy of individual achievement.

Kenyatta was confronted with a problem that haunted Kikuyu politics: how to define an (individual) authority that would not weaken mutual (and collective) trust.[18] In Kikuyu society, Kenyatta explained in *Facing Mount Kenya*, individuality was subsumed under "three governing principles": the family group (*mbari*, or *nyomba*), the clan (*moherega*), and the age-grading system (*riika*).[19] At the same time, individuals were the ultimate owners of land. That did not entail, however, any right to claim authoritative status.[20] Kenyatta was endorsing a specific trait of Kikuyu thought that Lonsdale described as "possessive individualism in the service of the community," defended by the tenants of generational history who opposed to the elders' view that land ownership lay soulely with *mbari* seniors.[21]

---

[16] Quoted in *Muigwithania*, July–August 1929, Vol. 2, Nr. 2, p. 8, KNA, DC/MKS/10B/13/1.
[17] Ibid.
[18] Lonsdale, "The Moral Economy of Mau Mau, Wealth, Poverty and Civic Virtue in Kikuyu Political Thought," 400.
[19] Kenyatta, *Facing Mount Kenya*, 1–2.
[20] Ibid., 21–22, 98. On Kikuyu culture and individualism, see Yvan Droz, *Migrations Kikuyus: des Pratiques Sociales à l'Imaginaire* (Paris: Editions MSH, 1999), 154; Droz, "L'Ethos du Mûramati Kikuyu."
[21] Lonsdale, "The Moral Economy of Mau Mau, Wealth, Poverty and Civic Virtue in Kikuyu Political Thought," 374 and "Contest of Time," 236. Ali A. Mazrui also referred to "possessive individualism in traditional Africa" to explain the emergence of a new generation of indigenous elites, who used their new economic status to claim extended social and political privileges. Mazrui sees in possessive individualism the prelude to "the cult of ostentation," characteristic of a "monarchical tendency" in African politics. See Ali A. Mazrui "The

The Family between Social Relations and Authority 43

This was carefully underlined throughout Kenyatta's thesis: individual land ownership should not be confused with individual *right* over land. No individuality could express itself outside of tribal authorities, namely the authority of the council of elders (*kiama*), and this was paramount to ensure that the well-being of the family (once the individual owner has built a family) is not jeopardized.[22] Translated in the politics of the time, individual ownership was necessary to protect the rights of a minority, the Kikuyu, against the white settlers. But the elders' supreme right and discretionary control over land ownership (the traditional authority Kenyatta was competing for) had to be safeguarded.[23]

Kenyatta further substantiated the distinction between individual and tribal authority. He not only denied individual rights, but condemned individualist behavior, which he saw as a product of colonial decadence – a thought that led the social anthropologist Bronisław Malinowski to reflect in the introduction of *Facing Mount Kenya* that his supervisee "might have been tempted to advise the writer to be more careful in using such antitheses as 'collective' vs. 'individual,' in contrasting the native outlook as 'essentially social' to the European as 'essentially personal'."[24] Kenyatta already wrote in *Muigwithania* that: "Let each person take his own road, that is the way by which we shall lose (throw away) our country."[25] A year earlier, in 1928, he implored his readers to "remember that 'Members of the same family do not lose their identity'."[26] Society could only survive through the

---

Monarchical Tendency in African Political Culture," *The British Journal of Sociology* 18 (1967): 231–250.

[22] Kenyatta, *Facing Mount Kenya*, 31.

[23] Lonsdale, "The Moral Economy of Mau Mau, Wealth, Poverty and Civic Virtue in Kikuyu Political Thought," 376. See also Fr. C. Cagnolo, *The Agĩkũyũ: Their Customs, Traditions and Folklore* (Nairobi: Wisdom Graphic Place, 2006).

[24] Bronisław Malinowski, "Introduction," in *Facing Mount Kenya*, ed Kenyatta, xi. Bronisław Malinowki taught anthropology in the United Kingdom (LSE) and in the United States. He was the founder and defender of anthropological functionalism, which considers society as a living organism, where social relationships are regulated by institutions – each institution playing a particular *function*, holding society as a coherent body. Functionalism aims at uncovering regular patters of behaviors, while myths and beliefs are seen as malleable and changing ornaments.

[25] Kenyatta, "Our Land," in *Muigwithania*, May 1929, Vol. 1, Nr. 12, KNA, DC/MKS/10B/13/1.

[26] Kenyatta, "Let Us Agree among Ourselves and Exalt the Kikuyu," *Muigwithania*, November 1928, Vol. 1, Nr. 7, KNA, DC/MKS/10B/13/1.

household, and individual property through the family. A prosperous society was a prosperous family, itself the guardian of a prosperous land. Society, family, and land depended on each other.[27] Only the nature and source of authority was left to be defined. To do so, Kenyatta distinguished ownership from use of land: he drew a line between private ownership and collective boundaries. More significantly, he distinguished the family both from the collective and from the tribe.

Kenyatta stressed that the family, vested with land rights, ultimately prevailed over the collective, which only demarcated territorial boundaries.[28] Although the collective embodied the general good, it was made of atomized voices, and, as such, was a European invention; it had no relevance when deciding over land issues. Kenyatta, in turn, set the family apart from what he called the Kikuyu "tribe": "the Gikuyu system of land tenure was never tribal tenure, nor was there any customary law which gave any particular chief or group of chiefs any power over lands other than the lands of their own family groups."[29] There could be no collective further than the supreme authority of the family: "Realise that there is nothing equal to a man's home, for it is it that leads him (i.e. actuates, impels him?) and is also his base" he wrote in *Muigwhitania*. The family only could be the fertile soil of political and economic social relations. Furthermore, it only could ensure trust among individuals by providing trust within society, in contrast to European commerce, which "serve[s the] interest of their party which rob all the other [sic]."[30] Kenyatta contrasted the cohesion of Gikuyu customs with the Europeans' "good jobs and good money."[31] He warned that the "time of being helped is coming to end," for were a man to leave his good job, he would be left with unreliable friends quick to forget the glory of his past. His ancestry too would fade away,

---

[27] For detailed anthropological studies of the relationship between land and generational organization, see Peatrik, "Un Système Composite"; Droz, *Migrations Kikuyus*, 116; Kershaw, *Mau Mau from Below*, 66–68.

[28] Lonsdale highlighted these contradictions in "The Moral Economy of Mau Mau, Wealth, Poverty and Civic Virtue in Kikuyu Political Thought," 335.

[29] Kenyatta, *Facing Mount Kenya*, 32, 26–27. It must be noted that Kenyatta invoked or condemned the term "tribe" at his own convenience throughout the rest of his book. All mentions of "tribe" or "tribal" should be understood as being in inverted commas and are directly referring to concepts used by Kenyatta.

[30] Kenyatta, "Let Us Agree among Ourselves and Exalt the Kikuyu."

[31] Kenyatta, "Money Making (or, Quest of Possessions)," *Muigwithania*, December 1928–January 1929, Vol. 1, Nr. 8, KNA, DC/MKS/10B/13/1.

and "HE WILL BE REDUCED TO EATING THE VERY SKIN OF HIS BODY."[32] Individual autonomy and dignity relied on home and land. Writing *My People of Gikuyu and the Life of Chief Wangombe*, Kenyatta insisted: "[a] good name, rather than material reward, was what every warrior looked for."[33] Trust was an internal and almost intimate process that no alien or superseding social or authoritative structure other than the family could ensure.

From Precolonial Kikuyu Moral Debate to the Kenyan Nation

Accession to independence, together with the formation of a Kenyan independent state challenged the boundaries of Kenyatta's political imagination: what and who was to be the "family" in a postcolonial Kenyan nation? Could the language of Kikuyu ethos and morality speak for all? Becoming president, Kenyatta met the difficult task of enlarging, without diminishing, his Kikuyu thought. It should be noted that working with Kenyatta's speeches and specifically their English version presents natural limitations: Kenyatta's public addresses to (especially rural) Africans were commonly made in Swahili, and sometimes in Kikuyu. His speeches were often impromptu and unscripted, colored with local metaphors, tales, or proverbs suggesting subtext often difficult to understand for an outsider, and even more difficult to render faithfully into English. Press or diplomatic reports offered at times inaccurate translations of such messages, while no original version in Swahili or Kikuyu was kept in the Kenya National Archives. Furthermore, Kenyatta was notoriously good at using different registers of languages, and even different languages, to suit varying political purposes, masquerading as different characters for different audiences – as when he portrayed himself as an ancient tribal leader on the cover of *Facing Mount Kenya*. All of these potential hurdles should neither make us accept him as just an enigmatic figure nor should they distract us from trying to understand his politics as a coherent, yet reactive, performance whose meaning can be deciphered through a more global interpretation. Great care was taken here to situate these speeches in their proper historical context, to cross-read them with his earlier writings, and to uncover their political motivations. What has

---

[32] Ibid.
[33] Kenyatta, *My People of Gikuyu and the Life of Chief Wangombe*, 17.

emerged is a description of Kenyatta's political ideas not seen exclusively through the lens of reported political speech, but one that weaves different fragments together (archives, early writings, and published speeches) to reconstruct the core ideas that defined Kenyatta's political career.

Kenyatta's distrust of individuals proved to be an enduring political dynamic that survived after independence. British high commissioner and friend Malcolm MacDonald wrote to the new president in 1964: "I know that you think (quite rightly) that individuals are unimportant" and "agree with you about the unimportance of individuals – except for the rare few, and Mzee Jomo Kenyatta is one of those few."[34] We touch here on an important aspect of Kenyatta's political imagination: politics are not a matter of individuals, they are a matter of families. In other words, individuals *alone* – that is, isolated from tribal institutions – have no power or any political relevance. Trust too remained a relevant feature of his speeches. Speaking at a KANU seminar on June 29, 1962, not even a year after his release from restriction, he bluntly denounced corrupt political behavior: "If a person can buy another, he too can be bought. If a person can offer himself to be bought by a leader, he is no better than a prostitute and cannot be trusted."[35] Trust had to remain rooted in a moral community.

The accession to independence nonetheless challenged the boundaries of his imagined moral community. It forced him to readjust the scope of his discourse to the now independent Kenyan state, and to adopt the nationalist vocabulary of the time, largely dominated by notions that accompanied African decolonization, such as African socialism, African culture and traditions, parliamentary democracy, or even human rights.[36] Kenyatta knew this vocabulary, since he participated in the fifth Pan-African Congress of 1945 in Manchester, and visited the Comintern Schools in Russia. Although his commitment to and interest in Pan-Africanism remains poorly studied, he

---

[34] Malcom MacDonald to Jomo Kenyatta, November 19, 1964, MacDonald Papers, MAC/44/1/2.
[35] Kenyatta, "Ministerial Mantle," *Suffering without Bitterness*, 185.
[36] See, for example, Göran Hydén, *African Politics in Comparative Perspective* (Cambridge: Cambridge University Press, 2012); ibid.; Fabian Klose, *Human Rights in the Shadow of Colonial Violence: The Wars of Independence in Kenya and Algeria* (Philadelphia: University of Pennsylvania Press, 2013).

made no secret of his stance against communism and socialism, ideologies he thought negated the tribal past he valued.[37]

Therefore, Kenyatta did use, more or less willingly, Africanist notions, although systematically connecting them to his earlier writings on Kikuyu history. Speaking in 1964 about the one-party system, he acknowledged the rising "momentum" of "Africanism" but was keen on distinguishing his own understanding from those for whom "Africanism means negritude."[38] As he explained,

> I submit that the Africanism to which we aspire in this country is the Africanism which combines the best from the past, present and future: the Africanism which seeks to fulfil what our people want to be, to do and to have. Indeed, this is the Africanism to which I dedicated my book ... in my early days in the political field, when I said that: "The dead, the living and the unborn will unite to rebuild the destroyed shrines."[39]

This definition directly echoed *Facing Mount Kenya*. The connection with his earlier writings is all the more obvious when it comes to land and tribal issues. During the 1964 independence celebrations, Kenyatta reasserted that land was not only the "greatest asset" for economic development in Kenya, but also ensured "our survival and salvation."[40] Although he reaffirmed that "all tribal land is entrenched in the tribal authority," he quickly added that the tribe should not replace the state, for "[a]t no time did the African tribes, or groups of tribes, see the State in the same way as the Greek City States. At no time did African tribes see themselves as tinpot 'nations'."[41] In fact, Kenyatta invoked an "African" past that was just as malleable as it was in *Facing Mount Kenya*, and that was tailored, once again, to serve his own political interests.[42]

---

[37] See Murray-Brown, *Kenyatta*; Gikandi, "Pan-Africanism and Cosmopolitanism"; McClellan, "Africans and Black Americans in the Comintern Schools, 1925-1934."
[38] Kenyatta, "Statement in the Capacity of the President of KANU," August 13, 1964, in *Suffering without Bitterness*, 227.
[39] Ibid.
[40] Kenyatta, "Television Broadcast," September 11, 1964, in *Suffering without Bitterness*, 232.
[41] Kenyatta, "A One Party System," August 13, 1964, in *Suffering without Bitterness*, 229.
[42] On the malleable use of the past, see Lonsdale, "The Prayers of Waiyaki"; Lonsdale, "Contest of Time."

The glow of the precolonial past could mask, justify, or decry, depending on convenience, the contradictions of a postcolonial Kenyan nation. One contradiction that had to be tackled at independence was the breach between the freedom fighters (ex-Mau Mau) and the loyalists. Kenyatta's calls to "forget and forgive" the past have been widely noted by historians, who pointed out that this was a convenient strategy to conceal his ambiguous relationship to the Mau Mau movement, while subsuming the freedom fighters' cause in the larger struggle for independence.[43] Forgetting the past was justified by the need for national unity: "all [a long history of setbacks and sufferings, of failure and humiliation] can be forgotten, when its outcome is the foundation on which a future can be built."[44]

Nevertheless, Kenyatta's notion of unity was as instrumental as it was confused, especially when it came to situating tribalism within the new nation. On the one hand, Kenyatta claimed that unity depended on the constant dedication to nation-building: "Whether this age of African opportunity becomes in fact the age of African achievement, depends on how we move, as one united team, towards a common goal."[45] Consequently, he vilified tribalism: "unity cannot be taken for granted ... There are some people who remain tribalists at heart, and who regard unity as their enemy."[46] On the other hand, unity did not dethrone tribalism. Instead, Kenyatta juggled with concepts. He was quick to admit that the colonial past could not be wiped away – just as he had done in *Facing Mount Kenya,* certainly because he knew the colonizers were part of his audience. He acknowledged that tribal politics mattered, under the cover of a culturalist argument: "Every man has the right to take a pride and interest in his tribe – its history, its culture and its customs."[47] He appealed for tribal feeling clothed in

---

[43] See in particular Murray-Brown, *Kenyatta*; Elisha S. Atieno-Odhiambo, "The Production of History in Kenya: The Mau Mau Debate," *Canadian Journal of African Studies* 25, no. 2 (1991): 300–307.

[44] Kenyatta, "Speech on Kenyatta Day," October 20, 1964, in *Suffering without Bitterness*, 241.

[45] Kenyatta, "Opening Address at the Kenya Institute of Administration," August 19, 1965, in *Suffering without Bitterness*, 282.

[46] Kenyatta, "Speech on Madaraka Day," June 1, 1965, in *Suffering without Bitterness*, 276.

[47] Ibid., 313.

From Precolonial Kikuyu Moral Debate to the Kenyan Nation 49

terms of a more democratic representation.[48] Yet again, when tribal animosities risked damaging his politics, he argued for unity. An *aide mémoire* preparing his forthcoming tour of Western province in April 1964 advised him:

> Western Region people consider themselves neglected by government. They urge redistribution of portfolios to give them an additional Minister. Your underlying theme, therefore, might be on UNITY, and that the strength of the State and Government depends on the loyalty of the people to their laws and respect for Human Rights and property.[49]

Kenyatta was taking advantage of the unsettled status of African traditions in a newly established republican context (Kenya became a republic in December 1964; see Chapter 3 for further details). Nevertheless, his use of concepts foreign to his own lexicon barely concealed patchy rhetorical constructions.

Given the sensitive and divisive nature of the issue of tribalism, Kenyatta used culturalist arguments to legitimate the remnants of tribal politics in the new, decolonized state institutions. Setting aside his assertion that tribes should not be states, he compared Kenya's state institutions to tribal authorities. The parliament "must give full modern expression to the traditional African custom, by serving as the place where the Elders and the spokesmen of the people are expected and enabled to confer."[50] When it came to the justification of the one-party state in 1964, he argued that, just as tribes had, from time immemorial, united against crises, the tribal council "was at once a Government and an expression of the very personality of each and every citizen."[51] The connection between tribal council and the state was "justified on the grounds that only therein could people find peace and security."[52]

---

[48] Kenyatta was already at pains to establish a parallel between Kikuyu culture and Western democracy in *Facing Mount Kenya* (see p. 33). As for his postindependence speeches, the references to "democracy" are multiple. See, for example, Kenyatta, *Suffering without Bitterness*, 229, 231, 260–261, 306, 347.
[49] Tours of Western province (Friday, April 23–Sunday, April 25, 1965), *aide mémoire*, KNA, KA/4/9.
[50] Kenyatta, "Speech for the State Opening of Parliament," December 1964, in *Suffering without Bitterness*, 260.
[51] Kenyatta, "A One Party State," August 13, 1964, in *Suffering without Bitterness*, 229.
[52] Ibid.

The frontiers between the nation and the tribe were fuzzy, and Kenyatta was, once again, at pains to reconcile ancestral tribes with the modern nation. Picking up on the *en vogue* concept of *"ujamaa"* ("familyhood" in Swahili, "sharing" by extension) popularized by the Tanzanian president Julius Nyerere, Kenyatta barely clarified the distinction, asserting "we have our own concept of *Ujamaa*, springing from our own culture here."[53] This was vague enough a formulation for Kenyatta to publicly hint at his antisocialist feelings.[54] Nevertheless, at a time when African socialism was defined through its neocolonial antithesis, liberal capitalism, Kenyatta could not politically afford not to take a position on this issue. Confronted with the accusation that his "African socialism" meant nothing at all, Kenyatta replied: "The essential of our African socialism can be defined as inspiration. We are seeking to inspire dedication, not in pursuit of an ideology or in search for power, but for the welfare of humanity."[55]

Kenyatta had never been a man of ideology and the political consequences of his insistence on values must be seriously explored. He was part of a movement of moral refoundation that was not limited to Kikuyu politics. At the time of his encounter with Bronisław Malinowski, indeed, colonial doctrine was undergoing change, becoming increasingly self-reflective as well as more critical. Colonial administrators, with the help of anthropologists who saw an opportunity to promote their own research agenda, started to rethink colonization, its progress, its techniques, and its legitimacy. This "second colonisation" aimed at rationalizing and modernizing colonization by fostering scientific knowledge and promoting, as a result, "a colonial science."[56]

---

[53] Kenyatta, "Speech for the State Opening of the Parliament," November 2, 1965, in *Suffering without Bitterness*, 286. For an in-depth analysis of the rhetorical use of the term *"ujamaa"* in Tanzania, see Marie-Aude Fouéré, "Julius Nyerere, Ujamaa, and Political Morality in Contemporary Tanzania," *African Studies Review* 57, no. 1 (2014): 1–24.

[54] See McClellan, "Africans and Black Americans in the Comintern Schools, 1925–1934."

[55] Speech by His Excellency the President at Diplomatic Corps Luncheon, July 29, 1965, KNA, KA/4/9.

[56] Terence Ranger, "From Humanism to the Science of Man: Colonialism in Africa and the Understanding of Alien Societies," *Transactions of the Royal Historical Society (Fifth Series)* 26 (1976): 115–141; Paul Cocks, "The Rhetoric of Science and the Critique of Imperialism in British Social Anthropology, c. 1870–1940," *History and Anthropology* 9, no. 1 (1995): 93–119; Jack Goody, *The Expansive Moment: The Rise of Social Anthropology in Britain and Africa 1918–1970*

Yet, this science was no ideology, entailing too moralizing a discourse. Moral virtues occupied a special place in Kenyatta's speeches. Comparing the notes prepared for his speeches, generally by an assistant minister or the attorney general, with the publicly delivered version, they were almost his personal signature. Just as he had done in *Facing Mount Kenya*, he continued to warn against the pervasiveness of "colonial mentality" and advised people "to be vigilant, and to rededicate yourselves today to building a nation deeply rooted in our own thoughts and ideas [so as to preserve] in many arts the African traditional forms and culture."[57]

Making politics an affair of civic virtue, law and order became a matter of individual behavior – not of collective action. Kenyatta's definitions of political loyalty and obedience to state authority were confined to the cradle of moral virtues – more precisely, to the family. Addressing administrative officers in March 1965, the president did not mince his words: "Those of you who fail to give your best are not only betraying yourselves and a shame to your families, but you are also failing in the trust which I as Head of the Republic of Kenya have placed in you."[58] Loyalty was invoked whenever law and order mattered, especially when it was about joining opposition, and thus abandoning "past loyalty to Kenya nationalism."[59] Moral virtues set the ultimate boundary between individuals and the state. Kenyatta expressed this clearly during the 1964 republican celebration: "All of us must safeguard the integrity of our State. And we must look on law and order not just as an institution of society, or a code of behaviour, but as the outward image of our self-respect."[60] The society Kenyatta

---

(Cambridge: Cambridge University Press, 1995); Véronique Dimier, "Enjeux Institutionnels Autour d'une Science Politique des Colonies en France et en Grande-Bretagne, 1930–1950," *Genèses* 37, no. 1 (1999): 70–92; Frederick Cooper, "Development, Modernisation, and the Social Sciences in the Era of Decolonisation: The Examples of British and French Africa," *Revue d'Histoire des Sciences Humaines* 10, no. 1 (2004): 9–38; Helen L. Tilley and Robert J. Gordon, eds., *Ordering Africa* (Manchester: Manchester University Press, 2007).

[57] Kenyatta, "Speech for the O.A.U. Day," May 25, 1964, in *Suffering without Bitterness*, 218.

[58] H.E. the President's Talk to Administrative Officers, March 12, 1965, KNA, KA/4/9.

[59] Kenyatta, "Broadcast Address to the Nation," April 26, 1966, in *Suffering without Bitterness*, 302.

[60] Kenyatta, "Republic Celebrations – 1964," December 12, 1964, in *Suffering without Bitterness*, 257.

defended was certainly not a nation (i.e., a collectivity not only defined by its belonging to the same territory, but by a notion of ruling for all), yet not a tribe either.[61] It was, instead, inherently atomized, and made up of individuals his state authority had no intent to unite, as we will now see.

Postcolonial Kenya: Virtue for All, State for No One?

Following Lonsdale's observation that Kenyatta imagined himself as a Kikuyu elder, that his authority was not at all an authority for all, it can be argued that Kenyatta never considered authority (and, by extension, the state) as an instrument of social change.[62] His conception of authority, his authority as president, did not extend beyond the realm of security, law, and order. Far from conceptualizing a strong state, it was, in fact, a minimal state. He repeated several times "you must know that Kenyatta alone cannot give you everything. All things we must do together."[63] On the eve of independence, setting aside his previous attraction to British parliamentarism (see Chapter 3 for further explanation), he asserted that the state could not be accountable to its citizens: "We reject a blueprint of the Western model of a two-Party system of Government because we do not subscribe to the notion of the Government and the governed being in opposition to one another, the one clamouring for duties and the other crying out for rights."[64] Rather, building on the Kikuyu ethos of "self-accomplishment," according to which individuals ought to seek their own means to fulfill their own lives and achievements – that is, to become adults – he asserted: "It is ... the responsibility of each individual to ensure that

---

[61] I want to emphasize here that Kenyatta's ideas of the "nation," "tribe," or "community," cannot be read outside of the context of the land issue. Kenyatta was not attempting to reinvent concepts to imagine the future post-colony. He was manipulating *en vogue* concepts (yet at no point was he an idealist) that would serve his *immediate* interest. For a similar reasoning on the concept of the clan in postcolonial Kenya, see Claire Médard, "Territoires de l'Ethnicité: Encadrement, Revendications et Conflits Territoriaux au Kenya" (Ph.D. diss., Paris 1, 1999), 240–241.

[62] Lonsdale, "Jomo Kenyatta, God & the Modern World," 49, 63.

[63] Kenyatta, "Independence Day, 1963," December 12, 1963, in *Suffering without Bitterness*, 217.

[64] Kenyatta, "Broadcast," September 21, 1963 and August 13, 1964, in *Suffering without Bitterness*, 211, 227.

he grows up into a person who can fit into his national society, thereby living contentedly with his fellow human beings."[65] Authority, state, and society were bound less by a traditionalist than a functionalist conception of community-making, inspired, perhaps, by his anthropological studies with Malinowski, where social cohesion comes first, myth and history second; at the same time, it was bound to a conservative and static understanding of the rule of law.

Kenyatta placed the Kikuyu principle of personal accomplishment at the basis of state-building in Kenya, and exalted it in virtually all his postindependence speeches. In line with his contempt for communist values and his ideal of a self-regulated society, he considered "self-help" (or self-mastery) as the cement of social order. Heading to London for the last independence conference in 1963, he carefully reasserted the supremacy of land property right – a principle that quickly became the crux of the politics of independence – in front of an audience of Kenyan businessmen crowded into Nairobi City Hall. He explained that, if the state was to protect property, at no point did it mean nationalization: "You must not interpret my remarks as implying nationalisation. We consider that nationalisation will not serve to advance the cause of African socialism."[66] He continued the line he had always taken since the early days of his political commitment: the supremacy of land property and the necessity to work for it. In the same speech on economic policy, he stated that

[t]he land is the place where the ordinary man and woman can do most to build the nation. When one farmer increases his cultivations and improves his farm by harder work, it is a personal achievement. When ten thousand farmers follow his example, it becomes a national achievement.[67]

It was only successful business, itself closely depending on working the land, that could lead to successful nation-building. All the state could and ought to do was to enable "individual men and women" (Kenyatta rarely referred to these individuals as citizens) to "[exercise] their

---

[65] Speech by His Excellency the President at Diplomatic Corps Luncheon, July 29, 1965, KNA, KA/4/9. See the following pages on self-accomplishment.
[66] Kenyatta, "Speech in the Nairobi City Hall on Economic Policy," September 29, 1964, in *Suffering without Bitterness*, 238.
[67] Kenyatta, "Speech for the State Opening of the Parliament," February 15, 1967, in *Suffering without Bitterness*, 336.

personal initiative and for the fulfilment of their individual ambitions."[68]

Kenyatta transferred, or rather enlarged, the Kikuyu principle of possessive individualism (which should not be simply reduced to Western conceptions of individual liberalism), the same individualism he praised in *Facing Mount Kenya*, to the new Kenyan republic. Individual undertaking (self-help) alone could lead to individual achievement (the ethos of the *mûramati*). Speaking to the Kenyan youth in 1966, he summarized this position: "Not everybody can reach the top of his profession and not everybody can enter the profession of his choice ... There is work in Kenya for all, but you must go out and seek it."[69] The solution to unemployment depended "equally on the efforts of the many thousands of our countrymen whose livelihood comes from the land."[70] Already in December 1964, he had stated: "Do your work honestly and well. For the State's obligation to you is no greater than your obligation to your fellow-men."[71] Yet, Kenyatta did not necessarily reduce his expectations on the state. Instead, possessive individualism materialized as his prime concern: the protection of land ownership and property by the new state. No matter whether he spoke of human rights or concepts related to African socialism, at no point did national expectations supersede his Kikuyu ethics. The state was meant to protect the integrity of property, not to create new opportunities. Therefore, any attack against property was an attack against the state. In a speech celebrating the birth of the Republic of Kenya, the notions of property and crime were barely masked by the ornamental, internationally acceptable expressions of "human rights" and "unlawfulness":

We must gear ourselves to a fundamental belief in individual human rights, as the basis of respect. And this respect must be extended, beyond what a man is or what he does, to what he *owns* and cherishes. Without respect for property, security of property, chaos can swiftly come to any State ... We are all moving now towards a common goal. We need, therefore, respect for a

---

[68] Ibid.
[69] Address by His Excellency the President at the Youth Festival on October 16, 1966 at 2.30 p.m., KNA, KA/4/11.
[70] Kenyatta, "State Opening of Parliament – 1967," February 15, 1967, in *Suffering without Bitterness*, 335–336.
[71] Kenyatta, "Republic Celebrations – 1964," December 12, 1964, in *Suffering without Bitterness*, 255.

Postcolonial Kenya: Virtue for All, State for No One?   55

new social conscience, in which the *criminal* is not just a candidate for punishment or pity, but a traitor to our purpose and an object of scorn.[72]

The state being an instrument of control, self-accomplishment could only be achieved outside of the realm of authority and power: at the margins of the state. At no point was self-accomplishment a state ideology.

Kenyatta considered community-making through the state as impractical and illusionary: since communal sense did not exist outside the individual, no authority could foster and protect it.[73] The state was at best "in the hearts and spirit of the people."[74] The spiel of virtues for all, yet state for no one, was adapted to all government's politics. As for concrete development issues, such as land possession and agriculture: it was "not the intention of government to go on pumping money indefinitely into large scale farmers in this area if these farmers do not follow the rules of good husbandry and the advice of the extension staff."[75] Banks could not "make something out of nothing and the government cannot by order, or 'fiat' grant to a printed piece of paper a value independent of the backing which it possesses."[76] (Although these lines may sound like colonial officialdom, Kenyatta was praising the indigenous communal organization such as "self-help" or "*harambee*," literally "let's pull together" in Swahili.) Individuals should obey state legislation – "there is no hope in our country if individuals take upon themselves to grab land" – and yet "it should be made clear to everyone that we will not be able to give everyone land."[77]

---

[72] My emphasis. Kenyatta, "Republic Celebrations – 1964," December 12, 1964, in *Suffering without Bitterness*, 254.

[73] It should be emphasized again that the individual is likely to be the male individual, as the individualization of land ownership also followed a colonial pattern that reinforced masculinity and the male individual as the rightful owner of land. See Médard, "Territoires de l'Ethnicité," 228.

[74] Speech by His Excellency the President at the Opening of the Secondary School and Technical Block at Starehe Boy's Central, July 15, 1966, KNA, KA/4/11.

[75] Speech to Be Delivered by the Minister for Finance on Behalf of His Excellency the President on the Occasion of the Opening of the Eldoret Show on March 4, 1966, KNA, KA/4/11.

[76] Speech by His Excellency the President Mzee Jomo Kenyatta at the Opening of the Central Bank on September 14, 1966, KNA, KA/4/11.

[77] Notes for the President on the Occasion of the Presentation of Certificates to the Former Squatters on November 25, 1966, KNA, KA/4/11.

Kenyatta and the Family

Kenyatta's vision of leadership was ingrained in the domestic realm of the family. He is often remembered for the cutting question he asked his Kikuyu opponent, former Mau Mau and socialist politician Bildad Kaggia: "what have you done for yourself?," when he publicly emphasized that building a large house, together with a large family, was the primordial aim for a self-respecting man.[78] I wish to push the argument further and show how he connected the politics of the state to the family household. To begin with, Kenyatta portrayed the good politician as a good farmer:

> I work during the day, and then after work I go home to my *shamba* and have a look at my bananas, potatoes, poultry and other things. If you elect somebody who spends all his time in Nairobi doing nothing: what good is that? What does such a person – whether an M. P. or a City Councillor or a KANU official – show us he is doing back at his home and in his *shamba*, where his parents are? Of what use is it roaming about in Nairobi in bars and hotels? This only brings poverty and prostitution in this country. Many of you write letters blaming the women, saying that these women prostitutes are spoiling Nairobi, but you do not tell the truth. It is the men who are prostitutes.[79]

His denunciation of the decadence of urban life adds a substantial nuance to the equation made between the ability to lead and the ability to farm. Kenyatta disliked town life, in particular in Nairobi, which he saw as a place of strangers, alienating Africans from their traditional way of life; once president, he even refused to sleep in the Nairobi state house, which he believed was haunted by ghosts.[80] More significant

---

[78] Kenyatta and Kaggia were arrested and jailed together. See Kaggia's own records of the event in Bildad M. Kaggia, W. de Leeuw, and M. Kaggia, *The Struggle for Freedom and Justice* (Nairobi: Transafrica Press, 2012), 271. Lonsdale highlighted the tension between leadership and self-mastery when he wrote that Kenyatta "made room for the self-mastery of others, by no means for all Kenyans but for all the more important ethnic vassals who, having had done with trifling, aspired to realize their ambition under an elder's shade." In Lonsdale, "Kenyatta, God, & the Modern World," 63. See also Hervé Maupeu, "Kikuyu Capitalistes. Réflexions sur un Cliché Kenyan," *Outre-Terre* 2, no. 11 (2005): 493–506. For more historical insights on Kenyatta's address to Kaggia, see Chapter 5.

[79] Kenyatta, *Suffering without Bitterness*, 347, see also 305.

[80] John M. Lonsdale, "Town Life in Colonial Kenya," *Azania: Archaeological Research in Africa* 36–37, no. 1 (2001): 211; Kenneth Kwama, "When 'Ghosts'

perhaps is his suggestion that town life not only led to women's prostitution, but that prostitution could contaminate men living in the city too. Hence, a detribalized town life would strip men of their manliness: leaving "land unattended" entailed an "attitude ... not only negative, but [which] promotes biggest waste in Kenya today," and was a "disgrace to ... manhood and to our society."[81] Hence, the rural family order protected manliness, as well as men's ability to lead.

Kenyatta was rooting the ability to lead not only in a milieu characteristic of traditional tribal life, but also in a patriarchal vision of political hierarchies and moral values. The male individual only could be both a family man and a man of power. His conception of women was as much inspired by Kikuyu mythical history as by colonial politics. The fundamental myth of the birth of the Kikuyu tribe that he recalled in the first chapter of *Facing Mount Kenya* suggested that women are unfit for leadership.[82] Instead, women ought to fertilize the tribe, ensuring the "bond of kinship" and ensuring the physical and psychological well-being of the family.[83] The association of women and fertility must be read in a longer perspective, passed on from precolonial to colonial history, and which Lynn Thomas described as "the politics of the womb," where women are confined to being non-political agents both within and outside the household.[84] At no point during his political career did Kenyatta challenge this patriarchal conception of the family, or the masculine definition of authority.

Finally, by comparing state-building to farming, Kenyatta set up the family not only as the ultimate social basis of the state itself, but as the ultimate frontier his leadership could not cross: "I am prepared to serve you with the life which is still left in me. I have not come to rule you so as to tell anyone do this and do that," he would tell his welcoming

---

Haunted Kenya's First President Mzee Jomo Kenyatta out of State House," *The Standard*, July 12, 2013.

[81] Kenyatta, "Television Broadcast," September 11, 1964 in *Suffering without Bitterness*, 233–234. The association of town and the loss of manhood was observable up until independence see Elisha S. Atieno-Odhiambo, "Kula Raha: Gendered Discourses and the Contours of Leisure in Nairobi, 1946–63," *Azania: Archaeological Research in Africa* 36–37, no. 1 (2001): 254–264.

[82] Kenyatta, *Facing Mount Kenya*, 3–8.   [83] Ibid., 13–14.

[84] Ibid., 3–8; Lynn M. Thomas, *Politics of the Womb: Women, Reproduction, and the State in Kenya* (Berkeley: University of California Press, 2003).

crowd in 1946.[85] After independence, and advocating the politics of *harambee*, he repeatedly insisted: "you must know that Kenyatta alone cannot give you everything."[86] The rhetoric of governing oneself, deep-rooted in the household, was elevated to the realm of state-building:

> I tell you this: nation building is not a matter of having money to employ, or of having authority to wield. It is a matter of patriotism and pride. In your work, whatever this is, and in your homes and in your districts, the smallest efforts to build and to improve are most important.[87]

Family was a Janus-faced concept. On the one hand, it demarcated acceptable social behavior, by safeguarding the sanctity of ownership of land and of the owners. It encompassed two opposite forces: individualism and tribalism. It restricted individuals from thinking that individual achievements would give them the right to have "authority to wield." And it was erected as the antithesis of tribalism, which, for the reasons previously explained, Kenyatta never considered a self-sufficient right to authority. At no point, however, was the concept of family in conflict with individualism and tribalism – or ethnicity. Ethnicity would remain the guiding strength from which Kenyans had to "[learn] how to master themselves in modern times," the only force to prove "that Kenya was a moral community precisely because its people were not detribalised."[88] But family boundaries set the boundaries of the state and of authority, as a state could never replace the people's duty to rule their own lives.[89]

However, the boundaries of the family were unclear, both in theory and in practice. In *Facing Mount Kenyatta,* the definition of the family was fuzzy and imprecise, perhaps because the family was, at that time already, a new concept in a new environment. As a result of the colonization of the fertile White Highlands, shortage of land hindered the formation of new and large *mbari* (clans) that had structured precolonial Kikuyu society, and these were thus reduced to the patrimonial families that could afford to acquire and cultivate land. Kikuyu society did not disappear, but disintegrated. Its basic unit shrank, and

---

[85] Lonsdale, "Henry Muoria, Public Moralist," 279.
[86] Kenyatta, "Independence Day 1963," in *Suffering without Bitterness*, 217.
[87] Ibid., 258; see also 273, 287, 347.
[88] Lonsdale, "Jomo Kenyatta, God & the Modern World," 51.
[89] On the tension between state and ethnicity, see John Lonsdale, "KAU's Cultures," 121.

its ideal became democratized: the *mûramati*, the Kikuyu accomplished man, owner of land and family, a man aspiring to leadership, was no longer subjected to the authority of the *mbari*, the clan. With the disintegration of clanship, the nuclear family took over the control and regulation of social relations.[90] In *Facing Mount Kenya*, Kenyatta described this transformation, yet without being able to solve the internal contradictions it posed to his Kikuyu history. At that time, his aim was to revive the ethos of personal accomplishment, while he himself aspired to be recognized as a *mûramati*, as the legitimate leader of his "clan."[91] He associated the family group with the *mbari*, literally the lineage or extended family, and gave a rather minimalist definition: the family "brings together all those who are related by blood; namely a man, his wife or wives and children and also their grand- and great-grandchildren."[92] This was a surprising definition, for Kikuyu society was regulated by rituals, not by blood ties.[93]

From a more practical point of view, Kenyatta took great care to marry into an influential Kikuyu family, especially once he returned to Kenya in 1946, seven years after the publication of *Facing Mount Kenya*. Before then, he had married twice, first, in 1920, Wahu, who was from Kiambu and with whom he had two children, Peter Muigai Kenyatta and Margaret Wambui Kenyatta; then, in 1942, when living in Great Britain, where he married Edna Clarke who bore him one son, Peter Magana Kenyatta.[94] In 1946, Kenyatta married the daughter of the powerful senior chief Koinange, Grace Wanjiku: this was a political act that linked him to a powerful Kikuyu clan and enabled him to claim to be a Kikuyu elder.[95] At the same time, he became brother-in-law to his long-time comrade and later powerful minister Mbiyu Koinange. Grace Wanjiku died while giving birth to their daughter, Jane Wambui Kenyatta. Kenyatta then married his fourth wife, Ngina Kenyatta, better known as "Mama Ngina," in 1952. Ngina was the daughter of senior chief Muhoho in Kenyatta's birthplace, Ngenda,

---

[90] Droz, *Migrations Kikuyus*, 117.
[91] See Lonsdale, "Jomo Kenyatta, God & the Modern World."
[92] Kenyatta, *Facing Mount Kenya*, 1.
[93] See Peatrik, "Un Système Composite."
[94] On Kenyatta's marriages, see Murray-Brown, *Kenyatta*, 79, 213–214, 229–232, 247.
[95] Murray-Brown, *Kenyatta*, 229–232; Kershaw, *Mau Mau from Below*, 199.

and this marriage secured another alliance with a trustee of a clan.[96] They had four children: Christine Wambui-Pratt, Uhuru Muigai Kenyatta, Nyokabi Muthama (born Kenyatta), and Muhoho Kenyatta.

Kenyatta's authority had been, from the early stage of his political career, deep-rooted in a Kikuyu system of power on which he continued to rely once he became president. More important, however, was the fact that his closest collaborators originated from Kiambu district, a pattern that led political analysts to talk about the government of a "Kiambu mafia."[97] Among them were, to mention but a few, the attorney Charles Njonjo (the son of the former colonial chief Josiah Njonjo), the minister of finance James Gichuru (Kenyatta's brother-in-law), and the minister of defense Njoroge Mungai (Kenyatta's cousin and personal physician).[98] Similarly, most of the PCs and heads of major parastatal institutions, as well as top police officers, were Kikuyu, and all either from Kiambu or Nyeri districts.[99] James Gichuru is said to have commented that: "It is not by accident that Kiambu was made the seat of power, it is not that they like it, it is because the god of the Kikuyu decided that Kiambu would be the head, Murang'a the stomach and Nyeri the legs."[100]

---

[96] Murray-Brown, *Kenyatta*, 247; John Lonsdale, "The Moral Economy of Mau Mau, Wealth, Poverty and Civic Virtue in Kikuyu Political Thought," 272.

[97] On Kenyatta's first marriages, see Murray-Brown, *Kenyatta*. For insights on the notion of "mafia" state and contemporary Kenyan politics, see Wrong, *It's Our Turn to Eat*. On the politics of the chiefs, see Clough, *Fighting Two Sides*.

[98] On the moral legitimacy provided by the association with former chiefs, see Throup, "The Construction and Deconstruction of the Kenyatta State." Njonjo, Mbiyu Koinange, and Mungai were referred in 1969 as the "inner cabinet" – that is, Kenyatta's "closest advisers ... often making decisions without consulting ministers or even Kenyatta." By 1969, 30 percent of Kenyatta's cabinet was Kikuyu; in 1964, the president, the attorney general, the foreign minister, the defense minister, the finance minister, and the commissioner of police, as well as the elite presidential guard Bernard Njinu and his bodyguard Wanyoike Thungu, were all from Kiambu, to mention only these few. Furthermore, "nine of the twenty-two permanent secretaryships [of the Civil Service, on which Kenyatta heavily relied to rule the country], four of the then seven [PCs] also [were] of the same tribe." Both quotes are from Tamarkin, "The Roots of Political Stability in Kenya," 302.

[99] Hornsby, *Kenya*, 255–256.

[100] Emman Omari, "When They Were Kings: How Kiambu's Power Men Ruled," *Daily Nation*, June 15, 2011.

Kenyatta and the Family

Kenyatta's preference for Kiambu-based loyalties puts into perspective his understanding of the family as a political unit more viable than the tribe as a whole. The nuance shows that, although Kikuyu identity was a crucial ingredient in enhancing his legitimacy, it was not sufficient, in a disrupted colonized world, for him to impose his political authority. Colonization had put a stop to one of the key elements of identity of the Kikuyu tribe – that is to say, the notion of a dynamic frontier – by means of the acquisition and cultivation of new areas of land.[101] By preventing Kikuyu expansion not only in Central province, but in the fertile land of the Rift Valley, colonization created and reinforced disparities within the tribe.[102] At the same time, integration into the colonial economy heightened both economic disparities and political schisms within the Kikuyu tribe.[103] As the district closest to Nairobi, Kiambu benefited from the socioeconomic modernization of the capital.[104] Regarding the burning land issue that set ablaze growing masses of disgruntled landless and squatters in other Kikuyu districts (in particular, Nyeri and Fort Hall, today's Murang'a), a more landed and wealthy class developed in Kiambu, thus limiting the influence of radical politicians in the district.[105] Such conservative history may explain why most of the moderate politicians from the KAU (which Kenyatta would come to chair in 1947) came from Kiambu district.[106]

The historical depth of these district rivalries may also explain why Kenyatta avoided speaking for the tribe as whole, but rather in favor of a family rooted in land, bound by shared moral virtues, and where

---

[101] Godfrey Muriuki, *A History of the Kikuyu 1500–1900* (Oxford: Oxford University Press, 1974), chapters 2 and 3.

[102] See the distinction made by Tignor between the ancestral Kikuyu practice of squatting or *kaffir* farming and the squatting during colonization, which entailed land dispossession, in Tignor, *Colonial Transformation of Kenya*, 107. I thank John Lonsdale for his generous advice on the historical formation of a Kiambu Kikuyu identity.

[103] Geoff Lamb, *Peasant Politics: Conflict and Development in Murang'a* (New York: St. Martin Press, 1974), 7.

[104] See Claire C. Robertson, *Trouble Showed the Way: Women, Men, and Trade in the Nairobi Area, 1890–1990* (Bloomington: Indiana University Press, 1997), chapter 3.

[105] Lamb, *Peasant Politics*, 12–14; Kanogo, *Squatters and the Roots of Mau Mau (1905–1963)*, 105–120, 140; Furedi, *The Mau Mau War in Perspective*, 88–90.

[106] Lonsdale, "KAU's Cultures."

blood ties mattered less than the community of interests.[107] Significantly, it is difficult to draw a clear line between Kenyatta's biological and political family, given the marital, political, and business alliances that tied his relatives and political collaborators before and after independence. In the end, the attempt to define Kenyatta's family brings us back to his intellectual training in functionalist anthropology with Bronisław Malinowski: family matters as a functional organ of society, not as an essential social body. Such a definition was best suited to adapt to the political, social, and economic disruptions caused by colonization. We may see, however, Kenyatta's notion of family as maintaining, rather than reinventing, the colonial pattern of "small-peasant farming on an individual basis."[108] We must remember, as Robert Buijtenhuis underlined, that Kenyatta had never been an economic nationalist.[109] He never questioned the colonial economic legacy, but continued it, as the next chapters will show. In fact, he might have seen the preservation of the colonial economic legacy as the only way to preserve (Kiambu) Kikuyu self-mastery as well as land ownership.

***

Kenyatta's postindependence speeches were clearly inspired by his earlier writings. Although deeply embedded in politics, they revealed a model of society and authority that Kenyatta established and defended. He did not believe in community-building, because he saw individual interests as paramount. Neither did he believe that individuals could wield authority alone. He liked to repeat that nothing is free, that people must work for themselves and should not expect any help from the state. Therefore, his conception of authority as state leader was confined to law and security: at no point was it an instrument of social transformation. By the same token, his moral authority remained rooted in the moral economy of the family.

---

[107] It is meaningful that Duncan Ndegwa, first secretary to the cabinet and head of the civil service, devoted a large part of the first 100 pages of his autobiography to Kikuyu culture; see Ndgewa, *Walking in Kenyatta Struggles*.

[108] Robert Buijtenhuijs, *Mau Mau: Twenty Years After: The Myth and the Survivors* (The Hague: Mouton and Co., 1973), 31. See also Leys, *Underdevelopment in Kenya*, chapter 3.

[109] Buijtenhuijs, *Mau Mau*, 54.

The discourse on the limits of state power was not antithetic with a moral and constitutionalist discourse. It was neither a specificity of Kenyatta's political imagination, nor a specific trait of patrimonial power. As historians have shown, the transformations brought about by colonization radically altered traditional representation of power, while fostering the emergence of new conception of legitimate authority and moral duties.[110] Recent research also emphasizes that conservatism was not necessarily at odds with liberal thoughts *en vogue* at the time.[111] Conservative ideas were increasingly centered on the reconstruction of a social and moral order – two central elements in Kenyatta's political imagination. At the same time, the emphasis on morality overshadowed the importance of the territory, which came second after the notions of political hierarchies and the definition of property.[112] Colonial disruption of state power fostered a quest for moral equivalence among a newly built, colonial-educated elite, which defined authority as a moral language entitling them to a new social status and political roles.

Kenyatta was no nationalist thinker, and never reflected on non-Kikuyu tribes; yet, neither was he a tribalist thinker, as he always avoided speaking for the tribe *per se*. Those who saw in him a tribalist failed to acknowledge the emphasis he put on the "family." Kenyatta was, above all, a *mûramati*, a family man, and, to accomplish himself, a man of power. Being Kikuyu, Kenyatta acted within a particular cultural frame: that of Kikuyu society, which shaped him profoundly, although his political imagination was augmented by the Western influences he experienced both in Kenya and abroad. Kikuyu ethnicity provided a necessary language to forge political loyalties, but we must

---

[110] Romain Bertrand, "Locating the 'Family-State': The Forgotten Legacy of Javanese Theories of the Public Domain (17th–20thc.)," in *Patrimonial Capitalism and Empire (Political Power and Social Theory, Volume 28)*, eds. Mounira M. Charrad and Julia Adams (Emerald Group Publishing Limited), 241–265; Derek R. Peterson, "'Be Like Firm Soldiers to Develop the Country': Political Imagination and the Geography of Gikuyuland," *International Journal of African Historical Studies* 37, no. 1 (2004): 71–101; Emma Hunter, "Languages of Freedom in Decolonising Africa," *Transactions of the Royal Historical Society* 27 (2017): 253–269.

[111] Hunter, "Languages of Freedom in Decolonising Africa"; Duncan Bell, *Reordering the World: Essays on Liberalism and Empire* (Princeton, NJ: Princeton University Press, 2016).

[112] Bertrand, "Locating the 'Family-State'," 254 and Peterson, "Be Like Firm Soldiers to Develop the Country," 73.

take his denunciation of tribalism seriously.[113] Important as Kikuyu culture was to his personal development and his political imagination, we should not forget that Kikuyu moral economy was constantly negotiated and underwent profound changes in Kenyatta's lifetime, in particular after independence, where he was confronted with the necessity of building viable alliances in which ethnicity was no longer the sole ingredient for building power.[114]

Last, but not least, Kenyatta had an acute sense of political realism, which was, in a way, the continuation of the politicized history that emerged in the 1920s. In 1965, Kenyatta claimed that "it would always be unwise to start by demolishing the whole structure created by the Colonial Government in favour of some untried experiment."[115] Independence could not be imagined *ex nihilo*: it had to be considered in the midst of the contradictions produced by colonization. Although ideas mattered in the struggle for decolonization, possibilities were ultimately determined by political constraints. Similarly, his understanding of Kenya's independence clearly displayed pessimism: "We have nobody else to rely on. Therefore, every contribution counts."[116] Kenyatta often repeated that the fruits of independence could only be harvested through work and effort.[117] Kenya was about to "to break the last links which chained us to a longer past" but "[w]ith the sunrise tomorrow, there will be no sudden fulfilment of all our ambitions and needs."[118] Perhaps unsurprisingly, Kenyatta shared an equally negative understanding of heroic figures. His repeated

---

[113] On the public and instrumental use of ethnicity, see Atieno-Odhiambo, "Hegemonic Enterprises and Instrumentalities of Survival."

[114] As Michael Chege wrote: "at the community level 'social capital' may be a more appropriate development determinant (especially when added to the right legal and macro-economic policies) ... Social capital varies with community, not ethnicity. Because it is premised on the intensity of voluntary civic engagement by private citizens, it is therefore a malleable human artefact." His article proposed a useful critic of "culture" and "ethnicity" as historical, social, and economic variables to explain the Kenyan economy, see Chege, "Introducing Race as a Variable into the Political Economy of Kenya Debate," p. 230.

[115] Jomo Kenyatta, "University Ceremony," March 26, 1965, in *Suffering without Bitterness*, 269.

[116] Kenyatta, "Inauguration Ceremony," *Suffering without Bitterness*, 258.

[117] Kenyatta, "Independence Day," December 12, 1963, *Suffering without Bitterness*, 216.

[118] Kenyatta, "Farewell to the Governor-General," January 3, 1964, *Suffering without Bitterness*, 250.

statements that he himself was no hero are countless: "We ourselves can save us, but nobody else ... These are not the words of Kenyatta. God Himself told the human race. He said He had closed the door with a lock, and had thrown the key into the ocean; that the door would never open again and there would be no more manna in the world"; he often repeated that "you must know that Kenyatta alone cannot give you everything."[119] To him, the post-colony started with an individual and moral commitment and so decolonization was an individual process, over which the state had no responsibility.

[119] Kenyatta, "Independence Day (1963)," *Suffering without Bitterness,* 216, 217.

2 From Prison to Party Leader, an Ambiguous Ascension (1958–1961)

In June 1958, Kenyatta's name was revived for the first time by the prominent Luo leader Oginga Odinga, from his seat in the LegCo. His move took both colonizers and nationalists by surprise. No one expected Kenyatta's name would suddenly burst onto the political scene. As this chapter shows, neither the British nor the Kenyan nationalists seriously imagined, and even less foresaw, the consequences of Kenyatta's political return. On the contrary, the campaign brought to the fore the deep fragmentation of Kenyan nationalist politics, which would eventually turn to Kenyatta's advantage – although much later. Although Kenyatta became a strong symbol, he was politically weak, and his political horizon obscure. Understanding how his weaknesses will turn into his greatest political resources will be crucial to the understanding of the premises of his presidential rule.

W. O. Maloba's work on Kenyatta's liberation campaign, which was published after I had conducted my archival research, narrates both the national and international intricacies of the Kenyatta campaign.[1] The British authorities, whether in the metropole or in the colony, and the white settlers wanted to prevent the campaign from getting out of hand and causing embarrassment internationally at a time when the British Empire was already being shaken by independences. At the same time, they hoped to gain time, working very closely with the most prominent African leaders from the KADU and KANU ranks. Maloba and I often used the same material: the Foreign and Commonwealth Office migrated archives, released in 2011 following the legal case brought by Kenyan Mau Mau veterans against the British government (a rich source that Keith Kyle, who also wrote on the topic in his 1999 book on the politics of Kenya independence, could not have used back then) and which brings new insights on

---

[1] Maloba, *Kenyatta and Britain*, chapter 6.

the local and international agitation surrounding Kenyatta's potential liberation.² Maloba has written an extensive and detailed account of the circumstances of the "Release Kenyatta" campaign. This chapter is not, strictly speaking, a competing account of the same events. While Maloba focuses on a chronological history of the events surrounding Kenyatta's rise to power, my interest is entirely dedicated to Kenyatta's emergence as a presidential candidate. Therefore, I emphasized different aspects of the campaign, such as the hostility, surprise, and uncertainty that characterized Kenyatta's political return.

This chapter argues that Kenyatta emerged as a national figure out of a not only deeply divided, but also inimical political scene. His main strength was that of his ambiguous past role with the Mau Mau movement, for which he had been sentenced and jailed. Once the Kenyatta campaign was launched, Kenyatta's so-called old-authority resurfaced, without anyone being able to define it. This ambiguous authority triggered political negotiations behind the scenes to understand what Kenyatta's political role could be, once released. In such fragile circumstances, Kenyatta was particularly careful, and refrained from speaking publicly, understanding that if he wanted things to change, things would have to stay as they were.

"Release Kenyatta": Between Political Maneuver and Old Authority

As Odinga recalled, his motivations to revive Kenyatta's name in the midst of a parliamentary session in June 1958 were triggered by "a letter from Kenyatta and the other four prisoners in Lokitaung complaining about the conditions under which they were detained."³ To him, these were the true political leaders Africans should fight for. His move was eminently strategic, for Kenyatta's name not only embodied the generational conflicts between the young generation of nationalists who had climbed the ladder of colonial power while the "old guard" (Kenyatta's generation of politicians) was in jail, but was also closely associated to the Kikuyu political influence the British had tried to

---

[2] Kyle, *The Politics of the Independence of Kenya*, chapter 6.
[3] Oginga Odinga, *Not Yet Uhuru* (Nairobi: East African Publishers, 1995), 156. See also Kyle, *The Politics of the Independence of Kenya*, 86–87.

undermine throughout the Emergency, and which was seen as a direct threat to the political ambitions of the "young" elite.

The colonial government actively enabled the emergence of an African educated and moderate political elite that they saw as part of the solution to the Mau Mau war. At the same time, constitutional reforms slowly progressed. In 1954, the first multiracial constitution named after the colonial secretary at the time, Oliver Lyttleton, was introduced. Despite strong resistance from the white community and condemnation of racialist features by African politicians, eight African representatives were, in 1956, nominated to the LegCo.[4] In March 1957, eight African members were elected: all ethnic groups but the Kikuyu were represented. Oginga Odinga (Luo representing Central Nyanza), Tom Mboya (Luo representing Nairobi), Bernard Mate (Meru for the Central province seat), Ronald Ngala (Mijikenda for the Coast seat), Masinde Muliro (Luhya for the Nyanza North seat), Lawrence Oguda (Luo representing the Gusii and Kipsigis for the Nyanza South seat), James Muimi (Kamba for the Ukambani seat), and Daniel arap Moi (Kalenjin for the Rift Valley seat) were elected. As they had no common political party, they formed the African Elected Members Organization (AEMO), with Mboya as secretary and Odinga as chairman.

Although the AEMO defended a vision of gradual political change, it opposed the segregationist principles established by the Lyttleton constitution. In April 1958, it finally succeeded to have it replaced by the Lennox-Boyd constitution, which expanded the number of African elected representative to fourteen (giving them parity with European elected members) and provided twelve "Specially Elected" members from "three races." The new elections in March 1958 brought a young elite to power: Jeremiah Nyagah (Nyeri-Embu), Justus ole Tipis (Masai), Taaitta arap Toweett (Kipsigis), and Julius Kiano (first Kikuyu to represent South Central province). *Uhuru* (Independence) was now their official slogan, and, in late 1958, they decided to boycott the LegCo to press for more reforms.[5]

Nevertheless, the AEMO united front could barely hide the internal divisions. Personal rivalries were a direct outcome of the colonial

---

[4] Hornsby, *Kenya*, 53.
[5] Ibid., 54–56. This new African elite eventually became the backbone of the political game of independent Kenya.

geography of Kenyan politics: as the Mau Mau movement had been defeated by 1954, the government allowed in June 1955 the formation of district-based parties, and this amounted to deep-rooted ethnic politics. Kikuyu politicians in particular were requested to show a loyalty certificate.[6] More generally, in order to sharpen their counter-insurgency strategies against Mau Mau fighters, the British had designed an electoral and bureaucratic system privileging a new, loyalist but also politically and economical divided elite, as Daniel Branch described it.[7] Their ideological divisions were subsumed under this constraining legal framework.[8] Anyone coveting nationalist electoral assets was heavily dependent on the local electoral support commanded by their competitors; it was thus difficult (if not impossible) for members of the nationalist elite to avoid such mutual dependency.[9] Reviving Kenyatta as a nationalist hero risked blurring electoral lines and shattering their political bases. At the same time, neither the British nor the African politicians seriously imagined the possibility (or the consequences) of Kenyatta's political return.

To the contrary, Kenyatta's release was perceived as "inopportune" by the African Elected Members, who took some time before forming a firm opinion on the matter.[10] As a symbol of colonial oppression, his name could be a promising tool with which to pressure the colonizers in the struggle for freedom. It was not yet exempt from the ambiguities that had led him to jail, however, and this is why taking positions on the issue was delicate.[11] Odinga might have known this very well, but he might not necessarily have fully anticipated the irremediable precedent his action was about to set. If he wanted to take the advantage of setting the pace of political activity and making way for his own

---

[6] Daniel Branch describes loyalists as those who "monopolized the benefits of the Africanisation of the bureaucracy and the partial political liberalisation ... Loyalists became integral to decolonizing the Kenyan nation-state." At the same time, "loyalism was initially a fluid allegiance beset by ambiguity," in Daniel Branch, "Loyalists, Mau Mau, and Elections: The First Triumph of the System, 1957–1958," *Africa Today* 53, no. 2 (2006): 28.
[7] Ibid.; Anderson, "Yours in Struggle for *Majimbo*," 547–564.
[8] Gertzel, *The Politics of Independent Kenya, 1963–8*, 9–10.
[9] David Goldsworthy, *Tom Mboya: The Man Kenya Wanted to Forget* (London: Heinemann, 1982), 94.
[10] Odinga, *Not Yet Uhuru*, 159; Goldsworthy, *Tom Mboya*, 102. For a detailed account of the political reactions at Odinga's statement see Maloba, *Kenyatta and Britain*, chapter 5.
[11] See, for example, Goldsworthy, *Tom Mboya*, 102.

interests, this was a risky move, for the symbolic politics could barely hide the question of Kenyatta's leadership that was looming in the back of everybody's mind. As Mbiyu Koinange and Joseph Murumbi tellingly wrote to Odinga:

We are indeed very disappointed to hear that some members of the Legislative Council have disagreed with you and what is worse, have openly attacked you. Their action can ... expose the obvious rift among African members of the Legislative Council and the latter is, you will agree, the last thing to be desired.[12]

Odinga's unexpected move eventually forced the whole nationalist class to align themselves with the so-called Kenyatta cult that was about to start. From 1958 until his final release, Kenyatta gradually became the marker of political maneuvers.[13] All nationalists "seized the cult of Kenyatta for their own nationalist ends" as a British journalist then described it, although no one knew what to expect from the Old Man.[14]

The Odd Development of the Kenyatta Campaign

From 1958 to 1960, Kenyatta seemed aloof from the agitation his name alone was causing, while the campaign triggered increasing concerns. In jail, no one was allowed to contact him, and political news was kept away from him. Wanting to avoid that Kenyatta becomes a political martyr, the colonial authorities were suddenly at pains to stifle any resources nurturing what appeared to be a "Kenyatta cult," looking for ways "to prohibit the importation of 'Facing Mt. Kenya' ... not so much on the grounds that the book itself is objectionable, as that its reproduction in a cheap edition would give a fillip to the growing Kenyatta cult, and so its importation would be contrary to the public interest."[15] They ultimately forbade him to wear "his

---

[12] Mbiyu Koinange and Joseph Murumbi to Oginga Odinga, September 16, 1958, KNA, MAC/KEN/72/4.
[13] Bennett and Rosberg, *The Kenyatta Election*, chapter 5.
[14] John Dickie, "Prison in Desert Is Their Shrine" in *News Chronicle*, November 29, 1958, BNA, CO 822/1247.
[15] H. D. Dent, "A.G.(2)," September 29, 1958, BNA, FCO 141/6766. See also Maloba, *Kenyatta and Britain*, 148–149.

symbolic staff and signet ring."[16] Their most difficult task, however, was to handle the numerous rumors about his state of health, which agitated the already troubled sea of politics.[17] These were all the more dangerous in that they proved the Old Man was not forgotten. On June 25, 1958, the director of intelligence reported that

> the vernacular newspaper "Jicho" published a photograph of KENYATTA in connection with a report on the Lokitaung letter. This led to a widespread rumour that KENYATTA had been released and as a result all copies of the paper sold including a reprint of 500 copies above the normal. The paper was purchased in Nairobi by members of all tribes, and there was considerable discussion, Kikuyu women were observed weeping over copies of the photograph in Burma market.[18]

Speculation was rife. Ghana's independence in 1957 stirred high hopes for change (the colonial authorities were constantly fighting against what they considered to be a mischievous comparison of Kenyatta with other famous nationalist leaders such as Kwame Nkrumah or Hastings Kamuzu Banda, who were themselves pleading for Kenyatta's release).[19] From 1958, they feared civil disobedience or a campaign of positive action would be out of control.[20]

The Hola Camp Massacre in March 1959 where eleven Mau Mau detainees were beaten to death by their prison guards and many more were injured, caused greater, and more importantly, international

[16] Confidential. The Minister for Internal Security and Defense to the District Commissioner, Turkana, Lodwar, "Kenyatta's Personal Belongings," April 9, 1959, BNA, FCO 141/6767.
[17] In a letter dated September 15, 1954 the executive officer of the Nairobi Extra-Provincial Council, Emergency Committee, confessed his worries to the secretary of defense about "the resurrection of the name of Jomo Kenyatta in public statements and in the press," listing the various on-going rumors: "(a) That the Government is negotiating with Kenyatta. (b) That Kenyatta is in custody in Nairobi. (c) That Kenyatta will issue orders for passive resistance, including the destruction of passbooks." BNA, FCO 141/6766.
[18] Secret. The Director of Intelligence and Security to the Permanent Secretary for Defense and the Permanent Secretary for African Affairs, July 10, 1958, BNA, FCO 141/6766.
[19] Secret. The Director of Intelligence and Security to the Secretary for Defense and the Secretary for African Affairs, "Jomo Kenyatta," May 28, 1957, FCO 141/6766 and Extract of K.I.C appreciation no. 10/58 for the Period September 10–30, 1958, BNA, CO 822/1247. See also Maloba, *Kenyatta and Britain*, 149–152.
[20] David A. Percox, "Internal Security and Decolonisation in Kenya, 1956–63," *The Journal of Imperial and Commonwealth History* 29, no. 1 (2001): 95–96.

embarrassment for the British. In the colony, the believed resurgence of the KLFA and secret societies supposedly linked to Mau Mau nurtured fears among the authorities, who hoped to retain the state of Emergency by all possible means.[21] The prospect of independence was becoming difficult to hold back. Following the British Conservative reelection in November, the MacMillan government was fully committed to liberal reforms. Independence was now a question of time. The AEMO elite knew that, but the prospect of an independent government only fed their personal ambitions and ethnic entrenchment.

The same day of the Hola Camp Massacre, on March 3, 1959, Kenyatta was called to testify in a trial that would greatly affect the political scene: Rawson Macharia, once a determining witness in the Kenyatta trial, had confessed he had accepted a bribe from the British to testify against Kenyatta; he had been arrested in January 1959, his case being reopened the same month.[22] Although the secretary of state for the colonies Alan Lennox-Boyd, was "satisfied that no evidence was disclosed at the Macharia trial which would justify the setting up of an independent inquiry into the conviction of Kenyatta at Kapenguria," the issue provided various politicians or political associations with another opportunity to denounce Kenyatta's now illegal and inhuman restriction.[23] Possibly surprising, the Macharia trial boosted the Kenyatta cult. As the journalist John Kamau noted, the day Macharia walked into People's Convention Party headquarters to declare that the British government had paid him to falsify his testimony during the Kapenguria trial gave Mboya an incredible opportunity for a political checkmate.[24] Besides his personal interests in the Nairobi seat for the LegCo, Mboya still had to carve a secure place for himself in the divided KANU. This could enhance his position among

---

[21] Ibid., 102.
[22] Rawson Macharia, *The Truth about the Trial of Jomo Kenyatta* (Nairobi: Longman Kenya, 1991), 30–38. See also Elkins, *Britain's Gulag*, 58, 404; Lonsdale, "Les Procès de Jomo Kenyatta," 191.
[23] The Secretary of State for the Colonies to the Officer Administrating the Government of Kenya, May 8, 1959, BNA, FCO 141/6768 and Extract from the Kenya Intelligence Committee Appreciation no. 12/58 for November 1959, BNA, CO 822/1247.
[24] John Kamau, "How Tom Mboya Used Rawson Macharia," in *Daily Nation*, December 18, 2008. See also Maloba, *Kenyatta and Britain*, 129, 145, 161.

the Kikuyu, and even radicalize his image, while still appealing to the moderates and the loyalist elite.[25]

The emerging possibility of celebrating Kenyatta Day (the day Kenyatta was arrested by British authorities) worried the colonial authorities even more. Nevertheless, reports showed that the Kenyatta cult was far from fostering spontaneous political unity. Political personalities were undecided. In Nairobi and Nyanza and Central provinces, where local people were more attentive to the Kenyatta case, there was little mobilization. Tom Mboya and his Nairobi People's Convention Party had not issued any definite call yet; in Nyanza, "only [the Luo politician] MAKASEMBO has mentioned observance of 'KENYATTA DAY' on 14 April and his efforts have met with little response."[26] In Central province, "in absence of a recognised leader, there are no plans for organised demonstrations or incidents on the day."[27] There was still a long way to go before the fierce demonstrations later organized in the year.

Rumors intensified about Kenyatta's condition. Radio Cairo was particularly effective in issuing dreadful information on Kenyatta's health, which they described as deteriorating "on the point of death."[28] Joseph Murumbi was one of the initiators of the radio enterprise, after Kenyatta encouraged him at the time of his Kapenguria trial to "go out and tell the world what was happening in Kenya."[29] Radio Cairo had been established with the help of the Egyptian government in the early 1950s, but was run by two Luos who gave allegiance to Odinga. With the Odinga–Mboya rivalry, the radio's activity turned out to be, to quote Murumbi's own words, "explosive."[30] This explains the hard line the radio took when it came to the Kenyatta issue. Its reports might not have had an effect on the indigenous population (because news was issued in English for India, Pakistan and Southeast Asia mainly, as well as in Somali), but some were "picked up by the B.B.C. Monitoring

---

[25] Kamau, "How Tom Mboya Used Rawson Macharia."
[26] Secret. The Director of Intelligence and Security to the Chief Secretary and the Permanent Secretary for Defense, April 14, 1959, BNA, FCO 141/6767. Dickson Oruko Makasembo was a Luo politician closely associated to Odinga's politics, and was the chairman of the Central Nyanza African District Association.
[27] Ibid.
[28] Extract from Cairo Radio "The Health of Jomo Kenyatta," October 19, 1959 and Afro-Asian News Service "Jomo Kenyatta Reported Dying," October 13, 1959, BNA, FCO 141/6768.
[29] Murumbi and Thurston, *A Path Not Taken*, 60.   [30] Ibid., 73.

Service," hence creating much discord and uncertainty among British colonizers.[31] The Colonial Office was struggling to disprove the news, answer straight away all the questions raised during the British parliamentary sessions, and counterattack the allegations frequently brought up by the nationalist press.[32]

To what extent did Kenyatta know about all this political turmoil? Very little information leaked out of jail. An extract from the Kenya Special Branch Summary reported that Odinga was shocked after receiving

> a letter signed by Kariuki Chotara, Paul Ngei, Kungu Karumba and Fred Kubai, the Lokitaung detainees [asking him] to refrain from praising Kenyatta or naming him as the African leader, as the detainees alleged Kenyatta is no longer a true African because he believes that Africans should co-operate with Government on a non-racial approach to politics and that he would be prepared to work for Government if he were released.[33]

By 1959, Kenyatta had finished his sentence. The question was to decide whether he could be released, but the colonial authorities, not reassured by the ongoing Kenyatta campaign, preferred to keep him under indefinite restriction. The newly appointed Governor Renison stuck to the belief that Kenyatta was the leader of Mau Mau and that his restriction was necessary to ensure security in the country.[34] Maloba underlined that Renison's obstinacy in considering his release only through the lens of security showed how much he was under the influence of the Kenyan settlers, at a time when the Colonial Office was much more conflicted over the issue.[35] Nevertheless, the quest to keep Kenyatta out of the political scene proved counterproductive. It opened the arena of imperial hegemony to contestation from within, providing nationalists with the official channels through which to voice

---

[31] Confidential. J. L. F. Buist to G. J. Ellerton, October 24, 1969, BNA, FCO 141/6768.
[32] Ibid. and Extract from Minutes of the Twenty-Ninth Meeting of the Central Province Security Committee Held November 6, 1959, BNA, FCO 141/6768.
[33] Extract from the Kenya Special Branch Summary no. 11/58, 1959, BNA, CO 822/1247.
[34] Secret. Sir Patrick Renison to Ian MacLeod, July 9, 1961, BNA, CO 822/1912.
[35] Maloba, *Kenyatta and Britain,* 163. Calder Walton showed how the belief that Kenyatta was the leader of the Mau Mau as well as a communist persisted within MI5 services, see Walton, *Empire of Secrets,* chapter 6.

The Odd Development of the Kenyatta Campaign 75

their cause.[36] On April 14, 1959, Kenyatta was transferred to Lodwar, still in northern Kenya, where he was held in indefinite detention.

The official ending of the Emergency in January 1960 did not affect the colonizers' stand. On the contrary, it was confirmed, if not reinforced, by the publication of the *Historical Survey of the Origins and Growth of Mau Mau*, also known as the Corfield Report, in May 1960.[37] At stake was the need to "get world opinion thinking about why Kenyatta should be detained behind bars at all."[38] It clearly "continued the war by other means."[39] Kenyatta was very much the centre of the report, for it fitted well in the attempt to denounce the evil role of Kikuyu in the advent of Mau Mau and, by extension, their evil obstruction of the (colonial) road to modernization.[40] In a public statement issued in May 1960, Governor Renison faithfully conveyed the gist of the report:

As I have said he planned for Kikuyu domination; he was an implacable opponent of any co-operation with other people; tribes or race, who live in Kenya. I have been here long enough to know that without such co-operation Kenya will not become a modern and developing nation but will split up into opposing tribes again and either stagnate with threatened return to savagery or be subjected to the fears of intimidation of a dictatorship.[41]

Kenyan politicians appeared comfortably indifferent to the Corfield report: "Kiano repeated that the publication would not embarrass

---

[36] Lonsdale, "Les Procès de Jomo Kenyatta," 197.
[37] Interestingly, Greet Kershaw alleged that Leakey (an anthropologist whose Kenyatta's *Facing Mount Kenya* greatly challenged) wrote some parts of the report, including the section on oaths. His ideas would become the official perspective the Mau Mau war, figuring prominently in its official history written by Frank D. Corfield in 1960 in Greet Kershaw, "Mau Mau from Below: Fieldwork and Experience, 1955–57 and 1962," *Canadian Journal of African Studies* 25, no. 2 (1991): 277.
[38] Secret and personal. W. J. Coutts to Granville Robert, April 27, 1960, BNA, CO 822/1909. See also Kyle, *The Politics of Independence of Kenya*, 113.
[39] Lonsdale, "The Moral Economy of Mau Mau, Wealth, Poverty and Civic Virtue in Kikuyu Political Thought," 291.
[40] Meaningfully, a note introducing the index warns that "No reference is made to Jomo Kenyatta whose name appears on almost every page of the History," in Corfield, *The Origins and Growth of Mau Mau*, 317. See also Branch, *Defeating Mau Mau, Creating Kenya*, 223.
[41] Statement by His Excellency the Governor, "Jomo Kenyatta," May 9, 1960, BNA, FCO 141/6769.

African Elected Members in relation to membership of the Government."[42] As the report showed that the Mau Mau movement was not African nationalism, but an attempt to ensure a Kikuyu-dominated country, "African Elected Members recognise[d] that it may assist them as well as us."[43] Some may have been reassured, like Mboya, who took his time before making up his mind on the Kenyatta issue, that the report was largely ignored in London, although it was certainly delaying African political participation in the independence talks.[44] Nevertheless, the Corfield report stumbled over the irremediable outcomes of the Kenyatta campaign, as no nationalist could avoid taking a public stance on the report. It was now a matter of showing off one's independence of mind, so to speak. This was, according to Kiano and Mboya, "bedevilling Kenya at the present time."[45]

The matter was taken to the heart of the first independence conference organized in Lancaster House in January 1960. Odinga riled the British and African delegations, and, more importantly, his rival Mboya, by appointing Peter Mbiyu Koinange as a second adviser, thus bringing in Kenyatta's political specter and rousing the radical voices claiming that there should be no conference without Kenyatta. Back in Nairobi, even Mboya's "lieutenants" attempted to use the Kenyatta issue to oust him from his political headquarters.[46] Governor Renison summed up the tricky situation they were all trapped in:

The question of what statement I should make in reply to all the pressures for the release of Kenyatta is much more difficult. It will be tragic after we have got so far with the African Elected Members if we lose them on this issue. But this is not an issue which we can avoid, and I do not see how I can delay for very long ... The African Elected Members have built it up to its present sise and look like putting themselves into the position of having to lose all that

---

[42] Secret. Inward Telegram to the Secretary of State for the Colonies, from Kenya (Sir Patrick Renison), April 28, 1960, BNA, CO 822/1909.
[43] Ibid. As David Anderson explained, KADU's fear of Kikuyu domination did not only result from anti-Mau Mau colonial; it had a deeper history rooted in colonial economic disruptive policies. See Anderson, "Yours in Struggle for Majimbo."
[44] Maloba, *Kenyatta and Britain*, chapter 5; Goldsworthy, *Tom Mboya*, 170; Tom Mboya, *Freedom and After* (Nairobi: East African Publishers, 1986), 44–47.
[45] Secret and Personal. W. J. Coutts to Granville Robert, April 27, 1960, BNA, CO 822/1909.
[46] Goldsworthy, *Tom Mboya*, 134–135, 137.

they have won if we cannot find them a way out. I can at present see no way out which I could possibly accept in my conscience.[47]

In their quest for a solution, they faced a major obstacle: "What is Jomo Kenyatta thinking today? We do not know."[48] For that, the Corfield report was of little help. They had to find out by themselves. Indecision was general.

Unmasking Kenyatta

With the end of the Emergency in January 1960, there was virtually no further barrier to Kenyatta's return to politics. Approaching him was still considered a sensitive task. In December 1960, Renison described him as "well informed on Kenyan politics and world affairs."[49] But, besides underlining his "very powerful personality," so powerful that he "could at present sweep the existing African parties out of existence if he wished on release," his report offered virtually no concrete information to understand Kenyatta's source of authority.[50] The colonial authorities were not better off with their various enquiries about his thought. Colonial officers who visited him agreed on his commanding although dangerous authority.[51] Numerous commentaries suggested Kenyatta was "above the parties," "the only person capable of producing unity," with a unique "influence."[52] His "old authority" was mentioned, in connection with a short and unexpanded mention of "the result of his teaching in Central Province."[53] But it is difficult to assess whether the colonial authorities, together with the chiefs and tribal police, saw there the signs of the evil power of manipulation they

---

[47] Secret, Private, and Personal. From Patrick Renison to Iain MacLeod, April 20, 1960, BNA, CO 822/1909.
[48] "Jomo Kenyatta," Draft Statement by His Excellency the Governor, April 20, 1960, BNA, CO 922/1909.
[49] Sir Patrick Renison, "Jomo Kenyatta. Appreciation of Action to Be Taken," December 1960, BNA, CO 822/1910.
[50] Ibid.
[51] Secret. File no. MLGH/OFF/1/15, March 30, 1960, BNA, FCO 141/6769.
[52] Outward Telegram from the Secretary of State for the Colonies to Sir Renison, April 11, 1961, BNA, CO 822/1911; Record from F. D. Webber to Sir Renison, December 9, 1960, BNA, CO 822/1910; Note on a Meeting that Took Place in the Kenya Office at 11 a.m. Tuesday January 10, 1960, BNA, CO 822/1911.
[53] Sir Patrick Renison to Ian MacLeod, July 9, 1961, BNA, CO 822/1912 and Sir Patrick Renison, "Jomo Kenyatta. Appreciation of Action to Be Taken," December 1960, BNA, CO 822/1910.

believed him capable of as a Mau Mau leader, being obsessed with the possibility of another outbreak of Mau Mau violence.[54] Writing to Ian MacLeod in July 1961, Renison described Kenyatta's "words and expressed intentions [as] moderate and constructive," but concluded that "it is unlikely that Kenyatta's character has changed. He is arrogant, dominating and satanic."[55]

The situation became trickier with negotiations for independence firmly underway. In the wake of the "wind of change," a phrase famously coined by Harold Macmillan in February 1960, and the beginning of the independence negotiations, African politicians reorganized.[56] Two main nationalist parties were formed in May and June 1960. The KANU was constituted by the largest ethnic groups (Kikuyu, Embu, Meru, Luo, and Kamba) and defended a centralized state authority, which would supersede ethnic divisions, as well as an open competition for (alienated) lands. James Gichuru presided, and Oginga Odinga was vice president. Its counterpart, the KADU, gathered ethnic minorities, which feared the domination of Kikuyu and Luo ethnic groups over the national agenda and the reallocation of lost lands. Its president was the Coast leader Ronald Ngala and the party was, at least in the beginning, strongly backed up by Europeans, who view KANU as a Kikuyu evil.

KANU, however, was born riddled with internal divisions: a very positive element for KADU, always prompt to "[welcome] the idea of dividing KANU," and, yet, whose hands were tied by the improbable "Kenyatta formula."[57] Indeed, the independence negotiations stumbled over the question of whether Kenyatta would become chief minister once released: an unacceptable prospect for KADU who feared he would only defend Kikuyu interests. Electoral competition grew fiercer. Kenyatta's authority appeared all the more ambiguous: on the one hand, no one seemed to know what he was thinking or what his political plans were, and, to many, his role in the Mau Mau

[54] David A. Percox, "Circumstances Short of Global War: British Defence, Colonial Internal Security, and Decolonisation in Kenya, 1945–65" (Ph.D. diss., University of Nottingham, 2001), 201.
[55] Patrick Renison to Ian MacLeod, July 10, 1961, BNA, CO 822/1912.
[56] "Harold Macmillan: Winds of Change," in *The Cold War: A History in Documents and Eyewitness Accounts*, eds. Jussi M. Hanhimäki and Odd Arne Westad (Oxford: Oxford University Press, 2003), 357.
[57] Secret. Outward Telegram from the Secretary of State for the Colonies to Kenya (Governor's Deputy), April 10, 1961, BNA, CO 822/1911.

movement was still unclear. On the other hand, there seemed to be a general, tacit yet obscure agreement that "[n]o African politician would ever be forgiven if he took portfolio now ... Anyone who took Kenyatta's seat would never be forgiven."[58] It seemed that the nationalist elites increasingly feared the authority of the Old Man. Kenyatta was a decisive actor. Although the governor still considered his release as a matter of security, he confided to MacLeod that Kenyatta should be released before the British lost their control over the political events.[59]

Nationalist politicians too were at pains to grasp Kenyatta's thought. Visits to Lodwar were as much envied as contested, and the restrictions issued by the governor on the constitution of the delegation only caused further divisions within KANU.[60] Njoroge Mungai explained to the British authorities that "Kenyatta was a very important figure during this time, and a large section of the people of Kenya, all Africans, loyalists, Mau Mau, Homeguard and very many chiefs have all agreed they would like him back."[61] Clearly, Kenyatta's ambiguities were his strongest asset, whereas other politicians, like James Gichuru, were believed to have supported the detention of Mau Mau leaders in 1954.[62] When Mungai added that Kenyatta's appeal was not restricted to Central province, but expanded through the whole country, he was certainly not exaggerating. He had been accused of being the leader of Mau Mau, and the governor had fueled this image over the years. He constantly denied it, but his refutations had never been believed by all.

The nationalist elite was agitated by the forthcoming general elections of February 1961, which could enhance their positioning during the independence negotiations. KANU was using Kenyatta's name to pressure the electorate.[63] Mboya, the masterful organizer of the KANU campaign, wanted to "assess Kenyatta's attitude by himself" and was

[58] Secret. Outward Telegram from the Secretary of State for the Colonies to Kenya (Sir P. Renison), April 11, 1961, BNA, CO 822/1911.
[59] Keith Kyle, "The End of Empire in Kenya," University of London, Institute of Commonwealth Studies Postgraduate Seminar Paper, March 14, 1996 quoted by Percox, "Internal Security and Decolonisation in Kenya, 1956–63," 100.
[60] Secret. Inward Telegram to the Secretary of State for the Colonies from Kenya, March 4, 1961, BNA, CO 822/1911.
[61] "Note of a Meeting Which Took Place in the Kenya Office at 11 a.m. on Tuesday 10th January 1961," BNA, CO 822/1911.
[62] Secret. Inward Telegram to the Secretary of State for the Colonies from Kenya (Acting Governor), December 30, 1960, BNA, CO 822/1911.
[63] See Bennett and Rosberg, *The Kenyatta Election*.

relatively slow to realize he could not usurp Kenyatta's unifying position.[64] He was certainly "concerned about his own immediate political future, being unsure he would get sufficient Kikuyu support to ensure his return (from Nairobi North) to Legislative Council."[65] In spite of KANU's huge victory (which proved its commanding influence on the popular vote), KADU, favored by Governor Renison, remained a powerful and unsquashable political force, and formed a coalition government with the European settlers' New Kenya Party.[66] The colonial authorities observed both nationalist parties exploiting the Kenyatta issue as a pressure tactic: Odinga used it to "turn on the more moderate elements led by MBOYA and GICHURU, who were then preparing to enter the government and temporarily eclipsed their influence"; whereas KADU, benefiting from KANU divisions over Kenyatta's confinement, "availed themselves of an invitation to consult him, thereby securing a minor triumph in that they were cordially received and returned bearing tidings of KENYATTA's disappointment (not to say criticism) that KANU had not seen fit to meet him."[67]

In the wake of the elections, it was clear that Kenyatta, although he was no real political force, had become an increasingly powerful symbol, as a survey revealed in March 1961.[68] Fittingly entitled "Kenya's Kenyatta," the purpose of the survey was "to determine whether public opinion supported the Governor in his stand, and whether the public electorate supported the stand taken by KANU and KADU since the Election, and finally to determine how well the public has understood the post-election issues."[69] The survey showed the unsurprisingly clear divide between the African electorate in favor of Kenyatta's release, and the Asian and European electorate averse to Kenyatta's comeback in politics. More surprising perhaps are the contrasting

[64] Goldsworthy, *Tom Mboya*, chapter 9.
[65] According to Renison, "Whatever they say publicly KANU will not regard themselves as unable to participate in Government without Kenyatta as member of Legislative Council or Chief Minister. This, however, you should not, of course, reveal in debate." Secret. Outward Telegram from the Secretary of State from the Colonies to Kenya (O.A.G.), June 28, 1961, BNA, CO 822/1912.
[66] David Anderson gave a detailed account of the relationship between KADU, the governor and the white settlers in "Yours in Struggle for *Majimbo*."
[67] Secret. "The Return of Jomo Kenyatta. A Review of the Period March–November 1961," Special Branch Headquarters, November 22, 1961, BNA, FCO 141/6772.
[68] See also Maloba, *Kenyatta and Britain*, 179–180.
[69] Kenya Survey, "Public Opinion on Kenya's Kenyatta," Poll no. 6, March 1961, KNA, MAC/KEN/69/1.

answers given to the two following questions. To "Who is the most outstanding leader in Kenya today?," the majority of African interviewees replied Mboya (67 percent) while only 20 percent supported Kenyatta.[70] Yet, to the obviously divisive question "Who should be the first Chief Minister of Kenya?," 65 percent chose Kenyatta. The survey exposed the fact that Kenyatta had become a nationalist political symbol. It even noted that "it would be political suicide for KADU to attempt to form a government itself [because] it is the opinion of all racial groups, including KADU itself, that the next government should be formed by a coalition of the best of KANU and KADU."[71] It clearly showed the uncertainty surrounding Kenyatta's leadership, but hinted at the fact that a political symbol could not stay too long outside of politics. As Maloba wrote, the "Kenyatta question could no longer be sustained. Political, strategic, and economic imperatives called for a quick resolution."[72] In the wake of the survey's results, and as its introduction mentioned, "African leaders have decided to visit Lodwar ... and it will be interesting to see the results of their interview there."[73] Even the visit, however, was a highly political issue.

KANU leaders were unable to settle their attitude toward Kenyatta and the symbol he represented. Their desire to participate in the constitutional talks was a matter of political survival.[74] Besides the fact that his name was used to draw political lines within the party, their uncertainty about Kenyatta's political opinion ultimately hindered their political moves. On March 11, 1961, Tom Mboya wrote a four-page-long letter to Kenyatta, to inform him about the postelection political situation. He described at length the "serious weaknesses" developing within KANU.[75] More importantly, perhaps, he noted that even the visit to Kenyatta was a source of divisions. When the governor forbade KANU to form its own delegation to Lodwar, Mboya commented that "Despite this, Gichuru and myself were ready to come until we saw that this would have caused serious internal split in KANU."[76] KANU politicians were trapped between the urgency of not losing political ground in the negotiations for independence, and

---

[70] Ibid. [71] Ibid. [72] Maloba, *Kenyatta and Britain*, 180.
[73] Kenya Survey, "Public Opinion on Kenya's Kenyatta."
[74] Outward Telegram to Kenya (O.A.G.) from Secretary of State of the Colonies, June 28, 1961, BNA, CO 822/1912.
[75] Tom Mboya to Jomo Kenyatta, March 11, 1961, KNA, MAC/KEN/70/4.
[76] Ibid.

the necessity to safeguard their symbolic stand facing the radicalization the Kenyatta campaign dragged them into. As such, Mboya's and Gichuru's readiness to come and visit Kenyatta is better understood once properly contextualized. In March 1961, Governor Renison reported:

> I have already gone a very long way with Mboya and Gichuru in discussing ministers and ministries and various other aspects of the new Government such as Parliamentary secretaries and Government whips. It is clear that they are eager to be part of such government if only they can get over the Kenyatta hurdle. They think they can do this by seeing him now and getting him to say they should go ahead. They think this will release them from election pledges not to enter Government unless Kenyatta is released.[77]

Kenyatta's vague political statements, "[preaching] the virtues of African unity," did not ease their task, being no more than a tactful political screen. When they finally met him, they all seemed to be greatly impressed: Odinga reportedly "[behaved] as if he had been in the presence of the Messiah himself"; Mboya felt "obliged to revise his own personal view that KENYATTA was a political 'has been'"; "KADU refused be over-awed by him," although its leaders acknowledged that Kenyatta was very much physically and mentally healthy.[78] His purported "old authority" seemed to take all the nationalist leaders aback. We can wonder, however, to what extent this so-called old authority suffices to explain Kenyatta's political revival. Was this seemingly magnetic, charismatic, and impassable influence *only* due to his "moral authority" as a Kikuyu leader? A crucial question remains to be answered: What did Kenyatta have in mind? And "[would] he retain his stature once he is the midst of the quarrelling and no longer a myth?," as the governor appropriately wondered.[79]

---

[77] Top Secret and Personal No. 6. Inward Telegram from Kenya (Sir Patrick Renison) to the Secretary of State of the Colonies, March 4, 1961, BNA, CO 822/1911. A handwritten note on the document indicates that the telegram should be treated as "secret."
[78] Secret. "The Return of Jomo Kenyatta."
[79] "The problem facing Kenyatta" from our Africa Correspondent, in *The Times*, Wednesday August 9, 1961, BNA, FCO 141/6764.

If We Want Things to Change, Things Will Have to Stay as They Are?

If the nationalist elites did not know how to brand their participation in a government of transition, Kenyatta himself seemed undecided. He probably knew that he had no stronghold on the political scene yet, and that his political future would depend on how much he could maneuver within the KANU/KADU rifts.[80] No one seemed able to anticipate what Kenyatta would do once released. No one really knew what his real intentions were, and he himself could not disclose too much if he wanted to protect his own political stake. For a time, some suggested he should be released and then sent to England, where his political ideas could be discerned without being feared too much. Kenyatta did not like this idea "for fear of his appearing to be 'running away' but would probably agree to it if he could announce at the time that he would be coming back."[81] On April 4, 1961, he was transferred to the slightly less remote Maralal. This was the last destination before his final release. The transfer was meant to ease visits, always in the hope of unraveling Kenyatta's state of mind, while the colonial government hoped that "access to Kenyatta" would "expose his failings and weaknesses as a possible national leader."[82] Visitors flocked to his house, to the point that, to the permanent secretary for defense "it seems to have degenerated into a game of one-upmanship and several of the delegations have confessed to rue that while they have no real need or desire to see Kenyatta, they cannot be left off the bandwagon."[83] As we will see, not only did the colonial government's policy fail, but one could argue that introducing Kenyatta to all the major political figures of his day gave him a unique sense of orientation

---

[80] It is significant that Kenyatta, in March 1961, requested to see Nyerere before seeing the KANU/KADU leaders, who were planning on visiting him in Lodwar. Governor Renison commented "Question on which I think he requires Nyerere's advice is whether or not he should release leaders from their public pledge not to participate in a government until he is unconditionally released." Secret and Personal No. 35. Inward Telegram to the Secretary of State for the Colonies from Kenya, March 19, 1961, BNA, CO 822/1911.

[81] Secret and Personal No. 26. Inward Telegram from Kenya (Sir Patrick Renison) to the Secretary of State of the Colonies, March 15, 1961, BNA, CO 822/1911.

[82] Maloba, *Kenyatta and Britain*, 182.

[83] The Permanent Secretary for Defense to District Commissioner, Maralal, "Kenyatta Visits," June 28, 1961, KNA, DC/MRL/1/6/9.

within the Byzantine Kenyan political scene; a sense that he would quickly turn into a political resource.

Seven days later (and five months before his restriction was officially ended) Kenyatta gave his first public conference, known as the Maralal Press Conference, on April 11, 1961. His general tone remained vague, and right from the outset he expressed his feeling of mistrust against the journalists themselves.[84] He defined his political views as a belief "in freedom of African people from Colonialism and Imperialism"; he refused to take sides for either KANU or KADU, for he did not know "the inside business"; he said the recent constitutional negotiations were "a step forwards," although he felt it "had in some of its aspects a kind of delaying tactic which is the chief weapon of the colonial powers"; he insisted that "the Communists have no place in African society as it is today." Most importantly, he denied, once again, his responsibility in the Mau Mau war, ingeniously replying to the pressing journalists that "many people in your country have respect for Her Majesty the Queen but nevertheless gangsters . . . are there but this does not mean that her Majesty is responsible for what they are doing"; he refrained from any strong and clear position on the role of the Mau Mau movement in the achievement of independence: "that is not for me to say because I think that in a democratic country everyone has the right to express his or her opinion."[85] When he was questioned on his views on the hot issue of land tenure, Kenyatta felt compelled to recall "history about granting titles of land," and as a perspicacious journalist asked him whether he would respect "the Kikuyu smallholder who has a title in the Central Province today granted by the Kenya Government," he vehemently replied that

no matter how twisted you might put it . . . the present system of land holding or smallholding in Central Province as I know it, the people are holding a title for land that belonged to their forefathers. There is nothing that has been given to them at all by the Government . . . That is, land was never owned by any person but by all people, it was owned and is still owned by clans.[86]

Clearly, Kenyatta did not depart from the principles he laid down some twenty years ago. On tribal customs, he also made clear that "my policy was and still is that some of those African customs could be

---

[84] A Transcript of Tape Recording Made by K. B. S of Mr. Jomo Kenyatta's Press Conference at Maralal on April 11, 1961, p. 1, BNA, FCO 141/6364.
[85] Ibid., 3, 4, 8.   [86] Ibid., 5.

kept and some of the European or Asian customs which are good could be adopted."[87]

At the same, time, he could not easily say much more. As a report from the Special Branch rightly noted:

> the circumstances were too artificial for KENYATTA to reveal much of his true line of thought ... The questions put to him were practically standard and invariably elicited a stock answer. It was not surprising therefore that comment on his moderation, farsightedness and liberal outlook should have been so widespread; KENYATTA knew he was on probation, and accordingly, played his hand close to his chest.[88]

Kenyatta refused to give any other interview, and the few interventions he made remained just as vague.[89] His strategy rather consisted in avoiding too great a political commitment by trying to set himself above political parties – hence his general plea for African unity. At the Maralal Conference, he not only affirmed that "disunity is harmful," but also that there was no difference between KADU's and KANU's policies.[90] Resolving personal rivalries was a Herculean task. To the KANU coalition, Kenyatta embodied the risk of Kikuyu domination and the revival of the old KAU. To ensure he would be "sufficiently far removed from influences of possible Kikuyu intrigues," plans were tailored for Kenyatta to become the president of a future East African federation between Kenya, Tanganyika, and Uganda.[91]

British officials too were worried, but their subsequent attempts to interpret Kenyatta's evasive answers, whether about his political return, the future of the white settlers, on internal independence, or

---

[87] Ibid., 5.   [88] Secret. "The Return of Jomo Kenyatta," 5.
[89] Confidential. Public Relation Officer to the Under Secretary, Ministry of Information and Broadcasting, "Press Visit to Kenyatta," April 19, 1961, BNA, FCO 141/6364.
[90] A Transcript of Tape Recording Made by K. B. S of Mr. Jomo Kenyatta's Press Conference at Maralal on April 11, 1961, p. 1, BNA, FCO 141/6364.
[91] The colonial authorities referred to a report stating that, during the London Conference in 1961, "Mboya contacted SAMUEL AYODO, another Luo MLC, with the request that he should make an immediate start on convincing his KANU colleagues, particularly Kamba MLCs, CHOKWE (Coast) SAGINI (Kisii) and NYAGAH (Embu) of the imperative need to thwart any revival of KAU – KENYATTA's old party – even if the Old Man wished to resuscitate it on his release. Perhaps even more significant was the report that MBOYA and NGALA had privately agreed: that in the event of an attempt by KENYATTA, the Kikuyu MLCs or OGINGA ODINGA, to reform the KAU, they were prepared to join forces to oppose it." Secret. "The Return of Jomo Kenyatta," 7.

the Somali and Masai claims for land, remained frustrating.[92] At the same time, reports from the colonial authorities might have been biased because of their unwillingness to believe him. On the one hand, they were at pains to overcome his mesmerizing character. One informer – Lord Lambton, a British MP – noted that he "found it easier to talk to him looking only at his left eye, which, without doubt, is not as powerful as is his right, despite its appearance." On the other hand, they might have been right in judging it was "just possible that he is now more practical than he was and realises that there is comparatively little time before him, and that a recurrence of violence might occasion another acute period of unrest, which he would not survive."[93] Kenyatta seemed to bide his time, and told them: "I have something cooking and I don't wish to spoil it."[94]

With the Maralal Conference, hopes rose for reconciliation between KANU and KADU, possibly under Kenyatta's leadership. His release was now certain, and the intelligence services, known as the Special Branch, considered that it was better for British interests to have Kenyatta released when they were still in power.[95] By July 1961, however, the "so-called spirit of Maralal had already worn rather thin" under the increasing dissensions between and within the two parties, in addition to KANU's refusal to be a mere "add-on" to KADU-dominated government.[96] On top of their ideological dissensions was the question of the repartition of powers in an independent government, and the redistribution of land. They were fighting to harvest the fruits of Kenyatta's release. KADU politicians were anxious to demonstrate that it was a "purely KADU exercise, since by it they hoped to rehabilitate themselves in Pan-African eyes and to offset the

---

[92] Very Private. (Notes by Lord Lambton on His Visit to Africa, July 10,1961), BNA, CO 822/1912.
[93] Ibid. See also Maloba, *Kenyatta and Britain*, 184–186.
[94] Confidential. R. A. Hosking to F. W. Goodbody, "Press visit to Mr. Kenyatta at Maralal," June 28, 1961, BNA, FCO 141/6364.
[95] Percox, "Internal Security and Decolonisation in Kenya, 1956–63," 206.
[96] Secret. "The Return of Jomo Kenyatta," 7. See also Kyle, *The Politics of the Independence of Kenya*, 141.

obloquy that had been engendered locally by their original decision to take part in government."[97]

Kenyatta's Indecisiveness and Party Leadership

In August 1961, Kenyatta was finally allowed to return to Kikuyuland, to his house in Gatundu. The triumph of his return (with people flocking to visit him in Gatundu) contrasted with the insecurity that characterized his political position. His strategy of setting himself above the political parties would prove short-lived. His name was still closely associated with Kikuyu hegemony, undermining his outspoken bid for African unity. His attempt to "play the part of the elder statesman unmoved by party rivalry" was all the more delicate in that it supposed he would not commit himself to any side, or on any hot issue, thus risking ready-made accusations of inefficiency. He was very much embarrassed by the various ethnic factions within KANU that seemed to confirm KADU's fears of "tribalism," and on which he himself would remain silent. At best, his call for African unity was "unrealistic."[98] He could only cut short the visit the prominent members of the KLFA paid him in August at Gatundu, insisting he disliked violence, but unwilling to make any "categorical condemnation": a very "deliberate" move, as a comment written in the margin of the document underlined.[99] Ambiguities could only worsen once his fellow detainee Paul Ngei was de-restricted and committed himself to disturbing KANU with anti-European speeches in Nairobi, forcing Kenyatta to take refuge in immobility and silence, once again – KANU leaders could afford to lose neither the landless Kikuyus' vote, nor the Kamba vote that Ngei commanded.[100]

KANU leaders were aware of Kenyatta's strategy of charismatic indecisiveness. They knew his leadership, at least symbolic, was unavoidable for KANU to show a united front during the

---

[97] Secret. "The Return of Jomo Kenyatta," 8. Ronald Ngala, KADU's leader, insisted "KADU must not lose to KANU the credit for securing Kenyatta's release." Secret and Personal No. 369. Inward Telegram to the Secretary of State for the Colonies from Kenya (Sir. P. Renison), July 19, 1961, CO 822/1912. For that matter, KADU insisted that neither the house that was being built for Kenyatta, nor the land, should be a gift from KADU, and not just handed over by the government, or cabinet. "Jomo Kenyatta," Memorandum by the Secretary of State for the Colonies, July 25, 1961, BNA, CAB 129/106/14.
[98] Secret. "The Return of Jomo Kenyatta," 14.   [99] Ibid., 10.   [100] Ibid., 15.

constitutional talks; they nonetheless continued to play the fluctuating Kenyatta card. The KANU parliamentary group demanded that Kenyatta be allowed to participate in the talks, although it had been previously agreed between KANU and KADU that he would not. KANU was obviously "[forcing] a trial of strength" with KADU.[101] This was an intolerable request for KADU. The KANU delegation walked out of the negotiations on September 7.

The Kenyatta card was conveniently double-faced. Mboya insisted Kenyatta should be admitted to the talks. This was also a way to force him to take a position on a series of sensitive and divisive issues, in particular, the question of land redistribution after independence: Should the land be freely redistributed, as Mau Mau fighters, landless, and land poor demanded, or should land titles be secured through a buy-and-sell system, just as the colonizers wanted? Clear-cut commitment was exactly what Kenyatta avoided. Subsequently visited by his fellow KANU politicians at Gatundu, Kenyatta refused to advise them on any point. He would not let himself become a puppet figure and

pointed out KANU had made him the subject of a previous deadlock with the government and had refused to participate in the formation of an administration after the General Election and he wished it to be made known to Parliamentary group that in future he would like to be consulted before they involved themselves in any further disputes over him.[102]

The KANU leaders, purportedly disappointed, decided to return to the talks. The entire constitutional talks stumbled on the land issue again. KADU feared that with independence and the return to the land, the Kikuyu (and therefore KANU) would exert a political and economic influence, which, if enshrined in a centralized government, would sign the political death warrant for minority ethnic groups. KANU sought Kenyatta's advice on the attitude to adopt toward KADU. But they were left with Kenyatta saying that no one had looked for his confidence beforehand, and, therefore, "he had no intention of becoming embroiled in any inter party acrimony."[103]

To the people, Kenyatta was a "second God," a pompous terminology used, once again, by Oginga Odinga, yet sufficiently evocative for the African church leaders to request a meeting him when he was

---

[101] C.C. (61) 61st Conclusions. Meeting of the Cabinet Held at Admiralty House, SW1, on Thursday November 9, 1961, BNA, CAB 128/35/61.
[102] Secret. "The Return of Jomo Kenyatta," 18.   [103] Ibid.

still in Maralal.[104] In May 1961, a delegation of six visited Kenyatta. They found a "Jomo [who] welcomed them with open arms, addressing some of them by their old nick names [sic], recalling past memories of their early youth contacts with four of them."[105] Kenyatta showed great care in reassuring the African church leaders of his Christian affiliation, whether by quoting the Bible from memory ("Psalm 23 'The Lord is the Shephered'... and so on") or by reassuring them of his pro-independent school past: "He said he was never opposed to Christianity, emphasized that at the Kenya Teachers' College, Githunguri, or other independent Schools, 324 of them, they had prayers in Church in the morning."[106] He, nonetheless, "refused to be pinned down to any denominational connection"; instead, he "respect[ed] all religions."[107] As the discussion drifted toward the land issue, Kenyatta asserted that "Land Consolidation was one of his ideas but this was picked from his papers which had been impounded by the Kenya Government on his imprisonment."[108] He was keen to reassure the Church leaders that he would interfere with neither land consolidation, nor the distribution of title deeds. Claiming that he was "the leader of light and prosperity and not darkness," he stated again that he would support neither KADU nor KANU.[109] He must have made a great and successful impression upon the delegation, whose report concluded that "Jomo Kenyatta is really a different man in his attitude to us Christians."[110]

Did Kenyatta avoid taking any strong position publicly because of a *"lack of confidence in himself,"* as a "Kikuyu source" informed the British intelligence?[111] He seemed rather fully confident that the

---

[104] Donald B. Thomas and Paul J. Nugent, "Walter Martin, 'Friends Visit Jomo Kenyatta at Maralal'," *Quaker History* 99, no. 1 (2010): 35–36. On Odinga's speech, see African Church Leaders Conference, Steering Committee, May 29, 1961, National Council of Churches of Kenya (NCCK) Archives, LIM/1/1/260. The religious comparison was also a politically loaded metaphor, see Cristiana Pugliese, "Kikuyu Pamphlets and Songs, 1945–1952," in *Mau Mau & Nationhood*, 97–120; Derek R. Peterson, "Gambling with God: Rethinking Religion in Colonial Central Kenya," in *The Invention of Religion: Rethinking Belief in Politics and History*, eds. Derek Peterson and Darren Walhof (New Brunswick, NJ: Rutgers University Press, 2002).
[105] African Church Leaders Conference, Steering Committee, May 29, 1961, NCCK archives, LIM/1/1/260.
[106] Ibid. [107] Ibid. [108] Ibid. [109] Ibid. [110] Ibid.
[111] Secret. From Director of Intelligence to Permanent Secretary for Defense, "Jomo Kenyatta/Private Opinions," September 19, 1961, BNA, FCO 141/6772. Underlined in the original document.

nationalist elite could not ignore him. By October 1961, after the constitutional talks broke down, personal rivalries emanating from KANU as well as KADU were no secret to anyone. A united façade was the less dangerous option, even if some could fear that it might well "prefigure a one-party under Mr. Kenyatta its leader." The political chaos in Congo was in everybody's mind; and Kenyatta himself would later make good use of the threat of Kenyan "little Katanga." Interviewed in Gatundu on October 11, 1961, he simply stated:

> It is difficult for me to say that there is any opposition to me from KANU because they have never opposed me, but there are personality differences in that party. The real trouble is that KADU are afraid of a national party whereas KANU have agreed to dissolve and form one. KADU are afraid they will be swallowed up by KANU, and they also want to keep 8 ministries because this would give them control of the council of ministers and, if you do not already know the secret I will tell you, – it has been agreed that a Chief Minister or a Prime Minister will be elected by the Council of Ministers, so KADU are trying to keep this control to keep me from being the Chief Minister, but that will not work.[112]

Clearly, he was just as confident in his aims. He must have understood that the myth he embodied, paradoxically reinforced by the ambiguities of his figure, prevented him from alienating himself from the popular masses. The colonial authorities too understood this well, stating that, although "Kenyatta the myth" might have been slightly disappointing, "Kenyatta the man" had not lost his influence, especially not in Central province, and remained concerned about the impact of his public declarations.[113] The problem was elsewhere: without a party machine it would have been impossible for Kenyatta to participate in the constitutional talks, especially if he wanted to become chief minister, and, as such, he was just as embroiled in partisan divisions. The Kenyatta campaign gave him a uniquely charismatic status, but this was barely sufficient to enforce loyalties and win over the scramble for governmental power. As the negotiations for independence were at a standstill, Kenyatta could no longer refuse the

---

[112] Secret. From the Director of Intelligence to the Permanent Secretary for Defense, "Jomo Kenyatta," October 24, 1961, BNA, FCO 141/6772.
[113] Secret. From the Director of Intelligence to the Permanent Secretary for Defense, "Jomo Kenyatta, Public Reaction in Central Province," October 7, 1961, BNA, FCO 141/6772 and interview with John Nottingham, May 16, 2014, Nairobi.

formal invitation KANU politicians issued for him to take the lead of the party. On October 28, 1961, he became president of KANU.

That day, the atmosphere of the meeting was openly strained. Kenyatta was summoned by KANU politicians to take a clear and open stand on his willingness to take over the party presidency. Opening the meeting, the chairman, James Gichuru, announced it was time to end the "fruitless efforts ... to bring about unity between KADU and KANU."[114] Kenyatta was pressed to stop "evading in order to stay away from the party." He had to take his responsibilities, as Ayodo warned him that "KANU people were dangerous and tricky and would destroy him if he was not careful and aware what he was taking over." Yet, those threats could not mask the fact that, by offering Kenyatta its presidency, KANU was playing its last joker: "people are looking for Mzee's leadership" said Wasonga Sijeyo; "[w]e cannot afford to have a crowd of leaders, but should follow one leader and that is Mr. Kenyatta," urged Dr. Julius Kiano, recalling, nonetheless "what Mr. Kenyatta had stated on the radio, that he was a general without an Army"; "KANU had no other shield except Mr. Kenyatta," acknowledged the Masai leader Koi ole Natu who began his intervention by recalling that his people were not willing to recognize Kenyatta's leadership; Mboya finally concluded, by underlining that, if the decision the whole country was awaiting for was not taken today, "KANU would find itself in a very awkward position."

Kenyatta, noting in passing that he needed to get to "know Kanu leaders" as well as their positions, and, probably in order to show he would resist intimidation, insisted "that KANU was rotten, but this should not cause fear." KANU leaders might well show unity today, but "he was not sure this unity existed before." He admitted he had thought for a time of building a third party that would be his own; and, if his attempt to build unity had failed, it was not out of lack of willingness: it was because of the joint conspiracy led by the governor and KADU to block any of his moves. Kenyatta finally declared his will to lead the party, and was given full power to "clean the organisation." The "long ovation" that concluded the meeting could barely hide the

---

[114] The subsequent quotes are from the minutes of the KANU Governing Council Meeting held on October 28, 1961 at Parliamentary Building, KNA, MAC/KEN/38/4.

multiple breaches within KANU. Now that he was an official representative of KANU, Kenyatta would have to confront the ongoing personal rivalries, just as his fellow politicians had been looking for him to do.

***

The making of Kenyatta as a nationalist figure (as he was not yet a nationalist leader) reveals that the path that eventually culminated with a presidential republic, was a fitful process, made up of shared weaknesses, far from any grand narrative of the "father of the nation" surfing on the tide of history. His accession to the KANU presidency shows that his strength was his comrades' insurmountable weaknesses. The Kenyatta campaign imposed nationalist logics onto the process of negotiation, without these logics being anchored in any nationalist party machine. Put differently, the campaign for Kenyatta's release unintentionally crystallized a nationalist front: it forced the different parties to align on a nationalist issue, yet, without constituting a nationalist alliance; and it provided Kenyatta with a nationalist audience, yet, without any nationalist organization.

The uncertainty created by the decolonization process was exacerbated by Kenyatta's unexpected return and fueled personal divisions and ambitions. Adding to the ethnic, regional, and political divisions inherited from colonization, personal rivalries prevented the formation of strong national alliances. Oginga Odinga's move to revive Kenyatta's name successfully neutralized his main adversaries, and brought KANU back into the negotiation process. Yet, Odinga had no control over the symbol Kenyatta had become, and failed to anticipate how Kenyatta's political return would affect the course of decolonization. The Kenyatta campaign further drove other nationalist competitors such as Ronald Ngala, Tom Mboya, or even James Gichuru further apart, disrupting their negotiations with colonial authorities and clouding their political future. The emergence of Kenyatta as national symbol rapidly overwhelmed the KANU leaders, as virtually none, whether KANU or KADU, could afford to take position against this sudden appearance as a nationalist figure. Whereas nationalist politics remained ethnically, regionally, and ideologically divided, politicians were urged to take position on a cause with unknown political aftermaths.

The Kenyatta campaign was complicated by the international dimension in the context of decolonization. Both the British authorities, whether in the metropole or in the colony, and the white settlers, wanted to prevent the campaign from getting out of hand and causing further embarrassment, when the British Empire was already being shaken by a wave of independences (Ghana became independent in 1957 and Nigeria in 1960). The British had not abandoned their suspicions of Kenyatta, "the leader to death and darkness." Yet, they seemed ready to readjust their views in order to better secure their interests (as the next chapter will show), and regularly reviewed the state of mind of both Kenyatta's competitors and allies. One element remains very much unclear until today: the contacts the British authorities had with Kenyatta in the aftermath of the campaign. These may have pushed Kenyatta's rapid transformation from "leader to death and darkness" into a potential chief minister. The available archives, scattered as they are, only hint at the possibility of such contacts. The next chapter suggests, however, that Kenyatta could count on the British favor only *after* his release, when negotiating the decolonization of the land issue with the British colonial authorities.

Kenyatta emerged as a national figure out of a not only deeply divided, but hostile political scene. At the same time, the absence of any viable leadership alternative highlights three defining traits of his political ascent. First, Kenyatta inherited a divided political machine he could barely trust. This may explain his disinterest in political party organization, although he never neglected the party as a useful tool to win over the electorate.[115] This may be one reason, as well, why he would eventually prefer to rely on the provincial administration, admittedly a colonial legacy, but more reliable for him to build his authority on. Second, he was very much dependent on KANU. His idea of a third party quickly faded away. Unlike other African leaders who managed to mobilize a party machine, such as the Senegalese Léopold Sédar Senghor or the Guinean Ahmed Sékou Touré, Kenyatta was left with a hostile party machine and no tradition of militant action. He had no choice but to rely on the most influential KANU leaders: his

---

[115] See Kenneth Good, "Kenyatta and the Organisation of KANU," *Canadian Journal of African Studies* 2, no. 2 (1968): 115–136; Nicholas Cheeseman, "The Rise and Fall of Civil-Authoritarianism in Africa: Patronage, Participation, and Political Parties in Kenya and Zambia" (Ph.D. diss., University of Oxford, 2007).

friend James Gichuru, and his two main competitors, Tom Mboya and Oginga Odinga: a political dependency which would prove to be enduring. A financial dependency might have aggravated his dependency. Kenyatta did not seem to possess any financial capital upon his liberation; how he acquired wealth in the following years will be a crucial question to answer, especially regarding the issue of land redistribution that was already looming by then. Third, and perhaps most importantly, the construction of the Kenyatta campaign shows how oppositions were subsumed under Kenyatta's figurehead, and how all actors reluctantly accepted his political return. These oppositions were far from being tamed, however. The future president was left with the task of winning over and institutionalizing a system that contained so much internal dissent and challenge against his leadership.

3 | *Kenyatta, Land, and Decolonization (1961–1963)*

Between November 1961 and December 1963, the Kenyan nationalist elite, the European settlers, and the British government met for three constitutional conferences to negotiate independence. The two crucial issues were land decolonization (the transfer of European land to Africans) and the future constitution. KANU called for rapid decolonization, championed a centralized government, and argued for an open competition for land beyond ethnic boundaries. KADU, instead, feared the domination of the Luo and Kikuyu. Although it supported liberal economic policies too (they were, after all, backed by conservative white settlers, who considered KANU politicians as radicals endangering their economic and political privileges), it defended a regional constitution, known as *majimboism*. Regional assemblies would be created to levy taxes and manage local government affairs, and the police, as well education, housing and social services policies.[1]

The vexed question of the decolonization of land complicated the independence negotiations: uncertainty on the future of ethnic minority rights in an independent Kenya was ubiquitous. At stake was the persisting conflict of colonial state-issued land titles versus indigenous claims to historical rights over the land.[2] The British government and European settlers had already started in the 1950s to consolidate and register land titles.[3] With the first independence conference in 1960, British colonials and settlers understood that total decolonization was inevitable and that the establishment of stable institutions to

---

[1] On the independence negotiations, see Ogot and Ochieng', *Decolonisation & Independence in Kenya*; Kyle, *The Politics of the Independence of Kenya*; Anderson, "Yours in Struggle for Majimbo"; Hornsby, *Kenya*, 62–70.

[2] Onoma, *The Politics of Property Rights Institutions in Africa*, 145. See also Sorrenson, *Origins of European Settlement in Kenya*.

[3] Harbeson, "Land Reforms and Politics in Kenya, 1954–70"; Paul Kelemen, "The British Labor Party and the Economics of Decolonisation: The Debate over Kenya," *Journal of Colonialism and Colonial History* 8, no. 3 (2007): 1–33.

decolonize, redistribute land, and secure land ownership was a necessity.[4] Complications during the independence negotiations emerged out of the multitude of interests involved, highlighting the contradiction between mutual economic interests (the purchase and transfer of land to ensure general economic stability) and politically divergent objectives (regionalism versus centralized government).

Land transfers, set up via land settlement schemes, were driven by a fear of political instability and economic breakdown that could shatter the European settlers' interests as much as that of the British government or Kenyan nationalist elites. As the main financial contributor to the schemes, the British government considered economic stability a priority, and tended to favor political consensus. At the same time, all parties involved were united in their quest for stability and the fear that landless Africans would revive the Mau Mau movement. The search for consensus preserved and strengthened the so-called tribal spheres of influence created by colonizers – that is, a political geography defined on ethnic boundaries – which no nationalist politician, whether from KANU or KADU, contested.[5] The early years of settlement schemes did not meet much opposition, but the prospect of independence coming closer, the thirst for land, the rising unemployment, and the risk of massive migrations of people to settlement zones made effective political action all the more necessary if leaders were not to lose control of their constituencies.

This chapter analyzes how the reshaping of central institutions for land transfer impacted both the decolonization process and Kenyatta's ascension to power. The setting up of the Central Land Board was a pressing matter in 1961, as the peaceful decolonization of land was the most important issue of the independence conference. This chapter shows that the British authorities, obsessed with security and political

---

[4] The history of land settlement and land policies established between the end of the 1950s and the early 1960s has been well researched, it is too vast to be summarized here. See in particular Sorrenson, *Origins of European Settlement in Kenya*; Wasserman, *Politics of Decolonisation*; Christopher Leo, *Land and Class in Kenya* (Toronto: University of Toronto Press, 1984).

[5] Ibid., 107. The expression "tribal spheres of influence" was already in use in the 1960s. Carey Jones notes that the claim was not directed, at first, against Europeans but was designed to balance indigenous tribal politics. As competition over economic resources grew, tribal ties become increasingly politicized. The geography of settlement also reinforced tribal politics. See Jones, *The Anatomy of Uhuru*, 139; Leo, *Land and Class in Kenya*, 110–111.

stability, favored KANU, and hence Kenyatta, as the safest political bet – abandoning the European settlers' and KADU's argument for *majimboism*. At independence, Kenyatta would not only be considered as the guardian of political order, he would also inherit an advantageously designed institutional framework to control the most valuable political and economic resource in Kenya: land.

Kenyatta's Land Politics

Upon his release, Kenyatta's position on the land issue, feverishly anticipated at first, finally appeased many. Although little information has transpired from the available archives on the possible discussions the British might have had with Kenyatta while he was jailed or under restriction, the British certainly sounded him out on this issue. A telegram addressed to the secretary of state by Governor Renison in August 1961, the month Kenyatta was released, stated that "When German Consul General saw him at Maralal Kenyatta said Settlement Schemes were essential and should go ahead without further delay."[6] The Germans, who contributed financially to the settlement schemes, might have visited Kenyatta to obtain the assurance that the settlement schemes would be financially viable under a KANU government. This gives us a glimpse of the extent to which Kenyatta, if he was not directly associated with the negotiations on the schemes, was powerful enough not to be ignored or excluded from them.

All expected him to make his position on the land question public during his Maralal speech in 1961, ending his charismatic undecisiveness. For his fellow Kikuyu politicians, it was a matter of leadership competition. What mattered to the British was Kenyatta's ability to reassure the settlers as to their economic future in Kenya, and, more generally, to appease the impatient, landless Kikuyu, striving for their land in the White Highlands. During his famous Maralal speech, Kenyatta made clear he did not want the land to be redistributed for free. Later, in 1962, he gave similar speeches while touring the country. He denounced practices of land grabbing and advocated, instead, the policy of "willing buyer–willing seller." His words were interpreted in various and contradictory ways. In a telegram sent in January 1962 to

---

[6] Secret. Decipher Telegram to Secretary of State, no. 714, August 29, 1961, BNA, FCO 141/6923.

the secretary of state, who had asked about "immediate local reactions" and the possible "implications" of one of Kenyatta's recent speech in Kiambu, the governor noted that

> East African Standard Monday edition reported Kenyatta as having said that Africans should not buy land from Europeans until after independence, for then they would get it for free. This is not in accord with Police account, but Police report that subsequent to the meeting the majority of Africans present appeared to have gained the same impression of Kenyatta's meaning as in Standard report. Kenyatta has refuted Standard report. Nevertheless impression among many Africans remains that Kenyatta has now revealed his thinking as the same as Ngei's.[7]

Why was the reception of the speech so varied and contradictory? Governor Renison believed that "the Standard reporter's note did not ... support the account published."[8] He believed Kenyatta was jockeying, very carefully, in a political sphere that had reluctantly accepted his political return: "He wished ... to present KANU policy in most attractive light and probably realised that his audience would interpret his words as meaning that Africans should not buy European land now."[9] The colonial correspondence on Kenyatta's ambiguous speeches showed no sign of alarm: the image of the "leader to death and darkness" was fading away.[10]

While the first Lancaster House conference was disturbed by the news of Kenyatta's release, the second conference, starting in February 1962, was meant to solve political divisive views. Political stagnation, coupled with tensions surrounding decolonization of land, not only crystallized party opposition, but was shaking nationalist parties from within. KANU was troubled by a latent internal war between the moderates Kenyatta represented, who considered political consensus and economic stability as the only possible guiding line for land policy,

---

[7] Telegram to the Secretary of State, no. 63, January 26, 1962, BNA, FCO 141/6923.

[8] Secret and Personal. Decipher Telegram to the Secretary of State, no. 35, January 25, 1962, BNA, FCO 141/6923.

[9] Ibid. Besides, the governor noted the technicality that Kenyatta might well have been referring to "the payment of 'settlement charges' rather than purchase price of land."

[10] Peter Knauss, "From Devil to Father Figure: The Transformation of Jomo Kenyatta by Kenya Whites," *The Journal of Modern African Studies* 9, no. 1 (1971): 131–137.

and the so-called radicals. Certainly better described as populists, they wanted land to be freely redistributed to the landless, among them were many former Mau Mau fighters. This divide barely hid a deeper leadership competition to take over KANU. Led by the ex-Mau Mau detainees Paul Ngei, J. M. Kariuki, and Bildad Kaggia, the "radicals" controlled districts crowded by the landless and poor (Machakos in the Eastern region, Nyandarua and Murang'a in the Central region), and represented a threat to Kenyatta's political legitimacy. The Luo leaders, the unionist Tom Mboya, who needed to appeal to the Kikuyu to build up his national aura, and the socialist Oginga Odinga, who did not directly endanger Kikuyu legitimacy, were potential national competitors and represented a threat in a future KANU government.

As the second independence conference was about to start, KANU initiated, under Kenyatta's leadership, a moderating turn on the land question.[11] The party published a memorandum on land usage in February 1962 confirming its preference for willing buyer–willing seller land transfers. Claiming the primacy of central government's decision over land issues, the memorandum anticipated all issues of which the British could have been wary.[12] The preamble reaffirmed the principle of productive land use: "no racial or tribal consideration should be permitted to interfere with the attainment of its maximum potential."[13] The security of title, the ultimate protection against land grabbing, came second on the agenda and was declared a "national responsibility." Objectives of economic growth emphasized private property, as well as the productive use and development of land.[14] In a twisted plea to central government, the memorandum stated that, in the White Highlands, "KANU cannot agree that tribal spheres of influence do or should exist within the Scheduled Areas ... Indeed this is a policy that should be aimed at throughout the country."[15]

The decolonization of the White Highlands, also referred to as the "scheduled areas," was of particular importance to both KANU and the British colonials. The latter, just like the white settlers, needed the

---

[11] Wasserman, *Politics of Decolonisation*, 118–119.
[12] The memorandum stated that "[a]fter the central government, through its Agricultural Department, has designated land as undeveloped and liable to acquisition, the local government authority shall decide on the use to which the land shall be put," Secret. KANU Memorandum on Land Usage, BNA, FCO 141/6923.
[13] Ibid.   [14] Ibid.   [15] Ibid.

Kikuyu leaders' cooperation to ensure that the settlement schemes would go as planned. They considered Kenyatta to be of great use to them, probably because of the ambiguity that surrounded his Mau Mau connections. In March 1962, in a settlement zone south of Central province, recently settled Kikuyu suddenly abandoned their settlement, driven away by rumors alleging that they would be allocated less land than promised. Kenyatta was probably not "consulted about the walk-off from Muguga scheme."[16] A report on behalf of the governor stated that all this happened because local KANU leaders felt the settlement schemes were negotiated in favor of KADU and the white settlers, and "therefore told the settlers that as Kenyatta has not approved, they must not accept land."[17] The report recommended the secretary of state to "try to induce KANU to publicize (out here) their approval of the Schemes," and suggested threatening KANU leaders with "adverse publicity" if they failed to do so.[18]

Kenyatta was certainly conscious of the sensitivity of the land issue as well as the fragility of his political base (be it African or British). The risk of seeing local KANU branches, those so-called local subordinates, slipping out of his control directly endangered his political legitimacy. He was willing to support the scheme and urge the settlers to return immediately, on the condition he was given "written assurance" from the governor that they would be given the promised acres of land. He seemed nonetheless "suspicious that he [was] being led into a trap."[19] For the acting governor, there was no trap at all but simply mutual interest: "With [Kenyatta's] support or even with his passive acquiescence we can make very rapid progress at very low cost."[20] The governor understood that he, like the colonial authorities in general, could take advantage of the common interest they shared with Kenyatta and his moderate comrades: the peaceful ongoing of the settlement schemes. The land rights issue brought the British closer to Kenyatta, elevating him to the position of unique intermediary and appeasing political force. This mutuality of interest would prove to be crucial

---

[16] Secret, Decipher Telegram to Governor, March 8, 1962, BNA, FCO 141/6923.
[17] Secret. Decipher Telegram to Secretary of State, no. 164, March 7, 1962, BNA, FCO 141/6923.
[18] Ibid.   [19] Ibid.
[20] Secret. Decipher Telegram to Secretary of State, no. 170, March 10, 1962, BNA, FCO 141/6923.

when it came to establishing new land institutions for the independent government.

At the end of the second Lancaster House conference, in April 1962, a KANU–KADU coalition government was formed. It was to discuss the drafted constitutional proposals, called the "framework constitution," which conceded much to regionalist dispositions.[21] Kenyatta became minister of state for constitutional affairs and economic planning; his adversary, the KADU leader Ronald Ngala, was minister of state for constitutional affairs and administration. KANU joined the coalition government, yet always with the aim to dismantle all regionalist concessions.

Prelude to Centralization: Negotiations over the Central Land Board

The inability to settle the question of regionalism and the stagnation of the ongoing constitutional negotiations could not indefinitely contain the tensions between KANU and KADU, nor the internal divisions of KANU itself. British colonials and settlers worried that a delayed independence could aggravate an already tense security situation. The smooth execution of land settlements had to be secure. That is, the decolonization of land had to be as little politicized as possible. Constitutional negotiations in 1961 planned to revive the Central Land Board in order to organize the purchase and transfer of land, as well as the execution of settlements. The powers of the Central Land Board had been a subject of heated debate since the first Lancaster House conference, precisely because they encroached on the arguments over regionalism.

When in 1962 it came to deciding on the scope of the decision-making powers accorded to this strategic body, dissent arose among the members of the Council of Ministers.[22] To many, electing and granting authority to the members of the board was linked to the distribution of regional powers. Throughout the second Lancaster House conference, the establishment of the board remained the "main sticking point."[23] Gary Wasserman noted that, at the end of the

[21] Kyle, *The Politics of the Independence of Kenya*, 150; Hornsby, *Kenya*, 70–71.
[22] Confidential. From Griffith-Jones to Webber, May 23, 1962, BNA, FCO 141/6923.
[23] Wasserman, *The Politics of Decolonisation*, 106.

conference, all political parties had agreed on the necessity for the board to be "divorced from political control."[24] Nevertheless, Wasserman focused extensively on cleavages between the British Colonial Office, European farmers, and the Ministry of Land. Leaving KANU's and KADU's interests aside, he overlooked the implications the attempted depoliticization of land politics had on KANU's ascension to power. Similarly, John W. Harbeson gave a very detailed account of the technicalities involved when negotiating the responsibilities of the various institutions involved in the land settlement schemes, especially regarding the allocation of funds to the Central Land Board. He nonetheless did not pay particular attention to the mutuality of interest that emerged between KANU leaders and the British colonial authorities, and its influence on the decolonization process.[25]

The establishment of the new board on April 7, 1962, along with the creation of the Ministry of Land Settlements and Water Development, sought to take into account the protection of regional interests. It was designed to overcome the administrative inefficiency of its ancestor, the Land Settlement and Development Board, through conserving its mission to inspire confidence among the white settlers.[26] The independence of the board from the ministry was safeguarded so that the land minister would not be suspected of bypassing the board's decisions: otherwise "he will surely be unable to avoid suspicion and attack, however unjustified, on the ground that he will be under political pressure to circumvent the Board's intentions."[27] The minister in question was Bruce McKenzie, a South African farmer and alleged MI6 agent, who had recently joined KANU, and would later become the powerful minister of agriculture during Kenyatta's regime.[28]

---

[24] Wasserman, *The Politics of Decolonisation*, 114, see also 140.
[25] John W. Harbeson, *Nation-Building in Kenya: The Role of Land Reform* (Evanston, IL: Northwestern University Press, 1973), chapter 4 and 218–233.
[26] Confidential. W. B. L. Monson (Colonial Office) to Governor Renison, August 14, 1962, BNA, FCO 141/6924. On the Land Settlement and Development Board, see Wasserman, *The Politics of Decolonisation*, 140–141.
[27] Ibid.
[28] T. A. Watts, "A Review of the Activities of the Land Development and Settlement Board" (January 1961–July 1962), July 31, 1962, BNA, FCO 141/6924. On Bruce McKenzie, see David A. Percox, "Mau Mau and Arming the State," in *Mau Mau & Nationhood*, 137; "McKenzie, Bruce Roy (1919–1978)," in *Historical Dictionary of Kenya*, eds. Robert M. Maxon and Thomas P. Ofcansky (Plymouth: Rowman & Litlefield, 2014), 223–224; Hornsby, *Kenya*, 225–226.

The British wanted to accelerate the setting up of the board by restraining the scope of administrative change, and ensuring its independence from the government.[29] Hoping to play down tensions over regionalism, appease the settlers' demands, and ensure the representation of ethnic minorities, the representative of the colonial office, F. D. Webber, asked Kenya's attorney general and acting governor, Eric Griffith-Jones, whether "it might be possible to begin to put into the present Board provincial representatives, in order to set the pattern for the future."[30] Griffith-Jones replied that "we regard the Board as semi-political, semi judicial independent body which would approve or reject settlement schemes submitted to it by the Government and would advise the Government on settlement policy."[31] The board was not settled immediately because the British had difficulties in finding a suitable candidate to be chairman. This was becoming a matter of urgency, if they wanted to assure the smooth transfer of European land to the Africans, given that a settlement of 1,000,000 acres of land was immediately pending.[32] To use the colonial office's terms, it was necessary to "take this particular settlement scheme 'out of politics'."[33]

Ironically, one of the main defenders and architects of the board was the minister of land himself, Bruce McKenzie, who was playing a dual role in the decolonization of land. As a minister, he was the link between the coalition government and the British Colonial Office, thus hoping to assure the financial and political viability of the settlement schemes. However, he was also a KANU politician designing the institutional future of his own ministry. The British colonial officials themselves doubted, in a brief telegram, "whether an obligation on the Board to use the Minister as their agent is consistent with the White Paper's approach."[34] McKenzie replied that, since the transfer of land

---

[29] Confidential. Webber to Griffith-Jones, May 2, 1962, BNA, FCO 141/6923.
[30] Ibid. On the British authorities' strategy and their relationship with white settlers, see Wasserman, *The Politics of Decolonisation*, chapter 5.
[31] Confidential. From Griffith-Jones to Webber, May 23, 1962, BNA, FCO 141/6923.
[32] The settlement planned "to settle African families on about one million acres of predominantly mixed farming land in the scheduled areas over the next five years." See Secretary of State, "Kenya Financial Talks," August 9, 1962, BNA, FCO 141/6923.
[33] Confidential. W. B. L. Monson (Colonial Office) to Governor Renison, August 24, 1962, BNA, FCO 141/6924.
[34] Ibid.

in the scheduled areas was the primary objective of the British and the white settlers, an independent board was politically untenable and financially too expensive. Instead, he hoped to redesign the relationship between the board and the government, on the grounds that

> it would be too expensive and complicated to set up new organisation which anyway would require to co-operate with other organs of Government at every point ... details of settlement too important to Government to leave to independent body not responsible to Government since they could seriously affect economy and law and order.[35]

McKenzie's influence would have long-lasting and far-reaching implications for Kenyatta's ascension to power. The minister was clearly looking beyond land transfers, already preparing postcolonial land politics. His argumentation presaged the turning of the tide in favor of KANU, considered as the only stabilizing force for securing land transfers.

The political agenda of land decolonization was complicated by the unstable and deteriorating political context. In July 1962, the publication of the Regional Boundaries Commission's report, originally intended to ease the transition to *majimboism* and to redesign certain regions to match ethnic criteria, drew attention to the risks inherent in mass movements of ethnic groups across regions, particularly from the Rift Valley into the Central Region.[36] In December 1962, McKenzie prepared a memorandum urging cabinet ministers to accept the acceleration of Kikuyu settlement in the Central Region as a political priority. His argument fell on sympathetic ears, as the governor also emphasized that "my advisors and I regard the situation as politically explosive," while "senior 'Kikuyu' experts see parallel with 1952 [sic]."[37] The governor himself took on the mission to explain the land settlement schemes and the present situation to KADU "behind the

---

[35] Further indicated reasons were that "(iii) Government will be borrowing the money for the schemes and will have the responsibility of repaying it; it must therefore have ultimate control; (iv) Board is an unsuitable instrument for devising and executing detailed schemes since they will not be selected for ability to do this, and resultant burden on Chairman too great." Decipher Telegram to the Secretary of State, no. 602, September 5, 1962, BNA, FCO 141/6924.

[36] Hornsby, *Kenya*, 73–74; Secret and Personal. Decipher Telegram to Governor, no. 473, December 13, 1962, BNA, FCO 141/6918.

[37] Secret. Decipher Telegram to Secretary of State, no. 813, December 8, 1962, BNA, FCO 141/6918.

scenes," preferring discrete diplomacy to open debate in the Council of Ministers.[38] From December 1962 to January 1963, the governor's team attempted to "soften up KADU," but stumbled over the party's irreducible refusal to concede any additional Kikuyu settlement.[39] However, both KANU and its adversaries were bound by their political dependency on the necessary funds to buy out land and to settle landless Africans: funds that the board would allocate.[40] Therefore, the urgency to access financial resources was too important for the creation of the board to be delayed because of irreconcilable political views.

Political and financial intricacies forced a consensus on land institutions. Although the "most influential Ministers of both parties" came round to the idea of an independent board, with Kenyatta personally giving his consent, the political competition for economic resources led to a much more politicized solution.[41] McKenzie did assert in a memorandum on accelerated settlement that "the settlement of Kikuyu should not be made at the expense of other tribes."[42] Nevertheless, the search for political consensus, bound by the untouchable principle of tribal spheres of influence and subjected to the security situation in the White Highlands, automatically favored the Kikuyu (read KANU) as the most reliable interlocutors. As McKenzie explained: "The Government would like settlement to be unrestricted by race or tribe, but in the present political and security situation, it is not possible ... The settlement schemes are designed to secure orderly settlement in the former scheduled areas."[43]

The purpose of the board, therefore, was not an attempt to make land politics apolitical. It was now intended, in the words of Governor Renison, to "minimise the political vulnerability under the new regime

---

[38] Secret and Personal. Decipher Telegram to the Secretary of State, no. 307, December 14, 1962, BNA, FCO 141/6918.
[39] Secret and Personal. Decipher Telegram to Secretary of State, no. 14, January 10, 1963, BNA, FCO 141/6918.
[40] Harbeson, *Nation-Building in Kenya*, 228–230.
[41] Secret and Personal. Decipher Telegram to Secretary of State, no. 30, January 16, 1962 and Extract of Council of the Sixty-Fourth Meeting of the Council of Minister Held on the December 17, 1963, BNA, FCO 141/6918.
[42] Secret. Council of Ministers, Accelerated Settlement, C.M.M.(63)10, January 16, 1963, BNA, FCO 141/ 6918.
[43] Bruce McKenzie to M. M. Madan, Honorary Secretary of the Federation of Chambers of Commerce and Industry in Eastern Africa, January 11, 1963, KNA, BN/81/161.

of our settlement programme."[44] The governor himself assured the secretary of state that he was "not particularly worried at the fact that two out of the three [ministers negotiating land settlement in London] will be KANU. Gichuru must be associated with the financial side of things, and McKenzie is the only one of the three with the detailed knowledge of settlement factors."[45] The main conflict was not, therefore, between the Colonial Office and the Ministry of Land, since the two agreed that political security was paramount. Rather, white settlers and minorities defenders were sidelined into minor political actors.

Although Kenyatta may not have played a (visibly) direct role within this process, the setting up of the Central Land Board was a key ingredient in his political ascension. KANU and KADU were left with very little room for maneuver if they wanted to remain included in the schemes, which safeguarded the spheres of influences they depended on politically. The independence, or "depoliticization," of the board conveniently accommodated multiple antagonistic interests: The British searched for ways to accelerate transfers of land concentrated mainly in the White Highlands; KADU foresaw the new board as a guarantee against tribal domination and, perhaps, a future route toward regionalism; and McKenzie and his KANU ministers hoped to divert regionalist concerns with a plea for law and order. Land settlement policies kept moving forward with very little political opposition, slowed down only by financial obstacles.

Most importantly, the creation of the Central Land Board showed that minorities' rights were not automatically safeguarded by regionalist dispositions.[46] In fact, the obsession with political and economic stability overshadowed the opposition between regionalism and state centralization. This may explain why Kenyatta did not question the

---

[44] Secret and Personal. Decipher Telegram to the Secretary of State, no. 235, April 11, 1963, BNA, FCO 141/6918.

[45] Secret and Personal. Decipher Telegram to Secretary of State, no. 37, January 19, 1963, BNA, FCO 141/6918.

[46] Sanger and Nottingham noticed that, already by 1962, the Regional Boundaries Commission's report showed that "regionalism would not necessarily provide minority safeguards," see Clyde Sanger and John Nottingham, "The Kenya General Election of 1963," *The Journal of Modern African Studies* 2, no. 1 (1964): 14. The point I wish to emphasise here is that the establishing of the Central Land Board further consumed links between regionalism and minority rights.

technical independence of the board, but supported it. Backed by his two influential KANU ministers, McKenzie and Gichuru, he could restrict his political activities to strategic public appearances. The tide of negotiations favored KANU as the leading partner, while the stagnation of KANU–KADU opposition would play against the latter. The real turn, however, came with the May 1963 legislative elections.[47] Kenyatta's popularity as a national hero detained by the British gave considerable political leverage to KANU. As the party would go on to win these elections, Kenyatta would become prime minister and inherit this advantageously designed institutional framework, providing him and his cabinet ministers with direct control over land.

The 1963 Elections and After

Land transfer remained an all-out war that subverted party lines. On January 3, 1963, *The Times* published an article entitled "Kenyatta Party Threatened by Tribal Rivalries," summarizing the factions tearing KANU apart. The Luo were split along leadership disputes between Oginga Odinga, Tom Mboya, the lawyer Arwings-Kodhek, and other minor politicians fearing Kikuyu domination. Paul Ngei, influential Kamba leader in the Eastern region, seceded in November 1962 and created his African People's Party.[48] There was also the Nairobi branch, constituting of "Kikuyu who are opposed to Mboya and followers of Dr. Munyua Waiyaki." The article concluded that "meanwhile Kenya African Democratic Union are silently jubilant."[49]

The Times correspondent said nothing about what held the party together. Or, more precisely, of what held all these moderate leaders together. As a note prepared for the governor's office on January 24, 1963 explained, "[b]oth factions, particularly in view of the resurgence of the Mau Mau 'old guard' and the growth of the Kenya Land Freedom Army, decided that Kikuyu support was indispensable and that it would be suicidal to split against Kenyatta."[50] It was suicidal

---

[47] Ibid.
[48] François Grignon, "Le Politicien Entrepreneur En Son Terroir: Paul Ngei à Kangundo (Kenya) 1945–1990" (Ph.D. diss., University of Bordeaux, 1997), chapter 4.
[49] "Kenyatta Party Threatened by Tribal Rivalries," *The Times*, January 3, 1963.
[50] Governor's Office, "The Political Situation in Kenya as at January 1963," January 24, 1964, BNA, DO 168/45.

because all needed "the advantage of Kenyatta's authority as a symbol of both African nationalism and of Kikuyu leadership."[51] At a moment when landless masses could easily be manipulated by more radical and more vocal leaders, no moderate politician had any interest in weakening Kenyatta's charismatic leadership.

Kenyatta did not seem much interested in party business. He had delegated the reorganization of the party to Joseph Murumbi. He nonetheless hoped to prevent organizational issues of the party from going public, as Murumbi later recalled.[52] Kenyatta was much more preoccupied by the security situation, especially in the Central region. In early January, he met local politicians in Meru, where Mau Mau resilience was particularly worrying, and risked tipping the balance over land politics. He informed the permanent secretary of the Ministry of Defence, J. K. arap Koitie, "how strongly he had emphasized to the politicians the necessity for full cooperation amongst themselves, so as to work for the ... prosperity of the District."[53] Kenyatta knew that there was a risk of acquaintance between KANU officials and former Mau Mau groups.[54] He had to prevent the decline of the Kikuyu old guard from strengthening the subversive KLFA. As security risks were spreading over Kenya, the Kenyan government feared losing control of key zones, especially where islands of European farmers were surrounded by landless squatters and risked turning into hot spots of political opposition (in particular Nyandarua, Ol Kalou, and Kinangop in the Central region, and Sotik and Naivasha in the Nyanza region). As the coalition government was stagnating, KANU hoped the 1963 elections would strengthen its majority in parliament. Its victory was overwhelming, and KANU formed an interim government on June 1.[55]

Most revealing is not so much the results of the elections, but the following constitution of the cabinet announced on May 30, led by Kenyatta who was to be sworn in as prime minister within days. Fifteen ministers, along with fifteen permanent secretaries were chosen,

---

[51] Ibid. [52] Murumbi and Thurston, *A Path Not Taken*, 124–125.
[53] Secret. J. K. arap Koitie to Civil Secretary Embu, January 10, 1963, KNA, BB/1/149.
[54] Anthony Swann to Jomo Kenyatta, February 8, 1963, KNA, BB/1/149.
[55] Anderson, "Yours in Struggle for *Majimbo*," 561–564.

with careful attention to guaranteeing regional and ethnic equitable representation.[56] Tom Mboya became minister of justice and constitutional affairs. Oginga Odinga was appointed minister for home affairs. Kenyatta, according to MacDonald's memories, insisted on his later appointment, although "my civil servants were dead against this." Kenyatta would have preferred not to appoint him, but feared this would be "denigrating him and his tribe."[57] MacDonald was worried that Odinga would be given control over the police, but, to avoid Kenyatta being exposed to criticism, he as governor took the decision to retain international affairs, defence, and security under his control. "Jomo said magnificent... The cabinet was announced. 'Double O' was thrilled at being Home Minister. But within five minutes of finding the police were not under his control, he rang me."[58]

Within Kenyatta's close circle of government, his Kikuyu comrades were given prominent functions. James Gichuru remained minister for finance; Kenyatta's personal physician, Njoroge Mungai, became minister for health; his long-time friend and brother-in-law, Peter Mbiyu Koinange, was appointed minister of state and Pan-African affairs; and the young Julius Kiano became minister for commerce and industry. His main adversaries Paul Ngei, J. M. Kariuki, and Bildad Kaggia remained outside of the government, but their respective districts were represented by three permanent secretaries – respectively – the Kamba Eliud Mwendwa, the Embu Jeremiah Nyagah, and the Meru Jackson Angaine – who would be promoted to minister of land and settlement shortly after. As for the Asian community, Chanan Singh was appointed permanent secretary in the prime minister's office.[59] Early in June, MacDonald noted that Kenyatta now "seemed to take on a wholly new lease of life and power. His party's victory at the polls had been unexpectedly great, and he therefore realised that he could now at last assert his authority unchallenged." The governor only worried that

---

[56] Sanger and Nottingham, "The Kenya General Election of 1963," 37; Hornsby, *Kenya*, 83.
[57] Kenya Personalities and Power. Interview Given on April 24, 1976 by the Rt. Hon. M. MacDonald to Arnold Raphael and Celia Curtis (for the East African Standard (Newspapers) Ltd.), Malcolm MacDonald Papers, 76/7/52.
[58] Ibid.
[59] Sanger and Nottingham, "The Kenya General Election of 1963," 37–38.

Kenyatta's "conciliatory moderation" risked alienating the KANU radicals.[60] How Kenyatta would deal with the opposition from both KADU and KANU sides would determine his ability to gain and stay in power.

After the 1963 general elections, the final stage of negotiations for independence took a new turn, with KANU as the official leading force. Kenyatta participated in the councils of ministers, preparing constitutional talks between January and February 1963. In the LegoCo, his interventions were limited to general statements, showing a dislike for detail, perhaps hiding some indecisiveness, and always supporting the long and meticulous speeches delivered by prominent KANU leaders, Mboya, Gichuru, or McKenzie.[61] Besides, the most sensitive aspects of the independence talks were negotiated informally and privately.[62] In November 1963, Jonathan Chadwick, officer at the Commonwealth Relations Office, cautiously noted in his report on the Lancaster House conference that "Kenyatta is by no means a spent force, as is sometimes suggested. [He] has a shrewd political instinct for where his interests lie."[63] These lay in three major issues: land, regional boundaries, and territorial integrity.

Although the KANU legislative victory was certainly reassuring, KANU was no less fragmented. Given the persisting internal divisions, and the competition for the control of the tribal spheres of influence, Kenyatta was heavily dependent on his KANU comrades, who were also his main adversaries. So the search for consensus was a sensitive task. On the one hand, he knew he needed the support of two rivals of national stature: Odinga and Mboya. He needed to secure KANU leverage over the negotiation process: "holding the Kikuyu/Luo alliance" had been "his fundamental policy since he assumed the

---

[60] Secret and Personal. Malcolm MacDonald, "Notes on Kenya on the Eve of the Independence Conference, September 1963," Malcolm MacDonald Papers, 45/2/16.

[61] Secret. Malcolm MacDonald to the British High Commissioner, Despatch No. 1. Nairobi, July 3, 1966, BNA, DO 213/204.

[62] Confidential. J. Chadwick to L. J. D. Wakely, November 14, 1963, BNA, DO 168/49. For more insight into the informal and secret politics, see Walton, *Empire of Secrets*, 258–273 and chapter 6 more generally. This informality explains the limited material available to trace Kenyatta's thoughts and action during the independence conference, and the fact that I will mainly rely on British reports of the negotiation for this chapter.

[63] Confidential. J. Chadwick to L. J. D. Wakely, November 14, 1963, BNA, DO 168/49.

leadership of K.A.N.U."; this would be an enduring commitment.[64] Ongoing rumors that Kenyatta was already an old man who would not live long fed nascent speculation over his succession. The British were especially worried that, were Kenyatta not to control this alliance, Odinga would take the advantage and force him into more radical policies.[65] On the other hand, Kenyatta was, unsurprisingly, dependent on the British, and more particularly on British aid to settle land issues. He had no illusion as to the "means" required to resist the British in the negotiation process: Kenya had none, a lack that undoubtedly further hindered political leverage.[66] His "attitude towards the European settlers," noted the British high commissioner, "was not prompted by pure altruism; it sprang also from a sense of enlightened self-interest. Kenyatta clearly recognised the essential role which the large European (and also the Asian) community could play in the economic development of the new Kenya." To British eyes, this was "an additional dimension to his wisdom."[67] But the British authorities nonetheless feared their advantage could be played upon: the more untenable the situation in the Central region, the more they were concerned that "as soon as Africans press, we pay."[68] They shared with Kenyatta a deep anxiety over security in Kenya.

Kenyatta's promptness to support the British policy of willing buyer–willing seller puzzled some of his contemporaries.[69] He knew that Kikuyu land had, since the early stages of colonization, been alienated and fragmented, while the Kikuyu tended to be scattered over the Central and Rift Valley regions. In 1962, the British director of intelligence mentioned that

[64] Malcom MacDonald to the Secretary of State for Commonwealth Relations, "Kenya: Plans for a Coup d'Etat in Kenya?" July 21, 1965, BNA, DO 213/65.
[65] Confidential. J. Chadwick to L. J. D. Wakely, November 14, 1963, BNA, DO 168/49; Kyle, *The Politics of the Independence of Kenya*, 179. On Mboya, see David Goldsworthy's very complete biography: *Tom Mboya*.
[66] Eleventh Constitutional Meeting, January 24, 1963, KNA, KA.1/11/73. On Kenyan bourgeoisie's dependency on British funds for land settlement, see Leo, *Land and Class in Kenya*, chapter 4.
[67] Secret. Malcolm MacDonald to the British High Commissioner, Despatch No. 1, July 3, 1966, BNA, DO 213/204.
[68] Record of Cabinet Meeting, November 21, 1963, BNA, CAB 195/23/21.
[69] See in particular the accounts Odinga and Kaggia gave in their memoirs: Odinga, *Not Yet Uhuru*; Bildad Kaggia, *Roots of Freedom, 1921–1963: The Autobiography of Bildad Kaggia* (Nairobi: East African Publishing House, 1975), chapter 21.

[i]t has been reliably reported that KENYATTA and a number of his Kikuyu colleagues now in London are inclined to the view that the Rift Valley Province is the only area where it will be feasible to re-settle landless and unemployed Kikuyu in sufficient numbers to relieve the congestion and suffering in the Central Province.[70]

The policy of monetized land transactions was perhaps a safeguard against what Kenyatta considered to be abusive tribalism. As he pointed out during a ministerial meeting on February 23, 1963, there was the "danger of the Kalenjin and Masai tribes, for example, adopting a dog-in-the-manger attitude if they could not afford to purchase land which was for sale, and the owner would thereby find that he was unable to sell his land."[71] The necessity to make land available to all – read "to those who could pay" – was bluntly justified in a memorandum on Central province that Kenyatta prepared, in which he insisted on the

necessity to apply Part II of the Public Security Regulations, which provides for villagisation and applies to the Kikuyu Land Unit ... [It] will ensure that [the unemployed and homeless people], who now constituted a *security risk* or an *embarrassment* to the *proper* development of farm land, may be moved from where they are *causing trouble* to a place where they will have a home and a chance of employment.[72]

Furthermore, security issues persisted – besides resilient Mau Mau elements in the Central region, the increasing number of squatters pressuring land settlement policies threatened the general stability, while Northern Frontier territory was plagued by the Somali threat

---

[70] In 1962, the British director of intelligence further reported: "It has been reliably reported that KENYATTA and a number of his Kikuyu colleagues now in London are inclined to the view that the Rift Valley Province is the only area where it will be feasible to re-settle landless and unemployed Kikuyu in sufficient numbers to relieve the congestion and suffering in the Central Province." Secret. From Director of Intelligence to the Permanent Secretary for Defense, "Jomo Kenyatta and Regionalism," March 22, 1962, BNA, FCO 141/6772. On the particular issue of Kalenjin land and the attempt by Jomo Kenyatta after independence to break down Kalenjin claims over land, see Médard, "Territoires de l'Ethnicité," 251.

[71] Ninth Meeting with the Secretary of State, February 23, 1963, Council of Ministers, Constitutional Meetings, KNA, KA.1/11/73.

[72] My emphasis. Confidential. Cabinet, "The Population Problem in the Central Region and Particularly in the Nyandarua District," Memo by the Prime Minister, Cabinet Meeting, KNA, AZG1.3.20.

to secede, which turned into the so-called Shifta War.[73] Setting apart the poor as a political and economic nuisance, Kenyatta was being fairly consistent with the idea of meritocracy he had defended in *Facing Mount Kenya*. The rhetoric of nation-building provided him with a convenient alibi to prove his point. In a plea against ethnic regionalism, he asserted that

> it was nonsense to say that the Regions should reflect the systems of Government existing in Kenya eighty years ago or more ... If a strong Kenya were to be built which could treat with other nations on an equal footing, tribal feelings must be forgotten and a strong Central Government established.[74]

Kenyatta was openly distinguishing regions from tribal groups. Again, this was in direct line with his assertion, twenty-five years earlier, that tribes were not small states. In the political context of the time, with the Somali threat of secession, Kenyatta was all the more wary of the contagious risk of tribal temptations to secede. He firmly demanded a "definite statement to the effect that the Kenya Government was not contemplating, and would never contemplate, secession."[75] When putting his scarce interventions all together, it becomes clear that, to him, security, land, and territorial boundaries were linked by one overarching concern: the need to ensure that all land was accessible to all – though the definition of "all" requires nuancing.

***

If Kenyatta did want a nation – after all, KANU propaganda was one of united nationalism[76] – it was a nation devoid of nationalism. The land issue was understood as the necessity to buy out *all* land – not

---

[73] On the origins of the Somali claims, the Shifta War, and Kenyatta's reaction, see D. Branch, "Violence, Decolonisation and the Cold War in Kenya's North-Eastern Province, 1963–1978," *Journal of Eastern African Studies* 8, no. 4 (2014): 642–657.
[74] Second Meeting. February 16, 1963, KNA, KA.1/11/173.
[75] He was just as unhappy with the parallel negotiations the British would conduct with separatist groups, be they Somali or from Zanzibar. Championing constitutionalism while defending central government, he clearly stated that "he did not ... like the reference ... to the people of the Coast strip being given the opportunity to make representations to the Governor, since this would mean giving special recognition to one section of the population." Ninth Meeting with the Secretary of State, February 23, 1963, KNA, KA.1/11/173.
[76] Anderson, "Yours in Struggle for *Majimbo*," 548.

necessarily to make it accessible to *all* the people of Kenya.[77] The definition of regional boundaries and the breaking of ethnic ties were not bound to ensure national feeling, but were meant to safeguard the integrity of the territory as a whole. Ethnic fragmentation was not antithetic to central government; the equation was made possible because the state was, first and foremost, imagined as a tool for security, law, and order. During the independence conference in 1963, Kenyatta intervened on the issue of the deprivation of citizenship by registration. He was concerned that "if a citizen by registration turned out to be a spy or a criminal, the Government should have powers to deprive him of his citizenship."[78] The colonial secretary replied that secure rights were indispensable for nation-building. This was a concern that Kenyatta did not seem to share.

---

[77] One should here emphasize Lonsdale's remark that, according to Kenyatta, the geographical frontiers of authority were those of moral ethnicity: "In Kenyatta's view – and this is vital – each locality deserved its own moral autonomy, to be responsible to its own ancestors, to obey its own theology of abundance. His was not a politics of ethnic difference but of moral equivalence." Lonsdale pointed out the necessary distinction between the modern idea of territorial nationalism and Kenyan history, which knows no kind of "ethnic nationalism." See Lonsdale, "Jomo Kenyatta, God & the Modern World," 49, 52.

[78] Confidential. Unofficial Record of Second Meeting of Kenya Independence Conference, BNA, CAB 133/216; Secret and Personal. The Governor to P. J. Kitcatt, July 27, 1963, BNA, CO 822/3117.

4 | *Independence and the Making of a President (1963–1964)*

Kenyatta had gained a substantial asset with which to negotiate independence. Surprisingly, however, the question of presidentship emerged relatively late in the negotiation process. The negotiations were, at first, barely preoccupied with the question of presidential powers, which emerged unexpectedly, first brandished by KADU defenders as a last attack against arguments for central government. They were joined by several KANU backbenchers, who feared central government would significantly reduce their institutional power and political resources. While independence was hastened and achieved in December 1963, the question of presidency was left on standby until Kenya became republic, a year later.

As these debates show, presidentialism was not simply inherited from colonial rule, but was a controversial issue and very fragile construction. This chapter explores how these political and institutional conflicts were resolved, and eventually subsumed within the new state. I argue that presidential rule emerged out of the weaknesses of KADU and KANU contenders, revealing the limits of the purportedly untouchable principe of tribal spheres of influence that were in fact devoid of any power, influence, or authority when it came to accessing state resources controlled from the center. Such weaknesses and divisions were intimately linked to the question of land and the access to land resources. These had already been settled by 1961, however, with the centralization of the Land Board. Throughout the process, Kenyatta played the role of the reconciler (just as he had entitled his newspaper *Muigwithania* thirty years earlier) with very little concern for KADU, as well as little care for state institutions, yet strongly supported by the British authorities. It is safe to say that, although he participated little in the negotiations over the decolonization of land, he was the key beneficiary of the institutional construction that he thereafter defended very tactfully yet with steady determination.

Negotiating Independence and Presidential Powers

Building on its May 1963 victory, KANU demanded to review the constitutional provisions on regionalism elaborated during the previous Lancaster House conferences. The councils of ministers may have been "far more hilarious" than those of the British Cabinet, it did not necessarily erase "the hottest differences of opinion [that] exist[ed] between the two rival African political parties," wrote the British commissioner, Malcolm MacDonald.[1] In spite of KANU's dramatic declaration that *majimboism* was now dead, and that constitutional provisions on regionalism should be reviewed, *majimboist* claims continued to divide.[2] As independence approached, the controversy revealed institutional implications that were far more ubiquitous. That is, the debate over regional powers slipped away from ethnic considerations to questioning both the scope of parliamentary powers and of the hitherto conveniently ignored presidential powers. Dissensions over regionalism and central government converged into a single issue: the appointment of the head of state, with KANU pushing for the election of a president and prime minister.

Kenyatta was not inclined to further discuss the supremacy of an independent central government, but was giving thought on how to secure his leadership.[3] First, he ought to restrain parliamentary powers in order to weaken regional and ethnic dissidence. Second, he needed to resist constitutional movements undermining the executive powers of a president. Indeed, debates regarding the East African Federation uniting Kenya, Tanganyika, and Uganda in a Pan-African spirit had been going on for three years. Although initially opposed to the federation, KADU leaders realized that defending international federalism might serve *majimboism*.[4] Meanwhile, KANU leaders stuck to a centralized federation, hoping to smother *majimboism* once and for all within the state institutions. The problem was that KANU was not a

---

[1] Malcolm MacDonald to Mrs. Presland, February 5, 1963, Malcolm MacDonald Papers, 46/2/89.
[2] Kyle, *The Politics of Independence of Kenya*, 189; Sanger and Nottingham, "The Kenya General Election of 1963," 38–40; Anderson, "Yours in Struggle for Majimbo," 561–564.
[3] Secret and Personal. Notes on Kenya on the Eve of the Independence Conference, September 1963, Malcolm MacDonald Papers, 45/2/16.
[4] See Joseph Nye, *Pan-Africanism and East African Integration* (Cambridge, MA: Harvard University Press, 1965), chapter 3.

nationalist force strong enough to tame a fragmented political scene. If Kenyatta wanted to get rid of *majimboism,* he had to co-opt its key defenders. This was the third issue he had to tackle.

Debates over parliamentary powers showed up wide dissent over the centralization of executive power, a dissent that went beyond the KANU–KADU divide. On June 11, 1963, K. N. Gichoya, KANU representative of the Gichugu constituency in Central province, proposed the motion "That this House urges the Government to take steps to make Kenya a Republic within or outside the Commonwealth Organisation."[5] With this motion, Gichoya was not interested in *majimboism*: he wanted to secure strong parliamentary rights. He was careful enough not to question, at first, his leader's authority: "Kenyatta as Kenyatta is respected [but] our Prime Minister is Prime Minister, and not President." He made clear that, were Kenya to become a republic, it "must be so contrived and arranged as to make it possible at times for the National Assembly to increase or refute the power of the Executive President."[6] Heated debates ensued.

Uncertainties over presidentship rallied MPs behind the same cause. The day before, on June 10, 1963, KADU members spoke up against this institutional imbalance: their chairman Ronald Ngala, also representative for Kilifi in Coast province, condemned the fact that "When it becomes difficult in Parliament here, the Government will not resign but the Government will use its power outside, and every time we will be frustrated"; the Masai Justus ole Tipis, KADU representative for Narok in the Rift Valley, decried what he saw as "a deliberate attempt to usurp the powers of this Parliament"[7]; the Kalenjin Daniel arap Moi, Rift Valley leader and KADU representative for Baringo, "warn[ed] the Government that the Parliament is the supreme authority which governs the country."[8] The Kikuyu Joseph Mwangi Kariuki, former freedom fighter and KANU politician, added that "Ministers must understand that we have a say in the Kenya Government through Parliament, but not only in an executive committee such as the Cabinet."[9]

---

[5] National Assembly Debates (Hansard), Vol. III, Part II, June 11, 1963, col. 134.
[6] Ibid.   [7] Ibid., col. 48.
[8] National Assembly Debates (Hansard), Vol. III, Part II, June 10, 1963, cols. 49 and 55.
[9] Ibid., col. 55.

The Kenyan government was trying to stifle debates over the constitutional making of a centralized state. J. Nyamweya, parliamentary secretary in the prime minister's office, argued that, since negotiations of the East African Federation were still ongoing, "it would be very improper for this House at this stage, when it may be possible the Government intends to make certain changes, to indicate the form of the republic which Kenya should have"; constitutional change was a slow process that could not happen "overnight."[10] The debate was serious enough for Kenyatta to appear in the House six days later, on June 17. He first reassured MPs that the acceleration of federation was also the government's aim.[11] Then, he accused KADU of being a "nuisance" to the process of federation, which they used as a disguised argument for *majimboism*. He warned that "If you want *Majimbo* you cannot have two things, *Majimbo* and federation at the same time. We are going to strip the *Majimbo* away and have proper federation."[12] Reaffirming that the federation that his government defended had always been one of a centralized government, he concluded his speech with a clear provocation: "Hon. Members, you can talk and I am very happy when I hear you talking because you give me a chance to know that you mean nothing, that you do not mean business, that all you do is talk. When it comes to acting you do not act."[13] His last words warned that only "constructive criticism" would be tolerated.[14]

Behind the disputed institutional imbalance lay a very concrete concern, for MPs understood that securing an independent political voice in the House of Representatives was necessary to secure political influence in their constituencies. Bearing in mind that no land would be given away for free, they were also anxious not to lose a grip on the ongoing provision for land purchase. The KANU chairman of parliamentary group, H. C. Wariithi, answering the MPs, justified the institutional discrepancy, arguing that parliamentary debates were new to their country, so time was needed before a smooth institutional balance could be achieved; "misunderstanding and confusion outside this House and in this House" should not, however, suggest a lack of confidence in the government.[15] The fear

---

[10] Ibid., cols. 146 and 152.
[11] National Assembly Debates (Hansard), Vol. III, Part II, 17 June 1963, col. 268.
[12] Ibid., col. 270.   [13] Ibid., col. 271.   [14] Ibid., col. 274.
[15] National Assembly Debates (Hansard), Vol. III, Part II, June 23, 1963, col. 483.

of being dispossessed of political influence was the factor behind the backbenchers' persisting malaise. While ministers were touring regions, summarized Ngala-Abok, KANU member for Homa-Bay, "we get nothing, not even a written letter asking for a programme to be made out by the people on the spot. [Ministers] just announce it in the Press, and then they start going ... Mind you a Permanent Secretary of civil servants in a political Government must be a little political minded [sic]."[16]

Kenyatta was wary of politicized parliamentary speeches enhancing local representativity. He considerably moderated his praise of constitutionalism and parliamentarism.[17] Speaking in July 1963 at the dinner of the Kenyan branch of the Commonwealth Parliamentary Association, he reaffirmed his attachment to a parliamentary system that he described as "in everybody's blood," but stated that the new, independent Kenya demanded to adapt such a system to "our own traditions and methods."[18] He left unclear what such an adaptation meant, however, and twisted the issue concluding "I am afraid I am rather at loss to express myself because I am not accustomed to such tame after-dinner speeches."[19] Malcolm MacDonald took seriously Kenyatta's "taste for the British system of democratic Parliamentary government in a modern State"; he believed Kenyatta did not reject "constant public criticism," yet neither had he "[banished] from his beliefs an African instinct for personal autocratic clan rule."[20] Finally, the debates on parliamentary powers climaxed with the more serious questions of the afterlife of the colonial governor's powers, and the appointment of a president. Merely substituting the "governor" for a "president" was too simple a solution, and one the opposition was not ready to accept, since the realm of presidential powers posed an obvious threat to the autonomy of regional authorities, and vice versa. KADU voiced its concern at the final Lancaster House conference as the last chance to defend its views on regionalism.

---

[16] National Assembly Debates (Hansard), Vol. III, Part II, June 30, 1963, col. 735.
[17] Lonsdale, "Ornamental Constitutionalism in Africa."
[18] Kenya News. Press Office Handout no. 720, "Prime Minister Speaks at C.P.A. Dinner," July 26, 1963, BNA, DO 168/45.
[19] Ibid.
[20] Malcolm MacDonald, Despatch no. 1, July 3, 1966, BNA, DO 213/294.

Presidentialism on Hold: The Monarchical Parenthesis

The nascent East African Federation (the establishment of which had been accelerated since the achievement of independence in Uganda and Tanzania in 1961) pressed for the settlement of an independence day for Kenya, and hence forced the question of the delegation of executive powers onto the negotiation table. Would the president appoint a prime minister (which presupposed the choosing of a successor) or empower the House of Representatives? As every Kenyan politician hoped that Kenya would solve its leadership divisions in order to achieve independence, Kenyatta was foreseen as having the role of president of the federation. Caught in an intricate diplomatic strategy opposing British officials with East African leaders, the Tanzanian Julius Nyerere and the Ugandan Milton Obote, Kenyan ministers started to press for Kenyan independence.[21] The uncertainties of the federation, and its final demise, had, however, little to do with Kenyan politics, but depended on Obote's domestic difficulties over Uganda's future within the federation. Mboya and Odinga imagined their potential future in the federation, but their projects faded away along with that of the federation when Obote finally declared his opposition to it.[22]

Facing still unacceptable KADU proposals on the one hand, and the uncertainty about the East African Federation on the other, Kenyatta opted for continuity. Supported by other KANU ministers, he demanded that Kenya remain a monarchy, with the British queen as sovereign, represented by a governor-general, until the constitutional modalities of the executing power be settled.[23] As he later confessed to MacDonald, "originally after June 1st KANU ministers thought of creating a Republic on the day of independence; but then some difficulties had arisen. They learnt that certain political elements would

---

[21] Secret and Personal. Inward Telegram to the Secretary of State from Malcolm MacDonald, June 7, 1963, BNA, DO 168/48.
[22] Kyle, *The Politics of Independence of Kenya*, 165–168, 188–189; Nye, *Pan-Africanism and East African Integration*, chapter 3.
[23] Lt. Col. the Rt. Hon. Sir Michael Adeane, September 7, 1963, BNA, CO 822/3117. See also Maxon, *Kenya's Independence Constitution*, 205–207. Despite the extreme richness of Maxon's analysis of the makings of Kenya's independence constitution, the political negotiations of the presidential powers is treated only in passing and argues that KANU's stance in the negotiations betrayed neocolonial tendencies.

oppose the appointment of a President, and be obstructive."[24] The monarchical option took KADU leaders aback, as they did not immediately foresee the constitutional implications of the proposal. When Tom Mboya announced, during the preparatory constitutional talks, the government's decision that Kenya was to become independent as a constitutional monarchy, Ngala's "initial reaction was that this would be acceptable."[25] It was only the next day that Ngala and KADU more generally raised their voice for Kenya to become a republic instead. If they did not fully grasp the scope of the constitutional provisions at first, they were however very much aware of the importance of not leaving any constitutional matter unsettled before independence. For British officials, KANU was playing a "waiting game" by arguing over the status of an independent Kenya.[26]

The British themselves were surprised by such a proposal. In a letter to Duncan Sandys in August 1963, MacDonald confessed that: "It did not occur to me that Ministers would seriously contemplate resisting the wish of the Kenya Government that Kenya should remain a monarchy."[27] Yet, the colonial authorities decided to take the demand seriously. One reason was that Dr. Hastings Kamuzu Banda, leader of Nyazaland (today's Malawi), supported by the British high commissioner there, had demanded that the country should remain a monarchy after independence.[28] It was difficult for the British, to accept that Nyazaland, and even Uganda, become a monarchy, to find a convincing argument to refuse Kenya this choice. The British authorities interpreted Kenyan ministers' "perpetual switchback" between monarchy and republic as "a matter of convenience to save them from having to find a candidate as President for the fairly short period which they envisage before Kenya becomes a Federation."[29] As such, Kenya

[24] Malcolm MacDonald to Duncan Sandys, September 18, 1963, BNA, CO 822/3117.
[25] Secret and Personal. The Governor to Peter (?), July 30, 1963, BNA, CO 822/3117.
[26] Secret and Personal. The Governor's Attorney to P. J. Kitcatt, July 30, 1963, BNA, CO 822/3117.
[27] Malcolm MacDonald to Duncan Sandys, August 12, 1963, BNA, CO 822/3117.
[28] Secret. Extract from Conclusions of a Meeting in the Cabinet Held in Admiralty House, SW1, on Tuesday, September 24, 1963 at 3.00 p.m., BNA, CO 822/3117.
[29] Secret. Kenya Independence Conference, "Republic or Monarchy: Appointment of Head of State," Draft Brief no. 10, BNA, CO 822/3117.

would not want to remain a monarchy for a "decent" time, which would presume that the queen too, who would eventually become the sovereign of an independent Kenya, "should be used purely as local political convenience."[30] Undecided at first, they agreed to submit Kenya's monarchical project to the queen's goodwill on September 7, 1963, perhaps because they had been informed by the governor of Kenya that "surprisingly, Kenya Ministers were genuinely anxious for Kenya to remain a monarchy and were only contemplating the possibility of becoming a republic in the context of an East African Federation."[31]

This was an uncomfortable compromise, and Governor MacDonald decided to try to convince Kenyatta that Kenya should become an independent republic. He was sure of Kenyatta's "great respect for the Queen."[32] Nevertheless, he reminded him in a "frank" conversation that, if Kenya was to remain a monarchy for a short time only, this would be treating the queen with great disrespect. MacDonald found Kenyatta "slightly embarrassed."[33] A month later, Kenyatta finally gave a clear answer, revealing that the monarchical option was to him as tactical – leaving aside the question of president – as emotional – proving his attachment to the queen:

He said candidly [that the] sole difficulty consists in three words, i.e. the official description as of the parts of "the Queen's Dominions." If those words did not exist, or if they could be altered, no difficulty would remain. But otherwise they would be used as a stick to beat the Kenya Government with. They could be presented as meaning that the whole land and people of Kenya were still part of the British Queen's possessions, and so people could argue that although Independence had been granted to Kenya, part of the old Imperialism nevertheless remained. Mr. Kenyatta said that Kenyans had great respect and liking for the Queen, but it would embarrass them politically to be regarded as part of her property ... He repeated that if those three words could be changed, the difficulty would disappear. Otherwise the Kenya Government might have to consider later some alternative device.[34]

---

[30] Secret. Inward Telegram to Kenya, the Rt. Hon. Malcolm MacDonald, August 2, 1963, BNA, CO 822/3117.
[31] N. Aspin to P. J. Kitcatt, September 20, 1963, BNA, CO 822/3117.
[32] Malcolm MacDonald to Duncan Sandys, August 12, 1963, BNA, CO 822/3117.
[33] Malcolm MacDonald to Duncan Sandys, August 17, 1963, BNA, CO 822/3117.
[34] Malcolm MacDonald to Duncan Sandys, September 18, 1963, BNA, CO 822/3117.

Although the monarchical option for an independent Kenyan was abandoned, Kenya did reach independence as a dominion in 1963. Intense politicking followed between June 1963 and December 1964 to decide on its constitution of the future Kenyan Republic.

Holding on to Fragmented Politics

Now in full charge of drafting the constitution, the KANU government needed a larger majority to amend it and establish centralized government.[35] During the late summer of 1963, and with MacDonald's support, Kenyatta packed secret meetings with the most influential regional leaders, promising they would be included in the delegation to the third Lancaster House conference.[36] Kenyatta courted the Rift Valley leader Daniel arap Moi, informing him that "the Prime Minister would always be ready to meet him and had chosen KADU colleagues for friendly, confidential consultations on co-operation in the interests of all the Kenyan tribes together"; thereafter, MacDonald commented, "those two congenial and statesmanlike political leaders were in regular private touch with each other."[37] Because of his control over the Rift Valley region, where so many Kikuyu had fled and settled in the past years, Moi's electoral support was essential for KANU's majority in parliament. But KADU's first defections came from comparatively less influential leaders: John Seroney, William Murgor, and Taaitta Toweett, who, according to MacDonald, "all resigned from KADU

---

[35] Hornsby, *Kenya*, 86. For a refined history of the constitution making and the constitutional issues entailed see Yash Pal Ghai and J. P. W. B. McAuslan, *Public Law and Political Change in Kenya: A Study of the Legal Framework of Government from Colonial Times to the Present* (London: Oxford University Press, 1970); Maxon, *Kenya's Independence Constitution*. See also Goldsworthy, *Tom Mboya*, 220–231.

[36] Secret. Malcolm MacDonald, Despatch no. 6, "The Political Situation in Kenya I. The Recent Past," May 24, 1965, BNA, DO 213/65; Malcolm MacDonald to Duncan Sandys, November 29, 1963, Malcolm MacDonald Papers, 45/2/29. See also Secret. Inward Telegram to the Secretary of State for the Colonies, no. 505, September 4, 1963; Secret. Inward Telegram to The secretary of State for the Colonies, no. 518, September 10, 1963, BNA, DO 168/48. For further insight on Kenyatta's meeting with the Kalenjin leader Daniel arap Moi and the Kamba leader Paul Ngei, see Lynch, "Moi: The Making of an African 'Big-Man'"; Grignon, "Le Politicien Entrepreneur En Son Terroir," 266.

[37] Secret. Malcolm MacDonald, Despatch no. 6, "The Political Situation in Kenya I. The Recent Past," May 24, 1965, BNA, DO 213/65.

but none of these Kalenjin personalities is individually of great importance."[38] Kenyatta continued to carefully watch the moves of the influential KADU leader in the Trans-Nzoia (Rift Valley), Masinde Muliro, and was "in very close confidential contact with" the powerful Julius ole Tipis (Narok, Rift Valley). These contacts did not disturb Moi, as long as that they respected regional order.[39]

Kenyatta was at pains to preserve this fragile balance. Since mid-September, a few days before the official opening of the Lancaster House conference, he had been in close contact with the British authorities to discuss future agreements between an independent Kenya and Britain.[40] He was also in charge of the KANU delegation. Anticipating Ngei's African People's Party (APP) rallying KANU in early September, he "urgently" asked MacDonald to increase the numbers in the government delegation to Lancaster, arguing that "this is of extreme importance because of certain tribal considerations."[41] He shared his "serious difficulties" with his friend the Governor MacDonald and "[begged him] to persuade [the secretary of state for the colonies, Duncan Sandys] to accept [that] Government delegation shall be increased to 12 while the KADU Opposition delegation is increased to 5."[42] The director of intelligence reported that "[p]ressure on Ngei has been continuous since 25th August" to cross the floor in favor of KANU. By September, Ngei "gave in as a matter of principle, [but] insisted it was better to delay crossing until after the Independence Conference."[43] The KANU government, represented in the persons of Odinga and Joseph Murumbi, minister of state in Kenyatta's cabinet, courted him promptly, and assured him he could join their delegation to the London conference; he finally disbanded his party and merged with

---

[38] MacDonald to Duncan Sandys, November 29, 1963, Malcolm MacDonald Papers, 45/2/26.
[39] Malcolm MacDonald to Duncan Sandys, November 29, 1963, Malcolm MacDonald Papers, 45/2/29.
[40] Secret. Inward Telegram to the Secretary of State for the Colonies from Kenya, September 16, 1963, BNA, CAB 21/4772.
[41] Secret. Inward Telegram to the Secretary of State for the Colonies, no. 505, September 4, 1963; Secret. Inward Telegram to the Secretary of State for the Colonies, no. 518, September 10, 1963, BNA, DO 168/48.
[42] Secret. Inward Telegram to the Secretary of State for the Colonies, no. 530, September 14, 1963, BNA, DO 168/48.
[43] Secret and Personal. Weekly Personal Report by the Director of Intelligence to the Private Secretary to H. E. Governor, September 7, 1963, BNA, CAB 21/4772.

KANU on September 12, 1963 – he would eventually be rewarded with the chairmanship of the Maise Marketing Board.[44] By September, the necessary 75 percent of votes to amend the constitutions was assured.[45]

Complex political arithmetic did not deter Kenyatta from opening the final Lancaster House conference with a fierce speech:

> Opposition is not only a small minority in Parliament but in the recent county and municipal elections it has failed to retain any real control even in its former strongholds ... We cannot agree that merely because the present Constitution was the result of agreements at the last Lancaster House Conference, it is sacrosanct ... The Central Government, which it was intended should be a strong and effective and the only one in the country, is obstructed and frustrated without physical representations or administrative image in the districts.[46]

The secretary of state judged the speech as having "not (repeat not) been helpful."[47] During the formal meetings, Kenyatta was not talkative. Behind the scenes, however, he was trying to maintain cohesion within his delegation during the whole negotiation process, from September 25 to October 19, 1963.

The presidential option was posed candidly during the third and last conference. According to a colonial officer, it had been previously misunderstood and the transfer of the governor's financial powers over land to the minister of finance had been overlooked. Few understood perhaps, that "[i]f this were done, the Central Government would be given a stranglehold upon one of the most important sources of Regional revenues"; if it was not given regional powers, at least they would have the means to "distort the relativities between the Regions." In September 1963, KADU tackled this very problem and pointed out

---

[44] Grignon, "Le Politicien Entrepreneur en son Terroir," 266.
[45] Secret and Personal. Weekly Personal Report by the Director of Intelligence, September 7, 1963, BNA, CAB 21/4772. See also Hornsby, *Kenya*, 85–86.
[46] Kenya Independence Conference, "Record of the First Meeting Held in the Music Room, Lancaster House, SW1 on Wednesday September 25, 1963 at 12.00 Noon," BNA, CAB 133/215.
[47] Secret. Outward Telegram from the Commonwealth Relations Office to Nairobi, September 25, 1963, BNA, DO 168/45.

that the regions should play a role in the appointment of the president.[48] The British, however, did not seem to attribute too much importance to the way in which a president would be chosen. A draft brief prepared by the governor's constitutional adviser noted that, should a president have to be chosen in a republican Kenya, "there is no substantial British Government interest, nor are we committed to any statement or agreements. The method favored by KADU would appear to be a possibility."[49] Nevertheless, KADU was still clinging to *majimboism*, while KANU refused any amendment that would sound like a retreat. Once again, negotiations were stagnating.

The most controversial point remained the attributes of executive power – that is, the control of police, the public services, and the provisions for constitutional amendment. It risked, according to the British administrators, endangering once again both the negotiations and the security situation. As stagnation started to border on chaos, MacDonald initiated a decisive move by siding with KANU, to avoid risk of a unilateral declaration of independence.[50] Although Kenyatta took KADU's threat seriously – on October 10, he "telephoned to Murumbi in the middle of [the] night" to instruct [him] to keep a close eye on KADU leaders coming back to Kenya from the conference – he refused any compromise.[51] The British authorities were trying at all costs to keep the negotiations going, and were desperate to find a settlement, lest the crisis between the two parties degenerate into generalized divisions. Sandys personally (without even notifying the rest of the Kenyan government) approached Kenyatta to "urge him to conciliate KADU."[52] MacDonald confided to Sandys that "[a]nything that a disgruntled KADU could do would be child's play by comparison with what a disgruntled KANU could do."[53] Kenyatta remained inflexible, and wrote back to Sandys that "H.M.G. can only either seek to achieve agreement with Government (which may not succeed) or

---

[48] Kenya Independence Conference. "The Head of State," Memorandum by KADU, September 26, 1963, BNA, CO 822/3117.

[49] Secret. To Kitcatt and Webber, Brief, Kenya Independence Conference, "Republic or Monarchy: Appointment of Head of State," BNA, CO 822/3117.

[50] Kyle, *The Politics of the Independence of Kenya*, 190–191.

[51] Secret and Personal. Inward Telegram to the Secretary of State for Colonies from Kenya, no. 571, October 10, 1963, BNA, DO 168/48.

[52] Secret and Personal. Inward Telegram to the Secretary of State from Kenya, no. 586, October 15, 1963, BNA, DO 168/48.

[53] Ibid.

Holding on to Fragmented Politics 127

impose Constitution which it would declare to be unacceptable." His obstinacy proved successful in gathering British support and rallying the secretary of state to KANU's cause.[54]

Kenyatta's inflexibility was certainly decisive for the British decision to finally abandon their early suspicions and to consider him the safest political bet to preserve their political and economic interests in an independent Kenya. The British considered Kenyatta as "the only moderate minister" and trusted his ability to discipline his own delegation.[55] In fact, by this time, only KANU mattered to the British, as MacDonald clearly explained that "[i]f we get the KANU government to agree to such amendments now, and to undertake publicly to respect the Constitution containing them, that should go a long way towards restraining them from tearing up the constitution."[56] The decisive element had been, for the British authorities, that Kenyatta alone could guarantee stability:

[he] has been firm and strong throughout in his loyalty to the London agreement, except when occasionally he did not understand the issue involved in some proposal, and was inclined to waver a bit on it. I got at him afterwards … he always backed our insistence that there should be no further changes in the Constitution and no breach of its proper implementation.[57]

On December 12, 1963, Kenya became independent. The British support for Kenyatta had been decisive. Because the British viewed the land issue as their priority, and because their most strategic (economic as well as political) interests lay in the Kikuyu highlands, their support for Kenyatta was entirely logical.[58] Early December, Duncan Sandys asked "McKenzie on a personal basis how he saw things developing.

---

[54] Secret. Outward Telegram from Commonwealth Relations Office to Nairobi, no. 176, October 14, 1963, BNA, DO 168/48.
[55] Secret and Personal. Inward Telegram to the Secretary of State from Kenya, no. 586, October 15, 1963; Secret. Outward Telegram from Commonwealth relations Office, no. 179, October 17, 1963, BNA, DO 168/48.
[56] Secret. Outward Telegram from Commonwealth Relations Office, no. 964, October 18, 1963, BNA, DO 168/49.
[57] Malcolm MacDonald to Duncan Sandys, November 29, 1963, BNA, DO 168/45.
[58] Confidential. Outward Telegram from the Commonwealth Relations Office, no. 536, October 4, 1963, BNA, DO 168/48.

McKenzie said that things would go well if Mr. Kenyatta stayed in control."[59]

The wave of politicians crossing the floor to join KANU revealed a generalized dependency on regional anchoring, but also that the question of regionalism had been settled well before the constitutional talks started. This dependency was mainly of a financial nature, and subverted political or ideological divisions. The newly established institutions such as the Land Bank and the Central Land Board, as well as the International Monetary Fund and the World Bank had already condemned regionalism.[60] Financial dependency materialized politically when prominent leaders realized their political mandates depended too heavily on fragile parliamentary powers. As representation in the government was also the key to accessing funds for land settlement, they preferred the land package deal to the constitutional one.[61] In endorsing a central government, minority leaders also accepted a consensual yet pragmatic form of regionalism, preserving, after all, their "tribal spheres of influence."[62] The land issues clearly set the tone of the decolonization process, only temporarily sidelining the question of the definition of presidential powers.

Kenyatta was left with the difficult role of holding together this fragile territorial, institutional, and political equilibrium. By November

---

[59] Extract of Minute by Gilmore, "Political Developments in Kenya," December 3, 1963, BNA, DO 168/45.

[60] KANU repeatedly argued that regionalism would be too an expansive system of government. For statistic on the amount of multi-lateral aid given to Kenya in the 1960s see John Lonsdale, "KAU's Cultures: Imaginations of Community and Constructions of Leadership in Kenya after the Second World War," *Journal of African Cultural Studies* 13, no. 1 (2000): 107–124.

[61] Secret and Personal. Malcolm MacDonald to Duncan Sandys, "Notes on Kenya on the Eve of the Independence Conference September 1963," October 30, 1963, Malcolm MacDonald Papers, 45/2/22.

[62] The importance of political tribalism in determining access to land is a recurrent pattern in African politics. For a comparative analysis of this issue Catherine Boone, *Property and Political Order in Africa: Land Rights and the Structure of Politics* (Cambridge: Cambridge University Press, 2014).
I wish to insist, however, that when it comes to the issue of presidentialism, logics of personal interest in search of political favors may prevail over "tribal" logics. Far from undermining the political importance of tribalism, the latter must be seen both as a historical and political construction. Joel Barkan made a similar argument in "Legislators, Electors and Political Linkage," in *Politics and Public Policy in Kenya and Tanzania*, eds. Joel D. Barkan and John J. Okumu (New York: Praeger, 1979), 74.

1963, with Mau Mau resilience looming, the British predicted that security questions would become decisive, since the whole mechanism of this fragile status quo depended on security: "The big question is how far Kenyatta and his Ministers will show resolution in taking the firm action which will no doubt be necessary at the risk of incurring political unpopularity with the 'Watu'" (the "people").[63]

Delaying the Republic

The monarchical episode and its hastened resolution gave way to an uneasy compromise: in December 1963, Kenya was independent, but would become a republic only a year later, in December 1964. As already pointed out, presidential powers remained a looming issue during the last two independence conferences. Central land institutions had been established, and so the question of presidential powers had been conveniently avoided. By December 1963, the principle of central rule was settled; its form remained to be decided. That would drive political negotiations in the following year. The new Kenyan state had to conciliate three mutually dependent, but also conflicting, issues: pursuing the buying out and redistribution of land, appeasing the landless' claims for land, and ensuring the institutional representation of smaller ethnic groups to contain them in their spheres of influence.

Between the end of 1963 and early 1964, security concerns continued to dictate the politics of land.[64] Two regions were particularly sensitive to the government: the Northern Frontier district, where Somali insurrection threatened the integrity of the territory, and the Central region, where increasing numbers of squatters flocking in search for land threatened general political stability. Furthermore, an attempted army mutiny in January 1964 caused major concern among the government, which feared losing control over the military force.[65] The autonomous government was eager to speed up the rate of the settlement programs; in early 1964, the "planning of the settlement

---

[63] C. H. Imray to J. K. Hickman, November 12, 1963, BNA, DO 168/45.
[64] In direct continuation of the general land politics since the 1950s, see in particular Leo, *Land and Class in Kenya*, 116–117.
[65] This was a major source of concern to Kenyatta and his ministers, see Timothy Parsons, "The Lanet Incident, January 2–25, 1964: Military Unrest and National Amnesia in Kenya," *The International Journal of African Historical Studies* 40, no. 1 (2007): 51–70.

was complete" and the "settlement went forward without pause."[66] Remaining islands of European land in the Central region, however, the so-called European compassionate cases (farms being sold to Africans at reduced prices), turned out to be hot spots of tension, forcing the Kenyan government and the British authorities to rush through complex negotiations to settle the future of European farmers surrounded by squatters and landless people.[67] Kenyatta was caught in an uneasy situation. His public statements against illegal squatting were intended to reassure the European farming community but risked alienating the landless masses against the Kenyan government, and further endangering regional stability. As the chairman of the Central Land Board, Richard Turnbull, described in a letter to Malcolm MacDonald,

> Even the hands of the Prime Minister are to some extent tied; for each occasion upon which he has made one of his statesman-like pronouncements concerning Kenya's need to retain the European farmers, has been marked by the return to the forest of one more group of Forest Fighters, and by accusations of betrayal by one more branch of the [KANU] Youth Wing.[68]

Such deadlock forced Kenyatta's government to switch priorities. They had to match words with action so as to assuage criticisms of their politics. They decided to "Africanise the European areas," "[moving] away from high density settlement schemes" and transferring European land to African ownership.[69] In a meeting with the commonwealth secretary, Bruce McKenzie reassured the British authorities that "there had been no change in attitude by the Kenyan Government, but that there was now strong feeling, particularly among Parliamentary back-benchers, that European farmers not becoming Kenya citizens should leave." The government bet on the

---

[66] Restricted. "Progress of Settlement," Memorandum by the Minister for Lands and Settlements, November 12, 1963, BNA, FCO 141/6919; Leo, *Land and Class in Kenya*, 141–142.

[67] Carey Jones and Norman Stewart, "The Decolonisation of the White Highlands of Kenya," *Geographical Journal* 131, no. 2 (1965): 190, 195; Harbeson, "Land Reforms and Politics in Kenya, 1954–70," 242.

[68] Confidential. Richard Turnbull to the British High Commissioner, February 4, 1964, BNA, DO 214/39.

[69] Confidential. "Kenya – Finance. Record of a Meeting on 5 March 1964 at 3.30 p.m. with Kenya Government in the Prime Minister's Office, Nairobi," BNA, DO 214/39.

premise that the new African owners would, on the one hand, prove to hostile backbenchers that land was truly Africanized, and, on the other hand, that they would be in a better position to "drive [squatters] off," thus providing a long-term solution to land squatting.[70] The commonwealth secretary was not convinced that "merely changing the ownership from individual European to Kenya government with the same Africans remaining on farms" would alleviate tensions. The change was meant to be a smokescreen against the vocal opposition the Kenyan government faced in the House of Representatives. Land was bought for urgent political reasons, rather than for urgent social needs.

The conflict between the Kenyan government and the backbenchers, rooted in fundamental disagreements on land politics, exposed Kenyatta's authority to "pressures within the party."[71] Kenyatta was in direct opposition with three members of his newly appointed government: Oginga Odinga, minister for home affairs, J. M. Kariuki, his private secretary, and Bildad Kaggia, junior minister of education. The three pressed for politics to be designed with the poor and the landless as priority, and for free access to land. They were influential leaders in the Nyanza and Central regions, already shaken up by the unresolved cases of European land in the areas of Sotik, Ol Kalou, and Kinangop. Their words and deeds could endanger the government's policies. The conflict between Odinga and Kenyatta was one of national leadership and ideology. As a socialist, Odinga fanned fears of communist penetration in Kenya – which was what personally worried Kenyatta, while the British believed he was less a communist than "a fellow-traveller whose attitude has been obligingly influenced by the large sums of money which he has been receiving for some years from Communist sources, predominantly from the authorities of Pekin."[72] At the same time, Odinga was indispensable in safeguarding the favors of the Luo sphere of influence, but had little chance to compete for national leadership without personally attacking Kenyatta, a tactic that could be hugely unpopular. To the British, he was a "subversive" element and there was no doubt that they "must of course back Kenyatta and

---

[70] Ibid.
[71] Confidential. W. G. Lamarque to Mr. Chatterton, "Ol Kalou," August 10, 1964, BNA, DO 214/46.
[72] Secret. Malcolm MacDonald, Despatch no. 6, "The Political Situation in Kenya I. The Recent Past," May 24, 1965, BNA, DO 213/65.

try to understand his every move."[73] Kenyatta, as long as his leadership was not directly endangered, could defer the matter until after Kenya become a republic.

In 1964, Kenyatta was mostly preoccupied by immediate threats over the land issues in the Ol Kalou salient. Located in the heart of the Nyandarua district, it was coveted by multiple ethnic groups, in particular by the Nyandarua leader J. M. Kariuki, who was becoming worryingly vocal. The Kenyan government feared that these calls for the landless to seize the land by force would set a precedent for land to be distributed for free. In July, Kariuki reiterated in a speech at the House of Representatives that although "it is not right for us to take European farms by force ... These farms ... we must take them by all means."[74] Kenyatta confessed to McKenzie that "as eight months has elapsed since his public undertaking in last December to settle Africans in Ol Kalou he did not see how he would resist Kariuki's motion [to take over, by November 1, all abandoned farms in Ol Kalou]."[75] Kenyatta and his government were desperately hoping for British financial support to be publicly announced as quickly as possible. McKenzie managed to convince Kariuki not to propose his motion, assuring him that he would visit London the following week after and press the British government to provide funds for Ol Kalou. That seemed to satisfy the Nyandarua leader, who would also be given later in the year, on order of a directive issued by Kenyatta, "a house and 100 acres of land ... as a reward for his efforts in the 'fight for independence'."[76] In his usual manner, Kenyatta subsequently gave a public conference on mismanaged farms, promising further settlement.[77] Shortly after, he spoke on collective farms and nonalignment, so as to pull the rug from under Oginga's rhetoric.[78] His public politics

[73] Malcolm MacDonald to Duncan Sandys, July 4, 1964, Malcolm MacDonald Papers, MAC/45/1/17.
[74] Kenya National Assembly (Hansard), Vol. III, Part III, July 28, 1964, col. 1032.
[75] Confidential. Inward Telegram to Commonwealth Relations Office, No. 1497, July 31, 1964, BNA, DO 214/46.
[76] Confidential. B. Greatbatch to W. G. Lamarque, February 3, 1965, BNA, DO 214/204.
[77] Inward Telegram to Commonwealth Relation Office, No. 1582, August 15, 1964, BNA, DO 214/46.
[78] H. S. H. Stanley, Inward Telegram to Commonwealth Relations Office, no. 1612, "Controversy over Kenya Land Policy," August 18, 1964, BNA, DO 214/46.

were carefully examined by the British, who now understood that they should refrain from correcting him, for they should not "give Kaggia and his henchmen opportunity to inflame land issue."[79]

The problem with Kaggia was all the more sensitive in that he was a former Mau Mau leader – arrested and jailed with Kenyatta in October 1952. The district he represented, Murang'a (Kandara constituency, Central region), had badly suffered during the Mau Mau war. He explicitly called for the "return of all lands belonging to Mau Mau fighters confiscated during the Emergency."[80] In his memoirs, Kaggia reconstructed the correspondence he had with different Kenyan ministers over the land issue between September 1963 and June 1964, the month he had to resign his ministerial office. Disappointed with the systematic refusal to consider his plea for the return of confiscated land, Kaggia issued a press statement on April 14, 1964 calling for the nationalization of land and for "the Government to reconsider its attitude towards European settlement in this country."[81] This greatly embarrassed the government. Kenyatta personally responded to Kaggia's letter on May 22, to condemn his antigovernment criticism.[82] Reaffirming the agricultural value of settlement schemes, Kenyatta invited Kaggia to resign if "he was unwilling to support ... any of the Government's acts or policies." In mid-June, Kaggia did resign – although, according to him, he was sacked.[83] The three most "subversive" political elements in Kenyatta's government – Oginga, J. M. Kariuki, and Kaggia – were temporarily tamed. The way was open to amending, without too great an opposition, the constitution, and to establishing a presidential republic.

The Making of a Presidential Republic

On August 14, 1964, Kenyatta made another of his rare appearances in the House of Representatives to announce the presidentialization of the future Kenyan Republic. After a brief overview of the negotiation process that had delayed the creation of a republic, he announced that

---

[79] Confidential. Inward Telegram to Commonwealth Relation Office, no. 1617, August 20, 1964, BNA, DO 214/46.
[80] Kaggia, de Leeuw, and Kaggia, *The Struggle for Freedom and Justice*, 181.
[81] Ibid., 190.   [82] Ibid., 191.   [83] Ibid., 192–193.

the Government has considered carefully the various forms of Republic Government, and has decided that it must be the one which suited Kenya. It should embody the fact of national leadership as seen in the eyes of the people, the concept of collective Ministerial responsibility and also guarantee the supremacy of Parliament.[84]

As he continued to detail the distribution of powers, KADU leader Ronald Ngala attempted to denounce the "destructive statement" but was stopped by the deputy speaker on the grounds that a statement called for neither answer nor debate.[85] Reporting Kenyatta's statement to the secretary of state for the colonies Duncan Sandys, H. S. H. Stanley from the Commonwealth Relations Office noted that, in spite of the "vague principle for presidential republic," the novelty lay in the "supremacy of Parliament," thus defeating "Mr. Kenyatta's own preference for an Executive Presidency on the Tanganyika model [which] was overruled by this Cabinet colleagues."[86]

The supremacy of parliament was not an absolute concept, and was to be of a superficial use only to appease dissenting voices among politicians. Kenyatta entrusted "the sole responsibility for the constitutional drafting to Mboya and his legal advisers," hoping to limit therefore "interference by other ministers or Party officials."[87] He had found an ally in Tom Mboya, who was very much aware of the need to "discipline back-benchers" and improve their relationship with Kenyatta's ministerial cabinet, while criticisms of the blurred powers of the cabinet became a common feature of parliamentary debates after August 1964.[88]

On October 27, Mboya introduced a motion to amend the Kenyan constitution. Amendment no. 28 of 1964 established a republic based on centralized government and presidential power. He spoke of the necessity of strong government and leadership, instead of an "illusory ... arrangement ... just not understood by our people."[89]

---

[84] Kenya National Assembly (Hansard), Vol. III, Part III, August 14, 1964, col. 1708.
[85] Ibid., col. 1710.
[86] British High Commission, Despatch no. 13, August 20, 1964, BNA, DO 213/161.
[87] Ibid.
[88] Tom Mboya to Henri Wariithi, April 30, 1964, KNA, MAC/KEN/38/5.
[89] Kenya National Assembly (Hansard), Vol. III, Part III, October 27, 1964, col. 3881.

He cut short Ngala's desperate plea for regionalism, asserting boldly that "it would not be true to say that this bill deals a death blow to *Majimbo*. It would be more accurate to describe it as a cutting out of the wood in the present Constitution which is already dead."[90] The amendment was mainly criticized by KADU leaders, but they were not alone. The KANU Luo lawyer Argwing-Khodek pointed out that the supremacy of parliament was a rubber-stamp against the extensive executive powers granted to the president. Their criticisms targeted in particular clause 11, chapter III, of the amendment:

Where by or under the amended Constitution the President has power to make any appointment or make any order *or do any other thing*, that power may be exercised by the President designate before 12th December 1964 to such extent as may in his opinion be necessary or expedient to enable the amended Constitution to function as from 12th December 1964.[91]

KADU leaders pointed out that the stated supremacy of parliament was de facto nullified by the vague wording concerning presidential powers. Ngala condemned the text, saying that "the amendment bill involves so many things, some of them completely detached from the republican status of Kenya"[92]; Moi forcefully warned he would be "the Father of the House"[93], Shikuku denounced the "dictatorial" practices meant to speed up the amendment and the creation of the republic[94]; Muliro foresaw the uselessness of the parliament as an institutional body when reduced to "a place of individuals because of the manoeuvres in the House by powerful Government Members"[95] (4,032). While KADU leaders avoided accusing Kenyatta personally, and reaffirmed their faith in their prime minister, they tactfully raised their concern for the continuity of the constitution once Kenyatta was no longer in office. They further criticized it as being drafted for one person: the prime minister, who "shall be the person who immediately before December 12, 1964 holds the office of Prime Minister under the Constitution."[96] In this way, KADU was desperately attempting to use the discussion of the bill as a last assault on central government.

---

[90] Ibid., col. 3888.
[91] My emphasis. "The Constitution of Kenya (Amendment) Act," no. 28 of 1964, 189.
[92] Kenya National Assembly (Hansard), Vol. III, Part III, October 27, 1964, col. 3877
[93] Ibid., col. 3941.   [94] Ibid., col. 3950.   [95] Ibid., col. 4032.
[96] "The Constitution of Kenya (Amendment) Act," no. 28 of 1964, Clause 8, p. 188.

Debates were noisy, agitated, often interrupted, exhausting, and stumbling over the irreversible determination of the Kenyan Government. Gichuru expressed obvious disdain, affirming he "has never been so bored before in this House as [he has] been today," while Tom Mboya inexorably and unshakably defended the text.[97]

The bill had also to be passed through the senate, where voices of dissent started to be timidly and confusedly raised, arousing concern among Kenyan ministers.[98] Shortly before the Amendment Bill was proposed, tumultuous debates had set the finance minister, James Gichuru, in opposition to senators he accused of abusing amendments in order to delay the passing of cabinet laws.[99] Tom Mboya introduced the bill with barely veiled allegations that senators were voting to safeguard their own institutional raison d'être. His speech, widely broadcast and attended by Kenyatta himself, developed into a crescendo, giving assurances of constitutional safeguards, yet concluding that "the vital question" was "as to why the Upper House exists at all."[100] Mboya found an ally in Oginga Odinga, who urged for an "end to confusion" and for the senate to accept the changes peacefully.[101] Outside the chamber, Kenyatta conducted several meetings with several tribal leaders, in particular those of Maasai and Kalenjin.[102] Four Maasai senators subsequently crossed the floor – some reportedly affirmed that they did not "wish to be left behind" – thus securing a majority for the amendment to be passed.[103] Two other Kalenjin senators (W. K. Rotich for Baringo, Daniel arap Moi's constituency, and Sen. J. K. Soi for Kericho) also disclosed their favorable vote.[104] A document circulated among British officials would later

[97] Kenya National Assembly (Hansard), Vol. III, Part III, October 27, 1964, col. 3925.
[98] *East African Standard*, "More KANU Branches State Opinions," October 30, 1964, 5.
[99] *East African Standard*, "House Attack on 'Obstructive' Senate Amendments 'Acting Beyond Its Power'," November 5, 1964, 3.
[100] *East African Standard*, "'Supreme Test' for Senate. Warning Given to £100,000 Waste," November 6, 1964, 1.
[101] *East African Standard*, "'End to Confusion' Urged. Minister Asks Senate to Accept Changes," November 7, 1964, 1.
[102] *East African Standard*, "Masai Chiefs Meet Premier," November 6, 1964, 17.
[103] *East African Standard*, "Masai Leaders Join KANU. Government Sure of Senate Majority," November 9, 1964, 1.
[104] *East African Standard*, "Kalenjin Vote for Changes. Kadu Holding Crisis Meeting Today," November 10, 1964, 1.

reveal that the two benefited from specially allocated plots of land (the so-called Z plots) the very same year.[105]

Voting for the amendment came to be framed as a vote on the personality and power of Kenyatta himself, as a symbol and a political force few leaders could afford to oppose. The passing of the motion revealed how fragile the institutional equilibrium was. Rumors quickly spread that the constitution would be further amended to suppress the senate, after Mboya stated in a speech to the Nairobi Chamber of Commerce that the senate would be only retained "for the time being."[106] Early December, Oginga reiterated his anxious call for "senators to pass quickly the Constitution of Kenya Amendment (no. 2) Bill, because there were only a few days remaining before the country became a republic," while even the radical politician and former Mau Mau leader Achieng-Oneko joined the cause to reassure senators once again of their constitutional safeguards.[107] All forty-one senators approved the bill.[108] Two weeks earlier, on December 1, the House of Representatives had also approved the bill, after three readings. Announcing KADU's dissolution in a parliamentary statement, Ngala wished "every luck and success to my friend the President-designate, the Rt. Hon. Mr. Kenyatta," to which Kenyatta responded that "the opposing for opposition's sake, [has] now died forever and ever. Amen ... We shall work as one team."[109]

Kenyatta was already making "detailed plans for the reconstruction of his Cabinet," as MacDonald wrote to Duncan Sandys,

---

[105] "Z" Category Plots, BNA, DO 214/107.
[106] *East African Standard*, "Kenyatta to Retain Senate 'For The Time Being'," November 24, 1964, 5.
[107] *East African Standard*, "Pass Bill Quickly Appeal by Minister in Senate," December 9, 1964, 3.
[108] *East African Standard*, "Senators Give Bill Unanimous Approval," November 10, 1964, 1. An episode from the day of the vote, which Kenyatta attended, testifies to the charismatic power Kenyatta exerted. The *East African Standard* reported that: "One Senator, Mr. Chemjor (Elgeyo-Marakwet), at first indicated he would abstain from voting but later changed his mind after four of his colleagues had walked over to where he was sitting and talked to him ... This brought a smile from the Prime Minister, who was on the other side of the Senate floor. A few minutes later Mr. Chemjor voluntarily rose from his seat and walked across the floor in the direction of Mr. Kenyatta, who smiled broadly at him as he went on to cast his vote in favour of the Bill."
[109] Kenya National Assembly (Hansard), Vol. III, Part III, November 10, 1964, cols. 4416–4417.

There may still be changes owing to political pressures (this is Africa ...) ... the composition ... takes account of unavoidable tribal and factional circumstances of present day Kenya politics. No one, except a very small inmost circle of Kenyatta's ministerial advisers (excluding Odinga) know the proposed composition.[110]

Few changes were made. Gichuru, McKenzie, and Angaine retained their respective portfolios for finance, agriculture, and land settlement; Kenyatta's close circle of – Kikuyu – advisers kept ministerial functions – Joseph Murumbi was minister for external affairs; Njoroge Mungai, his personal physician, became minister for internal security and defense; Mbiyu Koinange was minister for education; the young Julius Kiano was minister for commerce and industry. Paul Ngei was given the Ministry of Co-operatives and Marketing, while Argwings-Kodhek took over the Ministry of Information, Broadcasting, and Tourism. Tom Mboya left the Ministry for Justice and Constitutional Affairs for the Ministry of Economic Planning and Development. The novelty was the entry into government of the ex-KADU Daniel arap Moi, who replaced Odinga as minister for home affairs. Odinga was appointed vice president, yet "without either any special duties in the present or any automatic right of succession to the Presidency in the future." Anticipating Odinga's fury, Kenyatta informed him of the future change – for, as MacDonald wrote, "if he were to lean of his a-little-up-but-more-down translation only when it was published in the newspapers, he might be guilty of a public outburst of disappointed rage" – yet without specifying the scope of his future powers and without disclosing the other appointed ministers. Odinga pleaded to retain his position at the Ministry for Home Affairs, but without success. It was all too obvious to MacDonald, who concluded that "[t]he reconstruction of the Cabinet thus resulted in a considerable strengthening of the position of Mr. Kenyatta and the 'moderates' in the Government."[111]

* * *

---

[110] Top Secret and Personal. Telegram to the Secretary for Commonwealth Relations, November 22, 1964, Malcolm MacDonald Papers, 45/4/1.
[111] Secret. Malcolm MacDonald, Despatch no. 6, "The Political Situation in Kenya I. The Recent Past," May 24, 1965, BNA, DO 213/65.

As parliamentary debates show, the presidentialization of executive powers was not simply an inheritance from colonial rule. Few politicians expected the controversy over presidential powers, and the ensuing political battle for parliamentary powers was only brought to an end by an unclear and very fragile constitutional set-up. It can be said that presidential rule in Kenya emerged out of the weaknesses of KADU and KANU contenders, resting on the irreconcilable contradiction between the untouchable principle of the tribal spheres of influence, and the political urge to access state resources. Such weaknesses were intimately linked to the access to land resources. The centralization of both the Land Board and the Ministry of land had already lay the ground for centralized state institutions and a centralized redistribution of land resources. The issue regarding the decolonization of land stifled the debates over regional power, leaving little choice to its contenders but to climb on the presidential bandwagon.

The decolonization of land hence set a precedent for the independence negotiations, an observation that falls in line with the existing literature that has described decolonization as a hazardous, often poorly anticipated, and barely controlled chain of events.[112] Shrewdly defending their economic interests, the British contributed to the building of a system clearly advantaging KANU as a guarantee of stability. Aware of the scope of internal divisions paralyzing both nationalist parties, and with very little concern for KADU, Kenyatta strongly played his British support card. He relied on personal politics and co-optation to strengthen his presidential seat, along with the powers it

---

[112] R. Pearce, "The Colonial Office and Planned Decolonisation," *African Affairs* 83, no. 330 (1984): 77–93; J. Darwin, "What Was the Late Colonial State," *Itinerario* 22, nos. 3–4 (1999): 73–82; C. A. Babou, "Decolonisation or National Liberation: Debating the End of British Colonial Rule in Africa," *The Annals of the American Academy of Political and Social Science* 632, no. 1 (2010): 41–54. Frederick Cooper's latest book *Citizenship between Empire and Nation: Remaking France and French Africa, 1945–1960* (Princeton, NJ: Princeton University Press, 2014) sheds light, in an original and refreshing way, on African leaders' power of imagination and political agency during the decolonization process. His archival research revealed how dispute and competition between West African nationalist politicians sabotaged more innovative postcolonial constructions. Emma Hunter's work also highlighted the multiplicity of the "languages of freedom" during decolonization in Eastern Africa, see Emma Hunter, *Political Thought and the Public Sphere in Tanzania: Freedom, Democracy, and Citizenship in the Era of Decolonisation* (New York: Cambridge University Press, 2015); Hunter, "Languages of Freedom in Decolonising Africa."

entailed. His rise as a unique intermediary must also be read in light of a fundamental nuance to his (and KANU's) position on regionalism: although the latter was viscerally opposed to *majimboism*, they never called into question the regional, and much less the ethnic equilibrium inherited from colonization.[113] As such, they never questioned the backbone of *majimboism*: the tribal spheres of influence. What they opposed, however, was a federal distribution of executive powers. *Majimboism* was not to be replaced by, but subsumed under a centralized state, with highly concentrated executive powers.[114] Presidential rule revealed the limits of the purportedly untouchable principle of tribal spheres of influence that were in fact devoid of any power, influence, or authority when it came to accessing state resources controlled from the center.

---

[113] Anderson noted that *majimboist* debates survived the achievement of independence, see Anderson, "Yours in Struggle for *Majimbo*," 548.
[114] Ibid.

5 | Kenyatta, Meru Politics, and the Last Mau Mau (1961/3–1965)[*]

The independence settlement appeased, apparently at least, the white settlers, Kenyan ministers, and the landless masses, but left unclear how their diverging expectations could be fully satisfied. European settlers worried about losing their land, and continued to argue that a sudden, massive, and forced departure would lead to economic breakdown. Kenyan ministers feared that independence might cost them the British funds promised at independence to buy out European land. The landless and poor demanded that confiscated land be redistributed for free. The support of the landless was of strategic importance to the government's legitimacy, and their frustration was all the more alarming as the KANU government, the white settlers, and the Colonial Office feared it could stir Mau Mau resistance, under cover of the freshly revived KLFA.

Jomo Kenyatta seemed to be caught in a political crossfire, risking losing significant political assets. Yet, his public commitment to the willing buyer–willing seller land policy did not harm his popularity. His release from jail in 1961 gave hope to ex-Mau Mau fighters, who thought this Kiambu Kikuyu elder would defend their interests.[1] His immediate declaration that no land would be given for free did surprise and shock many landless Kikuyu. Even so, the uncertainty surrounding his politics and his Mau Mau background persisted.[2] Why did the resilient freedom fighters or the millions of landless fail to maintain revolutionary action? The military defeat of the Mau Mau movement

---

[*] This chapter is derived, in part, from an article published as A. Angelo, "Jomo Kenyatta and the Repression of the 'Last' Mau Mau Leaders, 1961–65," *Journal of Eastern African Studies* 11, no. 3 (2017): 442–459, available online: www.tandfonline.com/doi/abs/10.1080/17531055.2017.1354521.

[1] On the landless' surprise at Kenyatta's statement, see Kanogo, *Squatters and the Roots of Mau Mau (1905–1963)*. See also Wasserman, *Politics of Decolonisation*, 48; Kershaw, *Mau Mau from Below*, 259.

[2] Kanogo, *Squatters and the Roots of Mau Mau (1905–1963)*, 171.

does not suffice to explain why the landless and the Mau Mau fighters' land claims eventually fell into oblivion. Neither does it explain how Kenyatta succeeded in maintaining the ambiguity surrounding his relationship to the Mau Mau movement.

Surprisingly perhaps, little has been written about the governement's attitude to Mau Mau resilience after independence, particularly in 1965, the year that Field Marshal Baimungi, a resilient Mau Mau fighter from Meru, was killed by the police. Kenyatta's ambiguous political stance hence remained unaccounted for. This chapter investigates the connection between postindependence Mau Mau resilience and the shaping of the land ministry, attempting to explain what drove Jomo Kenyatta to appoint a Meru leader, Jackson Angaine, as minister for lands and settlement. It suggests that the repression of the Mau Mau must be read in light of Kenyatta's more astute political calculations about how to influence local politics: not directly, but by subjecting them to dominant personalities he could control. The Meru district, in Eastern province, will be my main focus. This was not only the Mau Mau's last bastion, it was also the home district of Jackson H. Angaine. A dominant political figure, Angaine was known for his ambiguous history with the Mau Mau movement, and for his just-as-ambiguous relationship to the local "tribal" authorities, Njuri Ncheke, which risked undermining the legitimacy of Kenyatta's government. To explain how and why the repression of the resilient Mau Mau movement in Meru coincided with the appointment of Angaine as minister for lands is the aim of the following pages.

The chapter shows that Kenyatta had known about the resilient Mau Mau fighters, particularly those in Meru district, since he took over the KANU presidency in 1961, but resisted any personal intervention. He relied, instead, on Jackson Angaine, who was a rising figure in the district and a convenient political proxy. Turning to the government's repressive politics against Mau Mau resistance, the chapter outlines how only the top leaders of the movement were targeted, while the government was always at pains to protect Kenyatta's political integrity. The highest spheres of power attempted to mask such repressive politics behind a subtle equilibrium between Mau Mau, pseudo-Mau Mau, and the loyalist government, and a strategic use of Mau Mau bodyguards as a convenient smokescreen in public meetings. All in all, Kenyatta's strategy was twofold: incessant repression prevented grassroot organization among Mau Mau while he deliberatly shrouded his ambiguous Mau Mau past in mystery, and thereby deprived residual Mau Mau of a clear target for mobilization.

Kenyatta, Mau Mau Resilience, and the Meru District

A close reading of the records shows that Kenyatta was aware of what the colonial, and thereafter postcolonial, government saw as the problem of resilient Mau Mau fighters, but always avoided becoming involved in the matter in any way at all, certainly to preserve the political benefits of his Mau Mau image. Although he owned his political rise, especially during the Kenyatta campaign, to his ambiguous relationship with the Mau Mau movement, which both his comrades and opponents conveniently avoided clarifying, Kenyatta never verbally rewarded the Mau Mau's struggle for independence.[3]

Mau Mau freedom fighters demands for free redistribution of land, for the eviction of all loyalists from the government, and for the integration of former fighters into the army were clearly running against the government's official policy. Yet, with independence achieved, resilient Mau Mau fighters were not calling for the overthrow of the new African government; neither did they represent an immediate political threat to the government. Their challenge was a predominantly moral one and targeted the government's land politics. It risked, however, delegitimizing Kenyatta's leadership, while feeding the opposition's complaints. With KANU controlling the autonomous government after December 1963, and Kenyatta installed as prime minister, time was ripe for him to tackle the remaining issue of the resilient Mau Mau fighters.[4]

Kenyatta had been informed that Mau Mau fighters were still active in Meru, in Eastern province. In Central province, Mau Mau leaders had either been killed or co-opted, like Waruhiu Itote, aka General China, who was arrested and jailed in Lodwar, where he became

---

[3] Buijtenhuijs, *Mau Mau*, 59.
[4] The number and strength of resilient Mau Mau is very difficult to assess. As Tabitha Kanogo observed, after independence the KLFA was considerably small due to the absence of open membership or intimidation, but also because the movement was afraid mass recruitment would expose it to betrayal. See Kanogo, *Squatters and the Roots of Mau Mau (1905–1963)*, 167–168.

Kenyatta's closest and most faithful friend among the inmates.[5] The capture and execution of General Dedan Kimathi by the British on February 18, 1957 signaled the official end of the Mau Mau insurgency.[6] Kimathi was nonetheless succeeded by his deputy leader, Field Marshal Baimungi Marete, who refused to surrender and, together with General Chui, another Kikuyu Mau Mau leader from Murang'a district, took over the command of the KLFA.[7] Another notable resilient leader was Field Marshal Mwariama, who, convinced he would live long enough to see Kenya become independent, revived Mau Mau oaths after 1957, and maintained a resistance throughout the district.[8] The government feared that, if not dispersed from their forest camps, remaining fighters and released detainees would be encouraged to form a separate community.[9] Kenyatta was "well aware of the situation in Meru" and committed himself to "do all he could to help."[10] His government was painstakingly looking for a durable solution to deal with the remaining freedom fighters, or, as they were now called, the terrorists.

The political situation in Meru was further complicated by the political divisions among local politicians, who seemed to be using Mau Mau oathing to boost their own popularity in the district. Colonial administrators suspected them all of "double talk" politics,

---

[5] Maina Macharia and Peter Kamau, interview, October 10, 2015, Nairobi. On General China and his Lodwar years with Kenyatta, see Elizabeth Watkins, *Jomo's Jailor: Grand Warrior of Kenya: The Life of Leslie Whitehouse* (Watlington: Britwell Books, 1996).

[6] Hornsby, *Kenya*, 47.

[7] Maina wa Kinyatti, *History of Resistance in Kenya (1884–2002)* (Nairobi: Mau Mau Research Center, 2008), 337. I rely on the interviews Kinyatti conducted with Mwariama in 1977.

[8] Samuel J. T. Kamunchuluh, "The Meru Participation in Mau Mau," *Kenya Historical Review* 3, no. 2 (1975): 208.

[9] Even in April 1964, the local administrator of the Eastern region, Mr. Oswald, stated that "from the security angle fighters were not considered to be a risk, at least for the time being." Oswald was speaking at a meeting held in the Office the Permanent Secretary to the Ministry of Home Affairs, which had been put in charge of dealing with the Meru district. Secret. Notes of a Meeting Held in the Office the Permanent Secretary, Ministry of Home affairs on April 15, 1964 to Consider Methods of Dealing with Meru Freedom Fighters, KNA, BB/1/149, Eastern Region Law and Order.

[10] Secret. W. B. G. Raynor to Permanent Secretary Ministry of Security and Defence, "Security – Meru," July 15, 1963, KNA, BB/1/149.

denouncing terrorist oathing, while themselves encouraging oathing to "ensure support for their party."[11] District colonial administrators held responsible the KANU chairman for Meru, Jackson Harvester Angaine, for such practices: "he is the source of all subversion, and indeed started the oathing campaign in 1960 in order to defeat [KADU leader Bernard] Mate's influence."[12] He was suspected of having close contact with ex-detainee KANU leaders, as well as with ex-fighters. These suspicions revived the old fears of a practice both the colonial authorities and the autonomous government saw as a sign of Mau Mau activity, and were at pains to stop.[13] Angaine systematically denied any subversive activity, or any populist use of oathing campaigns.[14] Suspicions persisted.

Kenyatta, who presided over KANU at the time, refused to intervene to settle Angaine's ambiguous politicking, despite being repeatedly asked to do so. In May 1962, the Central province commissioner felt bound to ask Kenyatta to "do everything he can" to convince Angaine to stop his "tactics."[15] The situation did not improve, and the issue finally reached the governor's office. The governor himself requested Kenyatta to take urgent action to discipline the politician, quoting Kenyatta's earlier "special plea ... to overlook Mr. Angaine's actions" and recalling that "it was yourself who said to me, when I spoke recently about the behaviour of another parliamentary secretary [Murgor], that it was necessary to have discipline in the Government."[16] Kenyatta must have felt politically cornered in Angaine's case. He showed no esteem for the latter: colonial administrators claimed that he was "more prepared to sack him" than any one else. He nonetheless avoided any personal interference with Angaine,

---

[11] Confidential. "Security – Meru," Regional Government Agent, July 2, 1963, KNA, BB/1/149.
[12] Ibid.
[13] Secret. "An Appreciation of the Present Situation in Meru," June 16, 1961; Secret. "Oathing in Meru District," District Commissioner Meru, June 5, 1961; Secret. The Director of Intelligence to the Permanent Secretary for Defence, "Oathing – Meru District," June 2, 1962, KNA, BB/1/149.
[14] Secret. Provincial Commissioner Central Region, "Meru Affairs," June 17, 1961; Secret. District Commissioner Meru to Provincial Commissioner Nyeri, "Illegal Meetings," February 23, 1962, KNA, BB/1/149.
[15] Secret. Provincial Commissioner to District Commissioner Meru, May 9, 1962, KNA, BB/1/149.
[16] Confidential. Governor Renison to Jomo Kenyatta, July 18, 1962, KNA, BB/1/149.

leaving the sensitive task of obtaining his resignation from his KANU seat in the LegCo to the governor himself.[17] Angaine did not resign, but finally "showed signs of being strongly pro-government of late," a change the colonial officer judged to be of personal interest only.[18] This was an opportune move for Kenyatta too, whose silence and even sudden favor toward Angaine showed that the future president foresaw in his future minister for lands a much greater political potential that he could use.

Jackson Angaine, Ambiguous Hence Indispensable

An exploration of Angaine's biographical background, and of how he became a prominent cabinet minister from 1961 to 1964, shows why Kenyatta wanted to stay aloof from the politics of the district, yet discreetly backed Angaine. Kenyatta understood that he needed to tame a district bordering his Kikuyu country, and where three well-rooted political forces challenged his authority: the traditional government of elders, KADU politicians, and former Mau Mau leaders.

If Jackson Harvester Angaine was an ambiguous, and at times even unreliable, political player, his family history made him nevertheless all the more strategic to the Meru political scene. He was born in 1903 under the name of Jackson Harvester M'Nchebere. "Angaine" was his father's name: Chief M'Angaine MBE, a colonial chief and prominent leader of the Njuri Ncheke, the council of elders and the "traditional" government in Meru.[19] Chief M'Angaine commanded an even greater respect in the district, as his own father was believed to have been a traditional Meru prophet, a Mugwe, who, according to Rev. Stephan Mûgambî (today's spiritual advisor of the Njuri Ncheke), had foreseen the insidious conflicts in Meru brought about by the

---

[17] District Commissioner Meru to Provincial Commissioner Nyeri, August 2, 1962; The Governor Sir Patrick Muir Renison to Jackson Angaine, August 20, 1962, KNA, BB/1/149.
[18] Secret. Regional Government Agent, "The Meru Security Situation," June 17, 1963, KNA, BB/1/149.
[19] Reverend Mûgambî (spiritual advisor to the Njuri Ncheke), interview, October 12, 2015, Nairobi. For a history of Njuri Ncheke, its origins (or "invention as a tradition"), emergence, and decline, as well as its rites, see Anne-Marie Peatrik, *La Vie à Pas Contés. Génération, Age et Société dans les Hautes Terres du Kenya (Meru Tigania – Igembe)* (Nanterre: Société d'Ethnologie, 1999), 455–470.

struggle for independence.[20] As for Jackson growing up in the colony, he was educated at the Alliance High School, like many of his fellow politicians.[21] After working as an accountant for some years, Angaine started to be politically active: he was the secretary of the Meru Local Native Council (1935–1948), and then became chairman of the KAU local branch (1948–1952), where he would also work with Jomo Kenyatta.

Angaine's relationship to the Mau Mau movement is poorly documented. In 1954, when the Emergency was declared, Angaine was arrested and briefly detained by the colonial government. It remains unclear whether this was primarily because he was suspected of belonging to the Mau Mau movement, or because he was accused of and prosecuted for the murder of his wife. The judgement proved inconclusive, and Angaine was acquitted for lack of any proof.[22] Nevertheless, his detention helped to establish him as a follower of the movement.[23] He was also believed to have a close relationship to the Mau Mau fighters: reports by the police tracking for ex-Mau Mau members in the district subsequently mentioned "friendship" with "Field Marshal" Baimungi.[24]

After joining KANU in 1960, Angaine was elected chairman of the Meru branch.[25] His links to both Njuri Ncheke and the Mau Mau movement accelerated his political career, and certainly did not play an insignificant part in Kenyatta's insistence that he should be appointed permanent secretary in his autonomous government, and later

---

[20] Ibid. For a history of the "mugwe" in Meru prior and during colonization, see Bernardo Bernardi, *The Mugwe: A Blessing Prophet: A Study of a Religious and Public Dignitary of the Meru of Kenya* (Nairobi: Gideon S. Were Press Ltd., 1959). See also Peatrik, *La Vie à Pas Contés*, 458.

[21] On the importance of the Alliance High School in training the Kenyan elite, see Benjamin E. KipKorir, "The Alliance High School and the Origins of the Kenya African Elite 1926–1962" (Ph.D. diss., University of Cambridge, 1969); Hélène Charton, "La Genèse Ambiguë de l'Elite Kenyane. Origines, Formations et Intégration de 1945 à l'Indépendance" (Ph.D. diss., Université Paris 7, 2002).

[22] Confidential. "Leading Personalities in Kenya, 1978," BNA, FCO 31/2314; K. M. Thimangu-Kaunyangi, interview, October 21, 2015, Kenjai. A "Detention Order" issued by the District Commissioner Meru in April 1954 and concerning M'Chabari s/o Mugaine, although misspelled, may well be to Jackson Angaine's detention order, KNA, VQ/11/7.

[23] Reverend Mûgambî, interview, October 12, 2015.

[24] Secret. F. R. Wilson to the District Commissioner Meru, May 9, 1962, KNA, BB/1/149.

[25] Maxon and Ofcansky, *Historical Dictionary of Kenya*, 23–24.

appointed minister for lands and settlements. By then, Angaine was a "senior" politician. Age was an important asset by which to impose leadership throughout the district.[26] Now a strong defender of the KANU party line, Angaine found himself in opposition not only to KADU leaders in Meru, such as the educated and teacher Bernard Mate, but also to the traditional government itself, the Njuri Ncheke. To colonial administrators, he was "slightly mad but dangerous."[27]

At the heart of the competition between Angaine and Njuri Ncheke was the control of the Meru vote, as well as the control over land transactions in the district. In both, Njuri Ncheke had become an indispensable political body. In the wake of the Emergency, it accumulated power and respect. In 1955, the colonial government saw it as a tool to further ensure that the Mau Mau movement would not gain ground in Meru district.[28] Njuri Ncheke was "recognised officially by combining it with the Local Government system of the District."[29] Members of the local district institutions were nominated through the Njuri Ncheke council, while the colonial government further advocated that "all Meru Government servants, upon invitation by Njuri, should be given the opportunity of joining the Njuri should they so desire."[30] Njuri Ncheke was thus empowered, as colonial officers acknowledged that their "elders are the only record of [land] holding and transactions" and "any decision which affect the laws and customs of the tribe must be discussed by them before any adjustment can be made."[31] This was a useful device by which to counter emerging Mau Mau claims. Already in 1950, the Njuri Ncheke elders decided that "any Meru who took an illegal oath would be dispossessed of all tribal

---

[26] John Kerimi, interview, October 19, 2015, Makutano, Meru.
[27] Confidential. "Security – Meru," Regional Government Agent, July 2, 1963, KNA, BB/1/149.
[28] "The upheaval caused by the Mau Mau has left us now with a choice of either developing or of abandoning the old structure of the tribe ... It has been decided in Meru to make an effort to develop the indigenous system which has shown itself to be capable of adjusting itself to the new times ... and build up on the framework of the Njuri system an institution which can take over the responsibility of the present day administration." Reconstitution Committee memorandum no. 1, KNA, DC/MRU/1/4/5. See also Peatrik, *La Vie à Pas Contés*, 467–468.
[29] Central Province Annual Report 1955, "Meru District," KNA, VQ/16/95.
[30] Office of the District Commission to All Heads of Government Department, Meru, May 11, 1955, KNA, DC/MRU/1/4/5.
[31] Reconstitution Committee Memorandum no. 1, KNA, DC/MRU/1/4/5.

rights and land."[32] Njuri Ncheke continued to oppose the Mau Mau movement throughout the decade, whether by organizing ceremonies to curse the movement or, later, organizing the rehabilitation of Mau Mau detainees in camps.[33] Counterinsurgency politics formalized a longer history of powerful influence, as well as collaborative politics with the government, and colonial officers described Njuri Ncheke as "most helpful" and praised their "invaluable assistance."[34]

The reinforcement of the authority of Njuri Ncheke over administrative business enhanced their control over land ownership in Meru, to the great displeasure of their Kikuyu neighbors. Njuri Ncheke was one of the main defenders of the integrity of the Meru land unit, which they saw as a guarantee for the cohesion of the Meru ethnic group against foreign intrusions, in particular that of the Kikuyu. In the late 1940s, ethnic integrity was a prominent concern among Meru chiefs and elders, who felt threatened by potential foreign migrations and institutional disruptions in the district.[35] Angaine's father himself defended "the importance of tribal unity" and the "strengthening of the tribal institution."[36] These ethnic tensions climaxed with the dramatic expulsions of Kikuyu from the Meru district.[37] The beginning of the Emergency further fuelled anti-Kikuyu feeling in Meru, particularly

---

[32] Meru District Annual Report 1950, KNA, VQ/14/86.
[33] Njuri Ncheke would "try and reform their ways, and as soon as the tribal authorities are satisfied that they [the detainees] can be safely released, they are returned to their homes but are, of course, kept under careful watch" in Annual Report Central Province 1952, "Meru District," April 2, 1952, KNA, VQ/16/81; Central Province Annual Report 1954, KNA, VQ/16/94. See also Kamunchuluh, "The Meru Participation in Mau Mau," 195.
[34] Meru District Annual Report 1950, March 12, 1951, KNA, VQ/14/86. Another government's report noted that "The Njuri system of government has all these three merits. It is well known and generally accepted, its simplicity allows for its operation at clan as well as tribal level, and its proved worth over two centuries of primitive society and two decades of the post-European era suggest that it should be the sound political basis for orderly development of a tribal community looking towards a larger share in the national life of Kenya." "Some Notes on the Working of the Indigenous Government of the Meru People," KNA, DC/MRU/1/4/5; Central Province Annual Report 1951, "Meru District," KNA, VQ/16/80.
[35] Notice of a Meeting of Chiefs Held at Meru on December 8, 1939, KNA, DC/MRU/1/4/5; Annual Report for Meru District, 1939, KNA, DC/MRU/1/4/5.
[36] Notice of a Meeting of Chiefs Held at Meru on December 8, 1939, KNA, DC/MRU/1/4/5.
[37] Meru District Annual Report, 1940, KNA, DC/MRU/1/4/5.

among the tribal authorities, as previously mentioned.[38] A few years after, in 1956, the Meru people won a decisive battle with the creation of the Meru Land Unit, which officially separated them from the former Kikuyu native land unit. This was, in the words of a British district officer, a "momentous occasion for the Meru people."[39] Meru land, its administration, and its relationship with the Kikuyu remained a sensitive question far from definitively settled. Upon independence, the revision of provincial boundaries would revive the debates surrounding the specificities of the Meru ethnic group, its history, and its enmity with the Kikuyu.

The prospect of an end to the Emergency, combined with the rise of nationalist parties, further complicated political mathematics. The 1959 report for the Meru district noted that "Njuri Ncheke [was] gradually losing its influence": the gap between the traditional institution and the rising educated, loyalist elite was widening rapidly. Most importantly, at a time when the colonial government was advocating the individualization of land titles (in the wake of the Swynnerton Plan), Njuri Ncheke, while clinging to the traditional tribal authority all over the Meru land, found itself at odds with the vast majority of the population.[40] Furthermore, as KANU and KADU increasingly dominated the political scene, the competition narrowed down to their prominent politicians, among them Jackson Angaine, who overshadowed Njuri Ncheke's authority.

Angaine's relationship to Njuri Ncheke has remained unclear until today, and so have his political maneuverings regarding the council of elders. He certainly inherited the respect his own father had commanded over the council, but his name and lineage were insufficient to establish a legitimacy to rule, and certainly not to join Njuri Ncheke.[41] The exact nature of the relationship is not known: was Angaine (really) a member of Njuri Ncheke? Reverend Mûgambî believes that the young Angaine assisted his father in keeping records of Njuri Ncheke decisions, and could not have done so had he not been

---

[38] On this issue see Branch, *Defeating Mau Mau, Creating Kenya*, 102–103.
[39] Annual Report Meru District 1956, KNA, DC/MRU/1/12/1.
[40] Meru District Annual Report 1959, KNA, DC/MRU/1/15/1. See also Peatrik, *La Vie à Pas Contés*, 469–470.
[41] Reverend Mûgambî, interview, October 23, 2015, Nairobi. On the complex relationship between generation set and clan system, see Jurg Mahner, "The Outsider and the Insider in Tigania Meru," *Africa* 45, no. 4 (1975): 400–409.

initiated into the council.[42] For the politicians who knew him, Angaine could not *not* have been a Njuri Ncheke elder: it was politically impossible, given the political importance of the council.[43] On the political front, however, Angaine clearly differed with the council, and at times even opposed it.

With independence approaching, Njuri Ncheke feared that a pro-KANU, centralized government would undermine their leadership. In the year 1961, the Njuri elders sent a delegation to visit Jomo Kenyatta in jail "to give good wishes to him and tell him that when he comes into power, he doesn't forget Njuri."[44] Early 1962, as the independence negotiations started, the elders requested several meetings with the colonial authorities to "seek advice as to how to ensure the usual safeguards so that they do not become Kikuyu vassals after Independence."[45] As they confessed to the then provincial commissioner of Eastern province F. R. Wilson, they feared their claims to authority and control over Meru land would be overlooked. The elders demanded to be represented and heard at the ongoing negotiations for independence in London. Wilson explained:

At the back of all this is their horror at recent trends in Meru resulting from Jackson Angaine's activities. A recent meeting of the Njuri was in fact broken up as a result of Jackson packing the meeting with K.A.N.U. adherents, including many Kikuyu, none of whom were members of the Njuri ... The Njuri are adamant, therefore, that the time has now come for them to press for the full their claims to live in a separate province or region to the Kikuyu.[46]

---

[42] Reverend Mûgambî, interview, October 23, 2015.
[43] To the question "Was Angaine a Member of Njuri Ncheke?," the personalities I interviewed in Meru replied with various degrees of ambiguity. Joseph Muturia asserted that "you could not lead if you were not a member of Njuri Ncheke at that time" (interview, October 21, 2015, Laare). Kaunyangi replied "I think so, but I am not sure. But by the time he was a Minister, he was a member of Njuri Ncheke" (interview, October 21, 2015, Kenjai). Reverend Mûgambî asserted that "No way could (Jakson Angaine's father) allow his son to be a leader without having initiated him into Njuri Ncheke," although he believed that "it is not everybody who knows" (interview, October 23, 2015, Nairobi).
[44] Julius M'Mworia (representative of Njuri Ncheke during the second Lancaster House conference), interview, Nairobi, October 24, 2015.
[45] R. E. Wainwright to the Provincial Commissioner, Central province, January 5, 1962, KNA, BB/11/36.
[46] Confidential. F. R. Wilson to the Chief Commissioner, Office of the Leader of the House, February 1, 1962, KNA, BB/11/36.

Njuri Ncheke elders eventually sent a delegation to the second Lancaster House conference in 1962 but their hopes turned out to be short-lived. In the memorandum that stated their claims, they avoided siding with any particular political party, and preemptively disassociated themselves from the KADU concept of *majimboism*.[47] Behind the formalities, Njuri Ncheke were clearly supported by KADU leaders, in particular Bernard Mate who helped in drafting the memorandum, whereas Angaine would have preferred Njuri Ncheke not to go to the conference.[48] Julius M'Mworia, who represented the Njuri Ncheke delegation at the conference, admitted that "Our policy as Njuri Ncheke was more on the KADU side than KANU ... KANU were saying there is no individual land, the land, the whole of it in the republic belongs to the government. And that we did not want, we did not want this to be free for everyone."[49] The elders got only a "non-committal" answer.[50] As the conference stumbled over the irreconcilable KANU–KADU views on regionalism, and with KANU leading the new government coalition, Njuri Ncheke's requests were forgotten: "we never talked about that again."[51]

In spite of KANU's national victory, local competition in Meru persisted, forcing Angaine to make sure that Njuri Ncheke would not further contest his leadership in particular and KANU policy in general. According to Reverend Mûgambî, one of Angaine's first moves against Njuri Ncheke was to invalidate the opening of the Njuri Ncheke headquarters in Nchîrû (Meru), also referred to as "the parliament" or "the shrine." Angaine is believed to have been responsible for bringing "six lorries of uncircumcised male adults" from Turkana to the opening.[52] As circumcision determines age and seniority, defines

---

[47] "We maintain that the so-called Njuri delegation is merely a group of people who represent nobody but themselves. We do not know who gave them mandate to speak on behalf of the Njuri and we will never recognize them. We only recognize the two Meru elected Members namely the Hon. J. Angaine MLC and the Hon. B. Mate MLO who virtue their election by the Meru to the Kenya legislative Council have the the mandate to speak on behalf of the Meru people [sic]." In "Memorandum of Elders of the Njuri Ncheke of Meru to Be Submitted to the Kenya Constitutional Conference to Be Held in London in February 1962," KNA, BB/11/36.

[48] Julius M'Mworia, interview.   [49] Ibid.   [50] Ibid.

[51] Ibid. On KANU–KADU conflicting views over regionalism, see Anderson, "Yours in Struggle for *Majimbo*"; Maxon, *Kenya's Independence Constitution*, 77–152.

[52] Reverend Mûgambî, interview, October 12, 2015, Nairobi.

the ruling generation, and legitimates its authority, the presence of uncircumcized men was not only contrary to Njuri Ncheke's constitutional organization, but "desecrated" the meeting.[53] A few months later, before the cleansing rituals were completed, the death of the Njuri Ncheke chairman, ex-Chief M'Mûraa wa Kairangi, raised the issue of his succession. There was no visible tension between M'Mûraa and Angaine, but the Njuri Ncheke elder might have been closer to KADU leaders, as Bernard Mate was his son-in-law.[54] He was replaced by a prominent Meru teacher, Norman Murechia, who came from the "same village" as Angaine – that is, the same division in the district.[55] The relationship between the two remained equivocal. According to Mûgambi, Murechia was "a loyalist" chosen by Angaine, who "paid lip service to the institution for almost 40 years."[56] Nevertheless, many testimonies reported tensions and even competition between Angaine and Murechia.[57] Murechia may have been wanting to strengthen his control over Njuri Ncheke.[58] As both men were from the same age group, Murechia had few chances to challenge Angaine's authority

---

[53] Reverend S. A. Mûgambî Mwithimbû, "Njûrî Ncheke: An Instrument of Peace and Conflict Resolution," in *Culture in Peace and Conflict Resolution within Communities of Central Kenya*, eds. Njuguna Gĭchere, S. A. Mûgambî Mwithimbû, and Shin-ichiro Ishida (Nairobi: National Museum of Kenya, 2014), 81. To compare with Njuri Ncheke's constitution, see "The Constitution of the Njuri Ncheke of Meru," KNA, BB/11/36. On the importance of circumcision in Meru tribes, see E. Mary Holding, "Some Preliminary Notes on Meru Age Grades," *Man* 42 (1942): 58–65. For a broader perspective on the history of the circumcision issue in Meru, see Lynn M. Thomas, "'*Ngaitana* (I Will Circumcise Myself)': The Gender and Generational Politics of the 1956 Ban on Clitoridectomy in Meru, Kenya," *Gender and History* 8, no. 3 (1996): 338–363; "Imperial Concerns and 'Women's Affairs': State Efforts to Regulate Clitoridectomy and Eradicate Abortion in Meru, Kenya, c. 1910–1950," *The Journal of African History* 39, no. 1 (1998): 121–145.
[54] Julius M'Mworia, interview.
[55] K. M. Thimangu-Kaunyangi and John Kerimi, interviews October 21, 2015 and November 4, 2015.
[56] Mûgambî Mwithimbû, "Njûrî Ncheke," 81.
[57] John Kerimi and Julius M'Mworia, interviews, October 19, 2015 and October 24, 2015.
[58] Julius M'Mworia, interview: "[Traditionally] no chairman would control others. They would coordinate the proceedings. The one who was involved in the control of the proceeding is Murechia, he is the one who tried to become a controller of Njuri Ncheke. He could refuse to accept what one would say. But previously we would discuss an issue, then what majority said is right and the chairman goes with it without any complain ... The people from the previous chairmen were not getting anything out of it ... But now things have changed,

and raise support within his political bastion. Therefore, he probably remained a minor political threat. Angaine was not trying to annihilate the traditional government; instead, he wanted to neutralize it so as to ensure Njuri Ncheke leaders would not overshadow his political influence in the district.[59]

Angaine's name and reputation provided him with significant, and even unique, assets to make his way through Meru politics. His public association to Njuri Ncheke, due to his father's name, overshadowed his opposition to the Council of Elders. Similarly, his ambiguous relationship to the Mau Mau movement would later overshadow a more treacherous opposition to it. A strong defender of the KANU line, Angaine was finally favored by Kenyatta himself, who, as previously mentioned, overcame his ill-feeling, to back his politics and make him one of the most powerful ministers of his cabinet. Later appointing Angaine as minister for lands, Kenyatta would ensure that neither Njuri Ncheke (he was said to see it as a "small nonsensical thing") nor the resilient Mau Mau fighters would challenge his leadership.[60]

By September 1963, Angaine was the leading politician in Meru and had a free hand to enforce political unity. The most disruptive KANU leaders and the elected members for Meru were simply evicted so as to ease the way toward political unity.[61] Colonial administrators now hoped Angaine would remain the "recognised head" of "political figures" in the district. Kenyatta himself left him in charge of political order in Meru when he went to London for the independence negotiations.[62] While the Njuri Ncheke were tamed, the question of resilient Mau Mau fighters remained.[63] Political unity among Meru leaders was all the more necessary as the government wanted to start a public campaign of disapproval against the freedom fighters, offering amnesty

---

you go somewhere, you get allowances, a chairman can get something. Murechia converted it."

[59] Joseph Muturia, interview.   [60] Julius M'Mworia, interview.
[61] Secret. RGA Embu to the Civil Secretary Embu, September 2, 1963, KNA, BB/1/149.
[62] Ibid.
[63] Surprisingly, Angaine was advised by the regional government agent for Meru to revive Njuri Ncheke and use it to give public politics a united front. This advice could either be read as the adminsitrators encouraging Angaine to rebuild a broken a link with Njuri Ncheke, or as a sign that Angaine's political actions against Njuri Ncheke remained fairly subtle. See Private and Personal. RGA Meru to J. H. Angaine, October 21, 1963, KNA, BB/1/149.

to those who surrendered before Kenya achieved independence on December 12. The aims of the campaign were not confined to Meru, but were to "safeguard the loyalists at and after Independence," to make sure KANU's moderate stance was "taken seriously by the people," and to prevent "wide repercussions" if the Meru KANU hierarchy chose the freedom fighters over "their commitment to the Prime Minister."[64]

Political unity remained a distant horizon, however, for many politicians feared losing ground by condemning Mau Mau fighters. In fact, the political situation was a deadlock, and political bickering was such that no leader did "and, for the time, will not condemn terrorists publicly," as the colonial authorities worried.[65] Angaine himself was "equivocal in the extreme and [said] that even if he did [condemn them], people would not believe he meant it."[66] Cooperation with politicians was all the more important as government administrators had little faith in the success of police operations. The police lacked the means to track the "gangsters" effectively: "the amount of luck required for the security forces to prevail in those circumstances is beyond all reasonable expectation."[67] Colonial administrators insisted on the "necessity for the government to make a new offer of surrender terms to the terrorists," arguing that recent *barazas* had been promising so far.[68] Angaine toured the district offering surrender terms to fighters who would hand over all weapons, ammunitions, and equipment, while the regional administration tried to keep up with "fixing the publicity and press arrangements."[69]

A question remains: Why did Kenyatta appoint a Meru politician as minister for lands at independence? One element of the answer to this question points to the dramatic history of ethnic relations between Meru and Kikuyu people, dating back to the 1930s. Timothy Parsons showed the complexities at work behind interethnic relationships in Meru district between the 1930s and the 1950s. Land shortage in Central province, and particularly in the Kiambu district, forced many

---

[64] Secret. RGA Embu to the Civil Secretary Embu, September 2, 1963, KNA, BB/1/149.
[65] Ibid.   [66] Ibid.
[67] Secret. P. E. Walters to the Permanent Secretary to the Ministry of Internal Security and Defense, September 3, 1963, KNA, BB/1/149.
[68] Ibid.
[69] Secret. RGA Meru to Civil Secretary Eastern Region, October 11, 1963, KNA, BB/1/149.

landless Kikuyu to settle in Meru, while the colonial authorities were at pains to find land to relocate them. Meru district appeared to become an ideal place, not only because land was available, but also because of the alleged similarities of Meru and Kikuyu tribal practices, which fuelled a debate about the purported tribal cohesiveness of the Mount Kenya people. Kikuyu politics were intensively involved in this debate. One of the KCA's most radical voices was that of Senior Chief Koinange (soon-to-be Kenyatta's father-in-law), who spoke against tribal mingling and assimilation, and against those, like the nationalist Harry Thuku, who defended a more flexible understanding of tribal identity.[70]

A KCA representative himself, writing his thesis in defence of the Kikuyu tribal identity, Kenyatta must have been aware of the ongoing virulent debates surrounding the migrations of landless Kikuyus and rights over land in other districts. In *Facing Mount Kenya,* he spoke about the importance of maintaining the unity of the Kikuyu tribe. An example can be found in his chapter about marriage, which he defined as "one of the most powerful means of maintaining the cohesion of Gikuyu society and of enforcing that conformity to the kinship system and to tribal organisation without which social life is impossible."[71] It could be that, at the same time, Kenyatta had learned about the Njuri

---

[70] Timothy Parsons, "Being Kikuyu in Meru: Challenging the Tribal Geography of Colonial Kenya," *Journal of African History* 53, no. 1 (2012): 75, 79. The security of land ownership in Meru has remained a problematic question until today, as the politics of issuing of land titles (prerogative of the Ministry of Lands) shows. See, for example, Phares Mutembei, "CS Charity Ngilu Urges Meru Residents to Avoid Court during Land Disputes," *The Standard*, November 30, 2014; David Muchui, "Land Shortage Hits Town as Individuals Grab 200 Plots," *Daily Nation,* February 24, 2015; "Nyambene Residents Desperate for Land Titles," *Daily Nation,* August 25, 2015. Finally, another parallel can be drawn between Kenyatta's awareness of the Kikuyu land and tribal issue spreading beyond Central province and the constitution, in 1970, the Gikuyu Embu Meru Association (GEMA) formally attempted to unite the Mount Kenya Region, and maintain the political and economic strength of the Kikuyu in the region. On Kenyatta and GEMA, see Branch, *Kenya,* 131–135; Onoma, *The Politics of Property Rights Institutions in Africa,* 170–171; Njenga Karume, *Beyond Expectations: From Charcoal to Gold: An Autobiography* (Nairobi: Kenway Publications, 2009), chapter 6.

[71] Kenyatta, *Facing Mount Kenya,* 164.

Ncheke elders, who were supported by the colonial authority in their effort to end Kikuyu migrations.[72]

Upon independence, the land issue in Meru stood in clear continuity with the past Kikuyu–Meru tribal disputes. At stake was the recognition (or not) of the Kikuyu migrants' land claims, and whether to secure (or not) their right over land through a land title – two issues against which Njuri Ncheke had been historically opposed.[73] The Njuri Ncheke memorandum for the protection of tribal land shows that the tensions had not vanished. The renegotiations of provincial boundaries, under the Regional Boundaries Commission in 1962, gave a vivid illustration of the persisting intertribal mistrust, as Meru people successfully disassociated themselves from the old colonial Central province (dominated by the Kikuyu) to join the newly formed Eastern region. The statements made by regional politicians to the Regional Boundaries Commission are particularly eloquent. Chief Jacob Mwongo, representing the Meru African District Council clearly stated that "They [his delegation] wish to be disassociated from the Kikuyu who have always tried to dominate them and prevent them from having responsible position in the Central Province organisations."[74] Nteere Mbogori, KADU representative in Meru, warned that if they were not separated, "Meru will use force."[75] Jeremiah Nyagah, representing the KANU Embu group, stated, however with more moderation, that Embu people should receive guarantees to protect their rights over land, local, and central administrative institutions and distribution of government's funds.[76]

A tentative argument would be that Kenyatta wished to secure a grand Kikuyu land unit that stretched over all the Mount Kenya tribes. Angaine was a convenient political pawn. His ability to control Njuri Ncheke and/or to maintain his Mau Mau aura depended on him having direct access to presidential favors. More than an elder or

---

[72] At least Kenyatta's Ph.D. *Facing Mount Kenya* was read by H.E. Lambert, the colonial officer in charge of the Meru tribe and the redesigning of tribal institutions such as Njuri Ncheke. See Parsons, "Being Kikuyu in Meru," 74.
[73] Ibid., 76.
[74] Report of the Regional Boundaries Commission, 1962, KNA Library, K2008–216/526-926762. See also Branch, *Defeating Mau Mau, Creating Kenya*, 103.
[75] Report of the Regional Boundaries Commission, 1962, KNA Library, K2008–216/526-926762.
[76] Ibid.

Mau Mau follower, he was "Kenyatta's friend."[77] The establishment of a centralized government and the subsequent repression of Mau Mau resilience simply stifled both Njuri Ncheke's and Mau Mau's claims to land: neither had any choice but to rely on Angaine, now minister for lands and settlement, to buy or even to request land.

Breaking the Last of the Mau Mau

Kenyatta never dealt personaly with the resilient fighters, but delegated the conduct of personal contacts and public meetings to prominent cabinet ministers. At the end of 1963, he sent Tom Mboya and Oginga Odinga to visit Meru district. They informed him about the "terrorists'" complaints as well as KANU divisions.[78] Several *barazas* were held throughout the district, spreading Kenyatta's promise of amnesty for Kenyan prisoners, targeting in particular some members of the Land Freedom Army, although without any visible result.[79] Kenyatta further delegated the negotiations to Mbiyu Koinange, to the despair of colonial administrators who repeatedly requested him to visit the district, and complained of being "completely in the dark" about both present and future negotiations.[80] The situation stagnated. The regional government agent for Meru wrote a worrying report in which he called for a change of political strategy: the number of "gangsters" was increasing and rumors of sabotage operations during the independence celebrations now circulated. He too pressed for Kenyatta to visit the district. Personally informed of the report at his Gatundu home, Kenyatta responded that he was anxious to do so as soon as possible.[81]

Kenyatta met only carefully chosen Mau Mau leaders in a meeting facilitated by Jesse Kariuki, Munyua Waiyaki, and Waruhiu Itote.

---

[77] Angaine's "friendship" with Kenyatta, as to explain his close connection and even dependency on the president, was a recurrent feature of the interviews with Joseph Muturia, K. M. Thimangu-Kaunyangi, John Kerimi, and Reverend Mûgambî.

[78] Secret. RGA Meru to Civil Secretary Embu, September 19, 1963, KNA, BB/1/149.

[79] *Daily Nation*, "Independence Amnesty for Kenya Prisoners," November 7, 1963, 1; Meru District Monthly Report. November 1963, December 6, 1963 (p. 113), KNA, BB/1/149.

[80] Secret. RGA Meru to Civil Secretary Eastern region, December 28, 1963.

[81] Secret. RGA Meru to Civil Secretary, Eastern region, November 14, 1963; Personal and Secret. P. E. Walters to G. J. Ellerton, November 16, 1963; Secret. G. J. Ellerton to P. E. Walters, November 27, 1963, KNA, BB/1/149.

Jesse Kariuki was a former KAU leader. Munuya Waiyaki was not only a descendant of the Kikuyu chief and anticolonial hero Waiyaki wa Hinga – a genealogy used by Kenyatta's government to enhance its legitimacy – he had been Kenyatta's medical doctor when the latter was restricted in Lodwar and Maralal; he was also an active player in KANU politcs.[82] Waruhiu Itote, formely known by his Mau Mau name "General China," had been imprisoned with Kenyatta, when the two eventually became closer.[83] On December 9, Kenyatta received "Field Marshal" Mwariama in his Gatundu house, in Kiambu, "to discuss the terms of the amnesty offered by the Prime Minister to people still hiding in the forests."[84] The visit was widely broadcast in the newspapers, and, a few months later, a general gathering was organized in Ruringu stadium, in Nyeri (Central province) for Mau Mau fighters to symbolically leave the forest and surrender their weapons to the government. The now famous picture showing Mwariama embracing Kenyatta immortalized the meeting.

Although Kenyatta's meeting with Field Marshal Mwariama was, and still is today, protrayed as an historic encounter: the absence of other Mau Mau leaders reveals both the limits of Kenyatta's willingness to deal with Mau Mau leaders, and the internal leadership battles that gnawed at the resistance movement. From Meru, only Mwariama's followers attended the meeting. Mwariama competed for leadership with his Meru rival General Baimungi: they fought for the title of Field Marshal.[85] Although they had previously agreed to all leave the forest, Mwariama made the first move to visit Kenyatta in Gatundu, without informing Baimungi, thus causing a rift between the two

---

[82] John Kamau, "Jomo's Foreign Minister Dr Munyua Waiyaki Dies at 91," *Daily Nation*, April 26, 2017; Hornsby, *Kenya*, 66, 160, 205.

[83] Kinyatti, *History of Resistance in Kenya (1884–2002)*, 361. On Waiyaki wa Hinga, see Lonsdale, "The Prayers of Waiyaki" Throup, "The Construction and Deconstruction of the Kenyatta State."

[84] *Daily Nation*, "Out of Hiding after 10 Years," December 9, 1963, 1.

[85] Kibiru Marete (former Mau Mau fighter and bodyguard of General Baimungi, today's chairman of the Meru branch of the Mau Mau War Veterans Association), interview, November 5, 2015, Makutano, Meru; M'Murungi M'Kobia (former Mau Mau fighter and bodyguard of General Baimungi), interview, November 6, 2015, Makutano, Meru, and Ciorukunga M'Kithumai (Mwariama's relative and former Mau Mau follower), interview, October 22, 2015, Makutano, Meru.

leaders. This might even have reinforced Baimungi's subsequent refusal to surrender and come out of the forest.[86]

In Ruringu Stadium, despite the joyful tone that the well-known picture of Mwariama embracing Kenyatta evokes, the atmosphere seemed more tense. A high level of security was deployed to protect Kenyatta in the stadium: "He was guarded by almost every soldier of Kenya" remembers Ciorukunga M'Kithumai, a relative of Mwariama and herself a Mau Mau follower.[87] Most interestingly, the arms and documents the Mau Mau fighters returned to the stadium were all taken away to places that remain unknown until today.[88] The same scenario took place in Kinoru Stadium, Meru, where a meeting was also organized for Baimungi's followers to surrender their arms to the government.[89] Similarly, General Baimungi's personal documents would also be taken away after his death.[90] Following the Ruringu meeting, Kenyatta declared that he extended the amnesty to December 16, until after the independence celebrations. Security reports stated that his statement had little effect, and continued to stress the ongoing security disturbances in the district.[91]

Early 1964, the Kenyan government reviewed its strategy to deal with the freedom fighters, turning away from generalized repression, useless promises and attempts to disrupt the movement. Kenyatta opposed the creation of camps for political reasons. "He felt," the inspector general of police R. C. Catling reported, "that for the Government to confine the 'forest people' in a camp or camps would bring upon Government the charge that they were just as heartless and indifferent to the 'Freedom Fighters' as previous governments."[92] The delegitimization and dispersion of any tentative groupings of former forest fighters was the government's preferred strategy.[93] The

[86] Ibid. [87] Ciorukunga M'Kithumai, interview.
[88] Grouped interview with Mwariama's followers: Simon Mtoruru John, Ciahampiu M'Munyi, Ciokirichiu M'Mutime, Ciorukunga M'Kithumai, Paulina Mwamunju M'Ndewa, Mgiliki M'Mumya, and Mukoiti M'Mukindia, October 22, 2015, Muthara, Meru.
[89] Kiburu Marete, interview. [90] M'Murungi M'Kobia, interview.
[91] *East African Standard*, "Warning to Forest 'Troops'. Law Breakers Will Be Prosecuted," January 9, 1964, 1; Secret. RGA Meru to Civil Secretary Eastern Region, February 10, 1964, KNA, BB/1/149.
[92] R. C. Catling, "Note," February 20, 1964, KNA, BB/1/149.
[93] *Daily Nation*, "Group Wanted Prime Minister as Patron," November 25, 1963, 16; "Minister Attacks Ex-Detainee Body," November 27, 1963, 24; "Ex-Detainee Association Changes Names," December 4, 1963, 2.

Breaking the Last of the Mau Mau 161

systematic prosecution of resilient fighters favored by Kenyatta was judged to be "unlikely to bear fruits" by the police inspector and by British administrators, because of the police's insufficient means to track and arrest all forest people.[94] Rather, they encouraged a legal solution: that of offering surrender terms, while firmly believing that Kenyatta's visit "only ... could influence any meeting of these Forest men."[95] However, Kenyatta continued to delegate the negotiations with the fighters. It was decided that "all the affairs of the 'Freedom Fighters' shall be dealt exclusively by the *Ministry of Home Affairs*."[96] Besides, forests fighters would "no longer be treated with by the Government as a group or groups."[97] Any attempt by former Mau Mau to advance their claims for land was dispersed and ignored.[98] A few eventually joined the army, responding to the government advertisements.[99] Their leaders were dealt with individually by different prominent figures of the Kenyan government, these interviews being sporadically reported in newspapers.

Dispersing the forest camps was difficult, however, as freedom fighters refused to cooperate, while the government knew it had limited options to convince them. The Kenyan government concluded that strong police action was needed, but knew that this would not be a sustainable solution, since a dispersed camp would automatically reform in a different location.[100] As the permanent secretary for the Ministry of Internal Security and Defense wrote to the attorney general and Kenyatta's close collaborator Charles Njonjo, government officers

---

[94] J. M. Oswald to P. E. Walters, February 24, 1964, KNA, BB/1/149. The debates over the police lack of means dates back to 1963, see Secret. RGA Meru to Civil Secretary Easter Region, August 30, 1963, KNA, BB/1/149.
[95] Secret. P. E. Walters to Permanent Secretary Minister of Home Affairs and Defense, February 11, 1964, KNA, BB/1/149.
[96] Emphasis in the original. Secret. Civil Secretary, Eastern Region to Permanent Secretary, Ministry of Home Affairs, "Proposals for Dealing with the Security Situation in the Meru District of Eastern Region, Arising from the Activities of Forest Fighters," February 6, 1964, KNA, BB/1/149.
[97] Ibid.
[98] *East African Standard*, "Moves to Unite by Fighters," January 21, 1964, 5.
[99] *East African Standard*, "30 Meru Youths Join the Army," March 13, 1964, 17.
[100] Secret. Civil Secretary Eastern Region to Permanent Secretary, Ministry of Home Affairs, "Proposals for Dealing with the Security Situation in the Meru District of Eastern Region, Arising from the Activities of Forest Fighters," February 6, 1964, KNA, BB/1/149.

doubted that legal solutions such as amnesty would suffice.[101] On February 18, Kenyatta gave his personal consent for a plan to disperse the Mau Mau forest camps, and signed restriction orders against some local politicians suspected of encouraging Mau Mau resilience.[102] A few days later, General Baimungi was arrested "for allegedly trespassing on a farm in Timau in Nyanyuki area."[103] Mwariama was also arrested, on charges that included "holding unlawful meeting and obstructing the police."[104] Released on bond the following day, he was arrested again for failing to appear in court. Whether these arrests were planned and organized by the highest circles of authority in Nairobi is unclear. At least, they took the British administrators by surprise. The latter commented that "[t]hese may well precipitate something."[105] According to Ciorukunga M'Kithumai, Mwariama was jailed after "some women came dancing praising Mwariama. But they were talking bad about the Kenyatta government."[106] A simple gathering would have triggered his arrest.

The Kenya government used Field Marshal Mwariama to tip the balance of negotiations in its favor, but kept quiet about the new strategy, giving only vague orders to local administrators. The government probably took the opportunity of Mwariama's arrest to bargain his release on the condition that he would personally support and promote the government's policy. Mwariama was portrayed in the newspapers as a more moderate leader, causing less trouble in the Meru district and condemning, in his speech, hatred, revenge, and brutality.[107] No Kenyan document tracing the chain of decision-making has been found. This was an "unavoidable" "switch of plan" leaving the local administrators largely uninformed of the ongoing discussion.[108] The British were nonetheless convinced that a deal had

[101] Secret. Regional Government Agent, Meru to Civil Secretary Eastern Region, "Freedom Fighters," February 10, 1964; J. Gethin (Permanent Secretary to the Ministry of Internal Security and Defense) to C. Njonjo, February 18, 1964, KNA, BB/1/149.
[102] Secret. R. C. Catling, "Note," February 20, 1964, KNA, BB/1/149.
[103] *East African Standard*, "Former Mau Mau Leaders Arrested," February 29, 1964, 1.
[104] Ibid.   [105] Confidential. J. M. Oswald to P. E. Walters, February 24, 1964.
[106] Ciorukunga M'Kithumai, interview.
[107] *East African Standard*, "Actions of Forest Fighters Condemned," January 8, 1964, 1.
[108] Confidential. P. E. Walters to the Permanent Secretary, Ministry for Home Affairs (for attention Mr. Kiereini), March 18, 1964; Secret. Regional

Breaking the Last of the Mau Mau 163

been struck, as Mwariama, "jailed for five years by a Meru magistrate, was released by the Government, without any announcement, and his prison sentence was rescinded."[109] During a meeting held in the Ministry of Home Affairs, the permanent secretary to the Ministry of Defense refused to comment on Mwariama, but Waiyaki added that he was released "so that he can go back to the Freedom Fighters against Baimungi."[110] P. E. Walters, civil secretary for the Eastern region, subsequently instructed the regional government agent for Meru, James Mburu, that

> you may *not* indicate to anybody that Mwariama has or has not obtained his release from prison by means of bargain with the government. He has obtained his pardon under provisions of the Independence Constitution of Kenya which accord this prerogative to His Excellency the Governor General. These are the facts to which you should give publicity.[111]

In the same letter, Walters requested that Mwariama receive assistance "to prosecute his personal propaganda campaign to persuade as many ex-forest fighters as possible to support the government."[112] The campaign was to be further "supported by a 'leaflet war'" and Mwariama's speeches widely broadcast over the radio "and regularly reported to Kenyatta."[113] The leaflets were to be dropped in specific locations, but were, in fact, never provided.

The government was entering the "second phase" of the strategy to disperse and silence the Mau Mau: the co-optation of their leaders, enforced by arrests of those who would not cooperate.[114] Mwariama was used as an intermediary with leaders unwilling to cooperate or

---

Government Agent Meru to Civil Secretary Eastern Region, April 6, 1964, KNA, BB/1/149.

[109] Confidential. From C. H. Imray to R. M. Tesh, May 22, 1964, BNA, DO 213/37.

[110] Secret. Notes of a Meeting Held in the Office of the Permanent Secretary, Ministry of Home Affairs on April 15, 1964 to Consider Methods of Dealing with Meru Freedom Fighters, KNA, BB/1/149.

[111] Secret. P. E. Walter to Regional Government Agent Meru, "Meru Forest Fighters," April 20, 1964, KNA, BB/1/149.

[112] Ibid.

[113] Ibid.; Secret. Notes of a Meeting Held in the Office of the Permanent Secretary, Ministry of Home Affairs on April 15, 1964 to Consider Methods of Dealing with Meru Freedom Fighters; RGA Meru to Civil Secretary Eastern Region, April 28, 1964, KNA, BB/1/149.

[114] Ibid.

negotiate, and was logistically supported by James Mburu, who "[used his] gifts and rewards vote for this exercise."[115] Mburu himself deemed the support he received insufficient, and he requested "additional funds as my one line vote is in red."[116] He found Mwariama's help "very useful," although he admitted that the latter "has not been very free with Administrative Officers and Police."[117] Mwariama was in regular contact with Kenyatta's office. But Mburu confessed he himself knew "very little of what goes on," while this absence of information allegedly made Mwariama "suffer from superiority complex, and it may be difficult to handle him later."[118]

Mwariama and some other generals were also allocated plots of land in Timau, a small location in the Meru district. Although specially selected for ex-freedom fighters, settlement in Timau was planned in totally disorganized haste, as the plot "was not in fact ready to receive settlers" and, "moreover the area [was] *only* suitable for use on ranching co-operative lines and certainly not for individual plots peasant subsistence agriculture [sic]."[119] The disorganization resulted from a conflict between the local Settlement Committee, which had been "formed very quickly" by Mburu and which refused to select freedom fighters on the grounds that the government did not consult the committee, and thereby reduced it to acting as a mere "rubber-stamp." This would be a recurrent issue throughout the country, as local committees in charge of settlement would often refuse to settle former freedom fighters, in order to demonstrate their authority. Eight plots of land were nonetheless allocated to Mwariama and some of his followers.[120]

A symbolic propaganda accompanied collaboration politics, subtly associating Kenyatta with the Mau Mau struggle for independence. Parallel to his denunciation of the Mau Mau "disease" (a phrase regularly used by his ministers and broadcast in the news) Kenyatta

[115] Confidential. Regional Government Agent Meru to Civil Secretary Easter Region, "Meru Forest Fighters," April 28, 1964, KNA, BB/1/149.
[116] Ibid.
[117] Secret. Regional Government Agent Meru to Civil Secretary Eastern Region, "Security Position," May 28, 1964, KNA, BB/1/149.
[118] Ibid.
[119] Confidential. P. E. Walters to the Permanent Secretary, Ministry of Home Affairs and the Permanent Secrety, Ministry of Internal Security and Defence, "Meru Forest Fighters," May 6, 1964, KNA, BB/1/149.
[120] Secret. P. E. Walters to Permanent Secretary, Ministry of Home Affairs, "The Security Situation in Meru," June 1, 1964, KNA, BB/1/149.

took great care to maintain the ambiguity surrounding his old reputation as the man the British had believed to be leader to death and darkness, and had put in jail.[121] In July 1964, rumors starting during debates in the senate, and circulated in the press, that Kenyatta was afraid of visiting the Meru district "because of the danger of the Freedom Fighters."[122] The rumor was promptly refuted, and the prime minister's visit to the district was announced – his first visit since taking office.

A month later, Kenyatta made carefully staged visits to Embu and Meru. He was, as the headline of the *East African Standard* had it, warmly welcomed in Embu.[123] The whole visit was turned into a ceremony celebrating Kenyatta as an "Uhuru" hero, an honor closely associated with Mau Mau symbolism. An "uhuru monument" was erected by the Embu Uhuru Celebration Committee, and dedicated to "the first great hero of the Kenya nation, Mr. Jomo Kenyatta, and also to all the people who suffered in the fight for freedom."[124] A Swahili inscription restated Kenyatta's traditional vow to eradicate poverty, ignorance, and disease.[125] Kenyatta thanked the Embu district authorities in a speech emphasizing that "the monument is aptly dedicated to the people who gave the lie to the saying that Africans could not defeat the strong colonialists. Independence is now no longer a myth; we have won it, so let us defend it and build the Kenya nation." Newspapers concluded that "Everywhere he stopped Mr Kenyatta urged the people to obey the laws of the land and work hard in the interest of nation-building."[126] When touring Meru a few days later, Kenyatta picked up on the government's campaign of collaboration politics, accusing the forest fighters who did not surrender, of "spoiling Meru's reputation," yet praising Mwariama for his cooperation with the government, and concluded by announcing some forthcoming financial donations to develop the district.[127] He then condemned Baimungi's followers who "had refused to work for their living and had returned to the

---

[121] See Kenyatta, *Suffering without Bitterness*, 52, 189.
[122] *East African Standard*, "Freedom Fighters under Control Senate Assured," July 29, 1964, 3.
[123] *East African Standard*, "Embu Gives Warm Welcome to Mr. Kenyatta," August 22, 1964, 5.
[124] Ibid.   [125] Ibid.   [126] Ibid.
[127] *East African Standard*, "Forest Men 'Spoil Uhuru' Meru's Reputation Marred Says Premier," August 24, 1964, 1.

forest so that they could live on other people through robbery and intimidation."[128]

As always, Kenyatta's strong words against resilient Mau Mau fighters were matched with ambiguous actions. After his visit to Embu, the regional government agent and chairman of Embu Urban District Council announced that a street was to be renamed after Kenyatta, and one after "'General' Kubu Kubu a freedom fighter who is alleged to have been burned to death after being captured by security forces during emergency."[129] The celebration of Kenyatta Day in October provided another occasion for even more symbolic politics and grandiose celebrations of Kenyatta as a hero and father of the nation. Prayers were also organized throughout the country to honor the then prime minister. A "country-wide campaign for blood donation, to symbolise the sacrifices made during the struggle for Uhuru" was organized by the minister for health and housing and Kenyatta's personal physician, Dr. Njoroge Mungai.[130] Perhaps even more symbolically significant, Kenyatta shared the podium with his five codetainees from Lodwar: Kungu Karumba, Paul Ngei, Bildad Kaggia, Achieng Oneko (now minister for information, broadcasting, and tourism), and Fred Kubai (permanent secretary to the minister of labor and social services).[131] He finally announced the release of eighty-two "people serving sentences for administering or taking illegal oaths."[132]

Baimungi's Last Days

Baimungi's refusal to surrender remained an embarrassing sign of defiance the government could not tolerate indefinitely. His resilience risked strengthening the voice of the populist opposition demanding land redistribution. After splitting from Mwariama, Baimungi visited

---

[128] Ibid.
[129] *East African Standard*, "Embu Street to Be Named for Premier," September 9, 1964, 5.
[130] *East African Standard*, "Kenya Prays for Prime Minister," October 19, 1964, 1; "Day of Jubilation for Kenyatta Nationwide Homage to Mr. Kenyatta," October 20, 1964, 1.
[131] *East African Standard*, "Former Detainees on Premier's Platform," October 21, 1964, 3.
[132] *East African Standard*, "Freedom for 82 Marks Kenya's Day of Joy," October 21, 1964, 5.

Kenyatta in Gatundu, where he was symbolically given several Kenyan flags.[133] Unlike Mwariama – who later confessed to Maina wa Kinyatti that poverty and his concern for the Mau Mau's welfare in the independent country obliged him to collaborate with Kenyatta's cabinet – Baimungi remained uncompromising. So he was portrayed by administrators: "he is not prepared to co-operate and he knows what he is doing. He knows Government's intention but he still stubbonly [sic] refuses to listen to any appeal and see the Government request. In simple terms he is not a person to compromise or reconcile."[134] Baimungi demanded that land be given to Mau Mau fighters, and considered the government's failure to do so as treason.[135] By September 1964, most of the other freedom fighter groups were described as having been "almost broken up" by repeated police actions and government's propaganda; Baimungi, however, kept active, although his activities were, as the regional government agent reassuringly put it, "reduced."[136]

Baimungi's affront escalated into a personal clash with Kenyatta. According to Kinyatti, his refusal to compromise aroused Kenyatta's ire, the latter coming to the inescapable conclusion that the country could not bear "two heads of state."[137] Kenyatta was particularly annoyed at Baimungi's public display of the Kenyan independence flag he himself had given to the fighters.[138] A showdown ensued between the government and Baimungi over this symbol of authority. Mburu reported that he had warned Baimungi not to attempt to question the government's authority, and that the government might "[become] annoyed and [decide] to remove the flag by force."[139] In spite of a verbal commitment, Baimungi did not lower the flag. Instead, he "threatened to confiscate all the flags now being hoisted at

---

[133] Kiburu Marete and M'Murungi M'Kobia, interviews. See also Kinyatti, *History of Resistance in Kenya (1884–2002)*, chapter 8.
[134] Confidential. Regional Government Agent Meru to Civil Secretary, Eastern Region, April 28, 1964, KNA, BB/1/149.
[135] M'Murungi M'Kobia, interview with the author.
[136] Confidential. Regional Government Agent Meru to Civil Secretary Eastern Region, September 10, 1964, KNA, BB/1/149.
[137] Kinyatti, *History of Resistance in Kenya (1884–2002)*, 365–366.
[138] *Daily Nation*, "Out of Hiding after 10 Years," December 9, 1963, 1.
[139] Confidential. RGA Meru to Civil Secretary Eastern Region, April 28, 1964, KNA, BB/1/149.

Government Headquarters in demonstration that is much more powerful than Government."[140] A police operation was launched late April to remove the flag. It was unsuccessful. Although the police encountered little resistance at Baimungi's largely deserted camp, they opened fire and were subsequently caught in a clash with another forest fighters' camp, causing "three deaths and a number of wounded."[141] As for the flag, "One of Baimungi's followers at scene pulled down the flag hurriedly and ran away with it into Mount Kenya Forest."[142]

The perceived deterioration of the security situation in Meru linked to Baimungi's persisting resistance ended with an arrest warrant against Baimungi in April 1964, signaling that more radical action was under way. It was not even a month after that Waiyaki revealed the government had released Mwariama to play him off against Baimungi, and, suddenly, perhaps unavoidably, switched its plans. In May, Baimungi and Chui were believed to be the most dangerous leaders, as Mburu wrote:

I am inclined to believe that [Baimungi] is not the same. He has all along been the greatest friend of Mr. J. H. Angaine. He could have listened to his advice ... He takes orders from his fellow criminal "General Chui". "Chui" undoubtedly is as dangerous as a wounded leopard. I hold the opinion that without Chui Baimungi could not be.[143]

In January, plans for an operation against the forest leader were considered, but the government was persuaded to postpone them because an increasing number of Forest fighters surrendered. Some of Baimungi's followers had already surrendered voluntarily, although most had been threatened by government authorities not to return to

---

[140] Ibid.
[141] Confidential. P. E. Walters to Permanent Secretary, Ministry of Home Affairs and Permanent Secretary, Ministry of Internal Security and Defense, May 6, 1964, KNA, BB/1/149. This version was confirmed in both interviews with Kiburu Marete and M'Murungi M'Kobia.
[142] Confidential. RGA Meru to Civil Secretary Eastern Region, May 7, 1964, KNA, BB/1/149.
[143] "Chui" means "leopard" in Swahili. Secret. RGA Meru to Civil Secretary Eastern Region, May 28, 1964, KNA, BB/1/149. It must be noted that this is one of the few documents where Jackson Angaine's name appears and is related to the government's correspondence over Baimungi and his followers.

Baimungi's Last Days 169

the forest and thus "were forced not to go back."[144] Few were present (around twelve people) the day Baimungi's camp was raided by the police.[145]

On January 26, 1965, Baimungi and Chui were both "killed by police in a dawn swoop on the forest," which the government was at pains to justify.[146] Five of their followers were killed alongside them, while the rest were taken to Kamithi prison, where some, like M'Murungi M'Kobia, would stay for five years.[147] Njoroge Mungai, the minister of defence, explained with blunt vocabulary reminiscent of earlier anti-Mau Mau propaganda that "All the forest outlaws were warned earlier ... that 'stern action' was planned on outlaws who ignored the Jamhuri amnesty offered by President Kenyatta."[148] The president's office issued a statement two days later through the newspapers justifying the police operation on the grounds that it "followed a fresh wave of intimidation, terrorism and cattle thefts in the Meru district."[149] In an attempt to delegitimize Baimungi, the government argued that the resilient fighters demanded "rewards ... such as land, high offices in Government and commissions in the Army."[150] They pressured the local inhabitants to supply them with food, and thereby forced the government to protect the terrorized population. The article concluded with Kenyatta's latest speech at Jamhuri Kiagutu secondary school "[warning] people against spreading rumours that there was no need to purchase land as free land would be provided."[151]

Kenyatta's direct implication in Baimungi's and Chui's deaths will probably never be proved or disproved. Orders to disperse Baimungi's camp and eventually to arrest the "General" did, however, come from the highest echelons of the government:

President's view that [forest fighters] are dispersed and sent to their homes without further delay and their long hair cut short. This view had been taken

---

[144] Interview with M'Murungi M'Kobia.   [145] Ibid.
[146] *Daily Nation*, "Baimungi Killed in Forest," January 27, 1965, 1.
[147] Kiburu Marete and M'Murungi M'Kobia, interviews.
[148] Ibid. On anti-Mau Mau propaganda during the Emergency, see Klose, *Human Rights in the Shadow of Colonial Violence*; Myles Osborne, "'The Rooting Out of Mau Mau from the Minds of the Kikuyu Is a Formidable Task': Propaganda and the Mau Mau War," *Journal of African History* 56, no. 1 (2015): 77–97.
[149] *Daily Nation*, "Baimungi Had Gone Back to Old Ways," January 28, 1965, 1.
[150] Ibid.   [151] Ibid.

owing to the failure by the forest outlaws to keep to their promise to get one of their leaders, Baimungi, out of the forest and to disperse to their homes within two weeks.[152]

The order, vague in its formulation, was transmitted informally to the top ranks of the administration, via the provincial commissioner of the Eastern province, Eliud Mahihu.

Protecting Kenyatta's political integrity was part and parcel of the government's policy. In an emergency meeting on January 23, gathering the provincial and district commissioners from Central and Eastern regions, as well as the respective provincial commissioners of police, Mahihu explained that they had been instructed to discuss and decide among themselves the appropriate method to disperse different forest outlaw camps around the Mount Kenya Forest. He concluded by "[warning] ... that whatever method was decided upon, care must be taken not to expose the President to political criticism."[153] To the "officers [who] generally criticised the lack of a written Government order to disperse forest outlaws," Mahihu "confirmed that the instructions he received were clear and left no doubt as to what line of action to be taken."[154] Mahihu later wrote to Duncan Ndegwa, permanent secretary to the Office of the President, that "[he wished] to explain in greater detail what exactly happened on the nights of 25th and 26th January, 1965" but specifically avoided doing so, arguing that Ndegwa had already taken note of their previous conversation.[155] Although he reported the two operations carried out on January 25 first, he did not comment on the operation of the 26th in which Baimungi and Chui were killed. He simply requested whether the president would have any message at all to be passed on during the forthcoming *barazas* organised throughout the district to "clear the air about the situation in Meru."[156]

---

[152] Secret. Note of the Emergency Meeting Held at the Provincial Police Headquarters Nyeri, January 23, 1965, KNA, BB/12/48.
[153] Ibid.   [154] Ibid.
[155] Secret. From Eliud Mahihu to Duncan Ndegwa, January 30, 1965, KNA, BB/1/48.
[156] Ibid.

The Aftermath: Kenyatta, Mau Mau Bodyguards, and Loyalist Government

The media soon forgot both Baimungi and Chui. As for public debate, a proposed question in May 1965 by the Kericho MP C. Kiprotich, relating to the "Treatment of Field Marshal Baimungi" was dismissed.[157] The forest leaders' names were not mentioned in the House until 2008, when Mau Mau veterans, suing the British government with accusations of torture during the Mau Mau war, opened a court case.[158]

This seeming amnesia shows that the large majority of the postindependence Kenyan elite took no interest (and had none) in the Mau Mau question. The shared silence highlights the legacy of the politics of cooperation that brought a loyalist class to power, as Daniel Branch has shown in great detail.[159] Yet, a loyalist establishment would not have sufficed to durably stifle Mau Mau agitation. It was only one ingredient in a wider strategy against residual Mau Mau alongside repression and co-optation. The available and declassified public records also tend to signal the British authorities' lack of concern over the repression of forest fighters. Out of the Commonwealth and Foreign Relations Office security files covering the period from 1964 to 1966 only two documents mentioned the Kenya government operation against Baimungi, whose name was variously misspelled on both occasions: "Barmangai" and "Barnamungai."[160]

More importantly, however, silencing, but not totally forgetting, the Mau Mau appears to have been the main goal of the Kenyan government's strategy. At no point did the government engage in a policy of total eradication of all Mau Mau fighters. It was determined, rather, to crush the Mau Mau as a *movement*, by disorganizing and atomizing its elements. Hence the government's repeated assertions that it "does not recognise the Freedom Fighters as a certain group of people. All who

---

[157] Kenya National Assembly (Hansard), May 7, 1965, "Questions Withdrawn, Disallowed or Dropped," cols. 2222–2223.
[158] Kenya National Assembly (Hansard), Wednesday October 8, 2008, "Demonstration of Appreciation to Mau Mau Veterans by Government," cols. 2549–2568.
[159] See Branch, *Defeating Mau Mau, Creating Kenya*.
[160] Secret. Defense Adviser Nairobi to MOD Army, January 11, 1965; Cypher, DDDSYE015, Priority 180820Z, Defense Adviser Nairobi to MOD Army, BNA, DO 213/159.

over past 70 years have suffered in the case of Kenya's freedom are freedom fighters."[161] This statement was meant to preserve Kenyatta's ambiguity regarding the Mau Mau movement, as his legitimacy to command authority from the whole Kikuyu tribe relied on his ability to be a Mau Mau and an anti-Mau Mau at the same time.

These observations do not explain what prevented a post-Mau Mau movement from reconstructing itself politically, given that the landless and squatters remained a painful reminder of the pending land issue. Postindependence Mau Mau history was not one of guerilla-like underground subversion – this may even explain why the Mau Mau question disappeared so suddenly from intelligence and security records, whether Kenyan or British. An easy answer would be that, as mentioned earlier, freedom fighters did not seek to overthrow the independent government, which they at first firmly believed to be headed by a friend of Mau Mau: Jomo Kenyatta.[162] Even today, Kenyatta's ambiguity persists. Although Kaggia declared and wrote in his autobiography that Kenyatta did not know about any Mau Mau business, many former Mau Mau fighters still believe that the latter "was the owner of Mau Mau," although he betrayed them after independence.[163] This seeming credulity of the people should not overshadow the fact that the Mau Mau was a secret society bound by powerful oaths, which may also explain the difficulty in bringing the issue into the open, even until today.

The power of the Mau Mau oath seems all the more relevant when we observe that Kenyatta's official discourse of national amnesia was subtly contradicted by the carefully chosen nominations of former Mau Mau leaders or followers to top positions within the state institutions. These nominations further enhanced his ambiguity relating to the Mau Mau, as it could possibly be deduced that Kenyatta too was bound by the oath of secrecy.[164] Jackson Angaine is one example, as is

---

[161] *Daily Nation*, "Government Is Urged to Honour Freedom Fighters," April 9, 1965, 4.

[162] Kiburu Marete and M'Murungi M'Kobia, interviews; Gitu wa Kahengeri (former Mau Mau from Central province and chairman of the Mau Mau War Veterans Association), interview, September 28, 2015, Nairobi.

[163] Kiburu Marete, M'Murungi M'Kobia, and Gitu wa Kahengeri, interviews; grouped interview with Mwariama's followers: Simon Mtoruru John, Ciahampiu M'Munyi, Ciokirichiu M'Mutime, Ciorukunga M'Kithumai, Paulina Mwamunju M'Ndewa, Mgiliki M'Mumya, and Mukoiti M'Mukindia.

[164] Maina Macharia, interview, May 15, 2014.

Paul Ngei, arrested with Kenyatta in 1952 and promptly co-opted at independence.[165] Even more significantly, when, in 1966, ex-freedom fighters were reported to be conducting sacrificial ceremonies, Kenyatta argued that "perhaps if we allowed them to do so under our supervision this may help to let off steam, and finally the emotion would cool down."[166] Hence, his constant plea to "forgive and forget the past" was not really about collective amnesia, for he knew very well that the Mau Mau could, but also should not, be forgotten.

Kenyatta's role during these early months of independence is not only symptomatic of his relationship to the Mau Mau movement, but perhaps even of his way of ruling in general. His use of cabinet ministers as intermediaries, whom he always met informally, would remain an enduring feature of his rule, making harder the task of tracing the chain of orders to the ultimate decision-maker. Perhaps more importantly, this use of intermediaries was only episodic. Baimungi's death in January 1965 put an end to Kenyatta's personal commitment to the fate of the forest fighters. In sharp contrast to past presidential preferential treatment of ex-Mau Mau leaders, neglect and distance followed.

After the operation against Baimungi and Chui, now that their leadership and power of organization was significantly diminished, Kenyan ministers lost interest in the forest fighters' cause. Former Mau Mau did not meet Kenyatta any more.[167] Any effort to provide sufficient means (mostly financial) to co-opt the remaining fighters was judged pointless, and became a residual matter left in the hands of powerless provincial administrators. Eliud Mahihu's repeated attempts, as early as March 1965, to obtain funding and support from the Office of the President remained in vain.[168] Mahihu, provincial commissioner for Eastern region, was convinced "that the help [to Mau Mau leaders] would go a long way in making their life a bit easier at the present moment," but was forced to admit that the district had "no spare funds" and that it would indeed probably be "'broke' in May this year."[169] He worried that Bildad Kaggia would exploit this

---

[165] See Grignon, "Le Politicien Entrepreneur en son Terroir."
[166] Confidential. Minutes of Provincial Commissioner's Meeting Held on February 15 and 16, 1966, KNA, BB/49/59.
[167] M'Murungi M'Kobia, interview.
[168] Secret. Eliud Mahihu to Duncan Ndegwa, March 11, 1964, KNA, BB/1/158.
[169] Ibid.

potential vacuum, rewarding the freedom fighters with his communist funds: Kaggia was, he wrote to Kenyatta's permanent secretary, Duncan Ndegwa, earlier on,

> trying to gain political survival, which he has lost tremendously since the death of Baimungi and I am convinced that he will do everything in his power to get these Forest Outlaws together and he is also trying to persuade the African Independent churches to be behind him. He has promised to give Shs.70,000/- to build a school at Kirua.[170]

Although Mahihu was well informed, his fears did not spark much reaction from the government.

Intelligence services too alerted the government to the undesirable alliance between the few still resilient freedom fighters and the government's political opponents like Kaggia and, to a lesser extent, Oginga Odinga. Kaggia was secretly visiting Mau Mau fighters in Meru, just as other Meru politicians (among them Senator Julius Muthamia and the MPs Jenaru Gituma, Stanley Lamare, and Abraham Gaciatta) tried to provide individual help and assistance to former, and often landless, fighters.[171] The main question remained that of (free) distribution of land. Several intelligence reports in 1965 concluded that Kaggia had attempted to "make full use of discontented Kikuyu ex-Freedom Fighters to further his political ambitions."[172] His actions were not just limited to the Meru district, as he made contacts with leaders from Murang'a and Nyeri, as well as from the Rift Valley.[173] In the same letter he addressed to Ndegwa, Mahihu requested that Kenyatta intervene personally to heal the political rifts in Eastern region in particular, where Ngei's former African People's Party remained active.[174] These appeals were ignored.

---

[170] Secret. Eliud Mahihu to Duncan Ndegwa, March 5, 1965, KNA, BB/1/158.
[171] Kiburu Marete, interview.
[172] Secret. Special Branch Weekly Intelligence Report for the Period May 18–24, 1965, May 27, 1965; see also Secret. Special Branch Weekly Intelligence Report for the Period March 2–8, 1965, March 12, 1965, KNA, BB/1/158. See Branch, *Defeating Mau Mau, Creating Kenya*, 191–207 for further detail on Kaggia's protests and the land issue.
[173] Secret. Special Branch Weekly Intelligence Report for the Period June 1–7, 1965, June 10, 1965, KNA, BB/1/158.
[174] Secret. Eliud Mahihu to Duncan Ndegwa, "Security Assessment in the Eastern Province," March 5, 1965, KNA, BB/1/158.

Although the Mau Mau movement remained an illegal organization, the government made a strategic use of Mau Mau veterans as personal bodyguards. *De jure*, gatherings of Mau Mau were forbidden, thus making the political reconstruction of the movement impossible. Surprisingly perhaps, the movement was banned and its supporters considered as outlaws and terrorists until 2003, when the Mwai Kibaki government lifted the ban of Mau Mau as an organization, opening a new, although no less tortuous, avenue for the telling of Mau Mau history.[175] On the ground, however, selected Mau Mau were employed as personal bodyguards for prominent ministers, and even for Kenyatta himself. His personal escort, entirely constituted of Kikuyu, gave prominent responsibility to former Mau Mau, such as Arthur Wanyoike Thung'u, his personal bodyguard.[176] As his permanent secretary, Duncan Ndegwa, recalled in his autobiography, this "provided constant, tangible reminders to Kenyatta's detractors that he still had Mau Mau links. It was no accident that the National Youth Service, a stabilising force that he could summon to back up forces loyal to him, was led by Waruhiu Itote, a former Mau Mau leader."[177] Thung'u was also known to the police for excesses that continued to stir up concern among the British officials who remained in charge of the escort training until the 1970s.[178] Commander Pearson, in charge of the escort, was said to believe that Kenyatta himself was

---

[175] On Kibaki and the new wave of Mau Mau history, see Daniel Branch, "The Search for the Remains of Dedan Kimathi: The Politics of Death and Memorialisation in Post-Colonial Kenya," *Past & Present* 206, no. 5 (2010): 301–320; Annie E. Coombes, "Monumental Histories: Commemorating Mau Mau with the Statue of Dedan Kimathi," *African Studies* 70, no. 2 (2011): 202–223; Lotte Hughes, "'Truth Be Told': Some Problems with Historical Revisionism in Kenya," *African Studies* 70, no. 2 (2011): 182–201. On the Mau Mau trial that subsequently opened in 2011, see David Anderson, "Mau Mau in the High Court and the 'Lost' British Empire Archives: Colonial Conspiracy or Bureaucratic Bungle?" *The Journal of Imperial and Commonwealth History* 39, no. 5 (2011): 699–716.
[176] Thungu is mentioned in Kaggia, *Roots of Freedom, 1921–1963*. The information has also been confirmed by Maina Macharia, interviews on May 5 and 15, 2014. Thungu was later accused of the killing of J. M. Kariuki in 1975, see Linus Kaikai, "When Kenyatta and Jaramogi Were Caught Up in Cold War Intrigues," *Daily Nation*, December 14, 2013.
[177] Ndegwa, *Walking in Kenyatta Struggles*, 275.
[178] Confidential. R. M. Purcell to T. J. Bellers, December 17, 1970; Confidential. T. J. Bellers to R. M. Purcell, December 29, 1970, BNA, FCO 31/597.

encouraging excessive violent behavior, leaving Pearson with the responsibility of "disciplin[ing] them."[179]

A British report on the presidential escort in 1972 pointed at Kenyatta's persisting concern for, and even fear of, remaining Mau Mau. The report gave an account of a private discussion with Isaiah Mathenge, then provincial commissioner for Central province, about Kenyatta's political position. According to the report, the president was

> scared of the Kikuyu have-nots. There were mainly people from mau mau villages who were still without land. He was desperately concerned that they were satisfied... Mathenge said that the President was afraid of driving such groups into the forest where he would lose control over them... The landless ex mau mau were such a group who would be well able to organise themselves from the forest... they would, if driven underground, be poised to assassinate ministers and senior public servants. Although the President himself might seem well guarded he had surrounded himself by ex mau mau toughs. Although now "tamed" they could still present a threat if provoked too far. Hence his desire to appease his own bodyguards by getting them farms.[180]

Such practices were also adopted by Jackson Angaine, who recruited former Mau Mau from his own area, Imenti, perhaps as a way to protect himself but certainly to control the remaining Mau Mau in Meru, and in order to be informed about the former Mau Mau attending his meetings.[181]

The strategy of personal escorts was known to former Mau Mau, who also knew that the entire top governmental functions were held by loyalists.[182] In the words of Gitu wa Kahengeri, former Mau Mau in Central province and today's chairman of the Mau Mau Veterans War Association, the Kenyatta government was made of those who "renegated [sic]" the Mau Mau movement.[183] Most of the prominent members of Kenyatta's government were selected and trained within a colonial administrative system (re)shaped during the Emergency, and part and parcel of the Mau Mau counterinsurgency (a Kenyan

---

[179] Confidential. T. J. Bellers to R. M. Purcell, November 17, 1970, BNA, FCO 31/597.
[180] Confidential. "Mathenge in Kikuyuland" by R. W. Newman, March 7, 1972, BNA, DO 226/11.
[181] Kiburu Marete and M'Murungi M'Kobia, interviews.
[182] According to M'Kobia, these bodyguards were "not real Mau Mau," interview.
[183] Gitu wa Kahengeri, interview.

specificity among the British colonies).[184] Those who were appointed provincial commissioners at independence were trained by T. J. F. Gavaghan, the brain behind the brutal rehabilitation politics during the Mau Mau war and later appointed in 1961 as training officer of the Kenyan provincial administration.[185] By 1965, two top members of the Office of the President were renowned loyalists: Duncan Ndegwa (permanent secretary) and Jeremiah Kiereini (under-secretary in charge of the provincial administration).[186]

***

The violent repression of the Mau Mau during the Emergency is not the sole explanation of why the movement was successfully, and permanently, silenced. Kenyatta's motto "forget and forgive the past" was subtly moderated by the public display of Mau Mau symbols, whether used by Kenyatta himself, by Jackson Angaine, or even by their Mau Mau bodyguards. Once woven together, the repression of resilient Mau Mau elements, the control of local politics in Meru, and the ascension of Jackson Angaine as minister for lands reveal how Kenyatta managed to forge himself a central position within a political machinery that was not just complex, but very much hostile.

---

[184] On the Africanization of the provincial administration, see Branch, *Defeating Mau Mau, Creating Kenya*, 162–174. As Branch noted, the "rapid promotion" of the prominent members of the postindependence administration has remained quite underresearched.

[185] Secret. Extract from Minute 32/60, P.C's Meeting of 27&28.9.60, KNA, BB/1/247. See Terence Gavaghan autobiography, *Of Lions and Dung Beetles* (Ilfracombe: Arthur H. Stockwell, 1999), chapters 20 and 21. See also Elkins, *Britain's Gulag*, chapter 10.

[186] Directory of the Government of the Republic of Kenya (1965), KNA, K.354.6762002. Other prominent loyalists who were trained by Gavaghan and later joined the Kenyatta top administration were P. K. Boit, E. Mahihu, I. Mathenge and J. Musembi (provincial commissioners), J. M. Malinda (director of personnel, Office of the President), P. Shikuyah and G. Gachati (permanent secretaries in the Ministry of Lands), and J. Michuki (Treasury), see "African District Commissioners, Appendix 'A'," KNA, BB/1/247. Interestingly, Keireini, as he wrote in his recently published biography, worked under Gavaghan's supervision as a rehabilitator in Mau Mau camps, and was even promoted by the latter to be in full charge of rehabilitation in the Mwea Camp. Thereafter, he was posted in Meru from 1958 to 1960 as a district officer, where he was in charge of land consolidation in the district. See Kiereini, *A Daunting Journey*, 98.

Kenyatta's and Angaine's political acquaintance served their personal ambitions well. An analysis of the archives shows that, in the early 1960s already, Kenyatta was carefully following Mau Mau agitation in the district, although he always refrained from intervening personally. Instead, he relied on Angaine, whose political prominence in the district was rapidly increasing. By supporting him, Kenyatta proved that he possessed a deep knowledge of Meru history, and had an acute sense on how to protect his interests. The examination of Angaine's early political career shows that, although Kenyatta had a low esteem for Angaine's politics, he anticipated that it was better to appoint a Meru man – and not a Kikuyu who could stand as a potential challenger or expose a penchant for political tribalism – as minister for lands, so as to tame both Njuri Ncheke and the resilient fighters, who posed a risk to undermining his leadership. Although Angaine was himself a powerful leader in Meru, he could compensate for his opposition to Mau Mau and Njuri Ncheke through his direct access to presidential favors, especially when it came to land claims or redistribution. From Kenyatta's perspective, Angaine might have been a useful asset in a potential scheme to acquire parts of Meru land, to fulfill the "grand Kikuyu land unit" that had historically suffered from a tense and complicated relationship between Kikuyu and Meru tribes.

Kenyatta's disregard for the Mau Mau claims can be linked to a much wider issue: his disinterest for a national policy of land redistribution. Kenyatta and his government firmly believed in the productive use of land, thus favoring large-scale settlement over smaller plots and poorer farmers. In order to achieve this, he would have to alloy his public legitimacy, based on his Mau Mau aura, with politics that intrinsically ran against the Mau Mau claims, and, by extension, the landless and poor masses.

6 | Taming Oppositions: Kenyatta's "Secluded" Politics (1964–1966)

Once the disruptive narratives of the liberation struggle were suppressed, Mzee Jomo Kenyatta was left with the challenging task of exercising presidential rule that had not only been hastily constructed, but was built on a very fragile institutional arithmetic. His ascension to power had been partly thanks to the benevolent support of the British authorities and he could not count on stable institutions (either party or parliament) to build his leadership. His decisive commitment to the willing buyer–willing seller policy was running against the main base of his popular support: the landless masses. The first year of independence forced him to attempt to save face not only with the British and white settlers, but also the landless and poor. The challenge was all the more critical as the scope of his presidential powers was still undefined, and his popularity depended on his future achievements.

This chapter explores how Kenyatta eventually succeeded in responding to these contradictory political expectations, and how his nascent presidential rule molded the institutional balance of the Kenyan postcolonial state. It argues that by controlling the funds and distribution of land resources, Kenyatta successfully isolated competing political actors and institutions, thus preventing various political grievances to spill over his government. The chapter first highlights the continuity between colonial and postcolonial land politics, but emphasizes the Kenyan government's agency in politicizing land accumulation. Upon independence, the British agreed to assist the Kenyan state with financial aid for land purchase, and eventually became Kenya's biggest international donor over the decade.[1] The Kenyan government was eager to secure British funds to send powerful signals to landless and squatters expecting Africanization of land ownership. Yet, governmental policies focused mainly on accumulating land and politicizing its redistribution. Throughout the process, Kenyatta was concerned

---

[1] Holtham and Hazlewood, *Aid and Inequality in Kenya*, chapters 3 and 4.

about sensitive land settlement scheme, but preferred to secure political order by marginal and well-timed adjustments, instead of profound reforms to change colonial economic structures and principles. Archival material reveals that he was not necessarily aware of the technical details involved. Far from being a sign of a deficit of authority (and certainly not of intelligence!), he consciously delegated technical aspects of the negotiations to his most loyal cabinet ministers, making his disinterest a hallmark of his rule.

The early politicization of land accumulation was the first step in the establishment of a "secluded" system of rule, as a Kenyan PC aptly described it at the time.[2] When it came to distributing regional powers, Kenyatta successfully strengthened his direct control over both parliament and provincial administration, without assuming the responsibilities such personal commitment involved. Instead, he used the civil administration as a rubber stamp against disgruntled MPs, insuring, at the same time, that civil servants could not become too politicized either. The sterile competition between parliament and civil servants (sterile, since there was virtually no room for them to increase their political sphere influence) further deprived civil society of representation. As the last section of this chapter shows, Kenyatta, despite his fear for discontented landless and squatters, paid very little attention to their needs. He contented himself with the appointment of a special commissioners of squatters, a position soon drowned into the internal competition of state institutions. Kenyatta's lack of familiarity with economic expertise revealed a general strategy of noncommittal politics that enabled him to remain above political battles, and to restrict his interventions to presidential favors and personalized promises. Such an informalization of powers had a great institutional consequence: by establishing a "secluded" state system, Kenyatta managed to neutralize the formation of any competing force against his government, either from within or without.

Kenyatta's "Back to the Land" Campaign

By 1964, Kenyatta's position on the land issue combined his earlier beliefs on land tenure and the long-lasting influence of British colonial

---

[2] Confidential. S. Nyachae to the Permanent Secretary, Office of the President, December 13, 1966, KNA, BB/49/59.

land policies. He feared squatters and landless flocking into abandoned farms, and rejected demands for a free redistribution of land. He was convinced of the need for productive use of land, and preferred the ownership of large plots instead of the subdivision of small holdings. As early as February 1964, Kenyatta discussed with his cabinet ministers the issue of the so-called illegal squatters, viewed by all as a threat to the smooth progression of settlement schemes throughout Kenya. Squatters should not be allowed to occupy land without the owner's consent: as the cabinet feared that the failure to contain squatting could set a precedent for the free allocation of land populist politicians demanded. Squatting could not feature alongside the willing buyer–willing seller policy the president had advocated since his political come back. With his cabinet ministers, Kenyatta considered the possibility to use police forces to remove illegal squatters. Furthermore, to enforce his appeal to take proper care of houses and not leave the land lying idle, Kenyatta ordered that "approximately 100 acres of preservation belt should be demarcated around each house."[3] Thus protected, the houses could be "disposed of either by offering them to individual Africans who can afford to pay for them, or by turning them over to Government Departments."[4]

Kenyatta outlined the main aims of his government land policy in a public speech on September 11, 1964. Although some of these ideas dated back to *Facing Mount Kenya*, they had been readjusted to suit the new independence deal, and still bore the mark of British colonial influence. In his "Back to the Land" speech, he insisted on the "value of land," urging "the people to begin to dirty their hands in the effort of nation building."[5] The speech was strongly colored by his Kikuyu philosophy of land use he exalted in *Facing Mount Kenya*, by his opposition to "radical" politicians, and by his rejection of Mau Mau claims. But Kenyatta also situated his pledge for authenticity within the modern economy of the newly independent country. The ancestral principle of rights to the land could be given juridical value now that Kenya was, he asserted, "governed by the normal pressures of a modern monetary economy."[6] Kenyatta explained that "in order to use our land efficiently and effectively, we must ensure that each farmer

---

[3] Confidential. Sett/pol/7/1/1A/2D, "Illegal Squatters," by Permanent Secretary, KNA, BB/88/20.
[4] Ibid.   [5] Kenyatta, *Suffering without Bitterness*, 232.   [6] Ibid., 233.

is certain of his land rights" and "has the kind of security to give him access to necessary credits and loans from Banks or other Government and private agencies."[7] To do so, he advocated land consolidation (a rationalized planning and distribution of land units) and the registration of land titles (unlike deeds registration, land ownership is entrusted in the land parcels) as the two pillars of the following "Back to the Land Campaign."[8] Priority was given to productive exploitation of land, and consecrated in private and individual ownership.

At a time when security reports systematically emphasized the political and economic sensitivity of all land matters, Kenyatta's stance was evidently influenced both by inherited colonial views of the landless and poor as a source of political instability, and by the unquestioned assumption that a new Kenyan government depended on British funds to buy land. Since 1963, and throughout 1964, worrying security reports alerted both British administrators and Kenyan politicians to the increase of squatters in Central province and the Rift Valley. As previously mentioned in Chapter 4, the Nyandarua district in Central province, where J. M. Kariuki was continuously voicing his opposition to government policies, remained an area of concern. Evaluating the risks, a memorandum drafted by the Ministry for Lands and Settlement warned that increasing numbers of illegal squatters would cause a drop in the "gross cash output" while the settlement holdings would mean owners of the holding could not "meet [their] loan repayment" and "obtain enough income in cash to support [their] family."[9] A political risk was spotted, too, that of the endangered "political faith of the people in the Nyandarua District and in settlement areas in other parts of the country."[10] Economic threats too took a prominent place in the cabinet's correspondences and memoranda. Both the Kenyan government and the British administration remembered the trauma of preindependence economic stagnation, when the uncertain outcomes of the negotiation of independence had led the colonial economy to a stop. Therefore, the fact that land transfer program would be tied to British funds was accepted virtually without any political debate in the KANU or KADU ranks.[11] The Kenyan government was responsible for the recovery of all the loan money spent, including that by the

---

[7] Ibid.   [8] Ibid.
[9] Secret. "Illegal Squatters on Settlement Schemes Holding," Draft Memorandum by the Minister for Lands and Settlements, KNA, BN/88/20.
[10] Ibid.   [11] Leys, *Underdevelopment in Kenya*, 58.

Central Land Bank on land purchase.[12] Preventing a deficit incurred by the failure to repay the loans was at the back of the mind of all cabinet ministers, who hoped to secure more funds to buy out land.[13]

The harmony surrounding the Kenyan–British consensus on land policy and funding was only superficial. The Kenyan government and British administrators did share a common fear of political breakdown shattering their control upon the decolonization process. They also shared a common disinterest for the sake of the landless and squatters, who remained a secondary issue. Nevertheless, diverging interests soon set British administrators against Kenyan cabinet ministers. The former were willing to stop funding settlement schemes they judged inefficient. The latter did not dispute the inefficiency of the schemes but wanted to accumulate land and argued that the landless' fury would be appeased if the government showed willingness to settle them. Kenyatta remained fairly distant from the negotiations and confined his role to general orders. When the growing opposition between British and Kenyan governments reached a deadlock, however, he intervened.

Accumulating Land, Turning Away from Settlement

The practical application of Kenyatta's "Back to the land" speech sparked a difficult correspondence within the Ministry of Lands and Settlement, opposing his closest cabinet ministers to land administrators, who were mostly drawn from the ranks of former colonial administration.[14] The heart of the matter was not a problem of objectives, since all agreed on the evils of the land issue, nor one of solutions, for Kenyatta's policy was not at odd with the proposals of the (colonial) administration. It was simply a matter of how to implement the proposed solutions. In the following paragraphs, I show that the apparent colonial continuity (and dependency) that influenced Kenyatta's stance on land politics must be nuanced in light of his cabinet ministers' agency, who aimed to acquire more land. Only then can we situate

---

[12] File No. CCNST/A/105, June 7, 1963, KNA, BN/82/21.
[13] J. Gichuru to J. Angaine, May 19, 1966; J. Angaine to J. Gichuru, June 14, 1966; P. Shikuyah, Paper no. 175, "Cash Flow of Expended Settlement Scheme," November 17, 1966, KNA, BN/84/7. See also Confidential. J. Gichuru to the Hon. M. MacDonald, February 22, 1966, BNA, DO 214/53.
[14] Deputy Sec. Barr (for P.S.), "Reference Attached Statement by the Prime Minister," September 18, 1964, KNA, BN/81/89.

Kenyatta's leadership within the new state, and understand his mode of operation with his ministers.

Land administrators could easily embrace two central ideas of Kenyatta's speeches, the productive use of land, and the consolidation of land holdings. The objectives of land consolidation and registration were explained in a memorandum entitled "A Project for the Acceleration of the Registration of Titles to Holdings of Trust Land," drafted by the commissioner for lands, J. A. O'Loughlin, and the permanent secretary to the minister of lands and settlement, P. J. Gachati.[15] It stated that "whatever our plans for the future, they must spring from a resolve to put to maximum production the land, however small the acreage our people may possess."[16] It linked the failure to exploit land to its fullest productivity to the "fragmentation of holdings ... owing to the large numbers of tiny widely-scattered fragments" as well as the "lack of defined boundaries and of secure title [which] has acted as a strong deterrent to the utilisation of the whole of any particular holding."[17] Just like Kenyatta's diagnosis and recommendations, the memorandum advised security in tenure of land holding, demarcation of clear boundaries, the need for expert agricultural advice, the extension of the marketing service for the full development of farms, and access to adequate loan capital.

Both land productivity and land consolidation draw a continuous line with the colonial land policy established in the 1950s under the supervision of R. J. M. Swynnerton, which was part of the British counterinsurgency strategy in the Mau Mau war.[18] The memorandum noted that

All this was included in the proposals set out in the Swynnerton Plan for Intensified Development of African Agriculture, but although this plan has been in operation for the past ten years progress in providing secure titles to

---

[15] Trust land refers to government-owned land.
[16] The Cabinet Development Committee, Memorandum by the Minister for Lands and Settlement, Draft, "A Project for the Acceleration of the Registration of Titles to Holdings of Trust Land," KNA, BN/81/89.
[17] Ibid.
[18] On the continuity of the establishment land settlement from the 1950s to the 1960s, see Harbeson, *Nation-Building in Kenya*, 209–211. For an analysis of the Swynnerton plan, see Berman, *Control and Crisis in Colonial Kenya*, 369–371; Simon Coldham, "Land Control in Kenya," *Journal of African Law* 22, no. 1 (1978): 63–77; Branch, *Defeating Mau Mau, Creating Kenya*, 174–178.

clearly demarcated holdings, and the services and loan-finance needed by the farmers has been very slow, mainly owning to the previous Government having been unable to provide adequate funds to implement the plan at a satisfactory pace.[19]

More than continuity even, the memorandum revived a colonial policy on the grounds that it had not been fully implemented. The link between the colony and postcolony lay in the enduring belief that fragmentation of land holdings impaired land productivity, whereas larger holdings would prove less expensive and more productive units.[20] Such belief defined Kenyatta's policy favoring large-scale farming and productivity, to the detriment of smaller and poorer farmers.

Land administrators and Kenyan ministers had diverging long-term interests, however, and differed on the feasibility of the program. With the "Back to the land" campaign, the ministry of lands and settlement wanted to accelerate land consolidation and registration, focusing on priority, and over two to three years, on selected districts of the Eastern, Rift Valley, Nyanza, Western, and Coast regions.[21] The principal land consolidation officer warned, in December 1964, that the scheme might be inhibited by the "lukewarm acceptance of registration" by the people, an obstacle already mentioned in the memorandum, and added that varying degrees of land fragmentation might also slow down the realization of the scheme. All administrators warned ministers against setting up unrealistic and infeasible goals, arguing that it was pointless to hope to "draw a formula covering the whole of Kenya," and that, due to lack of staff and funds, the proposed

---

[19] The Cabinet Development Committee, Memorandum by the Minister for Lands and Settlement, Draft, "A Project for the Acceleration of the Registration of Titles to Holdings of Trust Land," KNA, BN/81/89.
[20] See Kelemen, "The British Labor Party and the Economics of Decolonisation."
[21] The ministry hoped to consolidate 9,000,000 acres over the three years period. A. Davies to D. N. Ndegwa (permanent secretary, Office of the Prime Minister), October 23, 1964, KNA, BN/81/89. The chosen districts were: Machakos, Meru, Kitui, and Embu (Eastern region); Kajiado, Narok, Baringo, Elgeyo, Nandi, and Kericho (Rift Valley); Central Nyanza, South Nyanza, and Kisii (Nyanza); Kakamega, Bungoma, and Busia (Western region); and Taita (Coast region). See R. Giffard, "Increased Speed of Land Consolidation and Registration," October 14, 1964, KNA, BN/81/89.

timetable was untenable.[22] Nevertheless, the draft papers continued to circulate within the ministry, until they were merged into a single memorandum (entitled "A Plan for the Acceleration of Land Consolidation and Registration") with Angaine's name finally appended by the end of December 1964.

Cabinet ministers (James Gichuru, Daniel arap Moi, Jackson Angaine, Tom Mboya, and Julius Kiano) were deaf to the commissioner of land's calls for caution, and defended a vision of land politics that demanded the buying of more land. Meeting in November 1964, they reaffirmed that priority should be given to security of tenure and registration of land titles to accelerate agricultural development. Their main concern was "that at the current rate of progress registration would take approximately 20 years to complete."[23] They identified the same causes of slowness as the commissioner of land – that is, lack of funds, staff, landowners' "un-cooperative attitude," and lack of political support, as well as a lack of coordination between the ministries of lands and agriculture.[24] Their prime concern, however, remained the buying of more land, or, as phrased in their jargon, the "considerable development potential in the old tribal land units," which they hoped to "[exploit] to the fullest possible extent."[25] They also invoked the growth of the agricultural sector as well as job creation in rural areas as justifications. To cope with the slowness of the process, they recommended that more funds be allocated to accelerate land consolidation, and that legal procedures be shortened through an official amendment.

Obsessed with land productivity, the Kenyan government hoped to reduce settlements to take over farms and cut the ground from under the landless – this was clearly expressed by Bruce McKenzie himself:

---

[22] The commissioner of land's deputy wrote: "to date, local opposition has [in the Machakos District] prevented even the pilot scheme set on hand at Kangundo in 1956 from making any progress" and that "in an area such as Taita, where it is generally acknowledged that land consolidation is the only satisfactory solution to the Wataita land problem, the view was, I believe, recently expressed by local Politicians that land consolidation should not be supported." Confidential. F. E. Charnley (for Commissioner of Land) to the Permanent Secretary, Ministry of Land Settlement, November 4, 1964, KNA, BN/81/89.

[23] Secret. Minutes of the Meeting of the Cabinet Sub-Committee Appointed Under Minute 417 Held on November 26, 1964, in the Office of the Minister of Finance, KNA, BN/81/89.

[24] Ibid.   [25] Ibid.

with the Africanization of European areas on its way, "his Government now wished to move away from high density settlement schemes."[26] From 1962, intensive politics of settlement were gradually abandoned, a move much welcomed by the British authorities, who anticipated the limited efficiency of settlement schemes.[27] Nevertheless, the disproportion between the acceleration of land buying and the decrease of settlement alarmed the British administrators, the British government, and their financial advisers. Land administrators were still convinced of the necessity for further land transfer in politically sensitive areas. They wished, however, to maintain a balance between the political necessity of additional land buying, the pursuance of settlement, and the financial sustainability of the schemes and transfers.[28] Already by July 1963, British treasury officers planned to restrict and stagger land purchase until financial balance be achieved in 1965/1966, but stumbled on the Central Land Board's and Kenyan government's opposition, which demanded the full year's program to be executed for political reasons.[29] By the end of 1963, settlement was accelerated, and all land purchases planned for 1963/1964 were about to be settled.[30] In 1964, as internal politics were temporarily pacified, the question of the rate of settlement and the amount of funds to be allocated came up again. Tension arose as the Kenyan government requested further financial aid to buy more land, while the British were more and more concerned with the proper use of their funds.[31]

Settlement had only been a temporary answer to political pressures, as the government prioritized lucrative economic activity over land hunger among the poor and landless. Diverging views between cabinet ministers and land administrators soon disturbed their superficial harmony of interests. In May 1964, cabinet ministers formally asked the

---

[26] Confidential. Kenya Finance. Record of a Meeting with Kenya Government at 3.30 p.m. on March 5, 1964 in the Prime Minister's Office, Nairobi, BNA, DO 214/39.
[27] Wasserman, "Continuity and Counter-Insurgency."
[28] Holtham and Hazlewood, *Aid and Inequality in Kenya*, 81.
[29] W. G. Bristow to M. L. Woods, July 24, 1963, BNA, DO 214/40.
[30] To the Agricultural Settlement Fund Trustees. Report of Officer Administering the Fund, November 28, 1963, KNA, BN/87/26.
[31] The 1963–1964 transition is described by Wasserman, "Continuity and Counter-Insurgency," 142–148.

officer administering the settlement fund, chaired by Gichuru, McKenzie, and Angaine, to remove settlement as a priority "on the grounds that 'the back of settlement has been broken'." This was, according to the officer, "not correct," adding that "next year will see the biggest programme yet."[32] But the government preferred large-scale settlement and was turning away from small, fragmented plots of land. Large-scale cooperatives were also put on hold, with the argument that the "money made available from ... overseas sources ... cannot be used for any purposes other than those which are specified in the various agreements," and cooperative farming was not.[33] The government wanted, in fact, to "take over farms" specifically in politically sensitive regions, and "combat squatting." As with the Ol Kalou area (see Chapter 3), it was recommended that the land "could not be left to the hazard of pure co-operatives ... It was generally felt that to run the units as state farms would lead to difficulties, heavy overheads and the danger of trade union pressures on wages making the units non-viable."[34] This measure targeted populist politicians who were calling for the establishment and development of cooperatives, and thus standing in the way of the government's political and economic aims.[35] The colonial legacy inherent to the Kenya government's land politics was merely a tool to serve the political interests of the governing African elite.

The politics of land settlement became more controversial, and all the more divisive as the Kenyan government's excessive accumulation of land became obvious. In a draft letter to the Central Land Board chairman Richard Turnbull, Sir Saville Garner, from the Commonwealth Office, observed diverging views between the Department of Settlement and the Kenyan government over the end of the Million Acres Scheme.[36] The Kenyan Government was pushing to end high-density settlement but feared that an all too sudden ending of the scheme could have disastrous political consequences. According to

---

[32] Report of the Officer Administering the Settlement Fund, May 26, 1964, KNA, BN/87/26.

[33] J. H. Angaine, "Co-Operative Farming in Settlement Schemes," June 30, 1964, KNA, BN/81/164.

[34] "Ol Kalou Salient Settlement," March 14, 1964, BNA, DO 214/46.

[35] J. H. Angaine to C. Njonjo, May 9, 1964, KNA, BN/81/164.

[36] This very part of the letter was then crossed without any written comment in the margins. Draft Letter from Sir Saville Garner to Richard Turnbull, File no. 2-EAE 57/27/1, BNA, DO 214/40.

Turnbull, the Million Acres Scheme was a convenient façade to hide a different kind of politicking:

> the largest piece of cake has gone to the Kikuyu. Political and security factors make this inevitable; all the same, they have had more than their share and the other folk have had less than they were led to expect they would get ... If the scheme is closed ... that will be most damaging to Kenyatta and correspondingly advantageous to Oginga Odinga ... Kenyatta depends on [the Nyanza and Western Region] to keep Kanu in being as a party of (relative) moderation.[37]

The British, however, were obsessed by their finances and realized they had reasons to worry about a Kenyan land administration they always mistrusted.[38] Their aim was, as Neil Brockett from the British High Commission wrote, the "discharge of all disbursement made from UK."[39] By the end of 1964, a mishandling of the Kenyan land settlement accounts came to their ears. The controller and auditor general "experienced a good deal of difficulty in his audit of the land settlement accounts," and refused to certify the 1963/1964 accounts.[40] It was also pointed out that money was allocated by and between the settlement fund trustees, in particular Gichuru and Angaine, without proper control.[41] Shady distribution and use of land could hardly fail to expose political ambitions.

The politicization of land control and distribution sheds light on the political use of the land by the Kenyatta regime, and illustrates how, by deregulating and bypassing state institutions in distributing land, presidential power was strengthened. Early 1964, the officer administering

---

[37] Richard Turnbull to Sir Saville Garner, June 19, 1964, BNA, DO 214/40.
[38] Holtham and Hazlewood, *Aid and Inequality in Kenya*, 88. For a critical reflection on the idea of British neocolonialism in Eastern Africa, see Ichiro Maekawa, "Neo-Colonialism Reconsidered: A Case Study of East Africa in the 1960s and 1970s," *The Journal of Imperial and Commonwealth History* 43, no. 2 (2015): 317–341.
[39] F. N. Brockett to R. W. Wootton (East Africa Economic Department), August 28, 1964, BNA, DO 214/40.
[40] F. N. Brockett to M. L. Woods, July 15, 1964, BNA, DO 214/40; Confidential. Brief for Meeting with Mr. B. R. McKenzie, Minister of Agriculture, October 7, 1964, BNA, DO 214/40. See also Hornsby, *Kenya*, 118–119; Leo, *Land and Class in Kenya*, 162; John Kamau, "How Kenyatta Government Flouted Loan Deal So That Big Names Could Get Land," *Daily Nation*, November 11, 2009.
[41] Confidential. F. N. Brockett to R. W. Wooton, September 10, 1964, BNA, DO 214/40.

the fund noted a "lack of clear political leadership and political discipline" in the organization of settlement schemes.[42] In the same report, he dutifully reported that

> It is understood although I have not seen it, that the Prime Minister [Jomo Kenyatta] has issued a directive that certain houses should be preserved in their present condition and should have 100 acres of land around them excised from Settlement Schemes. We are seeking clarification on this matter since it would be very expensive and is outside the use of our loan money.[43]

A circular was issued by Jackson Angaine on May 11, 1964 to announce the government's decision. The land in question was reserved for political gifts and economic patronage, to further tie the African middle class and political elite to the government's settlement politics.[44] Disturbed by the discovery, the British authorities kept pressing Kenyan permanent secretaries to obtain fuller details.[45] By the end of September 1966, they were provided in dribs and drabs, with a list of farms referred to as "Z" plots. As Brockett commented, "the list is interesting in regard of some names."[46]

The list of allocated "Z" plots shows how land politics, and in particular land distribution, became, only a few months after independence, the linchpin of political loyalties. The list contains, apart from Jomo Kenyatta himself, the names of prominent members of the Kenyan political elite.[47] There were the ministers and permanent secretaries of the most influential ministries, in particular those of land and settlement and home affairs. Among these were Lawrence Sagini, minister for local government, who bought a 129.3-acre farm in Nyamiera district (Nyanza region) and Jackson Angaine, who acquired a 252-acre farm in Timau (Meru district, Central region); three permanent secretaries: A. S. Omanga (home affairs), P. Shikuyah (agriculture),

---

[42] To the Agricultural Settlement Fund Trustees. Report of Officer Administering the Fund, February 17, 1964, KNA, BN/87/26.
[43] Ibid. In 2008, a survey estimated that 20 percent of the 30,000 Kenyan population owns half of the arable land in Kenya, while 67 percent owns less than an acre, and 13 percent is landless. See Namwaya, "Who Owns Kenya?"
[44] Wasserman, "Continuity and Counter-Insurgency," 145.
[45] Confidential. F. N. Brockett to R. W. Wooton, February 11, 1966, BNA, DO 214/107.
[46] Ibid.
[47] Kenyatta bought a 139.5-acre farm in South Kinangop for £12,000, see "Z" Category Plots, BNA, DO 214/107.

and P. J. Gachati (lands and settlement), who respectively bought a 99.5-acre farm (Nyamira, Nyanza region), 157.5-acre farm (Kitale district, Western region), and 107.57-acre farm (Nyandarua district, Central province); finally, the chief agriculturalist J. Mburu, also president of the Central Region Assembly and later PC for North Eastern province (he also played a crucial role in the repression of resilient forest fighters, as mentioned earlier). Ironically, Mburu had written, a few months earlier, to Kenyatta to complain about the government's policy of settlement.[48] The PCs, pillars of the Kenyan administration, benefited greatly from the "Z" plots. Eliud Mahihu, powerful PC throughout Kenyatta's regime, acquired a 94-acre farm in Nyandarua (Central province); Daniel Owino, PC in Nyanza and later ambassador to the United Kingdom, bought a farm of 105 acres in Rift Valley; P. K. Boit, PC in Central province, bought 118 acres in Uasin Gishu district (Rift Valley); and K. M. Maina, who would in 1967 become district commissioner in Rift Valley, acquired 117.6 acres in Eldoret district (Rift Valley).[49] Others included KANU leaders (as A. Kimunai and A. Soi from Rift Valley); former Mau Mau and KAU leader Jesse Kariuki; S. Nyambati Nyamweya, a town clerk from Kisii (Nyanza); an area settlement controller, and later member of the Public Service Commission, L. Ngatia Mucemi; and the two Maasai senators mentioned earlier, R. Mwangi and K. Rotich.[50]

A clear hierarchy of rule was established, with President Kenyatta at the top intervening occasionally to allocate land to particular individuals. Although the "Z" plots helped the formation and strengthening of the provincial administration as an institution of power and privilege under the direct supervision of the president, the rewards given to powerful civil servants (who were, for the most part, Kikuyu) were also a way to limit the scope of action of the provincial administration itself.[51] The immediate control over the land distribution lay in the hands of the minister for lands, Jackson Angaine, who took over the

---

[48] Ibid. On James Mburu's letter, see To the Agricultural Settlement Fund Trustees. Report of Officer Administering the Fund, November 28, 1963, KNA, BN/87/26.
[49] Ibid. [50] Ibid.
[51] See Gertzel, *The Politics of Independent Kenya, 1963–8*; John J. Okumu, "The Socio-Political Setting," in *Development Administration: The Kenyan Experience*, eds. Göran Hydén, Robert Jackson, and John Okumu (Nairobi: Oxford University Press, 1970), 25–42; J. R. Nellis, "Is the Kenyan Bureaucracy Developmental? Political Considerations in Development Administration,"

task of selecting settlers from the provincial and district administration, giving priority to government officials.[52] Although British administrators were extremely upset by this system and feared a lack of efficiency, they found it difficult to criticize it, when they learned that the architecture of the system "was put forward by the President himself" and feared that by attacking the president, they might jeopardize British interests as a whole.[53] The "Z" plots hence continued to be allocated in this fashion until 1969.[54]

Kenyatta: Most Important Is to "Show Willing"

Despite their essential unwillingness to intervene in the Kenyan administration of land settlement programs (for issues of political sensitivity), the British authorities considered cutting funding so as to avoid the mishandling of their financial aid. Kenyan cabinet ministers feared such a move would impair their public political stance, and referred the matter to Kenyatta, hoping to secure his personal support. Early in 1965, the British government appointed an expert mission to review the funding process of the settlement schemes. The Stamp mission was appointed, with the consent and cooperation of the Kenyan government.[55] Its aim was to "to advise the British Government on the need for further scheme for the transfer of European farms to African ownership and if there is a need what form such a scheme should take."[56] Gary Wasserman and Christopher Leo examined the main ideas of the report, which was submitted in October 1965.[57] They did

---

African Studies Review 14, no. 3 (1971): 389–401. See also Harbeson, *Nation-Building in Kenya*, 243.

[52] A. B. Cohen to Mr. King, October 10, 1966, BNA, FCO 141/19010.
[53] Ibid.
[54] Ibid.; Wasserman, "Continuity and Counter-Insurgency," 145–146.
[55] Messrs. Maxwell Stamp (economist and leader of the mission), R. J. M. Swynnerton (agricultural adviser to the Commonwealth Development Corporation), Dr. A. M. M. McFarquhar (from the School of Agriculture of the University of Cambridge), and G. J. Caren (partner in a firm of chartered surveyors) all toured Kenyan mixed farming areas and led several meeting with various official from January 24, 1965 to the end of February, in "For the Record. Kenya Land Purchase and General Development," November 19, 1965, KNA, BN/81/24.
[56] Confidential. Stamp Mission – Terms of Guidance, BNA, DO 214/104. On the appointment of the team, see Harbeson, *Nation-Building in Kenya*, 257–258.
[57] Wasserman, "Continuity and Counter-Insurgency," 142–145; Leys, *Underdevelopment in Kenya*, 86–103.

not, however, explore the political consequences of the ensuing negotiations.

The Stamp mission quickly concluded that land transfers from European to African ownership did not contribute to the economic growth of the country. It recommended instead that "scare capital resources should be allotted to more remunerative development of African agriculture."[58] Kenyatta's ministers did not dispute the mission's finding.[59] A paper prepared by Mboya earlier the same year had equally concluded that settlement schemes "contribute[d] to practically nothing to Kenya growth."[60] The government nonetheless opposed the conclusion that settlement schemes should be put on hold.[61] Its line of argument was that the public advertisement of settlement schemes was a political necessity to guarantee stability and order within the country. During the negotiations that followed the final report, Kenyan ministers were at pains to have the report disregarded without having to contradict it. They wanted to retain British aid for settlements for their own ends.

In November 1965, a series of meetings took place at the Ministry of Overseas Development, where the Kenyan delegation repeatedly stressed, to no avail at first, the potentially disastrous consequences of disregarding the unstable political situation for purely economic reasons. They demanded, first, that the negotiations should be held independently of the Stamp Report; second, that land settlement and transfer should continue; third, that the Land Bank, instead of being reshaped, be more closely associated with the Agricultural Development Corporation, a parastatal organization chaired by McKenzie; and fourth, not to have British aid reduced too sharply.[62] McKenzie steadily defended an increase of land purchases, perhaps also motivated by his personal business with the Agricultural Development

---

[58] Commonwealth Economic Consultative Council, Meeting of Finance Ministers, September 1965, Brief by the Commonwealth Relations Office, BNA, DO 214/105.

[59] Ibid. [60] Kenya. Land and Agricultural Policies, BNA, DO 214/105.

[61] Confidential. Ministerial Committee on Overseas Development, Minutes of a Meeting of the Committee Held in Conference Room 'A', Cabinet Office, SW1, on Wednesday, November 3, 1965 at 4.00 p.m., BNA, DO 214/106.

[62] 1st Meeting. Report of Meeting Held at the Ministry of Overseas Development at 3 p.m. on Monday, November 8, 1965, To Discuss Future Kenya Development Aid, KNA, BN/81/24. The Agricultural Development Corporation was established in 1965 to undertake land transfer of large-scale farms, see Bethwell Allen Ogot, *Historical Dictionary of Kenya* (London: The Scarecrow Press, Inc., 1981), 14–15.

Corporation, which placed him in opposition to Mboya.[63] All three ministers repeatedly emphasized the political impacts of land purchases. "Strongly" supported by Angaine, McKenzie stressed that the

> President was already being challenged, particularly by Africans outside Kenya, for being too accommodating in his relations with Europeans. Gichuru said that if it were not for considerable political pressures the Kenya Government would not insist on a higher rate because they appreciated that it did not contribute to development.[64]

The British government, however, had been warned by officers from the British High Commission in Kenya to expect such a line of argument, and, consequently, did not take the gravity of these purported political problems too seriously.[65] To convince them of the contrary, Kenyatta became personally involved in the negotiations.

Kenyatta's supervision of the negotiations was distant as usual, yet undoubtedly influential. He must have given his assent to the appointment of the Stamp mission to Kenya, already discussed by November–December 1964. Indeed, it was probably he who wrote to the commonwealth secretary about the difficulties surrounding the publicity given to the mission.[66] He feared the volatility of public opinion and knew he had to refrain from any public declaration on the issue, which could have led to unpopular statements on land policy. He made his position clear to British authorities, "[acknowledging] that European farmers who farm well were welcome to remain."[67] Nevertheless, he did not lead the formal negotiations himself, but delegated them to his most trusted ministers, Bruce McKenzie, James Gichuru, and Jackson Angaine.

Although Kenyatta was kept informed by his cabinet ministers throughout the process, he showed little understanding of the

---

[63] 2nd Meeting. Report of Meeting held at the Ministry of Overseas Development at 10 a.m. on Tuesday, November 9, 1965, to discuss Future Kenya Development Aid, KNA, BN/81/24.

[64] Ibid.

[65] Confidential. B. Greatbach to W. G. Lamarque, August 25, 1965, BNA, DO 214/105.

[66] Confidential. Inward Telegram to Commonwealth Relations Office from H. S. H. Stanley, no. 2368, "Kenya Land Settlement," December 2, 1964, BNA, DO 214/104.

[67] Confidential. Notes of Meeting Held in Mr. King's Office at 4:15 p.m. on Thursday, March 4, 1965, BNA, DO 214/104.

technicalities at stake, but great concern for political disturbances. Anticipating the negotiations, Angaine requested Kenyatta in writing that some officers from his own ministry join the delegation, noting in passing that it was necessary for him to defend the legitimacy and raison d'être of his ministry, already seriously undermined by the Stamp Report. He pointed out that the report recommended:

> halt Settlement schemes for our poor Africans for two years. I am convinced that Your Excellency will support me in stressing the need for entertaining some form of Settlement Schemes, at least, otherwise we would be leaving the door open for the Kaggia type of politicians to talk nonsense.[68]

Kenyatta was also briefed by McKenzie, whom the British described as the "'overlord' of the Stamp Mission affairs."[69] Nevertheless, he had scant knowledge of the details involved, and limited his intervention to general statements mirroring his cabinet ministers' arguments. It is worth quoting at length a land administrator who had just met Kenyatta and reported that the latter was

> evidently not (repeat not) fully aware of the distinction, in context of Stamp report, between settlement and other forms of use of transferred land, but was very worried by prospect both of decelerated transfer of European mixed farms and of decelerated settlement. He asked me to emphasize the great importance in present circumstances of enabling him to give and answer to "hotheads" who might accuse him of doing nothing to secure the transfer of land to the landless. He also asked me to emphasize the need to keep European farmers contented until their turn came to be bought out: this entails in his view a very much shorter period of buy-out than is implied by the rate of 80,000 acres per year.[70]

Before the November negotiations started, Kenyatta discussed the core issues with MacDonald and his attorney general Charles Njonjo, guardian of all constitutional secrecies pertaining to the land politics.[71] He expressed his "strong hope" that the British government would not suspend land purchase; because of political pressure, he doubted he

---

[68] Jackson Angaine to Jomo Kenyatta, October 26, 1965, KNA, BN/81/24.
[69] Confidential. "Comments on the Stamp Mission Report," BNA, DO 214/106.
[70] Ibid.; Confidential. Mr. Pumphrey to Commonwealth Relations Office, no. 1969, November 10, 1965, BNA, DO 214/106.
[71] Médard, "Charles Njonjo"; Mordechai Tamarkin, "Recent Developments in Kenyan Politics: The Fall of Charles Njonjo," *Journal of Contemporary African Studies* 3, nos. 1–2 (1983): 59–77.

would "be able to keep ... within bounds."[72] Assessing these political risks, he was finally backed up by MacDonald who confirmed to London ministers that he was "sure, from recent casual conversation I have had with Bildad Kaggia and other critical Members of Parliament that this appreciation is correct."[73]

To the Kenyan government, the truth of the Stamp Report should not be publicly exposed, so as not to prepare the grounds for radical, antigovernment arguments. The government had already been very much embarrassed earlier in February when Maxwell Stamp publicly declared that European farmers should stay in Kenya.[74] The statement inflamed radical politicians such as Kaggia and Oneko, forcing cabinet ministers and Kenyatta to publicly disassociate themselves from the Stamp Report, while McKenzie was trying, behind closed doors, to persuade Kaggia not to bring up the matter in the House of Representatives.[75] After only a month, McKenzie reassured the British High Commissioner that "for the time being, other distractions have diverted attention from the Stamp Mission, and this has enable Ministers to avoid difficulties in the Cabinet."[76]

As negotiations around the report risked stagnating, Kenyatta insisted on the necessity of having land settlement continue as a political and social smokescreen to assuage various claims arising from the land issue. He reaffirmed, in a private conversation with the commonwealth secretary,

the urgency of favourable response from the British Government on assistance with Land Settlement. He emphasized that it was most important to "show willing" (even if in fact progress was not particularly rapid) since otherwise a handle was given to extremists who could demand confiscation.[77]

---

[72] Confidential. MacDonald to Commonwealth Relations Office, no. 1925, November 3, 1965, BNA, DO 214/106.
[73] Ibid.
[74] *East African Standard*, "Difficult if European Farmer Left," February 23, 1965, BNA, DO 214/104.
[75] Confidential. Note of a Conversation between British High Commissioner and Maxwell Stamp, February 27, 1965, BNA, DO 214/104.
[76] Ibid.; Confidential. MacDonald to Walsh Atkins (Commonwealth Relations Office), March 8, 1965.
[77] Confidential. Extract from a Minute Dated November 2 from Sir S. Farner to Sir A. Snelling (1965), BNA, DO 214/106.

Although the November meetings revealed irreconcilable British and Kenyan views, Kenyatta reinforced his position, in what came to be a determining and successful intervention. He sent a personal message to the British prime minister himself, stating that he "would be very happy if you could help Mr. McKenzie and Mr. James Gichuru." Quoting his ministers almost word for word, the message went on to argue that "our urgent need is to be able to push land settlement as quickly as we can"; Kenyatta demanded that a minimum of 160,000 and 200,000 acres be secured, as well as British financial help to buy out European farmers wishing to leave Kenya, and be able to do so in less than "seventeen years."[78] The British would finally concede to continue funding land settlements in spite of the Stamp Report's recommendations, and to extend figures for purchase from 80,000 acres to 100,000 acres per year for the next four years; as well as the exclusion of the compassionate case (i.e., European farms) from the £18 million land aid they agreed on.[79]

British unwillingness to pay was less motivated by fear of not being reimbursed, than by skepticism toward the economic viability of land settlements schemes – disregarding their historical responsibility in that regard. British land policy had always been dominated by the so-called developmental view that took little interest in squatters and landless, who were ignored for the sake of political stability preserving the benefits of a colonial economy.[80] British funds were not designed for land reforms, but for a transfer of ownership favoring former European owners.[81] The Kenyan government was certainly tied to international credit (from both Britain and the World Bank) and repaid nearly 60 percent of British funds. Far from being aid, these funds were bound to high repayment interests, forcing the Kenyan government into strict financial discipline. Nevertheless, it can be disputed whether these financial constraints were critical to British influence over Kenyan political affairs, given the shared economic and political interests that linked the African elite to its former colonizer, and the absence of debate over a change of the colonial economic structure.[82]

---

[78] Confidential. Commonwealth Secretary's Distribution, no. 1970, November 10, 1965, BNA, DO 214/106.
[79] Confidential. MacDonald to Ministry of Overseas Development, NO. MODEV 1185, November 22, 1965, BNA, PREM 2179.
[80] Holtham and Hazlewood, *Aid and Inequality in Kenya*, 81.   [81] Ibid., 87.
[82] Leys, *Underdevelopment in Kenya*, 60–62.

Some even questioned whether alternative economic models would have challenged or undermined British political influence over the decolonization process. This argument resonates with the lack of viable political alternative at the time.[83] The political and economic consensus established in the wake of the Emergency was critical to KANU's (and Kenyatta's) regaining political prominence. At the same time, the British government had only limited choices for supporting another leader. Oginga Odinga was considered a dangerous socialist because of his populist discourse and Eastern communist support. The British would have preferred to oust him from government, had they not met Kenyatta's refusal to do so (see Chapters 2 and 3). Tom Mboya, meanwhile, was supported by the United States, another foreign power trying to gain influence in the politics of the region.[84] As I have previously argued, no other moderate Kikuyu leader was charismatic enough to compete with Kenyatta, while the more "populist" politicians (such as Bildad Kaggia), risked endangering the political and economic assets of a loyalist elite. KADU leader Ronald Ngala lacked nationwide support. To British administrators, only Kenyatta's leadership could preserve the political status quo in the White Highlands. Hence, they felt bound to accept the illegal practices of the Kenyatta government regarding the land issue. Cabinet ministers themselves showed very little concern for their economic dependency, feeling free to politicize land resources for their own ends.

Kenyatta's disinterest in land efficiency would prove to be enduring, as several despatches sent by the British High Commission in the early 1970s noted his lack of will and capacity to ensure the coordination of state institutions tackling key social and political issues, such as land settlement or unemployment.[85] The president's disinterest in land settlements fit a system exclusively based on land productivity and large-scale farming. Back in 1963, Kenyatta had given his approval to settle Kikuyu families from the Rift Valley in a settlement zone

---

[83] Holtham and Hazlewood, *Aid and Inequality in Kenya*, 101.

[84] Tom Shachtman, *Airlift to America: How Barack Obama Sr., John F. Kennedy, Tom Mboya and 800 east African Students Changed Their World and Ours* (New York: MacMillan, 2009).

[85] Confidential. Eric Norris to Sir Alec Douglas-Home, "Kenya: The Internal Political Situation," July 28, 1970, BNA, FCO 31/596; The British High Commission in Kenya to the Secretary of State for Foreign and Commonwealth Affairs, "Kenya: The Annual Review for 1970," January 12, 1971, BNA, FCO 31/851.

situated in Mpanda, Tanzania.[86] Land there was of poor quality and, more importantly, difficult to access. The Nakuru district commissioner himself warned the Kenyan authorities that the Kikuyu families settled there were living in dire social, economic, and sanitary conditions, a situation which did not leave visiting KANU representatives unconcerned.[87] It would take a few months, however, before the officers in charge abandoned the scheme, and stopped forcing unwilling Kikuyu families to depart.

The strategy of increased land buying signaled much wider institutional consequences, discarding, on the one hand, the landless and poor from being of national concern, and, on the other hand, strengthening the direct control of the Office of the President over land issues, at the expense of other state institutions. After 1965, as the White Highlands were virtually all transferred to Africans, the Kenyan government coveted the Rift Valley, "the next target for Kikuyu expansion," as one British administrator put it, as well as Maasai land and even Coast land to expand its lucrative farming business at the expense of settling the landless (on the squatter issue, see the following section; see the next chapter for further details on the Rift Valley, Coast, and Maasai land).[88] Two main interests were served. First, individual enrichment (self-achievement) was firmly defended.[89] Second, buying out land remained both the end and the means to reduce the power of regions, so as to enhance state central control over political and economic affairs. These two objectives were bound to stir political resistance, as the transition to independence had only temporarily tamed radical politicians.

Resilient politicians continued to stir hopes among the landless of a free redistribution of land. Radical agitation was becoming

---

[86] R. E. Wainwrights to J. A. H. Wolf, July 15, 1963, KNA, BN/81/8; R. St. J. Matthews (Regional Government Agent Nakuru) to the District Traffic Superintendent, August 22, 1963, KNA, PC/NKU/13/20.

[87] J. C. Nottingham to the PC Rift Valley, September 3, 1963, KNA, PC/NKU/13/20.

[88] O. G. Griffith to T. Duffy, January 18, 1965 and T. Duffy to O. G. Griffith, January 21, 1965, BNA, DO 214/104. For a concise overview of the history of land-buying politics in the Rift Valley, see Catherine Boone, "Land Conflict and Distributive Politics in Kenya," *African Studies Review* 55, no. 1 (2012): 75–103.

[89] On Kikuyu capitalist ethic, see Maupeu, "Kikuyu Capitalistes"; John Iliffe, *The Emergence of African Capitalism: The Anstey Memorial Lectures in the University of Kent at Canterbury 10–13 May 1982* (London: Macmillan, 1983).

increasingly vocal, blaming the government for failing to distribute the fruits of *uhuru* (independence), and denouncing corruption and individual enrichment. Although Mau Mau sympathizers had been considerably weakened by the deaths of Field Marshal Baimungi and General Chui, they had not been completely silenced. In Central province, Mau Mau rhetoric and oathings continued to resurface.[90] While dealing with the negotiations of land economics, Kenyatta's government faced the difficult task of disciplining the state and its politicians. How did Kenyatta combine such a blunt disdain for the poor, and yet maintain his popularity and legitimacy throughout his regime? And how did he combine such distanced personal commitment to political negotiations with such a strong hold over his government? These questions call for further inquiry into the balance of institutions in Kenyatta's presidential system of rule.

Getting over "Radical" Politicians and Backbenchers

In 1965, not even a few months after Kenyatta was sworn in as president, enduring political upheaval shook Central province, setting up the president against so-called radical politicians. The government closely scrutinized Bildad Kaggia's activities. More specifically, the attorney general's office was patiently waiting for sufficient justification to initiate prosecution against the district leader.[91] Despite having made history, Kenyatta's exclamation addressed to Kaggia "What have you done for yourself?" had a rather injurious immediate effect. In April, reports by the Special Branch noted that

> the reaction to the President's speech, whilst favourable insofar as the law abiding majority of the population is concerned, has only served to harden the attitude of malcontents towards the present government. The landless have been so conditioned over the past years to expect free land at Independence that they now feel resentful and cheated when told that this is not practicable.[92]

---

[90] Branch, *Defeating Mau Mau, Creating Kenya*, chapter 6.
[91] K. C. Brooks to Provincial Police Officer Central Province, "Speeches at Public Political Meetings Central Province," March 19, 1965, KNA, AAC/1/51.
[92] Secret. Special Branch Weekly Intelligence Report for the Period April 6–12, 1965, April 15, 1965, KNA, BB/1/158.

A week later, another report noted "an increase in clandestine meetings" of a resilient branch of the Mau Mau, the Mitarukire in Fort Hall (todays Murang'a, Central province), "resulting from the public criticism of Kaggia by H. E. The President."[93] The landless remained a potential force the government could not ignore, especially given the depth of the political divisions within KANU. The Special Branch reported with uneasiness that "there is distinct lack of support amongst the lower echelons of the national party."[94] This lack of support was clearly exposed at the last KANU delegate's conference, where "a majority of district spokesmen supported by a member of the National Executive attacked the government during their speeches," specifically targeting ministers who had acquired large houses and farms.[95] With the land issue ongoing, the political opposition risked becoming more uncontrollable; a prospect ever more unsettling to the government.

Kenyatta was the target of growing public criticism that revealed the depth of KANU division within both the party and the national assembly, and the growing frustration within various strata of the population. In March, the Special Branch listed as sources of discontent the "effect of continuous criticism of Government policy and of H. E. the President by certain KANU politicians" along with the wave of industrial unrest, dissensions with the national party, dissatisfaction among former freedom fighters, and rising ranks of unemployed and landless.[96] Just a month earlier, the MP Pio da Gama Pinto, mastermind of Odinga's political organization and himself a radical politician, had been murdered. He had been preparing a policy paper criticizing the government's economic policy and was planning to table a motion of "no confidence" in parliament.[97] Pinto's murder further stirred antigovernment sentiment.[98] This combination of various

---

[93] Secret. Special Branch Weekly Intelligence Report for the Period April 20–25, 1965, April 29, 1965, KNA, BB/1/158. On the Mitarukire, see Karuti Kanyinga, "Land Redistribution in Kenya," in *Agricultural Land Redistribution: Toward Greater Consensus*, eds. Hans P. Binswanger-Mkhize, Camille Bourguignon, and Rogier J. Eugenius van den Brink (Washington: The International Bank for Reconstruction and Development, 2009), 101.
[94] Secret. Special Branch Weekly Intelligence Report for the Period April 6–12, 1965, April 15, 1965, KNA, BB/1/158.
[95] Ibid.
[96] Secret. Special Branch Weekly Intelligence Report for the Period February 23–March 1, 1965, March 4, 1965, KNA, BB/1/158.
[97] Hornsby, *Kenya*, 147.   [98] Ibid.

grievances was all the more dangerous for the government, as it was uniting very different individuals in search of more practical means to impact politics. Disgruntled former forest fighters in Central and Eastern provinces were a potential political force coveted by dissident KANU politicians and MPs. Dissident politicians themselves were trying to establish tighter connections with more prominent politicians such as Bildad Kaggia (whose popularity in Central province was a unique asset) and Oginga Odinga (who was clearly trying to rally politicians to his socialist ideology). All in all, the divisions had the potential to subvert the balance of state institutions, bringing MPs together against government ministers and administration, and defying regional confinement by building a cross-district opposition block.

Eastern province, in particular the Meru and Embu districts, remained a hot spot, precisely because the repression of Mau Mau leaders gave populist politicians and discontented backbenchers a reason to voice their dissent against both KANU and the government. In Meru, divisions were rife since the deaths of Field Marshal Baimungi and General Chui. Already in January 1965, Eliud Mahihu, the PC of Eastern province, informed the Office of the President that "Meru politicians are divided on the issue of Baimungi's death, some accusing Angaine for being responsible for his death and Angaine's group accusing Julius [Muthamia, Senator] and so on and so forth."[99] The situation became so tense that Mahihu wrote to the Office of the President asking for Kenyatta to "intervene and get all the MPs and Senators at a Round Table Conference with the intention of having open discussions as to reasons for disagreement."[100] As argued earlier, these political divisions were used by Bildad Kaggia to provide support to resilient forest fighters.[101] In the neighboring Embu, the KANU

[99] Secret. Eliud Mahihu to Duncan Ndegwa, "The Forest Outlaws," January 30, 1965, KNA, BB/12/49.
[100] Secret. Eliud Mahihu to Duncan Ndegwa, "Security Assessment in Eastern Province," March 5, 1965, KNA, BB/1/158.
[101] From May to September 1965, the Special Branch reported continuously on Bildad Kaggia's political relations with radical politicians and ex-freedom fighters, warning that he was to make use of discontent and divisions within Kanu. See Secret. Special Branch Weekly Intelligence Report for the Period May 18–24, 1965, May 27, 1965; Secret. Special Branch Weekly Intelligence Report for the Period June 1–7, 1965, June 10, 1965; Secret. Special Branch Weekly Intelligence Report for the Period August 17–23, 1965, August 26, 1965; Secret. Special Branch Weekly Intelligence Report for the Period September 7–13, 1965, September 16, 1965, KNA, BB/1/158.

chairman John Kamwithi, was said to be "in the Russian camp," meaning that he was a follower of Odinga's dissident group.[102] Odinga, in particular, was believed to be trying to "capture leaders of district who could be exploited for his own cause when the times come."[103]

Both Kaggia's and Odinga's support for the political agitation in Meru and Embu risked turning district dissidence into national unrest. The Special Branch reported in June 1965 that the "rift between the 'Kenya Group' [pro-government] and the 'Progressives' within the National Assembly was further widened when the former succeeded in wrestling control of the Back Bencher's Association from the latter," encouraging the progressives toward more aggressive opposition.[104] From June onward, the Special Branch reports became increasingly alarmed, pointing to a possibility of the formation of a new subversive opposition party.[105]

To settle these issues, Kenyatta made sure there would be no spillover beyond the affected districts, or any kind of political exposure, and directed his loyal minister and civil servant, Jackson Angaine and Eliud Mahihu, to handle the situation themselves. While available archives referring directly to Kenyatta's way of rule are scarce, PC Eliud Mahihu's papers reveal useful information. A top secret correspondence between Mahihu and Angaine shows how Kenyatta instructed them both to ensure loyalty within his government, but also freed their hands when it came to taking action. On June 17, 1965, Jackson Angaine informed Eliud Mahihu (copying his letter to Kenyatta himself) that

I have been to see the President, His Excellency Mzee Jomo Kenyatta and explained to him what is going on in Meru. I told him quite frankly that most of the Civil Servants in Meru are not loyal to our government. I mentioned

---

[102] Secret. Eliud Mahihu to Duncan Ndegwa, "Security Assessment in Eastern Province," March 5, 1965, KNA, BB/1/158.
[103] Secret. Eliud Mahihu to Duncan Ndegwa, "His Visit to Embu and Meru on 9th May 1965," May 15, 1965, KNA, BB/1/158.
[104] Secret. Special Branch Weekly Intelligence Report for the Period June 16–22, 1965, June 24, 1965, KNA, BB/1/158.
[105] Secret. Special Branch Weekly Intelligence Report for the Period June 16–22, June 24, 1965; Secret. Special Branch Weekly Intelligence Report for the Period June 20 – July 6, 1965, July 8, 1965; Secret. Special Branch Weekly Intelligence Report For the Period July 20–26, 1965, July 29, 1965, KNA, BB/1/158.

their names which I do not want to disclose in this letter, and the President asked me to get into touch with you and explain this to you so that myself and you should work as a team to put each and everything right in Meru.[106]

The letter fits into the wave of unrest previously described, and highlights once again the importance of Meru's security for Kenyatta's regime. At the end of it, Angaine did mention a few names: the MPs Abraham Gaciatta and Bernard Mate, Senator Julius Muthamia, and the KANU chairman in Embu, John Kamwithi Munyi. All were involved in the progressive group, and, more importantly for Meru's political order, they contested Angaine's leadership.[107] Mahihu called a meeting with police officers in charge of Meru district, and the district special branch officer.[108]

Although no other archive documents the outcome of Kenyatta's orders to Angaine and Mahihu, we can only observe the gradual eviction of undesirable MPs in the Meru district that followed and the tightening of Angaine's leadership over the district. In 1965, Abraham Gaciatta was accused of false mileage claims and arrested by the police.[109] He subsequently lost his seat, and was replaced by K. M. Thimangu-Kaunyangi, the son of the advisor of a local chief and himself a civil servant. According to Kaunyangi himself, he was picked by the local KANU branch because he was one of most educated of his area (he had been to the Alliance High School and Makerere College). It certainly mattered that he was not a member of KANU, and was nonetheless parachuted into the office of vice chairman of the KANU Meru branch by Angaine himself.[110] Kaunyangi's election as an MP was also strongly supported by Eliud Mahihu, who "came [to Meru], just at the beginning of elections campaign, and made meetings and instructed the chiefs at that time, how they should conduct the elections, because they are the one supervising the elections."[111] Besides,

---

[106] Top Secret. Jackson Angaine to Eliud Mahihu, June 17, 1965, KNA, BB/1/158.
[107] Interviews with K. M. Thimangu-Kaunyangi, Joseph Muturia, and John Kerimi.
[108] Top Secret. Eliud Mahihu to Provincial Police Officer (Eastern Province), June 25, 1965, KNA, BB/1/158.
[109] Interviews with K. M. Thimangu-Kaunyangi, Joseph Muturia, and John Kerimi.
[110] K. M. Thimangu-Kaunyangi, interview. [111] Ibid.

Angaine launched a discrediting campaign against Julius Muthamia.[112] By 1965, his unopposed domination of the Meru district earned him the (slightly ironic) nickname of the "King of Meru," and ensured his prominent role within Kenyatta and Moi's regimes for the next five decades.[113]

When it came to the Embu agitator John Kamwithi Munyi, the government mixed its repressive tactics with apparently unsound plans for institutional unity. Kamwithi Munyi, a Russian-educated politician who had been successfully elected senator in August 1965, was a known follower of Kaggia's and Odinga's "Lumumba Institute," a communist political center.[114] Munyi was attacking the connivance between government ministers and chiefs, calling for the expulsion of chiefs and the free redistribution of land, thus greatly embarrassing the Kenyatta administration.[115] The government's takeover of the Lumumba Institute in April 1965 was part of an attempt to stifle dissident activities.[116] More generally, the government attempted to foster greater unity in its administration, through a series of meetings bringing together ministers, PCs, and MPs, organized under the auspices of the Ministry of Internal Security and Defence. Little is known about the content of these meetings. One letter of caution written by Eliud Mahihu to the permanent secretary of the Ministry of Internal Security, hints at violent interrogations of MPs, condemning "such tactics," that risked being revealed and further damaging a hard-won governmental harmony that Mahihu was "determined to maintain ... at all costs."[117]

To further tame the backbenchers, Kenyatta personally took care of limiting their activities, deciding to dissolve the backbencher group after a parliamentary group met under his chairmanship in the summer

[112] Ibid.
[113] Kenneth Kwama, "Jackson Angaine Dominated Politics in Eastern Province for over Five Decades," *The Standard*, November 15, 2013.
[114] John Kamau, "Coup Haste That Saw Lumumba Institute Collapse," *Daily Nation*, March 13, 2010.
[115] Secret. Eliud Mahihu to Duncan Ndegwa, "Security Assessment in Eastern Province," March 5, 1965; Secret. Special Branch Weekly Intelligence Report for the Period August 31, 1965–September 27, 1965, KNA, BB/1/158. See also Irungu Tatiah and Jeremiah Nyagah Trust, *Jeremiah Nyagah. Sowing the Mustard Seed* (Seattle: Rizzan Media, 2013), 182–183.
[116] Kamau, "Coup Haste That Saw Lumumba Institute Collapse."
[117] Secret. Eliud Mahihu to the Permanent Secretary, Ministry of Internal Security and Defense, August 16, 1965, KNA, BB/12/48.

of 1965. The issue at stake was to prevent his opponents from gathering support among the backbenchers and forming a dissident political party. Kenyatta's role was therefore that of meeting tribal leaders so as to secure their allegiance, either visiting their districts or hosting courtesy visits in his Gatundu house.[118] Parallel to this absorption of locally elected members, the buying out of MPs enabled Kenyatta to strengthen his authority against Odinga.[119] Their "firm" commitment to Kenyatta only diminished their deeper divisions, as "in practice most of them owe a secondary allegiance to various personalities or factions in Parliament."[120] As the struggle against Odinga's politics intensified, and following the minister's complaints that "it was now time that they asserted themselves," Kenyatta became more assertive.[121]

Thereafter, the president often chaired KANU parliamentary groups, but repeatedly attempted to discourage greater political emancipation.[122] When speaking to KANU MPs, Kenyatta would not hesitate to warn "that the Government was strong enough and would not hesitate to take any action against the dissidents" or to blame their "colonial mentality," a conveniently emotionally loaded expression to expose their purportedly divisive behavior.[123] He would remain vague, however, when addressing concrete and precise complaints raised by the MPs, delegating them to his permanent secretaries and ministers of state. Kenyatta's direct connections with the MPs were also a way to torpedo any undesirable public debates, as the KANU MPs were asked to contact the Office of the President "preferably before bringing any

---

[118] S. O. Josiah to the Permanent Secretary, Office of the President, November 1, 1966, KNA, BB/49/59.
[119] Secret. Malcolm MacDonald, Despatch no. 6, "The Political Situation in Kenya. II – The Present," May 24, 1965, BNA, DO 213/65.
[120] Ibid.
[121] From H. S. Stanley to Norman (?), April 12, 1965, BNA, DO 213/65.
[122] H. W. O. Okoth-Ogendo clearly expressed this phenomenon when he wrote that "[i]n Kenya, where the politics of charisma have been the dominant feature, parliamentarisation in fact led to presidentialism" in "The Politics of Constitutional Change in Kenya since Independence, 1963–69," 29.
[123] Minutes of KANU Parliamentary Group Meeting Held in the Conference Centre, Harambee House on April 26, 1966 and Minutes of KANU Parliamentary Group Meeting Held on July 4, 1967, KNA, MAC/KEN/38/5.

questions or notices of motions in the House."[124] Neither KANU nor the parliament escaped the grip of governmental rule. KANU remained an empty shell; the parliament (merged with the senate in December 1966) an artificial and ineffective counter-power.[125]

Later attempts to attack the one-party state were met with the government's iron fist. In 1966, Odinga formed the Kenya People's Union (KPU) to directly attack the government's pro-West capitalist orientation and to demand redistributive land politics.[126] The government thereafter further tightened its control over the state institutions. Parliamentary seats were conditional on KANU membership, so as to discourage MPs from defecting from KANU, and the party regional branches were taken over by leading regional leaders loyal to Kenyatta, so as to hinder KPU's national and regional expansion. Kenyatta reshuffled the government, replacing former vice president Odinga with his long-time comrade Joseph Murumbi and maintained tribal and political balance within his government – just as he had done at independence – by appointing new faces, notably the former KADU chairman Ronald Ngala, the radical and Mboya-ally Clement Arwings-Kodhek, and the young Kikuyu Mwai Kibaki, freshly trained at LSE. Foreign affairs were taken over by the Office of the President.[127] To further prevent local political expression, the provincial administration became increasingly dominated by influential Kikuyu loyal to the president, although their power of action, as we will now see, were significantly hampered by the Office of the President.[128]

---

[124] Minutes of KANU Parliamentary Group Meeting Held on Wednesday March 22, 1967, KNA, MAC/KEN/38/5.
[125] On KANU during Kenyatta's regime, see Widner, *The Rise of a Party-State in Kenya*; David Anderson, "Le Déclin et la Chute de la Kanu," *Politique Africaine* 2, no. 90 (2003): 37–55. On Kenyan parliament, see Jay Edward Hakes, "The Parliamentary Party of the Kenya African National Union: Cleavage and Cohesion in the Ruling Party of a New Nation" (Ph.D. diss., Duke University, 1970); Ghai and McAuslan, *Public Law and Political Change in Kenya*; Throup, "The Construction and Deconstruction of the Kenyatta State"; Hornsby, *Kenya*, 167–169.
[126] On the formation of the KPU, see Mueller, "Government and Opposition in Kenya, 1966–9"; Odinga, *Not Yet Uhuru*, chapter 14.
[127] Hornsby, *Kenya*, 161–162.
[128] J. R. Nellis, *The Ethnic Composition of Leading Kenyan Government Positions*, Research Report no. 84 (Uppsala: The Scandinavian Institute of African Studies, 1974); Hornsby, *Kenya*, 175, 221; Report of the Truth, Justice, and Reconciliation Commission, vol. IIB (2013), 45, 48–49, 53–54.

After 1965: The Office of the President versus the Provincial Administration

Kenyatta's ability to remain above political divisions rested on his reluctance to distribute institutional responsibilities, preferring the symbolic role of the presidential patriarch: omnipotent yet distant and often making promises he would neither fulfill nor take responsibility for. To do so, he needed an intermediary body that would both connect him with and shelter him from people: this role was ascribed to the provincial administration. Kenyatta used it as a "shock absorber" against dissident politicians, as Gertzel rightly described it, and as a buffer for people's political grievances.[129] Whereas the historiography depicts the provincial administration as Kenyatta's political arm in the regions, a close reading of the PCs' files shows that they struggled to get active support from the president. To the great anger of the PCs, the latter was almost inaccessible and delegated relations with the provincial administration to his ministers. Remaining aloof from the provincial administration's responsibilities and burdens, Kenyatta was ruling a system in which he, the president, was politically invisible.

The independence constitution stipulated that the provincial administration, modeled after the former colonial civil service, ought to remain independent and apolitical. Provincial administrators were meant to execute the government's policies, ensure security in the regions, and were answering directly to the Office of the President.[130] The direct connection to the president has often been interpreted as a sign of empowerment, as the government preferred to use provincial and district commissioners as its regional representatives against "the politicians" – that is, KANU party members and MPs.[131] Indeed, civil servants were given just enough power to disrupt and even neutralize the political activities of dissident MPs. The Office of the President regularly received a plethora of complaints about civil servants, either on behalf of local citizens or of the MPs themselves. These denounced the officers' authoritarian behavior and deplored difficult relationships between district officers and district leaders, whether local chiefs, MPs, or senators.[132] Kenyatta seems to have been occasionally informed of

---

[129] Cherry J. Gertzel, "The Provincial Administration in Kenya," *Journal of Commonwealth & Comparative Politics* 4, no. 3 (1966): 208.
[130] Ibid., 202.   [131] On the conflict between PCs and politicians see ibid.
[132] A. W. Benaya to the President, (not dated), KNA, KA/6/10.

The Office of President versus Provincial Administration 209

some of the complaints. But it was Charles Njonjo, the attorney general, who was charged with informing the permanent secretary of the president of potential legal boundaries and to discuss further action, or nonaction.

A closer reading of provincial administration files shows, however, that its power fitted the system of "disempowered regionalism" mentioned in the introduction. PCs were constantly at pains to organize their actions and defend their prerogatives and responsibilities. They faced political, administrative, and financial obstacles that obtrued their efficiency and for which the under-secretary in charge of administration and the permanent secretary to the president's office, also head of the civil service, had little authority to act upon.[133] They struggled to get formal and personal support of the president himself, but more often than not they were disappointed. Attending a meeting of PCs, a rare appearance, in November 1965, Kenyatta said he would "visit the Provinces as often as possible."[134] Although the president reassured the civil servants that they were "the authority in their Province or District," he also reminded them that, when allowing political meetings or organizing ministerial visits in provinces, they should always refer to the Office of the President for ultimate permission.[135] He insisted that he did value contacts with his PCs and ordered his assistant minister to visit provinces and their officers regularly. But discipline was required: "He warned ... that he may request the Assistant minister to visit the provinces sometimes without prior warning."[136]

In fact, nowhere were the boundaries of the PCs' role and responsibilities defined, thus creating tension between PCs and government officials, and PCs were trying to restore this substantial disadvantage. Acting as "the authority in their Province or District," as Kenyatta

---

[133] Ibid., 204. See also Hornsby, *Kenya*, 109.
[134] Confidential. J. Musembi to the Permanent Secretary, Office of the President, "Minuted of Provincial Commissioner's meeting held on November 29–30, 1965," January 3, 1966, KNA, BB/49/59. As Kara Moskowitz showed, Kenyatta carefully planned his public ceremonies. Settlement ceremonies, in particular, gave him the opportunity to "augment the carefully curated image of Kenyatta as a personal granter of land." See Moskowitz, "Are You Planting Trees or Are You Planting People?."
[135] Confidential. J. Musembi to the Permanent Secretary, Office of the President, "Minutes of Provincial Commissioner's meeting held on the November 29–30, 1965," January 3, 1966, KNA, BB/49/59.
[136] Ibid.

expressed it, they nonetheless needed to refer to the Office of the President to allow political meetings or organize ministerial visits in provinces.[137] Presidential circulars organizing the government's function always mentioned that the Office of the President was responsible of the "Administration including the Provincial Administration."[138] Reacting to the president's circular in 1966, Eliud Mahihu, PC for Eastern province, asked vehemently: "Has there been any other directive on the subject giving the responsibilities to any other Minister apart from the President?"[139]

Furthermore, PCs were aware of the fact that their political power lacked economic resources. They complained that they were "expected to run more services than finances could meet."[140] They also denounced the "secrecy" that surrounded the allocation of resources, which amounted sometimes to a parallel system of decision-making, especially with regards to the allocation of land.[141] Nevertheless, control over the distribution of the state's financial resources had been settled during the independence negotiations: Kenyatta and KANU wanted the central government to control the funds allocated to regions so as to control the main source of political and economic patronage. To Kenyatta, "[t]here was no intention of dismantling local authorities. The idea of transfer was intended to control the public funds and direct the work of the County Council so that the wanachi [citizens] could benefit."[142] The hands of the provincial administration were tied.

---

[137] Ibid.
[138] "Organisation of the Government of the Republic of Kenya," President's Circular No. 1 of 1968, No. 1 of 1967, and No. 3 of 1965, KNA, KA/5/25.
[139] Confidential. Eliud Mahihu to the Permanent Secretary, Office of the President, November 9, 1966, KNA, BB/49/49.
[140] Confidential. Notes of a meeting between the PCs and the Permanent Secretaries of the Office of the President, Ministry of Economic Planning and Development and Ministry of Local Government held on June 28, 1967, KNA, BB/49/59.
[141] Confidential. P. K. Boit to Permanent Secretary Office of the President, "Provincial Commissioner's Meeting," October 12, 1967, KNA, BB/49/59.
[142] Confidential. F. M. Nthenge to the Permanent Secretary, Ministry of Cooperatives and Social Services, "Distribution of Funds and Effectiveness of the Provincial and District Committees," June 8, 1970, KNA, BB/59/49.

PCs complained that ministers downgraded them, and that they were criticized in return for their lack of cooperation.[143] They further denounced the interference from the Office of the President regarding the nomination of administrative officers, in total disregard of their views.[144] Indeed, Kenyatta relied heavily on his ministers to interact with the provincial administration. Their depoliticization, constantly advocated by Kenyatta, and the reason he favored the provincial administration as a whole, was also their main weakness. If PCs were cut off from both political and government institutions, their functions were virtually reduced to a smokescreen. As Simeon Nyachae, the Rift Valley PC, wrote to Kenyatta's permanent secretary, "you should really go into the question as to why we feel there is a necessity for the Minister of State to attend the PCs meeting."[145] He concluded that it was "wrong to underestimate our intelligence to the extent of expecting us not to know that there is a Minister who deals with political issues."[146] The PC for Western province, S. O. Josiah, also demanded to be further associated with ministers' decision-making, while James Mburu, the North Eastern province PC, demanded that Kenyatta chair the PCs meetings.[147] What the PCs were fighting was in fact a "secluded system" of rule, as Nyachae would call it, which stripped them of any power of decision-making and significantly reduced their efficiency as a coordinated institution.[148]

Ultimately, however, cabinet ministers treated all complaints, whether by politicians or administrators, with relative disinterest and skepticism. As Mbiyu Koinange wrote to Njonjo, "often most of the

---

[143] Confidential. Notes of a Meeting between the PCs and the Permanent Secretaries of the Office of the President, Ministry of Economic Planning and Development and Ministry of Local Government held on June 28, 1967, KNA, BB/49/59.
[144] S. Nyachae to Permanent Secretary, Office of the President, "Provincial Commissioner's Meeting," October 5, 1967, KNA, BB/49/59.
[145] Confidential. S. Nyachae to the Permanent Secretary, Office of the President, December 13, 1966, KNA, BB/49/59.
[146] Ibid.
[147] S. O. Josiah to the Permanent Secretary, Office of the President, November 1, 1966 and J. G. Mburu to the Permanent Secretary, Office of the President, October 27, 1966, KNA, BB/49/59.
[148] S. Nyachae to the Permanent Secretary, Office of the President, "Provincial Commissioner's Meeting," October 5, 1967, KNA, BB/49/59.

complaints taken out of context could be somewhat misleading and exaggerated."[149] Such disinterest would persist well after 1965. Civil servants were asked to be loyal, apolitical, and impartial, and yet the "general feeling that local authorities cannot be treated in isolation from Central Government" continued to unite PCs against government ministers.[150] The conflict continued to smoulder and as a PC meeting noted "the practice of writing angry letters had become common among some PC."[151] The latter were subsequently asked to "write such letter in a calm state of mind, in order that they may avoid possible repercussions."[152] 1966 saw further readjustments to the depoliticization of civil servants, as the government requested any civil servant to resign from KANU.[153] In 1969, civil servants were prohibited from standing for elections as members of the National Assembly.[154] Those who would choose to resign from the civil administration could not be reinstated.[155]

The secluded system of rule that Nyachae denounced was not only isolating the provincial administration from the president. It was also forcing the population to deal with a Kafkaesque bureaucracy. The president used the provincial administration as an intermediary that would absorb all grievances without taking responsibility for any of them. The separation of institutions and its impact on the population was most blatant when it came to the issue of land, the landless, and the squatters.

---

[149] Mbiyu Koinange to Charles Njonjo, February 21, 1967, KNA, KA/6/10.
[150] Confidential. Notes of a meeting between the PCs and the Permanent Secretaries of the Office of the President, Ministry of Economic Planning and Development and Ministry of Local Government held on June 28, 1967, KNA, BB/49/59.
[151] Confidential. Minutes of the PC's meeting held on March 15/16, 1967, KNA, BB/49/59.
[152] Ibid.
[153] Personnel Circular no. 36 by J. D. M. Malinda, "Prohibition of Membership of Political Associations," November 21, 1966, KNA, AAC/3/5.
[154] Personnel Circular no. 15 by G. K. Kariithi, "Prohibition of Standing for Election as a Member of the National Assembly," October 2, 1969, KNA, AAC/3/6.
[155] Personnel Circular no. 10 by J. A. Gethenji, "Prohibition of Standing for Election as a Member of the National Assembly," July 18, 1969, KNA, AAC/3/6.

The President and the Squatters, Landless, and Poor

Although both the negotiations of land buying and land settlement were meant to deal with the persistent issue of the squatters, landless, and the poor, the latter remained a missing voice. Their conspicuous absence from most of the government's correspondence shows that negotiations on the land redistribution and the political stability remained, purposely, mutually exclusive political issues. As seen earlier, the mere existence of the landless and poor masses justified speaking of development, which was, in turn, merely invoked to seek more funding. They never fitted into a grand narrative of national development, for the Kenyan government had none.

The absence of ideological commitment was coherent with the absence of any idea of the "nation" or "national community" in Kenyatta's political imagination. The lack of any reflection on the connection between state-building and national development runs against the rather intuitive belief that a new independent state should be less democratic and more repressive to enhance economic growth – an argumentation that the Senegalese Léopold Sédar Senghor, as well as the Ghanean Kwame Nkrumah attempted to justify shortly after they were elected presidents.[156] On the contrary, Kenyatta treated the shortage of land and the ensuring "squatter issue" – that is, landless people spontaneously occupying land despite any land rights – as a side issue that deserved only secondary treatment. As moneymaking became the driving force of land politics, the government was confining itself to a mind-set that excluded squatters. The squatter problem revealed a wider institutional divide between "radical" politicians

---

[156] Martin Shipway, "Colonial Politics Before the Flood: Challenging the State, Imagining the Nation," in *Decolonisation and Its Impact: A Comparative Approach to the End of the Colonial Empires*, ed. Martin Shipway (Malden, MA: Blackwell, 2008), 35–60; Cooper, "Development, Modernisation, and the Social Sciences in the Era of Decolonisation," 15–50; J. Tischler, "Cementing Uneven Development: The Central African Federation and the Kariba Dam Scheme," *Journal of Southern African Studies* 40, no. 5 (2014): 1047–1064. On Nkrumah's state ideology, see Kwame Nkrumah, *Consciencism: Philosophy and Ideology for Decolonisation and Development with Particular Reference to African Revolution* (London: Heinemann, 1964). On Senghor, see Janet G. Vaillant, *Black, French, and African: A Life of Léopold Sédar Senghor* (Cambridge, MA: Harvard University Press, 1990). For comparative perspective on African leaders' and state-building, see Prasenjit Duara (ed.), *Decolonisation: Perspectives from Now and Then* (London: Routledge, 2003).

attempting to defy the government's policy and cabinet ministers defending and protecting their responsibilities. The separation (or "seclusion") of state institutions channeled the landless' and squatter's dissatisfaction into a heavily bureaucraticized and unending process.

Squatters and landless had long remained second-class political issues, left to security and police forces, to the great disquiet of many administrators and politicians, and in spite of Kenyatta's full knowledge of the political sensitivity of the matter. From 1963 to the beginning of 1965, the government did not depart from its conviction that there would not be enough land for all, and that the squatter issue, although a direct consequence of colonial land alienation, could only be partially addressed. As Angaine explained:

> we are trying to acquire land in the central region as quickly as possible, but who goes on this land is a matter for the president of the central regional assembly to decide, and it is unlikely that Settlement Schemes will be able to absorb a very high proportion of landless and unemployed from other areas.[157]

Combating squatters, and employing police forces to do so if needed, was seen as a reasonable measure to preserve the grand economic architecture settled at independence.[158] Giving a press conference on March 6, 1964, Kenyatta reaffirmed that the government was committed to take firm action against squatters on European or Africans farms, and even on the settlement schemes themselves.[159] Police operations, however, were insufficient to erase a problem all deemed political. Despite the various meetings and committees established on the

---

[157] Angaine to the President of Eastern Region and the President of Central Region, "Landless Kikuyu in the Embu district," September 17, 1963, KNA, AVS/15/41. See also Moskowitz's "Are You Planting Trees or Are You Planting People?"

[158] Speaking of European mixed farms, Bruce McKenzie reassured European farmers stating the "Government's decision to take drastic police action very soon against the squatters in the Naivasha area of the Rift Valley Region ... ; if the squatters were not dealt with effectively now lawlessness would spread and the government be undermined." In "Extract. Nairobi Despatch (3) Land Policy," March 12, 1964, BNA, DO 214/39.

[159] Confidential. Inward Telegram no. 508, "Land Settlement: Parliamentary Questions," March 9, 1964, BNA, DO 214/39.

subject, the government was not ready to commit further means and funding to the squatters. On the contrary, the government continued to view squatters as a "disease" compromising its purportedly modern land policies.[160] In a secret document sent to all civil secretaries and regional commissioners of police, the Ministry of Defense passed on Kenyatta's views that "illegal occupation of land belonging to other people would not be tolerated," that "the Government was not going to be blackmailed into handing out land and money to buy off these squatters," and that "regions starting up local settlement schemes apart from those organised by the Central government" should be warned.[161] The document ironically concluded that "If at any time you need any specific assistance from the Central Government (excluding limitless funds and limitless land!) you may be sure that any request will be supported as far as possible."[162]

By 1965, however, as the topic became publicly discussed, Kenyatta was forced to adjust his attitude, although he subtly avoided altering it substantially. In February, squatters' evictions were debated in parliament, as Bildad Kaggia presented a motion on the issue.[163] Immediately after the motion was deposed, the government ordered the cessation of any violent eviction.[164] In March, Godfrey K. Kariithi, permanent secretary to the Ministry of Agriculture and Animal Husbandry (headed by Bruce McKenzie), brought the government's doubts into the open, blaming the old attitude of "let us evict them and put them on the roadside as the law provides" that was no longer, according to him, "really the answer."[165] Noting the alarming increase of population in all areas, Kariithi pleaded that "something more constructive must be worked out."[166] In the meantime, Njoroge

[160] "Precis of the Report on the Squatter Problem by the Special Commissioner for Squatters," by A. Davis, Under-Secretary, Ministry of Lands and Settlement, March 7, 1966, KNA, BN/97/3.
[161] Secret. J. Gethi, Permanent Secretary, Ministry of Internal Security and Defense to Civil Secretaries and Regional commissioners of Police of Coast, Nyanza, Rift Valley, Eastern, Central, Western Region, October 23, 1964, KNA, ACW/27/76.
[162] Ibid.
[163] National Assembly Debates (Hansard), Vol. IV, February 26, 1965, cols. 321–345.
[164] Confidential. F. N. Brockett to R. W. Wootton, April 26, 1965, BNA, FCO 141/18985.
[165] G. K. Kariithi, "Illegal squatters," March 17, 1965, KNA, ACW/27/76.
[166] Ibid.

Mungai, minister for defense, reported to Kenyatta that the Office of the President had given instructions "not to cooperate in any action taken by the police to remove illegal squatters."[167] To what extent Kenyatta was responsible for these instructions is unclear. Nevertheless, he clearly took a new stand on the issue as the situation worsened and risked contaminating public politics.

In May 1965, Kenyatta finally appointed a special commissioner to document the squatter problem and to advise the government accordingly, although at no time did the government intend to compromise its politics.[168] Interestingly, the appointment was not to be made public and not to be discussed in the press, at least "for the time being."[169] This was a clear sign that the government was undergoing a superficial makeover only, and was not ready to initiate any substantial political change. As discussed on April 23, while the decision to appoint a special commissioner was probably already contemplated, ministry officials agreed that "The plan for dealing with the squatter problem must therefore be based on dealing with urgent cases such as those squatters whose presence prevented the economic development of farms or constitute a security risk."[170] Land productivity being the unshakable principle of government policy, it was advocated, instead, to repatriate squatters on inexpensive lands.[171] Even more telling was the fact that Kenyatta considered that the post of special commissioner for squatters would only exist for two years, a period during which the "problem of squatters will have been reduced considerably."[172] The

---

[167] Confidential. Dr. Njoroge Mungai to the President, March 11, 1965, KNA, ACW/76/27. It is not clear if Njoroge Mungai wrote to Kenyatta after or before the Kariithi's letter, as his letter dated March 11, 1965 mentions a meeting dated the March 18, 1965.
[168] Memorandum by the Minister for Agriculture and Animal Husbandry, "Squatter Problem," KNA, ACW/27/76.
[169] Minutes of the First Liaison Committee Meeting on Squatters Held on May 21, 1965 at 3 p.m. in the Conference Room, Ministry of Agriculture, KNA, ACW/27/76.
[170] Confidential. Minutes of a Meeting of Officials on Squatters Held at Harambee House, Cabinet Room on April 23, 1966, at 9.30 a.m., KNA, BN/97/3.
[171] Inexpensive lands being listed as mismanages farms, vacant state land, or areas to be excised from forests. Ibid.
[172] Secret. Duncan Ndegwa to Permanent Secretary, Ministry of Internal Security and Defense, April 22, 1965, KNA, ACW/27/76.

government eventually chose Z. B. Shimechero, an assistant commissioner of police, to occupy these new functions.[173]

From then on, Kenyatta disassociated himself from the matter and left ministers and government officials deal with the special commissioner, his mission, his requests, and, more problematic even, the scope of his legal powers. Kara Moskowitz showed how the administration was deregulated and powerless to face squatters' political resilience and how Kenyatta's personal style of rule added confusion to a government burdened by ministerial infighting, as he made personal promises and commitments to delegations of squatters that could not be fulfilled.[174] The same pattern is observable when it came to negotiating the powers and purpose of the special commissioner of squatters, as conflict of authority grew between Schimechero and the minister of lands, Jackson Angaine. Although the archives document a stagnation of the tensions (that continue well after 1966), no evidence was found that Kenyatta had intervened in the matter.[175]

The establishment of a "secluded" system of state institutions may explain why Kenyatta's government quickly ceased to view the squatters and landless as a political threat and continued to ignore land hunger or social decay. The frustrations of the squatters and landless masses were confined to an administration insulated from the Office of the President. Kenyatta's subtle control of institutional infighting undermined the administration's proper functioning. The landless were forced to turn to the self-help solutions that Kenyatta advocated, although many desperately continued to seek presidential support, either by organizing delegations to the State House or writing to the Office of the President pleading for help.[176] The political and administrative treatment of the squatters effectively disempowered them. Meanwhile, Kenyatta enjoyed great popularity, which may explain why so many landless and poor continued to believe he would redistribute land – and waited.[177]

* * *

[173] Ibid.
[174] Moskowitz, "Are You Planting Trees or Are You Planting People?"
[175] See in particular the KNA files ACW/27/76 and BN/97/3.
[176] See Moskowitz, "Are You Planting Trees or Are You Planting People?"; Githuku, *Mau Mau Crucible of War*, chapter 5. Assessing how the politics of self-help might have been used against the government would be an interesting topic of study which goes beyond the scope of this book.
[177] Report of the Truth, Justice, and Reconciliation Commission, vol. IIB (2013).

Kenyatta succeeded in treating the financial negotiations with the British, the squatters' claims over land, and the radical political agitation as separate issues, despite the close connection to the land issue that they all involved. Like most of his cabinet ministers, Kenyatta was interested in encouraging land purchase both for political and personal ends and supressing political divisions, no matter how contradictory these two objectives would be. His willful ignorance of the details involved in political negotiations, disputes, or dissent showed that he wanted to be, and act as, a distant and discreet politician. The silencing of radical claims concerning the most controversial political topic in Kenya – that is, land redistribution – was inspired by his disinterest in national politics, and his disregard for land settlement and the landless, among them many Kikuyu. This conception was influenced by his Kikuyu ethos, although not exclusively. The making of his presidential rule bore the legacy of his own ascension to power: Kenyatta had always been cut off from grassroots politics. At independence, he seized strong presidential powers with a weak and fragile state. He had no real choice but to be a discreet president: at once direct, for his control of the state machine was his only resource, yet distant, for he had to remain above politics.

7 | Ruling over a Divided Political Family (1965–1969)

The political developments of the second half of the 1960s saw an increasing repression of the opponents to Kenyatta's regime, a fact that has been well documented in the literature.[1] Political agitators became increasingly vocal, blaming the government for failing to distribute the fruits of *uhuru* (independence), and denouncing corruption and individual enrichment. Meanwhile Jomo Kenyatta's health was declining and the president was gradually distancing himself from formal politics. The period, however, also saw another political development, on which much less has been written: the politicization of the land market after 1965 and its impact on the make-up of Kenyatta's regime.[2] Cabinet ministers and politicians sought to secure their access to economic and political patronage as they feared, as early as 1966, that the "Old Man" could pass away any time. They put two issues on the agenda: the Africanization of landownership and the question of presidential succession. At issue was the protection of land titles owned by the Kenyan elite and the slow exclusion of non-Kenyan citizens (even non-Africans) from the land market. Although the debate over the Africanization of land was framed in racial terms, race was only one element in a larger game to secure the control of the state and its resources even after Kenyatta's potential death.[3]

---

[1] For a detailed history of politics at that particular time, see Susanne D. Mueller, "Political Parties in Kenya, Patterns of Opposition and Dissent 1919–1969" (Ph.D. diss., Princeton University, 1979); Branch, *Kenya*. For a general history of the period, see Gertzel, *The Politics of Independent Kenya, 1963–8*; Ogot and Ochieng', *Decolonisation and Independence in Kenya, 1940–93*, chapter 4; Hornsby, *Kenya*, chapter 4.

[2] I thank John Lonsdale and an anonymous reviewer for their suggestions on how to better conceptualize this idea.

[3] R. Rathbone emphasized that the debate over the Africanization of land was more than a racial bargain in "Review. *Racial Bargaining in Independent Kenya: A Study of Minorities and Decolonisation*. By Donald Rothchild," *International Affairs* 50, no. 4 (1974): 665–666.

Although demands for Africanization had been a central feature of anticolonial discourse, the independence settlements emphasized the need to retain and continue to attract foreign capital to boost the Kenyan economy.[4] Arguments for Africanization receded while economic pragmatism and political prudence were on the rise.[5] The Kenyan government sought to retain foreign capital, aid, technical assistance, and the dominance of the private sector, whenever it would best protect and stabilize its economic interests.[6] Africanization was most rapid and visible in the civil service and legislature, but barely altered the foreign domination of key sectors of the economy and finance inherited from colonization and expanded after independence. These were strategic moves Kenyatta had always supported: with the government's policy of willing buyer–willing seller, foreign capital was central to securing land titles (and in particular access to loans and credit).[7]

Africanization, a synonym, at times, for decolonization, was a useful cover for government ministers tightening their control over lucrative businesses, taking over the top positions of parastatals, or private enterprises.[8] Many observed the simultaneous "Kikuyuisation" of the government, pointing at how the purported Africanization impacted the definition of citizenship. Noncitizens, in particular those of Asian and European origin, were seen as dangerous competitors who risked impeding the Africanization of the government and the development of the economy. A series of amendments was issued to further control trade permits and the land market, clearly targeting non-African Kenyans. The right to citizenship for commonwealth citizens became

---

[4] Donald Rothchild, "Kenya's Africanisation Program: Priorities of Development and Equity," *American Political Science Review* 64, no. 3 (1970): 737–753.

[5] Leys, *Underdevelopment in Kenya*, 147; Rothchild, "Kenya's Africanisation Program."

[6] Donald Rothchild, "Changing Racial Stratifications and Bargaining Styles: The Kenya Experience," *Canadian Journal of African Studies* 7, no. 3 (1973): 419–432; Leys, *Underdevelopment in Kenya*, 128–148. See also Arthur Hazlewood, *The Economy of Kenya: The Kenyatta Era* (New York: Oxford University Press, 1980), chapter 5; Swainson, *The Development of Corporate Capitalism in Kenya, 1918–77*, chapter 6.

[7] Rothchild, "Kenya's Africanisation Program," 738, 748. Branch also recalled that upon independence, when Kenyatta' land policy was being criticized, the president stated that "one day, all our farmers will be black," see *Kenya*, 95.

[8] *Who Controls Industry in Kenya? Report of a Working Party* (Nairobi: East African Publishing House, 1968); Leonard, *African Successes*.

cancellable after five years of residency.[9] Most significant perhaps, was the passing, in 1967, of the Land Control Act, which was meant to regulate land acquisitions and transactions and to tackle the complicated issue of landlessness, but which resulted in the gradual exclusion of noncitizens from the land market.[10] Such exclusion resonated with the dramatic expulsion of Asians from economic activity from 1967 to 1969.[11]

To what extent Kenyatta influenced such a turn of the tide is unclear, and neither the existing historiography nor available archives provide satisfactory answers. Historians and political analysts have shown that he remained firmly in control, but have also noted that his cabinet ministers enjoyed increasing leeway of action and decision-making regarding government affairs.[12] The two main sources of archives explored for this chapter – land files and political reports of the time – show Kenyatta's role as a suspiciously distant one. In fact, the scarcity of available archives prevents us from fully retracing his actions over the period. Precisely for that reason, however, a reflection on the evolution of presidential rule in the second half of the 1960s is needed. It must acknowledge the cabinet ministers' substantial political influence as Kenyatta retreated into a strategic waiting game – although he certainly remained a powerful and overarching leading figure.

This chapter traces how, after 1965, Kenyatta's presidential style became ever more erratic. The scope of his presidential powers had been, since independence, loosely defined, and, despite the fact that he had been surrounded by an extremely divided (at times even hostile) political elite, no competitor could afford to contest his statue as "father of the nation." He decided to play the role of a "reconciler," a title he had even given to his newspaper before independence: *Mugwithania*. It is in this role that he approached the two central issues

---

[9] Hornsby, *Kenya*, 167.   [10] Ibid., 196.
[11] See Richard Plender, "The Exodus of Asians from East and Central Africa: Some Comparative and International Law Aspects," *The American Journal of Comparative Law* 19, no. 2 (1971): 287–324; Donald S. Rothchild, *Racial Bargaining in Independent Kenya: A Study of Minorities and Decolonisation* (London: Oxford University Press, 1973). For a fictional account of Asians lives in Kenya since independence, and to read one of a few fictional yet realistic portraits of Jomo Kenyatta, see M. G. Vassanji, *The In-Between World of Vikram Lall* (New York: Vintage, 2005).
[12] Daniel Bourmaud, *Histoire Politique du Kenya: Etat et Pouvoir Local* (Paris: Karthala, 1988), 112–121; Branch, *Kenya*, 67–69.

dominating his government's affairs after 1965. Concerning the issue of the Africanization of land ownership, he clearly supported the demands of the Kenyan elite, but continued to reassure European farmers that they had no reason to worry. At the same time, his readiness to take over land, and even to settle Kikuyu in regions other than the Central province (in particular in Maasailand and in the Coast province) resonates with what the previous chapters showed: that Kenyatta never conceived a nationalist project. When it came to the presidential succession, most cabinet ministers preferred the status quo, waiting for the "Old Man" either to show his hand in the game and appoint a successor, or, alternatively, to die. Yet, Kenyatta used the same strategy that had salvaged him during the "Release Kenyatta" campaign: for things to change, everything has to remain as it is. He was left with the role of ruling over a divided political family, using his unrivaled access to state resources.

Kenyatta: Arbitrator of an Increasingly Politicized Land Market

By 1965, the government's increasingly brutal and merciless repression of political agitation was accompanied by increasingly oligarchic practices regarding land affairs. The sensitive context of the Cold War risked amplifying the voices of "socialist" critics who denounced the lack of radical redistribution of land and endangered the government's legitimacy and popularity. As a response to such critics, the government published, in 1965, a paper on African socialism, eloquently drafted by Tom Mboya. As Joseph Murumbi later recalled, Tom Mboya himself was "by no stretch of imagination a socialist. He was a capitalist. Now I don't believe there is any type of socialism called African Socialism."[13] The publication of the paper did not entail any political or economic reorientation. It was instead an ideological smokescreen few countries could do without during the Cold War. On the one hand, the competition between the two blocs boosted the value of international aid, further tightening African leaders' dependency on international patronage.[14] On the other hand, the fresh

[13] Murumbi and Thurston, *A Path Not Taken*, 148.
[14] On Kenya, see in particular William Attwood's memoirs (Attwood was the American ambassador to Kenya from 1964 to 1966): William Attwood, *The Reds and the Blacks: A Personal Adventure* (New York: Harper & Row, 1967), 150–152, 179, chapters 18 and 19. For more general insight on the issue, see

accession to independence forced African leaders to adopt a language of nonalignment. While some saw alignment with the West as a sign of neocolonization, others, like Kenyatta or the Senegalese Leopold Sédar Senghor, attempted to conceptualize positive cooperation with the two blocs invoking the sake of development.[15]

Besides vague commitments to positive non-alignment, the paper reasserted the productive use of land and the necessity to attract foreign aid to boost the development of the country – no matter how much these two ideas contradicted an already dubious socialist spirit.[16] The paper built on Kenyatta's repeated plea not to leave land lying idle, and affirmed that land ownership lay with those who would develop the land. It also advocated the protection of property and the expansion of land tenure, which supposed the individualization of land ownership rights.[17] The government's move away from settlement schemes was reaffirmed, and so was the plan to focus more exclusively on the development of land rather than the transfer of land.[18]

The paper formalized the continuity between colonial and postcolonial land discourses. On the one hand, the Kenyan government's rhetorical attacks against land lying idle echoed colonial arguments used in the early stages of the conquest, that land should be cultivated or, put differently, be civilized.[19] Civilizational discourse was not

---

Laëtitia Atlani-Duault and Jean-Pierre Dozon, "Colonisation, Développement, Aide Humanitaire. Pour une Anthropologie de l'Aide Internationale," *Ethnologie française* 41, no. 3 (2011): 393–403. For an analysis of the 1970s to 1900s, see Thad Dunning, "Conditioning the Effects of Aid: Cold War Politics, Donor Credibility, and Democracy in Africa," *International Organization* 58, no. 2 (2004): 409–423. For a conceptual interpretation of African states' financial dependency, see Jean-François Bayart, "L'Afrique dans le Monde: Une Histoire d'Extraversion," *Critique Internationale* 5, no. 5 (1999): 97–120.

[15] See in particular Matthew Connelly, *A Diplomatic Revolution: Algeria's Fight for Independence and the Origins of the Post-Cold War Era* (Oxford: Oxford University Press, 2002); Robert J. McMahon, ed., *The Cold War in the Third World* (Oxford: Oxford University Press, 2013). On Senghor, see his speeches and political writings, in particular, "Décoloniser pour Créer" (Fourth UPS Congress in Dakar, July 1963) and "Problème de Développement dans les Pays Sous-Développés" (Inaugural Lecture on Public Administration for Asian and African Francophones Interns, Ottawa University, September 20, 1966) in Léopold Sédar Senghor, *Liberté 4. Socialisme et Planification* (Paris: Seuil, 1983), 114–167, 276–301.

[16] Republic of Kenya, *African Socialism and Its Application to Planning in Kenya* (Nairobi, 1965), 24, 29.

[17] Ibid., 17.   [18] Ibid., 27–33.

[19] Berman and Lonsdale, *Unhappy Valley*, book two, 322.

simply a moral ornament of colonial psychology: it demarcated participation in or exclusion from the political arena, forcing opposing voices to adapt their political claims to civilizational logics. At stake in colonial Kenya was a very concrete objective: establishing moral rights to occupy land.[20] This had been a central concern for Kenyatta since his early literary and political career. In *Facing Mount Kenya,* he attacked Western civilization to assert his own intellectual legitimacy and authority.[21] To overcome the tricky circumvolution of the civilizational discourse, however, he emphasized the act of writing Kikuyu history as the materialization of a civilization itself. Writing history, John Lonsdale explained, was a competition for civilization, and

[20] The land issue was structured along a central element of the civilizational rhetoric: for its occupation to be morally justified, land had to be cultivated and its history documented. Settler colonialism built on the ancient conception that land property was an attribute of nobility, and its conquest was justified on the grounds that settled agriculture was an eminently superior form of culture. See A. Dirk Moses, "Das Römische Gespräch in a New Key: Hannah Arendt, Genocide, and the Defense of Republican Civilisation," *The Journal of Modern History* 85, no. 4 (2013): 878. On the importance of classics to colonial officials, see Ranger, "From Humanism to the Science of Man." The Kikuyu had to provide British colonizers and white settlers with historical evidence that they were the first to occupy the land, and, more importantly, that they did not get it through the use of force. In sum, they had to prove not only that their history went back, to employ Kenyatta's recurring words, to "time immemorial," but that their acquisition and use of land was itself civilized. This not entirely new to Kikuyu history, however. The Kikuyu themselves opposed the rustic hunters and gatherers against their farmers who "worked" and therefore transformed and civilized the land, see J. L. Lonsdale, "La Pensée Politique Kikuyu et les Idéologies du Mouvement Mau-Mau," *Cahiers d'Études Africaines* 27, no. 107/ 108 (1987): 329–57; "Contest of Time," 222–224

[21] Kenyatta, *Facing Mount Kenya,* 119–120, 140, 187–190, 204, 297, 298. See also Kenyatta, *Kenya,* 5, 11, 19, 23. It must be mentioned that his critique of Western civilization, and more generally of the colonial civilizing mission, became a strategic device to assert his own political authority. When they first met, Malinowski was seeking an opportunity to further his knowledge of the "Dark continent," championing the "scientificity" of anthropology in academic and political circles. See Cocks, "The Rhetoric of Science and the Critique of Imperialism in British Social Anthropology, c. 1870–1940"; "The King and I: Bronislaw Malinowski, King Sobhuza II of Swaziland and the Vision of Culture Change in Africa," *History of the Human Sciences* 13, no. 4 (2000): 25–47; Adam Kuper, *Anthropology and Anthropologists: The Modern British School* (London: Routledge, 1996), chapters 1 and 4. To Kenyatta, anthropology was an opportunity to gain credibility within colonial institutions. See Berman, "Ethnography as Politics, Politics as Ethnography," 313–314; Berman and Lonsdale "The Labors of *Muigwithania*"; "Custom, Modernity and the Search for Kihooto."

historical evidence was necessary to substantiate claims over land.[22] Competition for historical rights over land became a salient political issue – and has remained one until today.[23]

On the other hand, the paper on African socialism reenacted the supremacy of individual land ownership, perpetuating the colonial emphasis on individual private property at the expense of communally owned land. As previously seen, Kenyatta and his party embraced the concept of willing buyer–willing seller at independence, and, by doing so, dismissed indigenous discourses over land rights as illegitimate. After 1965, land consolidation and adjudication continued to spread, warmly supported by all the political elite, in particular the backbenchers.[24] In spite of its poor results and very slow progression, land consolidation remained a useful way, in politicians' view, of securing land ownership. Eager to secure their ownership and anticipating potentially threatening indigenous claims, cabinet ministers and prominent civil servants became increasingly influential in policing land affairs.[25] They were the architects of an Africanization of land ownership that favored African landowners over rich white farmers and protected land titles against communal claims.

---

[22] Lonsdale, "Contest of Time"; "Soil, Work, Civilisation and Citizenship in Kenya," *Journal of Eastern African Studies* 2, no. 2(2008): 305–314.
[23] Francesca di Matteo, "The Fora of Public Action in Kenya: From the Origins of the National Land Policy to Its Politicisation," *Mambo!* 12, no. 4 (2014); Gabrielle Lynch, "What's in a Name? The Politics of Naming Ethnic Groups in Kenya's Cherangany Hills," *Journal of Eastern African Studies* 10, no. 1 (2016): 208–227; Bruce Berman, "Ethnic Territory, Land Tenure and Citizenship in Africa: The Politics of Devolution in Ghana and Kenya," in *Territorial Pluralism: Managing Difference in Multinational States*, eds. John McGarry and Richard Simeon (Vancouver: UBC Press, 2015), 240–264. For Pan-African comparisons, see Catherine Boone, "Land Tenure Regimes and State Structure in Rural Africa: Implications for Forms of Resistance to Large-Scale Land Acquisitions by Outsiders," *Journal of Contemporary African Studies* 33, no. 2 (2015): 171–190; K. Klaus and M. I. Mitchell, "Land Grievances and the Mobilisation of Electoral Violence Evidence from Côte d'Ivoire and Kenya," *Journal of Peace Research* 52, no. 2 (2015): 622–635; Alan C. Tidwell and Barry Scott Zellen, *Land, Indigenous Peoples and Conflict* (London: Routledge, 2015).
[24] Ministry of Lands and Settlement, "Recent Land Reforms in Kenya," June 4, 1968, KNA, BN/81/87.
[25] A. Davies to Permanent Secretary, October 3, 1966; Confidential. J. M. Waiyaki to the Permanent Secretary, Ministry of Lands and Settlement, June 8, 1968, KNA, BN/81/87.

The productive use of land and the individualization of land titles dominated the government's correspondence after 1965. The Africanization of land ownership was a central concern for cabinet ministers, who feared they were losing grip of the land market. In October, a cabinet meeting presided over by Kenyatta concluded on the necessity to ensure that land valuations be "fair" to African buyers.[26] As Jackson Angaine explained in a letter to Charles Njonjo, the attorney general, his ministry feared that the land market was being dominated by a handful of rich Europeans who were failing to publicize sales, selling the land at too high a price, and thus "ridiculing" other African buyers.[27] Angaine was seeking legal advice from Njonjo to reconsider the principle of willing buyer–willing seller established at independence: in his view, the principle risked being translated into practise as non-Africans selling to non-Africans.[28] Angaine wanted to allow land institutions (in particular the local Divisional Land Control Boards) to refuse particular transactions even when there was only one applicant.

A general feeling prevailed that African ownership of land was hindered by price valuations too sympathetic to Europeans, and too high for African buyers. The minister of finance James Gichuru took on the difficult task of convincing the British government that this dissatisfaction should not lead to the cutting down of financial aid. Writing to the former high commissioner, Malcolm MacDonald, he noted that "[t]he question of the price paid for the land is still a live issue in Kenya politics" and reminded his reader that, at the time of independence, settlement policies served both governments' interests, before concluding, with a touch of provocation perhaps, that "memories are short."[29] Nevertheless, cabinet ministers were divided on this issue. The Ministry of Economy defended lower valuation prices, but its minister Tom Mboya defended a conception of development

---

[26] Extract from Cabinet no. 270 of the Meeting Held on 28.10.1965, CAB (65) 16A Min. 270 "Valuation of Properties Purchased by Government," KNA, BN/82/1.
[27] Strictly Confidential. Jackson Angaine to Charles Njonjo, August 31, 1966, KNA, BN/96/2.
[28] Ibid.
[29] Confidential. James Gichuru to Malcolm MacDonald, February 22, 1966, BNA, DO 214/53.

increasingly criticized, and which set him in opposition to Jackson Angaine.[30] Bruce McKenzie, at the Ministry of Agriculture, feared low valuations would break the morale of British farmers.[31] According to British accounts, however, McKenzie was more concerned with land productivity and hoped to make his personal business flourish with the Agricultural Development Corporation (ADC), the institution managing international loans provided to finance land purchase. McKenzie's business credo greatly influenced the government's policy, as "in some cases [they] were not anxious to buy farms [which] would not be ... profitable at all under African management; the value of the farm was therefore different for the two types of ownership."[32] At the same time, the ADC activities sparked much resentment, and Angaine in particular had his eye on the corporation, for his Land Ministry to take it over.[33]

Despite these divisions, most cabinet ministers and leading politicians from every province were anxious to control land transactions, invoking the domination of the land market by foreigners to legitimate their claims to Africanization. The concern was openly discussed during a KANU parliamentary group meeting chaired by Kenyatta. The president reminded his anxious audience that the constitution guaranteed property owned by noncitizens, and, although the government had no means to pay financial compensation for all, it would attempt to control land transactions and "[stop] foreigners from buying land for speculation purposes."[34] Kenyatta had perhaps been alerted by the situation in Thika, Central province, where large estates

---

[30] Note by B. Greatbatch, March 21, 1967, BNA, FCO 141/19010; Confidential. Edward Peck to Sir Andrew Cohen, July 4, 1967, BNA, FCO 31/32.
[31] Confidential. Edward Peck to the Ministry of Overseas Development, Modev. No. 768, September 9, 1966; R. W. Wootton to B. Greatbatch, September 21, 1966; Private and Confidential. Bruce R. McKenzie to Edward Peck, July 20, 1965; Edward Peck to Bruce McKenzie, September 29, 1966, BNA, DO 214/53.
[32] Notes of Meeting in the Minister's Room at Ministry of Overseas Development at 3 p.m. on Tuesday, July 11, BNA, FCO 31/32.
[33] Confidential. L. Bevan to B. E. Rolfe, July 4, 1967, BNA, FCO 141/18960.
[34] KANU Parliamentary Group. Minutes of the Meeting held on December 20, 1966 at 10.00 a.m. at Jumba la Baraza, Harambee House, Nairobi, KNA, KA/2/21.

were being bought by foreigners. He had been informed by Angaine himself, who wrote extensively on the matter.[35]

The government had to draw the line between non-Africans and Kenyan citizens, without hurting British feelings and jeopardizing international financial aid. "Kenyan Africans" constituted a distinguished category that the government was at pains to define. A draft memorandum on the control of transactions and transfer of agricultural land, probably prepared and reviewed by Angaine himself, shows handwritten notes systematically crossing out mentions of "Africans" and replacing them by "Kenyans" or "Kenyan citizens," while "non-Africans" became "non-citizens."[36] Such changes would entail amendment of the constitution itself, since both the principle of willing buyer–willing seller and the protection of private property for all citizens were enshrined constitutionally. To avoid such an extremely sensitive political change, Angaine wanted to convince cabinet ministers that the president could use his veto over land transactions, a solution that would enable them to remain within the bounds of legality.

The multiplicity of interests involved (whether of cabinet ministers or politicians) shows that Kenyatta was far from being the sole architect of what appeared to be a deregulation of the land market. Kenyan ministers' views on valuation and ownership eventually dominated, as British officials noted the increasing deregulation: "there was no longer a free market in land. Only Kenyan citizens could acquire land and this meant that only small farms, which African farmers could afford to buy, changed hands on the open market."[37] Breaking away from the principle of willing buyer–willing seller had been Angaine's aim, and it was achieved, at least in practice. His ministry further attempted to

---

[35] Jackson Angaine to Mzee Jomo Kenyatta, October 12, 1966; Strictly Confidential. Jackson Angaine to Charles Njonjo, August 31, 1966; Confidential. C. K. Kariithi to Peter Shikuyah, October 14, 1966; Confidential. The Cabinet. Development Committee, "Transfer to African Ownership of the Land," Memorandum by Jackson Angaine, October 25, 1966, KNA, BN/96/2.

[36] Confidential. The Cabinet, Development Committee, "Transfer to African Ownership of the Land," Memorandum by Jackson Angaine, October 25, 1966, KNA, BN/96/2. It must be noted that the title of the memorandum itself was corrected and replaced by "Legislation for Control of Transaction in Agricultural Land."

[37] Confidential. "Land Policy in Kenya," Note of a Meeting in the Ministry of Economic Planning on April 21, 1965, BNA, FCO 141/1895.

Africanize the post of commissioner of lands, but found it difficult to find the "right calibre," that is "a mature-minded person, who ... has to administer all public land on behalf of the Government, in a way that it would not *appear* corrupt," and, what is more, one who could keep silent in public about land affairs.[38] Although the scarcity of available archives prevents a more refined understanding of the dynamics at play, it can be suggested that the general politicization announced the definite "turn to land as patronage" and the enactment of politics as a business.[39]

Archives reveal that cabinet ministers, under the guidance of the powerful attorney general Charles Njonjo, strengthened their influence by further centralizing the control over land legislation. Land legislation had been at the center of the independence negotiations, in particular when it came to discussing the centralization of the regime.[40] To what extent this legislation was amended, by whom and under which circumstances are questions that go well beyond the scope of this book. Nevertheless, fragments of archives signal that behind the attempts to stifle the debates on the squatter issue, and control that of land ownership, cabinet ministers were seeking to strengthen their control over public land policies and protect private interests vested in land. In November 1965, only a few months after the appointment of the special commissioner for squatters, the commissioner for land, J. O'Loughlin, raised his concerns after he learned of a draft bill that "would unify the whole system of land control for all areas to which it [land control] was applied throughout Kenya."[41] The same month, a bill proposing to cap individual land ownership was put forward by Kaggia and rapidly dismissed.[42] By December 1965, the Central Land

---

[38] Emphasis in the original. Strictly Confidential. P. Shikuyah to J. D. M. Malinda, October 21, 1966, KNA, BN/81/31.

[39] I borrow the expression from Jacqueline M. Klopp, "Electoral Despotism in Kenya: Land, Patronage and Resistance in the Multi-Party Context" (Ph.D. diss., McGill University, 2001).

[40] Charles Njonjo, "Recent Constitutional Changes in Kenya," *East African Law Journal* 1, no. 2 (1965): 98–107; Okoth-Ogendo, "The Politics of Constitutional Change in Kenya since Independence, 1963–69," 21–34.

[41] J. A. O'Loughlin to the Director of Agriculture, November 12, 1965, KNA, AVS/3/5.

[42] Kenya National Assembly (Hansard), Vol. VII, November 9, 1965, cols. 199–203. Kaggia proposed the bill on the grounds that it fitted the government's (alleged) pursuance of African socialism. The Sessional Paper no. 10 on African Socialism introduced in 1965 by the government mentioned that a "working

Board was officially dead, and its powers were transferred to the settlement fund, which was run by three prominent cabinet ministers, James Gichuru (minister for finance), Bruce McKenzie (minister for agriculture), and Jackson Angaine (minister for lands).[43]

By the end of 1966, British administrators were trying to ascertain that "certain secret directions had been issued to Divisional Land Boards [*boards controlling land transacations in a local area*] not to approve the sale of land to anyone expect Africans."[44] The information they received revealed a clear rift between the government elite, mainly between the attorney general, Charles Njonjo, and Duncan Ndegwa, then head of the civil service, while it was not clear whether the decision was supported at all by the president. The British believed "Ndegwa ... had been the driving force behind this move. It was stated that this meeting was being held to advise the President on what should be done and that no policy decision had in fact been taken." Njonjo opposed the decision on legal grounds, arguing "that the whole matter should be reconsidered and properly processed through the various interested Ministries."[45] In fact, institutional skirmishes continued long after 1965. As for Kenyatta, he continued appeasing concerned European farmers, as in October 1967, when he met the leader of the conservative and white settler dominated Kenya National Farmers' Union, and gave "the clear impression that the services of the large-scale European farmers were valued and still wanted in Kenya."[46] It must be noted that, in 1968, only four of the top fifty directors of private companies in Kenya were African, so the government depended heavily on foreign capital.[47]

---

party might be established to consider the need and practicability of establishing a ceiling on individual ownership of property." Mboya answered that the paper made no mention of the government's obligation, while affirming that various recommendations were being acted upon. Republic of Kenya, *African Socialism and its Application to Planning in Kenya*.

[43] Draft letter from the Minister of Land to His Excellency Jomo Kenyatta, sometimes in 1966, BNA, FCO 141/18963.
[44] Confidential. B. Greatbatch to R. W. Wootton, December 2, 1966, BNA, DO 214/53.
[45] Ibid.
[46] Record of a Meeting between the Commonwealth Secretary and Representatives of the Kenya National Farmer's Union at the High Commissioner's Residence, 2 Tchui Road, Nairobi on Sunday, October 29, 1967, at 5 p.m., BNA, FCO 31/33.
[47] Hornsby, *Kenya*, 190.

Whether the president was aware of the changes planned by his cabinet ministers or whether the latters' prerogatives grew out of the weaknesses or loopholes of his presidential rule is difficult to say: too few documents remain to answer this question satisfactorily. As previous chapters have shown, Kenyatta used his ministers as intermediaries to carry out his orders, but granted them sufficient power to build their own authority. Furthermore, he did not concern himself with the detail of political disputes and negotiations. That he preferred to delegate power does not mean, however, that he did not know about his ministers' actions. Rather, it means that he did not judge it necessary to know about them. Duncan Ndegwa wrote in his autobiography, at times surprisingly candid, that when Kenyatta was released from jail, he "had no time to acclimatise himself with the nitty-gritties of governance" and, that, once president, Kenyatta "never liked working through groups. He depended on individuals whom he had won over and through whom he systematically spread his influence. In the post-independence days, Kenyatta delegated quite effectively to ministers and ministries."[48]

Kenyatta could afford such a "marginal" role, since all cabinet ministers depended on him to maintain stability within the government's politics. The informal meetings he operated with prevent us from forming a clear and nuanced understanding of his practice of presidential rule. The British high commissioner noted in September 1966 that "there is little doubt that Kenyatta intends to keep power on final decision making on important matters for himself; but it is difficult to assess how much influence this close circle of Ministers has in persuading him."[49] By 1965, however, a whole new period opened up, defined by the growth of patronage in land allocation, greater personal competition, greater personal enrichment, and stronger personal rule.

Kenyatta, Maasailand, and the Coastal Strip

The politicization of the land market should not obscure a wider phenomenon that had been in evidence since independence but that intensified after 1965 with the end of settlement schemes in the White Highlands: namely, the attempts by the government and its cronies to

---

[48] Ndegwa, *Walking in Kenyatta Struggles*, 5, 256.
[49] Confidential. E. Peck to E. Posnett, September 6, 1966, BNA, DO 213/69.

secure land titles throughout the country. Campaigns for land adjudication and consolidation facilitated land redistribution, which was the backbone of the government's strategy to create new loyalties within an ethnically and politically fragmented national territory. Unsurprisingly, prominent landowners were increasingly anxious to protect their land tenure from potential contesting claims. This was notably the case in Maasailand, which bordered Kikuyuland and covers today's Narok and Kajiado districts. In 1968, the director of land adjudication summarized the gist of the situation: "a number of influential Masai have indulged in extensive land grabbing [and] would like to secure that land with a Title, but ... such an allocation of land would be unacceptable to the majority of people and to the Government."[50] Similarly, archives from Coast province suggest that the government, supported by the president himself, was seeking to take over land on the coastal strip to counter the political opposition, secure lucrative interests, and prevent European landowners from establishing too firm a stake in the region.

Security of land tenure in the Rift Valley, Maasailand, and Coast province had been at the heart of the KANU–KADU competition during the independence conferences in Lancaster. Pro-*majimbo* KADU leaders feared that landless Kikuyu who were forced to migrate outside of Kikuyuland during colonization would prevent minority tribes from recovering tribal ownership over their land. KANU leaders opposed tribal land rights, precisely because they feared such rights would force a Kikuyu exodus. Although *majimboist* claims were defeated at independence, they never died, as David Anderson observed.[51] In fact, the balance of regional loyalties established by Kenyatta at independence was supposed to secure the loyalty of the formerly KADU regions, in particular in Coast province and in Maasailand, bastions of prominent ex-KADU leaders – among whom were the Maasai Justus ole Tipis, John ole Konchellah, John Keen, and the Mijikenda (Coast) leader and former KADU chairman Ronald Ngala. Just as Kenyatta managed to secure the Meru vote and access to Meru land through Jackson Angaine, he carefully worked on co-opting the

---

[50] Confidential. J. M. Waiyaki to Permanent Secretary, Ministry of Lands and Settlement, June 8, 1968, KNA, BN/81/87.
[51] Anderson, "Yours in Struggle for *Majimbo*," 548, 563–564.

most prominent Maasai and Coast leaders in his independent government.[52]

Land ownership in Maasailand remained a divisive political issue inherited by the Kenyan postcolonial government from its colonial predecessor. The colonial government alienated 50–70 percent of Maasailand, forcing Maasai people to live in reserves, condemning them to increasing impoverishment that continues today.[53] Maasai people feared their land would be taken over by wealthy Kikuyu after independence. They had voiced their concerns during demonstrations organized after Kenyatta declared, in the early 1960s, that Kikuyu people should have the right to remain in the Rift Valley, anticipating that the statement might well apply to Maasailand too.[54] During the second Lancaster House conference in 1962, Maasai leaders demanded land tenure be transferred back to them. As might be expected, the KANU government deemed these claims not only unacceptable, but also illegitimate, and responded with more assertive policies to annihilate communal land claims and rights.[55]

---

[52] Xavier Péron, *Occidentalisation des Maasaï du Kenya: Privatisation Foncière et Destructuration Sociale chez les Maassaï du Kenya*, two vols. (Paris: L'Harmattan, 1995), 67–77; Lotte Hughes, "Les Racines Historiques des Conflits Socio-Politiques en Pays Maasai, Kenya," in *Politique de La Terre et de l'Appartenance. Droits Fonciers et Citoyenneté Dans Les Sociétés Du Sud*, eds. Jean-Pierre Jacob and Pierre-Yves Le Meur (Paris: Karthala, 2010), 301; Marcel M. E. M. Rutten, "The Kenya 1997 General Elections in Maasailand: Of 'Sons' and 'Puppets' and How KANU Defeated Itself," in *Out for the Count: The 1997 General Elections and Prospects for Democracy in Kenya*, eds. Marinus M. E. M. Rutten, Ali Mazrui, and François Grignon (Kampala: Fountain Publishers, 2001), 405–440.

[53] For further insights on the political history of Maasailand, see J. G. Galaty and Munei Ole Kimpei, "Maasai Land, Law and Dispossession," *Cultural Survival Quarterly* 22, no. 4 (1998); Lotte Hughes, "Malice in Maasailand: The Historical Roots of Current Political Struggles," *African Affairs* 104, no. 415 (2005): 207–224; Esther Mwangi, "The Footprints of History: Path Dependence in the Transformation of Property Rights in Kenya's Maasailand," *Journal of Institutional Economics* 2, no. 2 (2006): 157–180; Parselelo Kantai, "In the Grip of the Vampire State: Maasai Land Struggles in Kenyan Politics," *Journal of Eastern African Studies* 1, no. 1 (2007): 107–122.

[54] H. Kulundu, "Historical Background to Law Review Squabbles," quoted by Hughes, "Les Racines Historiques des Conflits Socio-Politiques en Pays Maasai, Kenya," 287.

[55] Kantai, "In the Grip of the Vampire State." On the opposition between communal versus individual land tenure rights, see Angelique Haugerud, "Land Tenure and Agrarian Change in Kenya," *Africa* 59, no. 1 (1989): 61–90; Simon Coldham, "The Effect of Registration of Title upon Customary Land Rights in

Kenyatta had been concerned with Maasai land claims from a very early stage in the decolonization process. As previously mentioned, he had pointed out during the independence negotiations, and referring specifically to the Maasai "tribes," that there was a danger of them "adopting a dog-in-the-manger attitude if they could not afford to purchase land which was for sale," which would prevent land owners from selling their land.[56] Besides, both Kenyatta and KANU leaders showed awareness of economic interests in Maasailand, in particular with the Magadi Soda Company, a British company established in the early days of colonization in Maasailand and a lucrative concern the Kenyan government wished to retain after independence.[57] In a cabinet meeting in August 1963, it was decided that Maasai land lying idle was unacceptable but that Maasai people should be given "recompense on a sufficient scale" so as to avoid political trouble.[58] After independence, the government opted for the creation of individual ranches in Maasailand – that is, larges farms that could be owned by one individual with the consent of the community and the authorization of local county councils, and which could be registered communal land as privately owned.[59] Nevertheless, the intricate relations between politics

Kenya," *Journal of African Law* 22, no. 2 (1978): 91–111; Jean Ensminger, "Changing Property Rights: Reconciling Formal and Informal Rights to Land in Africa," in *The Frontiers of the New Institutional Economics*, eds. John N. Drobak and John V. W. Nye (San Diego, CA: Academic Press, 1997), 165–196.

[56] Council of Ministers, Ninth Meeting with the Secretary of State held in the Council Room at Government House at 10 a.m. on Saturday, February 23, 1963, KNA, KA.1/11/73.

[57] Council of Ministers, Second Meeting with the Secretary of State held in the Council Room at Government House at 10 a.m. on Saturday, February 16, 1963, KNA, KA.1/11/73. For a history of the Magadi Soda Company since colonization, see Lotte Hughes, "Mining the Maasai Reserve: The Story of Magadi," *Journal of Eastern African Studies* 2, no. 1 (2008): 134–164.

[58] Secret. "Settlement for Unemployed and Landless. The Use of Empty Land," Memorandum by the Ministers for Lands and Settlement and Agriculture and Animal Husbandry, August 28, 1963, KNA, AZG1.3.20. On the construction of Maasai ethnicity and the enduring conceptions of the Maasai as pastoralist people, see Thomas Spear and Richard Waller, eds., *Being Maasai: Ethnicity and Identity in East Africa* (London: James Currey, 1993). For further insight on KANU concerns for economic interests during the independence conferences, in particular regarding oil finding in the Tana region, see Council of Ministers. Tenth Meeting with the Secretary of State, Held in the Council Room at Government House at 5 p.m. on Thursday, March 7, 1963, KNA, KA.1/11/73.

[59] Mwangi, "The Footprints of History," 169.

and business in Maasailand favored wealthy Maasai land buyers, who were themselves supported by wealthy and politically influential non-Maasai leaders or businesses. Many of them were Kikuyu, and were thus able to set foot in the area and buy large plots of land.[60]

Similar requests to Africanize land ownership arose in Coast province. They were all the more contentious in that land settlement schemes had been neglected in the region and that dissident politicians were using the rising number of squatters to push for government action. The slow rate of settlement schemes at the coast since independence was due to the political fragmentation of the region and its heterogeneous population – mainly African/Somali, Asians and Arabs – and the high cost of land, which deterred the central institutions from buying it out.[61] By 1965, the government was becoming increasingly concerned about the rising numbers of squatters that impeded "progressive farming" and fueled antigovernmental discourses by Coast politicians.[62] Although KADU had dissolved upon independence, its chairman, Ronald Ngala, continued to be active, while the government believed that "there are indications that serious attempts will now be

---

[60] Mwangi, "The Footprints of History"; Péron, *Occidentalisation des Maasaï du Kenya*. On the politics of group ranches, see Marinus M. E. M. Rutten, *Selling Wealth to Buy Poverty: The Process of the Individualisation of Landownership among the Maasai Pastoralists of Kajiado District, Kenya, 1890–1990* (Saarbrücken: Verlag breitenbach Publishers, 1992); John G. Galaty, "'The Land Is Yours': Social and Economic Factors in the Privatisation, Sub-Division and Sale of Maasai Ranches," *Nomadic Peoples*, no. 30 (1992): 26–40; Kamau Kimani and John Pickard, "Recent Trends and Implications of Group Ranch Sub-Division and Fragmentation in Kajiado District, Kenya," *The Geographical Journal* 164, no. 2 (1998): 202–213; Esther Mwangi, "The Puzzle of Group Ranch Subdivision in Kenya's Maasailand," *Development and Change* 38, no. 5 (2007): 889–910.

[61] On the slow rate of settlement, see N. S. Carey Jones to Civil Secretary, Coast Region, "Land Problem – Coast Region," July 25, 1963, KNA, CQ/20/30. On population and land claims in the Coast, see Karuti Kanyinga, *Re-Distribution from Above: The Politics of Land Rights and Squatting in Coastal Kenya* (Uppsala: Nordic Africa Institute, 2000), chapter 5; Jeremy Prestholdt, "Politics of the Soil: Separatism, Autochtony and Decolonisation at the Kenyan Coast," *The Journal of African History* 55, no. 2 (2014): 249–270.

[62] Secret. C. Njonjo to Ministry of Home Affairs, February 5, 1965 and Memoradum by the Minister for Lands and Settlement, Jackson H. Angaine, "Development Committee. Land Policy in the Coastal Strip," July 1965, KNA CA/10/3/2.

made ... to 'coastalise' KANU Branches in existence in the Region."[63] The government had disregarded the politics of the region. Murumbi wrote to Kenyatta in 1965 that "we have neglected the Coast for too long and the time has come that we should closely supervise the reorganisation."[64] A few months later, Mboya would take over the reorganization of the KANU branch in the province and organize elections so as to enable Ngala to make his entry in the KANU hierarchy.[65] As Richard Stren minutely documented, the inherently factional nature of Coast politics, and the depth of the divisions that set their leaders against each other enabled Kenyatta to control them individually and efficiently, without involving himself too much.[66] But Kenyatta was also playing the rush to acquire coastal land.

Despite the fears that the political situation might worsen, the government invested very little in settlement schemes, concluding almost inevitably that no funds could be allocated.[67] Meanwhile, the richer, landed elite was riveted by the large plots of land. Dubious processes of selection of settlers for land settlement filled government correspondence. It was revealed, in 1969 that hand-picked "civil servants and some well-to-do members of the public" were being preferred for some settlement schemes.[68] In fact, land buying became part and parcel of

[63] Secret. Coast Region Intelligence Committee, "Draft Summary No. 12/64 for the Period November 28 to December 28, 1964," KNA, CA/39/3. Stren further noted that "by the time Ngala had dissolved KADU in November, 1964, his popularity among the Mijikenda and other Coast people was ascendant." In Stren, "Factional Politics and Central Control in Mombasa, 1960–1969," 42. See also Justin Willis and George Gona, "Tradition, Tribe, and State in Kenya: The Mijikenda Union, 1945–1980," *Comparative Studies in Society and History* 55, no. 2 (2013): 448–473 for an in-depth study of the postcolonial creative politics of the "Mijikenda" identity.
[64] Secret. Joseph Murumbi to Mzee Jomo Kenyatta, May 15, 1965, KNA, MAC/KEN/70/3.
[65] Stren, "Factional Politics and Central Control in Mombasa, 1960–1969," 43.
[66] Ibid.
[67] I. M. Mathenge to Provincial Police Officer, February 9, 1967, KNA, CQ/9/30.
[68] This was particularly the case with the Mtwapa settlement schemes in 1969. As the permanent secretary of land explained, "the Special Commissioner Squatters informed me that 20 people, composed mainly of civil servants and some well-to-do members of the public have been allocated with plots in that area. Furthermore it is learned that the usual machinery for selection of squatters for settlement has not been followed and that the 20 or so aforementioned have been handpicked by the District Agricultural Officer, Kilifi." See Confidential. S. B. Ogembo to Provincial Commissioner, Coast, July 29, 1969, KNA, CA/10/3/3. Later in the year, another permanent secretary of land wrote to the Office of the President that

the construction of political constituencies.[69] Just as in Maasailand, the government was determined to enable Kikuyu to settle in Coast province. Jackson Angaine reminded land officers that the constitution itself demanded that settlers be chosen regardless of their "tribal qualifications," while it was reported that "large numbers of Up-country tribes [were settled] in many areas in the [Kwale] District" without the prior approval of local authorities.[70]

Prospects of profitable business on the Coast, combined with communal land claims, triggered great competition over the Africanization of land in the province, especially since this was mostly freehold land, thus with potentially high sale prices.[71] On the one hand, remaining European landowners were clearly targeted. The Office of the President judged "foreign" land owners "uncooperative," and was, again, at pains to finds a legal solution to take over their land.[72] In 1967, Kenyatta had set up a committee of ministers to "consider all applications affecting non-citizens" so as to better control land transactions.[73] Central control of land tenure was hence reinforced, as all representatives of central institutions, whether the provincial, district commissioners, or the commissioner for land, were requested to approve any land transaction before such transactions were sent to regional bodies of decision-making.[74] On the other hand, the competition took on an

it is "extremely difficult for me to find a genuine reason to satisfy the House concerning the procedure which had been adopted in allocating the plots in question." See Confidential. J. K. arap Koitie to Permanent Secretary, Office of the President, December 4, 1969, KNA, CA/10/3/3.

[69] Kanyinga, *Re-Distribution from Above*, 87.
[70] Memorandum by the Minister for Lands and Settlement, Jackson H. Angaine "Proposed Legislation to Effect Change in the Procedure for Selection of Settlers on Land Settlements," March 1965, KNA, CA/10/3/2; Clerk to Kwale County Council to the Hon. R. S. Matano, October 20, 1968, KNA, CA/10/3/3.
[71] R. T. Jackson, "Problems of Tourist Industry Development on the Kenyan Coast," *Geography* 58, no. 1 (1973): 63–64.
[72] Confidential. Permanent Secretary, Office of the President to All Provincial Commissioners and District Commissioners, February 22, 1968, KNA, CA/10/3/3.
[73] Confidential. Peter Shikuyah to All District Commissioners, July 3, 1967, KNA, CA/10/3/3.
[74] Z. K. A. Kirui to Provincial Commissioner Mombasa, November 10, 1967, KNA, CA/10/3/3; C. N. Lotty to All District Commissioners, "The Land Control Act, 1967," October 31, 1970, KNA, CQ/9/16. For in-depth insights on the gradual demise of the land documentation system and the abuse of property right institution by influential con men, see Ato Kwamena Onoma, "The Contradictory Potential of Institutions the Rise and Decline of Land

intertribal character. In 1969, G. K. Kariithi, permanent secretary in the Office of the President, reported to Eliud Mahihu, freshly nominated provincial commissioner in the Coast, that "there has ... been a movement by various leading politics to try to induce expatriate landowners to sell land only to inhabitants of the districts in which that land is situated. This movement is wrong and is subversive."[75]

A telling example of the rush for land in Coast province, and the most significant for a grasp of Kenyatta's actions, lies in the beach plots owned by Europeans, or simply coveted, as the tourist industry boomed in the 1960s.[76] As the district commissioner for the Kilifi district described in a letter to the provincial commissioner Isaiah Mathenge in 1967: "I received an average of about ten Europeans a months who come inquiring about beach plots ... the plots should go to Africans or at least to Kenya Citizens, but there are no Africans whose financial positions are good enough to pay for these expensive plots."[77] Mathenge subsequently ordered district commissioners that "to ensure that no more plots on Government land are alienated to non-Africans. If the Commissioner of Lands advertize seafront plots in your respective districts you must report the matter to me before accepting and processing applications."[78] At the same time, influential politicians were increasingly involved in land grabbing.[79] A list of owners of beach plots featured Kenyatta's name, together with his wife's, Mama Ngina, and those of the cabinet ministers James Gichuru, Njoroge Mungai, and the attorney general Charles Njonjo, as well as the minister for commerce and industry, Julius Kiano.[80] Taking over coast land remained an inherently political process closely bound to presidential power and favors, as testified in a letter by the provincial commissioner Isaiah Mathenge to the commissioner of lands in 1968:

Documentation," in *Explaining Institutional Change: Ambiguity, Agency, and Power*, eds. James Mahoney and Kathleen Thelen (Cambridge: Cambridge University Press, 2009), 63–93.

[75] Secret. Geoffrey K. Kariithi to Eliud Mahihu, May 23, 1969, KNA, CA/10/3/3.
[76] Jackson, "Problems of Tourist Industry Development on the Kenyan Coast."
[77] Secret. C. P. Okech to I. M. Mathenge, February 22, 1967, KNA, CA/10/3/3.
[78] I. M. Mathenge to the District Commissioners – Kwale, Mombasa, Kilfi, Lamu, Galole, February 23, 1967, KNA, CA/10/3/3.
[79] See John Kamau, "How Mahihu Got Kenyatta to Sign Away Beach Plots," *Business Daily*, November 19, 2009.
[80] "Beach Plots. Section I – Mainland North," "Beach Plots. Section V – Mainland South," KNA, CA/10/3/3.

Recently H. E. the President Mzee Jomo Kenyatta while walking along the beach to the Dolphin Hotel noticed that the above plot was vacant. He asked me find out why the plot was unoccupied. On checking, I discovered that the lease which had been issued to Mr. Cecil John Green expired in 1966 and I informed the President on the matter. The President directed that this plot should be allocated to Mr. Duncan Ndgewa, the Governor of the Central Bank [Ndgewa was appointed in 1967].[81]

It was also politically risky enterprise, stirring voices of discontent among Kenyan citizens. In 1969, a report on security in Mombasa noted negative public reaction after a speech by Kenyatta when opening a clinic in the city: "they [the people] concluded commenting that the government Mzee would appear to be dictatorial like that of Dr. Nkrumah. They criticised Mzee by saying that he sought the advice of people like Mboya and Njonjo but not of the wananchi [citizens]."[82] Public opinion could be of little weight, however, against a political system, and a political territory even, increasingly dominated by a sprawling central government. As previous pages attempted to show, the scope of presidential powers must be read in the light of the increasingly dominating role played by cabinet ministers and prominent civil servants – Ndegwa's role is remarkable, for example, as he appears both as a leading figure in the Africanization and deregulation of the land market and as a beneficiary of Kenyatta's presidential favors. Such nuanced reading of presidentialism fits well with what scholars have analyzed as a "political sub-system," in which all political players, whether allies or enemies, and at all levels of the political hierarchy, are tied by a shared condition of dependency on patronage.[83] What mattered to Kenyatta was to control key regions through key personalities, as patterns of political alliances were, since

---

[81] Confidential. I. M. Mathenge to the Commissioner of Lands, August 21, 1968, KNA, CA/10/3/3.
[82] Secret. J. K. Ngoloma to the Director of Intelligence, January 22, 1969, KNA, CA/39/1.
[83] Bourmaud, *Histoire Politique du Kenya*, 138–150; Githu Muigai, "Jomo Kenyatta and the Rise of the Ethno-Nationalist State in Kenya," in *Ethnicity & Democracy in Africa*, 200–217; Branch and Cheeseman, "The Politics of Control in Kenya." See also how such subsystem affected political languages and meetings in Haugerud, *The Culture of Politics in Modern Kenya*. On how such a subsystem eventually affects patronage and decentralization, see Nic Cheeseman, Gabrielle Lynch, and Justin Willis, "Decentralisation in Kenya: The Governance of Governors," *The Journal of Modern African Studies* 54, no.1 (2016): 1–35.

independence, less organized along ethnic lines than by fierce personal battles played (and often solved) among regional blocks.[84] It was less the creation of an all-powerful president with monarchical ambitions, than the product of shared political ambitions and dependencies.[85]

Ruling over a Divided Political Family

The post-1965 era was also that of the beginning of a new type of political competition: that for the succession to the president. Kenyatta, despite his old age and declining health, seemed very much in control of the infighting that grew among his cabinet ministers. The succession struggle froze the political scene, just like before independence when no political leader could openly confront the "Old Man" – further comforting and strengthening Kenyatta in his arbitrator's role. Since independence, Kenyatta had been a safety net for an inherently divided political elite, who had had no choice but to accept the presidential status quo to access state resources. Oginga Odinga himself declared in September 1963 that he worried about the possibility of Kenyatta dying "within five years," before he could "place reliable party men

---

[84] Scholars have emphasized since the 2000s that ethnicity should be conceptualized as a changing political language and a created identity used in particular political contexts. The importance of personal alliances in regional ethnic blocs has been very well shown by Gabrielle Lynch, who pointed out in a recent article that leaders react to changing voting patterns and always seek the most strategic alliances to secure their interests in a particular region. See Lynch, "Electing the 'Alliance of the Accused'." For critical reflections on the logic of ethnic block voting, see Jacqueline M. Klopp, "Can Moral Ethnicity Trump Political Tribalism? The Struggle for Land and Nation in Kenya," *African Studies* 61, no. 2 (2002): 269–294; Gabrielle Lynch, "The Fruits of Perception: 'Ethnic Politics' and the Case of Kenya's Constitutional Referendum," *African Studies* 65, no. 2 (2006): 233–270; Jeffrey Steeves, "Beyond Democratic Consolidation in Kenya: Ethnicity, Leadership and 'Unbounded Politics'," *African Identities* 4, no. 2 (2006): 195–211; Jill Cottrell and Yash Ghai, "Constitution Making and Democratisation in Kenya (2000–2005)," *Democratisation* 14, no. 1 (2007): 1–25; Michael Bratton and Mwangi S. Kimenyi, "Voting in Kenya: Putting Ethnicity in Perspective," *Journal of Eastern African Studies* 2, no. 2 (2008): 272–289.

[85] For an interpretation of Kenyatta's presidential rule as a monarchical rule, see Mazrui, "The Monarchical Tendency in African Political Culture"; Bourmaud, *Histoire Politique du Kenya*, 153–173.

Ruling over a Divided Political Family 241

in all the key positions of Government."[86] Odinga understood Kenyatta's unique ability to unite a divided elite. At the same time, Kenyatta himself was aware of the limits of his leadership. He knew that being a Kikuyu – and even both a Mau Mau and not a Mau Mau – did not suffice to enforce loyalties.[87] He also knew he ought to refrain from politics that is too repressive lest it generate general rebellion.[88] Finally, he was certainly aware that his government coalition was unstable, no matter how much unity the repression against dissidents created.[89] The one issue that remained was the fundamental opposition between Tom Mboya as the only serious national competitor (especially after Odinga's political demise) and Kenyatta's inner circle of ministers.

Kenyatta's declining health brutally revived struggles for his succession, reviving tensions between cabinet ministers.[90] His old age had always been a source of concern (and hopes) within the Kenyan elite (as seen in Chapter 2), so the prospect of his succession hardly was a new issue. Yet, Kenyatta was unlikely to name any successor: as a British officer commented in March 1966, it risked endangering his own power, and would provide an opportunity for his opponents to coalesce against his successor.[91] Since his release from jail in 1961, his strategy had always been to avoid taking any side.

Historians and political scientists observed that the Kenyatta succession was less about the president himself than about a competition to secure political resources.[92] The struggle for the presidency was an

---

[86] Secret and Personal. Weekly Personal Report by the Director of Intelligence to the Private Secretary to H. E. Governor, September 7, 1963, BNA, CAB 21/4772.
[87] A British official wrote: "latent political unrest in some parts of the Central province suggests that we should be ill-advised to believe that President Kenyatta can count upon the loyalty of all his kikuyu." Report from C. H. Imray to Posnett, January 31, 1966, BNA, DO 213/65.
[88] Secret. Mr. Posnett to M. Scott, February 3, 1966, BNA, DO 213/65.
[89] The government's attempt to stifle backbenchers is a significant example. In July 1965, Kenyatta resolved to cease backbenchers' meeting groups, retaining only parliamentary meeting groups. According to a British official, "the new arrangement probably appeals to the Government since it will hope to exercise power influence over a potential ginger group," Imray to unknown, July 22, 1965, BNA, DO 213/65.
[90] Branch, *Kenya*, 67, 82–83.
[91] J. L. Pumphrey, "After Kenyatta, Who? – And What?" March 28, 1966, BNA, DO 213/69.
[92] Anyang' Nyong'o, "Succession et Héritage Politiques"; Mordechai Tamarkin, "From Kenyatta to Moi: The Anatomy of a Peaceful Transition of Power,"

eminently internal one, playing out in the highest spheres of power. Among the potential contenders were the Luo nationalists (and rivals) Oginga Odinga and Tom Mboya, who had both nurtured nationalist ambitions since independence. Another key contender was the Kalenjin Rift Valley leader and minister for home affairs, Daniel arap Moi, who was appointed vice president in replacement of Odinga and then Joseph Murumbi in 1967. Finally, among the Kikuyu politicians were James Gichuru, finance minister, Dr. Njoroge Mungai, Kenyatta's personal physician and minister of defence, and the former Nairobi mayor Charles Rubia. Daniel Branch has noted that senior cabinet ministers became increasingly powerful after Kenyatta's severe stroke in 1968, but that the president "did not notice the difference."[93]

Paradoxically perhaps, the main force driving the strengthening of presidential rule was that of both opponents and potential successors. One of the main actors behind Odinga's demise had been his Luo rival, Tom Mboya, to the great surprise and satisfaction of Kenyatta's ministers.[94] Mboya played a crucial role in leading the political operations against Odinga and his party. He took charge of reorganizing KANU so as to marginalize KPU branches throughout the territory, regularly informing the "Old Man" about his work and not missing an occasion to pledge his loyalty.[95] Kenyatta signed every KANU nomination paper and is believed to have suggested the idea of administrative action against the KPU.[96] Mboya was also supported in this task by the ex-KADU leader, Ronald Ngala, who used his parliamentary powers to move a motion of no confidence in Odinga, to have him excluded from KANU parliamentary group.[97] Ngala was but a temporary ally to KANU, however, for the party used him only to serve its

Africa Today 26, no. 3 (1979): 21–37; Dauch and Martin, *L'Héritage de Kenyatta*; Karimi and Ochieng, *The Kenyatta Succession*; Vincent B. Khapoya, "The Politics of Succession in Africa: Kenya after Kenyatta," *Africa Today* 26, no. 3 (1979): 7–20; Rok Ajulu, "Kenya: One Step Forward, Three Steps Back: The Succession Dilemma," *Review of African Political Economy* 28, no. 88 (2001): 197–212; James Kariuki, "'Paranoia': Anatomy of a Dictatorship in Kenya," *Journal of Contemporary African Studies* 14, no. 1 (1996): 69–86.
[93] Branch, *Kenya*, 68.
[94] Secret. Kenya Internal Political Situation, March 26, 1968, BNA, FCO 31/209.
[95] Goldsworthy, *Tom Mboya*, 266–267. See Mboya's letters to Kenyatta about KANU reorganization (1961–1966) in KNA, MAC/KEN/38/8.
[96] Secret. B. Greatbatch to Michael Scott, August 14, 1968, BNA, FCO 31/206.
[97] Eric Masinde Aseka, *Ronald Ngala* (Nairobi: East African Educational Publishers, 1993), 24.

best interests – hence Kenyatta's only sporadic interventions to settle conflicts, as Richard Stren has shown. Kenyatta did not act against Ngala before 1968, when he finally judged the latter's action "too tribalistic."[98] He ordered that the mayor of Mombasa be replaced, while the KADU Revival Committee was declared illegal in 1969.[99] The banning of the KPU in October the same year rang the death knell not only for Odinga's politics, but also for political opposition in general, since the increasingly authoritative state successfully deterred most MPs and politicians from defecting from KANU.[100]

Mboya's responsibilities in Odinga's demise ricocheted on his own political career. "Senior ministers," a British source believed, "[were] seriously worried at the prospect of the support which Mboya would command in terms of votes of MPs if Kenyatta suddenly disappeared from the scene."[101] Hence, cabinet ministers, led by Njonjo, used their control over legislative powers to kill two birds with one stone. The repression against Odinga's KPU was accompanied by a series of constitutional amendments to strengthen presidential power, but also tailor-made to weaken Mboya's chances of succeeding the "Old Man." In May 1966, the amended Preservation of Public Security Act permitted detention without trial; in 1967, the Societies Act gave the president greater control over associations and societies; in 1968, the Public Order (Amendment) Act prohibited displays of national symbols. The Provincial Advisory Council was also abolished, strengthening the government's power to define district boundaries. Finally, a tenth constitutional amendment ruled that the president would be elected directly in a national poll. Presidential candidates would be chosen by parties, and required the support of 1,000 people – the KPU thus being de facto excluded from the presidential race. Such a move specifically targeted Mboya, ensuring that individual MPs and parliament as a whole – where Mboya still had the support of half the MPs – would no longer have a say in the elections process. Attempts were also made to forbid candidates under forty to run, a proposition that would have

---

[98] Stren, "Factional Politics and Central Control in Mombasa, 1960–1969," 47.
[99] Secret. B. Greatbatch to British High Commission, October 8, 1968, BNA FCO 31/209; "Kadu Illegal Sociaty, State Official Warns," *Daily Nation*, July 4, 1969, 3.
[100] Mueller, "Government and Opposition in Kenya, 1966–9."
[101] Secret. Kenya Internal Political Situation, March 26, 1968, BNA, FCO 31/209.

excluded the thirty-seven-year-old Mboya from the race, but which was successfully blocked by the parliament.[102]

Kenyatta mistrusted Mboya too, as the two had been fighting each other with the same ambition: presidential power.[103] Another issue, besides Mboya's worrying political ascent, was the question of redistributive policies, which was at least a common point he had with Odinga, and which ran against the government's policies, as we saw in the first section of this chapter. After 1967, tensions between the Kikuyu ministers and Mboya worsened.[104] Kenyatta did use his influence to weaken Mboya, yet only sporadically, as he seemed to be quickly bored by what he judged petty conflicts – for example, he intervened in trade union battles for leadership, thus cutting into Mboya's main political resource.[105] Mboya was eventually shot dead in Nairobi on July 5, 1969. His death and the political turmoil it caused have been well studied, but it is worth noting here that his assassination seemed to have more to do with internal cabinet politics than personal discontent emanating from Kenyatta, while Njonjo might have played a much more decisive role than Kenyatta.[106]

---

[102] See Gertzel, *The Politics of Independent Kenya, 1963–8*, 152–155; Okoth-Ogendo, "The Politics of Constitutional Change in Kenya since Independence, 1963–69"; Mueller, "Government and Opposition in Kenya, 1966–9."

[103] From C. H. Imray to Robert (?), POL Z 78/19/3, June 20, 1965, BNA, DO 213/65.

[104] Branch, *Kenya*, 72; Malcolm MacDonald (on behalf of Margaret Rothwell) to Sir Saville Garner, June 1, 1967, BNA, FCO 31/3.

[105] Njonjo reported to MacDonald that one reason to release the trade union leader, James Akumu, "was to try to undermine Mboya's influence in the trade unions. Recent strikes were stirred up by Lubembe, instigated by Mboya, to discredit Kiano, the present Minister of Labour. Regarding those strikes, Kenyatta had taken a tough line, and instructed Kiano to do the same. But Kenyatta had suddenly got tired of having to do this. He then decided to let Akumu out of jug as a warning to Mboya and Lubembe to discontinue their actions, and as a threat to them that if they persist in making difficulties, Akumu would succeed Lubembe as the head of the trade union movement." See Malcolm MacDonald (on behalf of Margaret Rothwell) to Sir Saville Garner, June 1, 1967, BNA, FCO 31/3. On Kenyan trade unions, see Richard Sandbrook, "The State and the Development of Trade Unionism," in *Development Administration*, 252–295; Leys, *Underdevelopment in Kenya*, 142.

[106] Branch, *Kenya*, 85; Goldsworthy, *Tom Mboya*, chapters 18 and 19.

Ruling over a Divided Political Family 245

By 1968, Kenyatta was clearly favoring Daniel arap Moi, and had encouraged him to prepare to present himself as presidential candidate.[107] British officers could hardly believe that Moi would have the support of Kikuyu ministers, and even less that of Kenyatta. They were nonetheless speculating, as early as 1966, that, as "curious" as it were, "one result of the Kikuyu-Luo struggle in the Cabinet may be a significant step towards the detribalisation of Kenya's internal politics."[108] This detribalization, however, was more of a readjustment of the balance among the tribal spheres of influence that had been set up at independence, as Moi's presence in the government de facto secured precious access to the Rift Valley, and tamed his influential tribal group, the Kalenjin.[109]

Tribal balance was of much more strategic importance to Kenyatta than tribal domination. With Mboya's demise, the struggle for succession involved a very close elite circle, opposing Moi against Kenyatta's personal physician and minister of defense, the Kikuyu Njoroge Mungai. Behind these two men were two clans, with tribal feelings firmly entrenched in economic and commercial interests.[110] Moi was supported by Bruce McKenzie, "increasingly absorbed in moneymaking," as the British authorities saw him, and by Njonjo, who was convinced "that on the commercial place Mungai is committed to interests which are hostile

---

[107] Branch, *Kenya*, chapter 2.
[108] J. L. Pumphrey to Mr. Scott, April 20, 1966, BNA, DO 213/66.
[109] Moi's choice to join Kenyatta's government at independence has been well described by his official biographer, who wrote that Moi "assured the President-in-waiting that he could now count upon the allegiance of one and a half million Kalenjin. As one of the Kalenjin delegates, Philemon Chelegat, recalled: 'it was a tactic. Moi often says that if you go as an individual you lose credibility. By going with so many you show that you are the leader of your people'." Most importantly, perhaps, his biographer noted that "If Moi fitted into Kenyatta's tribal equation, he also entered into his political arithmetic. Moi was an ally at the high table, sharing completely the conservative views espoused by Kenyatta, Gichuru and Mboya." Andrew Morton, *Moi: The Making of an African Statesman* (London: Michael O'Mara, 1998), 85–86. For broader historical and political perspectives on the importance of Kalenjin to the Kenyan government, see Gabrielle Lynch, "Courting the Kalenjin: The Failure of Dynasticism and the Strength of the ODM Wave in Kenya's Rift Valley Province," *African Affairs* 107, no. 429 (2008): 541–568.
[110] For a detailed account of the economic interests tearing apart cabinet ministers over the presidential succession, see Karimi and Ochieng, *The Kenyatta Succession*.

to his own future prosperity."[111] He also attracted very ambitious Kikuyu politicians, such as Julius Kiano, Mwai Kibaki, or J. M. Kariuki.[112] As for Mungai, he was heavily reliant on the Kenyatta family and Kikuyu commercial business in Kiambu. He was counting on the support of James Gichuru, Mbiyu Koinange, Jackson Angaine, and Paul Ngei.[113] Although Kenyatta was himself from Kiambu, he would be ready to abandon his fellow Kikuyu minister whenever Mungai risked undermining his state leadership – as he would do later on in 1973: "Mungai was out of favour at the moment... The President was annoyed with him for breaking the negotiated pact and working against Moi."[114] Political favors, however, did not necessarily override tribal privileges, as the report noted that "the President did have a soft spot for Mungai. He likes him. [We believe] he had recently given him a large sum of foreign exchange so that he could buy a couple of properties in London."[115]

Exclusive tribalism was not Kenyatta's greatest political asset. Unlike other leaders who were heavily dependent on their tribal sphere of influence, Kenyatta had always tried to avoid such dependency. Significantly, all the vice presidents he appointed were non-Kikuyu – Odinga (Luo), Murumbi (Maasai/Goan) and, in 1967, Moi (Kalenjin). The debates surrounding his succession, and which he himself avoided, nonetheless revived tribal feelings as an ultimate political tool. It is worth noting that tribalism was at its peak when ideological issues were diluted in the one-party state machine. This was the case at independence, when *majimboist* arguments were defeated, and the land package deal rallied most tribal, nationalist leaders. Political tribalism (the manipulation, "from above," of tribal identities) reappeared after the demise of the radicals – led by Odinga and Kaggia – leaving political debates in the hands of the moderates – Mboya, Moi, and the Kikuyu ministers. After Mboya's death, tribalism resurfaced as minority tribes *and* internal tribal groups – such as the Kiambu Kikuyu – felt it necessary to "ensure that the new President will be adequately under their control."[116] The

---

[111] Secret. W. L. Allison to S. Y Dawbarn, March 7, 1973, BNA, FCO 31/1496.
[112] Confidential. A. Duff to Sir Alec Douglas-Home, October 22, 1973, BNA, FCO 31/ 1496.
[113] Ibid.
[114] British High Commission, from A. Duff, August 10, 1973, BNA, DO 226/13.
[115] Ibid.
[116] Ibid.; Confidential. A. Duff to Sir Alec Douglas-Home, October 22, 1973, BNA, FCO 31/ 1496.

most striking example is the oathing campaign that followed Mboya's assassination in 1969. Kenyatta had been wary of using oathing campaigns when it came to defeating Kaggia back in 1965.[117] By 1969, the "Gatundu oath" started to be administered in his home in Gatundu. If it primarily served his fellow Kikuyu ministers' interests, it also heightened tribalism as a political resource throughout the country.[118]

After Tom Mboya's assassination in July 1969, Kenyatta's regime became increasingly tribalized, while factionalism and political jockeying among cabinet ministers grew fiercer. Although the political motivations behind Mboya's murder remain largely unclear, the ensuing "polarisation of tribal lines" signaled the widening gap, not only between the Kikuyu elite and the Luo politicians, the latter being greatly affected by the loss of it leaders, but, more generally, between the Kikuyu elite and the masses.[119] No Kikuyu minister attended Mboya's funeral, while Daniel arap Moi, who represented the government, had his car stoned.[120] When Kenyatta attended Mboya's requiem in church, he was the target of "unprecedented demonstrations."[121] In their 1969 dispatch, the British commented on the "Kikuyuisation" of the state and parastatal bodies, noting that "Kikuyu ambition, acquisitiveness and drive are matched only by their indifference to public relations," proving that "the Kikuyu seem to have learnt little or nothing from last year's disturbances," in reference to Mboya's funeral.[122] Kenyatta remained surprisingly silent.[123]

---

[117] Report from Imray to Posnett, January 31, 1966, BNA, DO 213/65.
[118] Ben Knighton, "Going for Cai at Gatundu: Reversion to a Kikuyu Ethnic Past or Building a Kenyan National Future" in *Our Turn to Eat: Politics in Kenya since 1950*, eds. Daniel Branch, Nicholas Cheeseman, and Leigh Gardner (Berlin: Lit Verlag, 2010), 107–128; Branch, *Kenya*, 85–88.
[119] Confidential. Diplomatic Report from Eric Norris to the Foreign and Commonwealth Office, "Kenya: Annual Review for 1969," January 12, 1970, BNA, FCO 31/593.
[120] Goldsworthy, *Tom Mboya*, 281–282.
[121] Ibid.; Confidential. Diplomatic Report from Eric Norris to the Foreign and Commonwealth Office, "Kenya: Annual Review for 1969," January 12, 1970, BNA, FCO 31/593.
[122] Ibid.
[123] The British high commissioner noted his surprise at the president's silence: "It would have been reasonable to expect him to make some sort of appeal to the nation either after the assassination itself or after the disturbance in Nairobi on 8 July. According to Bruce McKenzie, he certainly used his influence behind the scenes to prevent the 'Kikuyu back-lash' after the stoning of his car from getting out of hand. But apart from a message of grief and condolence issued

British dispatches continuously reported that he "lack[ed] either inclination or resolution to restore unity" while there were "murmurs of complaint about his unwillingness either to delegate authority or to interest himself in many aspects of internal administration and in economic matters."[124]

* * *

Presidential rule took on a new character after 1965. Cabinet ministers became more and more influential, and Kenyatta more and more distant, yet not necessarily less influential. Rather than a transformation, however, these developments are reminiscent of the preindependence situation, when the negotiations on presidential rule unveiled the intrinsic and irreducible divisions of the political elite. Thus, Kenyatta could afford to be both distant and authoritative precisely because none of his opponents or potential successors had the political, as well as economic, resources to claim national representation. The government's repression against Odinga's KPU from 1966 to 1969 fostered unsound alliances within Kenyatta's cabinet ministers, but these were superficial, and vanished as soon as Odinga was removed from the political scene. The succession struggle then intensified internal divisions.

The rise of tribalism, by the end of 1969, signaled a new turn in Kenyan politics. This was barely surprising, as the commodification of land, unleashed after 1965, tended to inflame ethnic politics.[125] At the same time, tribalism itself became a political resource, well exemplified by the creation of tribal associations like GEMA. Nevertheless, this chapter has shown that tribalism was not Kenyatta's greatest asset until it was turned into a much wider system of rule, a form of

---

immediately after the murder, the president remained silent until yesterday (by which time the internal situation had been quiet for several days) when he appeared on TV to make an anodyne and generalised appeal for calm and national unity." Confidential. Eric Norris to Sir John Johnston, July 16, 1969, BNA, FCO 31/356.

[124] Confidential. Diplomatic Report from Eric Norris to the Foreign and Commonwealth Office, "Kenya: Annual Review for 1969," January 12, 1970, BNA, FCO 31/593.

[125] Rutten, "The Kenya 1997 General Elections in Maasailand," 431.

noninstitutionalized federalism, or, as I called it, "disempowered regionalism," which Kenyatta built and used throughout his career.[126] The late 1960s did not simply indicate Kenyatta's retreat from power: they marked the consecration of presidentialism as an untouchable system of rule.

[126] Widner expressed this idea of noninstitutionalized federalism when observing that the establishment of GEMA contributed to the "rise of KADU-style federalism within the KANU shell" in *The Rise of a Party-State in Kenya*, 118.

8 "Kenyatta Simply Will Not Contemplate His Own Death" (1970–1978)

The 1970s were not only marked by the succession struggle, but also by an authoritarian control of state institutions, ever more land acquisitions, and a distinctive Kikuyuization of the government. The one-party state was strengthened under Charles Njonjo's auspices to counter the rising opposition led by J. M. Kariuki. His rhetoric pandering to underprivileged Kikuyu worried the government because it was weakening Kikuyu political unity. At the same time, the polarization of tribal lines already triggered by Mboya's assassination was reinforced, particularly through the creation of the Gikuyu Embu Meru Association (GEMA) in the early 1970s. Officially defined as a cultural association, GEMA was, in fact, a political body controlled by the Kiambu-based Kikuyu elite in order to tighten its control over political and economic resources throughout the grand Kikuyu land unit.[1] At a time when both party and parliament were atrophied, GEMA reflected a new type of political mobilization, one that took the form of "community boundaries" legitimized by the malleable concepts of ethnicity and culture, better suited to factionalized politics.[2]

By 1970, Kenyatta was already in his seventies, his age and declining health becoming a source of constant worry: the British administration discussed his state of health at length and Kenyan politicians were busy positioning themselves for a potential succession that many thought was imminent. But the succession struggle lasted eight long years during which Kenyatta became ever more autocratic. Political

---

[1] Widner, *The Rise of a Party-State in Kenya*, 92; Karimi and Ochieng, *The Kenyatta Succession*, chapter 5.

[2] Widner, *The Rise of a Party-State in Kenya*, 111. It is worth noting here that GEMA was far from fostering natural unity within the "grand Kikuyu land unit." In Meru and Embu, it met the opposition of many politicians. Angaine in particular, was believed to oppose from inside GEMA, which he saw as an instrument used by the Kikuyu PC, Eliud Mahihu, along with some of his Meru and Embu adversaries, to oppose his politics in the region. M. Mutua, "Why the Meru and Embu Have Never Been GEMA," *Daily Nation*, May 5, 2012.

developments in this period have been widely documented and there is no point in retracing them in detail.³ What this chapter aims to provide is rather a portrait of Jomo Kenyatta during this decade.

The president spent his last years in power attempting to remain above tribal or political factions. Although he remained unmoved by the rising number of landless, Kenyatta feared assassination attempts or a coup and sought to tighten discipline within his government. The empowerment of the one-party state came with greater control over MPs and parliamentary activities. Kenyatta never spoke openly about the need to revitalize the party and resisted attempts to create other parties.⁴ Despite KANU's complete ineffectiveness and its lack of parliamentary coordination, "politicians realis[ed] that while the president lives there is small hope of establishing a viable new party since his still immense prestige is linked to the KANU party."⁵ Kenyatta resisted the establishment of any association that could outgrow his authority. He also prevented political emancipation of the GEMA leadership, which was actively involved in the succession struggle and supported a Kikuyu candidate against the president's purported favorite Daniel arap Moi.⁶

Aging President, Stagnating Politics

All annual dispatches sent by British high commissioners to the East African Department in London depicted the president as a man whose dominating political personality was feared by cabinet ministers. In 1970, the British high commissioner, Eric Norris, described the president as "becoming more and more unpredictable and whimsical," failing to restore order among a decaying and increasingly corrupted administration, while his personal powers grew unlimited.⁷ He attributed the persisting political stability to the president's "formidable personality, daunting nearly all his Ministers and officials," although

---

³ Karimi and Ochieng, *The Kenyatta Succession*; Dauch and Martin, *L'Héritage de Kenyatta*; Branch, *Kenya*, chapters 3 and 4; Hornsby, *Kenya*, chapters 5 and 6.
⁴ Widner, *The Rise of a Party-State in Kenya*, 94, 107.
⁵ Restricted. R. J. S. Edis to R. M. Purcell, June 29, 1970, BNA, FCO 31/596.
⁶ Widner, *The Rise of a Party-State in Kenya*, 117.
⁷ Confidential. Diplomatic Report No. 53/71, "Kenya: Annual Review for 1970," January 12, 1971, BNA, FCO 31/851.

it was also an "additional source of delay and inefficiency."[8] Upon his arrival in 1969, Norris had already sensed that Kenyatta's unchallenged charismatic powers were key to "holding things together."[9] At the same time, Kenyatta was uninterested in routine affairs, plunging the government into limbo that lasted longer than anyone could have expected. By 1969, the government would meet four mornings a week and Kenyatta would seldom receive official visitors in the afternoon or evening, and "very rarely" make public appearances in the second half of the day.[10] Thereafter, he would "very often spend most nights of the week from 8.30 to as late as 12.30 watching tribal dancing" – to the great displeasure of his wife Mama Ngina who, according to a British administrator, did not enjoy it at all.[11] Eric Norris further noted that Kenyatta had "an increasing aversion to being hurried into decisions," yet he was indispensable: "nothing of any importance [was] decided without reference to him."[12] With time, government meetings became even more sporadic. In 1972, it was reported that "the Cabinet has met six times ... , against some 30 or 40 times in 1971," while Kenyatta showed "a growing predilection for taking decision, when he has to, alone or with a few cronies."[13]

The succession struggle, combined with Kenyatta's calculated passivity, paralyzed government politics. Although the battle to gain local support was fierce, the main contenders, Daniel arap Moi and Njoroge Mungai, depended on Kenyatta's favors and goodwill to position themselves on the national political scene, the latter refusing to delegate power so as to stay aloof from the hustle of Kenyan politics. The British high commissioner Antony Duff (who replaced Norris in 1972) reported with clairvoyance that Kenyatta

can and does assert himself to discipline and control individuals or groups which appear to be threatening the establishment or which might bring it publicly or obviously into disrepute. He does interest himself in the morale

---

[8] Ibid.
[9] Covering Confidential. J. G. Wallace to Mr. Dawbarn, April 7, 1972, BNA, FCO 31/1197.
[10] Confidential. Eric Norris, "Kenya: First Impressions," June 16, 1969, BNA, FCO 31/1197.
[11] Restricted. W. L. Allison to Mr. Clay, August 16, 1972, BNA, FCO 31/1191.
[12] Confidential. Eric Norris, "Kenya: First Impressions," June 16, 1969, BNA, FCO 31/1197.
[13] Confidential. Diplomatic Report No. 79/73, "Kenya: Annual Review for 1972," January 17, 1973, BNA, FCO 31/1497.

and control of the Army ... though his reaction is almost invariably to keep himself and his Government as uninvolved as possible ... It has become his practice to bide his time in a manner which suggests passivity, but which is in fact a deliberate refusal to yield to immediate stimuli, in a favour of a deliberate attempt to ensure a continuity of policy.[14]

Later in 1974, British officials continued to believe that Kenyatta "was clearly concerned to distance himself from his Ministers" and would not miss an opportunity to blame the "KANU Government" for the faults and shortcomings of his regime.[15]

Meanwhile, reports of corruption at the top of government implicating the Kenyatta family directly became routine topics in British diplomatic correspondence. Administrators noted the appalling and unabated practices of corruption. They were less concerned with moral implications than with the potentially disruptive effect it could have on the reputation of the president and, by extension, on the succession struggle. Kenyatta was said to be interested in

land / money for himself and/or members of his family
land for his tribe.
Kikuyu appointments and promotions within the hierarchy.[16]

Corrupted land acquisitions were not only on the rise, but had become part of a much wider system of government involving top ministers and civil servants expanding their shady businesses internationally.[17]

Resentment and internal dissent against the president were increasing. His popularity was degrading and criticism of his regime was growing. "Ministers and senior officials," Antony Duff wrote, were "beginning to criticise [the President] privately and to discuss amongst themselves his foibles, his weaknesses and his acquisitiveness."[18] Two years later, in 1974, a monthly political report mentioned

a story is current in Nairobi that during a recent speech at Nakuru praising the Government's achievement in buying out the white settlers, the President

[14] Confidential. Antony Duff to the Right Honourable Sir Alex Douglas-Home, October 18, 1972, BNA, FCO 31/1191.
[15] Confidential. C. T. Hart to Miss S. Darling, June 5, 1974, BNA, FCO 31/1707.
[16] Confidential. Antony Duff to the Right Honourable Sir Alex Douglas-Home, October 18, 1972, BNA, FCO 31/1191.
[17] Branch, *Kenya*, 104.
[18] Confidential. Antony Duff to the Right Honourable Sir Alex Douglas-Home, October 18, 1972, BNA, FCO 31/1191.

exclaimed "Who has the land now" and a voice from the back shouted "You!" There are thinking people who no longer believe that the national interest would suffer if the change at the top came sooner rather than later.[19]

Kenyatta responded to these criticisms by denouncing and warning "those who went around spreading rumours that the Government had done very little for the people."[20] In 1972, speaking (in Swahili) at a Madaraka Day rally, he alleged that he had outmaneuvered those plotting against his government a year earlier. According to British commentators, "he may have wanted to warn trouble makers that Big Brother was watching them" or this was an act of "showmanship" hoping to stir a more passionate response from an audience whose size seemed to have been overestimated in the media (the Kenyan government announced 300,000–500,000 people, whereas British administrators counted only 30,000).[21] Yet, his "routine speeches," as some called it, were met with ever less enthusiasm.[22] An imposed cult of personality filled the gap: the portrait of the president was, by 1971, the only one permitted in shops and business premises and, in 1973, "businesses, sports, political and ethnic associations were required by law to stop using the title "president" for their heads."[23]

Kenyatta and his government further estranged themselves from the public. The Kikuyuization of the government ensured tranquillity of business for the elite: top government positions, the civil administration, and the security forces were increasingly dominated by Kikuyus, linked through overlapping formal and family networks.[24] Tribal diversity in the government was only meant to ensure stability. As Isaiah Mathenge, PC for Central province, explained to British administrators in 1972:

---

[19] Private and Confidential. "Report on Kenya, September 1974," BNA, FCO 31/1707.

[20] Confidential. B. T. Holmes to Miss S. Darling, February 27, 1974, BNA, FCO 31/1707.

[21] Secret. D. Y. Dawbarn to Mr. Smedley, June 21, 1972 and Confidential. E. Clay to A. Joy, June 3, 1972, BNA, FCO 31/1191.

[22] Confidential. Edward Clay to J. G. Wallace, October 24, 1972, BNA, FCO 31/1191.

[23] Hornsby, *Kenya*, 258.

[24] Throup, "The Construction and Deconstruction of the Kenyatta State"; Hornsby, *Kenya*, 254–260.

non-Kikuyu ministers were selected not so much for their ability as for the political weight they carried in their own tribal areas. The President was afraid to eject any of them autocratically because he feared making heroes of them in their own areas, where they could stir up ... trouble for the Government.[25]

In the same report, Mathenge explained that the expected KANU elections had been postponed to 1974, as key government Kikuyu leaders felt the context was not favorable: "Delaying tactics were employed in giving receipt books to those whose views differed from 'ours'." The elections had been postponed because they were not yet sure of being able to oust all the undesirables."[26]

By then, J. M. Kariuki was the leading opposition figure. Odinga had been completely eclipsed: since the banning of the KPU and despite his release from detention in 1971, he was kept outside of politics and would be regularly barred from attending Luo delegations visiting Kenyatta. In 1978, it was reported that "the two men had not met for some 10 years."[27] Kariuki continued to denounce land policies and to call for a greater redistribution of resources to the landless and more recognition of Mau Mau sacrifice in the struggle for independence, themes that had a considerable power over Kikuyu masses.[28] Kariuki knew his attack against government interests were sensitive. He endured regular intimidation, bans, and trials. Yet he believed that his closeness to the president (he had served as the his personal secretary in the early 1960s) would protect him and that Kenyatta would not dare fire a popular icon from his government.[29] In 1973, almost bankrupt, he openly supported Moi as a presidential candidate. In return for his support, the attorney general, Charles Njonjo assured him the protection from physical attack and financial collapse – enough guarantees to enable him to run for the forthcoming parliamentary elections in 1974.[30]

The government was attempting to contain political opposition. Kenyatta wanted to make sure that political meetings during the pre-election campaign were first approved by the PCs and resisted any

---

[25] Confidential. "Mathenge in Kikuyuland" by R. W. Newman, March 7, 1972, BNA, FCO 31/1191.
[26] Ibid.
[27] Confidential. C. D. Crabbie to D. Carter, April 19, 1978, BNA, FCO 31/2322.
[28] Dauch, "Kenya"; Branch, *Kenya*, 93–94, 105–110.
[29] Branch, *Kenya*, 106–107.   [30] Ibid., 107.

attempt to bypass their control.[31] He forcefully resisted temptations to form a new party expressed by dissidents such as J. M. Kariuki and two other prominent opposition politicians and MPs, the Kalenjin Jean-Marie Seroney and the Luhya Martin Shikuku (two former KADU members). He was growing particularly impatient and angry at the great independence of thought and speech displayed by MPs.[32] Despite manipulated nominations (ex-KPU leaders were barred from the election, a decision personally taken by Kenyatta), anomalies in registration, and interdiction of several rallies (in particular that of J. M. Kariuki) the elections results were a major blow to the government and to Kenyatta.[33] Over 50 percent of the sitting MPs lost their seats. The blow was particularly hard for Njoroge Mungai, who had had his eyes on the presidency but lost his seat in Dagoretti.[34] Kenyatta would personally reinstate Mungai as a nominated MP to limit the humiliation. The aftermath of the 1974 elections was bitter. Kenyatta's ire against insubordinate MPs intensified and lead to an unabashed muzzling of parliament. His style of arbitrary rule intensified forcing Kenyan politics and economy into inertia.

Repression and Inertia

Despite the crisis, the 1974 elections changed little in the organization of the government. Kenyatta's close cabinet ministers remained in their posts, among them Mbiyu Koinange, James Gichuru, and Charles Njonjo (Kenyatta's traditional confidents), as well as Daniel arap Moi, Julius Kiano, Mwai Kibaki, Jeremiah Nyagah, and Jackson Angaine. The proceedings of government meetings remained centered around Kenyatta's patriarchal figure. The British high commissioner Antony Duff described the submissive climate that reigned as follows:

in small meetings or in large ones, Kenyatta's Ministers and senior officials continue to shuffle their feet and their heads in his presence, for all the world like a lot of junior schoolboys. (I myself in one such gathering found myself

---

[31] Confidential. B. T. Holmes to Miss Darling, June 12, 1974, BNA, FCO 31/1707.
[32] Hornsby, *Kenya*, 273–274; Confidential. Diplomatic Report No. 103/75,"Kenya: Annual Review for 1974," January 14, 1975, BNA, FCO 31/1886.
[33] Hornsby, *Kenya*, 275.   [34] Branch, *Kenya*, 109.

raising my hand for permission to speak, so strong was the classroom atmosphere).[35]

No one dared to defy Kenyatta.

Opposition leaders were excluded from the government. MPs Martin Shikuku and Jean-Marie Seroney became increasingly vocal. They used their parliamentary tickets to make themselves publicly heard, attacking in particular the unlimited scope of presidential powers. In February 1975, and to Kenyatta's greatest displeasure, Seroney was elected deputy speaker of the National Assembly, despite the government attempts to co-opt him by offering him a post of assistant minister.[36] The open hostility of the parliament was a painful thorn in the government's foot. Seroney was a man who, according to a British administrator, knew "the National Assembly well and certainly better than the Government's advisor, Njonjo, who has had to resort to bribery and intimidation to regain control of the majority lost earlier this year."[37] By 1975, Kenyatta's regime grew increasingly merciless in its hard line against political dissent.[38]

The government hit back hard. On March 2, 1975, J. M. Kariuki's tortured and mutilated body was found near Nairobi the day after his death, although Kariuki was officially said to have gone out of the country.[39] The news of his death a few days later on March 11, triggered mass public demonstrations, while hostile backbenchers forced the government to investigate the case, a procedure that lasted several months. In such an atmosphere of public hostility, neither Kenyatta nor his closest ministers attended Kariuki's funeral.[40] In Nairobi, tension was palpable and the police remained "in evidence."[41] Upon the news of Kariuki's death, the National Assembly demanded an investigation on the murder and appointed a select committee, which included Shikuku and Seroney, among others, to

---

[35] Confidential. Diplomatic Report No. 310/75, "Valedictory Despatch," August 20, 1975, BNA, FCO 31/1885.
[36] Confidential, D. Wigan to Miss Southworth, February 10, 1975 and Confidential. P. R. A. MAnsfield to R. A. Neilson, January 15, 1975, BNA, FCO 31/1833.
[37] Confidential. C. T. Hart to D. Wigan, September 10, 1975, BNA, FCO 31/1885.
[38] Hornsby, *Kenya*, 281.   [39] Ibid., 283.   [40] Ibid.
[41] Confidential. Telegram from Duff, FM Nairobi 151ø23Z, March 17, 1975, BNA, FCO 31/1883.

conduct the investigation.[42] Up until today, Kariuki's murder has remained unsolved although much ink has continued to be spilled. Nevertheless, the report of the select committee involved the names of Kenyatta's closest collaborators, namely Mbiyu Koinange, his bodyguard Wanyoike Thung'u, and Ben Gethi, the commander of the Government Security Unit. Kenyatta reportedly tore out the last page of the report mentioning Koinange's name to avoid both public and personal exposure – some commented that "the evidence leaves no doubt that [the president] is so determined in any situation where his prestige is affected."[43] So was the report "published without its last page."[44]

J. M. Kariuki's infamous murder dealt a real blow to Kenyatta's and his family's reputation: both became the subject of increasing popular resentment.[45] In response, the government organized a public display of its force and authority: Kenyatta paraded with the military in downtown Nairobi on March 23, 1975; further loyalty ceremonies were organized throughout Central province. Meanwhile, presidential rule grew "increasingly arbitrary."[46] The president continued to show an "inability, or unwillingness to control the acquisitive greed of his family and close cronies [while] his ruthless suppression of any political opposition on issues of importance to his position have caused widespread concern."[47] Antony Duff reported a conversation with Charles Njonjo, who allegedly confessed: "he had 'never wished that man ill' but now he was forced to the conclusion that 'the sooner it happened' the better."[48]

Yet, Kenyatta remained dedicated to reinforcing his authority and his control over state institutions. His intolerance against political dissent grew fiercer. In October 1975, Seroney and Shikuku were arrested in the middle of a parliamentary session: they were accused of having publicly said that KANU was dead, triggering the

---

[42] Hornsby, *Kenya*, 283.
[43] Confidential. P. R. A. Mansfield to M. K. Ewans, November 19, 1975, BNA, FCO 31/1885.
[44] Hornby, *Kenya*, 284.
[45] M. K. Ewans to Mr. Aspin, January 23, 1976, BNA, FCO 31/2020. See also Hornsby, *Kenya*, 285–286.
[46] Confidential. Diplomatic report No. 54/76, "Kenya: Annual Review for 1975," January 2, 1976, BNA, FCO 31/2020.
[47] Ibid.
[48] Confidential, Antony Duff to H. of C., "Political Situation," March 24, 1975, BNA, DO 226/15.

government's brutal response in the arm wrestling started by MPs.[49] The two MPs were subsequently jailed without trial – they would be released on presidential favor in late 1978, after Kenyatta's death. Their arrest, probably ordered by Kenyatta himself, was a sign that the government was to kill, once again, the emancipatory dreams of dissident parliamentarians. A British administrator later commented that

> Seroney was a serious threat ... because he was the master parliamentarian and was seeking through his Select Committee to amend standing orders as a means of emasculating the President's powers. But he showed his hand too early and the President moved in on his Committee, almost depriving it of a quorum and threatening to close it down.[50]

After Seroney's and Shikuku's arrest, the parliament was almost completely subdued. Kenyatta thereafter "addressed MPs in camera for about 80 minutes. According to parliamentary sources he said that he had personally signed the detention orders for Seroney and Shikuku. Others would be detained if they continued to oppose the Government."[51] His threatening speech against dissidents impacted the MPs' morale. The parliament was reduced to an empty arena, where fear of repression reigned. A British report noted that "Attendances dropped from 80-100 down to under 30 and the House was often without a quorum ... since no-one knew who would be next month's victims there were few who dared to speak at all and none who dared to speak frankly."[52] Repression of any dissident voices – whether from MPs or intellectuals like the writer Ngugi wa Thiong'o, whose politicized fictions would land him in jail in 1977 – together with the halted succession struggle, enabled the president to remain aloof from popular criticism. As the new British high commissioner Stanley Fingland noted early in 1976: "The President is skilled at containing ... resentment, but it washes off on his whole regime and any legitimate successor would have greater difficulty in dealing with it."[53] All diplomatic reports continuously noted a significant erosion of what was but a semblance of democracy.

[49] Hornsby, *Kenya*, 288.
[50] Confidential. C. T. Hart to EAD, October 19, 1976, and Confidential. C. T. Hart to Mr. Rosling, August 17, 1977, BNA, FCO 31/2121.
[51] Restricted. C. T. Hart to D. Wigan, October 17, 1975, BNA, FCO 31/1885.
[52] Confidential. C. T. Hart to D. Wigan, November 4, 1975, BNA, FCO 31/1885.
[53] Confidential. Diplomatic report No. 54/76, "Kenya: Annual Review for 1975," January 2, 1976, BNA, FCO 31/2020.

The succession struggle further aggravated the deleterious state of affairs. Kenyatta was careful enough to preserve the status quo to ensure his prestige and authority remained unchallenged. Despite his clear preference for Moi, he "took good care to let it appear that he has no mind of his own. In photographs in the press, Moi usually looks as though he is dancing sheepishly to the President's tune."[54] In the meantime, Kenyatta's health continued to deteriorate. He would spend most of his time on "busy working holiday" at his residence on the Coast, or most frequently in the Rift Valley; and as the British high commissioner noted, Kenyatta "[appeared] most animated at the endless daily entertainments by traditional dancers and choirs at his home."[55] The president was increasingly isolated from the public opinion, entrenching himself in the close circle of his "cronies."[56] Such isolation continued to put the political life of the country on hold. In July 1977, Kenyatta postponed, once again, national elections (they were already postponed in April 1977 due to the president's health issues), for he had been "alarmed at the extent of the national divisions between the Moi and Mungai camps."[57] As an Australian diplomatic report, circulated in London, put it, the president was simply "not [contemplating] his own death, ... he is determined to prevent any one man acquiring too much power and that he fears a diminution in his own influence if a successor is too obviously singled out."[58]

It was in the midst of this political fatigue and seemingly endless struggle for succession that Kenyatta died, on August 21, 1978, in Mombasa. His health had been continuously worsening, yet his death came as a surprised and the "shocking news," as one newspaper put it, was, on that day, circulated with great secrecy.[59] Two of Kenyatta's sons, Peter Magana and Peter Muigai, and his wife Mama Ngina

---

[54] Confidential. P. R. A. Mansfield to M. K. Ewans, May 19, 1976, BNA, FCO 31/2019.
[55] Confidential. Diplomatic report No. 68/77, "Kenya: Annual Review for 1976," January 6, 1977, BNA, FCO 31/2120.
[56] Confidential. Stanley Fingland to Rt. Hon. Dr. David Owen, October 25, 1977, BNA, FCO 31/2121, 27.
[57] Confidential. C. T. Hart to Mr. Hunt, July 5, 1977, BNA, FCO 31/2121.
[58] Confidential. Despatch No. 4/77, W. P. J. Handmer, High Commissioner to the Honourable Andrew Peacock, "Kenya: The Postcolonial Challenge," October 28, 1977, BNA, FCO 31/2321.
[59] Hornsby, *Kenya*, 327; "The Day the President Died," *The Weekly Review*, September 1, 1978, 8–9.

handled the matter with great tact, calling with utmost discretion their political allies in fear that political vacuum and uncertainty might work against them. They first called the PC of Coast, Eliud Mahihu (Kikuyu) and summoned cabinet minister Munyua Waiyaki (Kikuyu) to come down to Mombasa. Vice president (and future president) Daniel arap Moi was informed shortly before Geoffrey K. Kariithi (Kikuyu), the head of the civil service who eventually organized the transferral of Kenyatta's body to Nairobi. Only after this were Peter Mbiyu Koinange, together with Margaret Wambui Kenyatta and Kenyatta's other children informed. Finally, Bernard Hinga (Kikuyu), commissioner of police, James Hanyotu (Kikuyu), director of intelligence, as well as Mwai Kibaki (Kikuyu), minister of finance and economic planning (who eventually succeeded to Moi), were all summoned to the Mombasa state house, where Kenyatta's body was resting.[60] They were perhaps the last pillars of the Kenyatta state after fourteen years of presidential rule and destructive divisions. They were also a sign that, by the end of the 1970s, Kenyatta's political family was reduced to a handful of trusted politicians from handpicked institutions that barely resembled Kenyatta's state at independence.

Back to Kenyatta's Family

The attempt to sketch the Kenyatta family highlights the importance of picturing political relations as a process of socialization. The lack of sources or exact information about his family's political and business connections allows only for a general picture encompassing the period from the 1960s up to today, without proper chronological distinctions. The Africanization of the Kenyan economy and the increasing tribalization of politics in the 1970s were accompanied by a gradual reinvention of the codes of socialization among the elite after independence, which gave a prominent place to the cultural attributes of power and success.[61] Although Kenyatta's family was (and still is) an eminently politically active and economically powerful one, the establishment of

---

[60] "The Day the President Died," *The Weekly Review*.
[61] Dominique Connan, "Race for Distinction: A Social History of Private Members' Clubs in Colonial Kenya" (Ph.D. diss., European University Institute, 2015).

other political dynasties and economic empires has spread and mushroomed within the Kenyan elite.[62] Nevertheless, a reflection on who and what the Kenyatta family is emphasizes that socialization is more a reflection of state power, rather than its primary source.[63]

Of Kenyatta's seven children, four served prominent political functions. Peter Muigai Kenyatta became an MP, KANU chairman for the Juja branch in Kiambu, and assistant minister for foreign affairs; Margaret Wambui Kenyatta was Nairobi mayor from 1970 to 1976 and Kenya's ambassador to the United Nations from 1976 to 1986; Jane Wambui Kenyatta married Udi Gecaga, who would be appointed to the London board of the media group Lonrho in 1973, providing the government with an opportunity to better control Kenyan newspapers; and Uhuru Muigai Kenyatta was elected president of Kenya in 2012.[64] It is worth recalling that Kenyatta had also family connections with Mbiyu Koinange (his brother-in-law) and Njoroge Mungai (his cousin and personal physician), two of his most prominent ministers.

The political influence of the Kenyatta family must be read in the light of its economic resources – it must be noted, however, that its estate has been and still is a subject of both fascination and speculation, so accounts should be taken at face value.[65] Land estate is estimated at 500,000 acres, "approximately the size of Nyanza province," as a Kenyan journalist noted in 2004.[66] Most of the land properties were supposedly acquired during the 1960s and 1970s, although the means

---

[62] Hornsby, *Kenya*, 674. See also Peter Mwaura, "Koinange's Death Marks the End of a Dynasty That Reigned in Kiambu," *Daily Nation*, September 7, 2012; Victor Juma, "Kenyatta Business Empire Goes into Expansion Drive," *Business Daily*, November 11, 2013; Patrick Nzioka and Bernard Namunane, "Political Families Own Half of Private Wealth," *Daily Nation*, February 20, 2014; Peter Kagwanja, "Generational Change of Guard and the Odinga Dynasty," *Daily Nation*, October 25, 2014; Benson Wambugu, "Thirty-Two Years On, Koinange Family Fights over Estate as Brokers Profit," *Daily Nation*, July 6, 2016; "Is It the End of the Affair for Kenya's Oligarch?" *Daily Nation*, November 12, 2011.

[63] Connan, "Race for Distinction," 178.

[64] On Kenyatta's family members and their political functions, see Hornsby, *Kenya*, 315. On Udi Gecaga, see Peter J. M. Kareithi, "Multinational Corporations and Foreign Owned Media in Developing Countries," *Crime, Law and Social Change* 16, no. 2 (1991): 204.

[65] In 2016, Forbes magazine estimated Uhuru Kenyatta's wealth at $500 million, with land as the main capital asset. See "Africa's 40 Richest. #26 Uhuru Kenyatta," *Forbes*.

[66] Namwaya, "Who Owns *Kenya*?"

of acquisition, and their legality, remain unclear; journalists, NGO activists, and historians reported that settlement schemes or land funds were diverted to increase personal fortunes.[67] No exhaustive list of the Kenyatta's' land holdings exists – past or ongoing land transactions further complicate the creation of such a list – but the estate supposedly covers fertile lands in Central province (in Dandora, Gatundu, Juja, Kasarani, Muthaiga, Nairobi, Ruiru, and Kahawa Sukari), the Rift Valley (in Endebess, Nakuru, Naivasha, and Rumuruti), and Coast province (in Nyali and Taveta).[68] Charles Hornsby describes Kenyatta as a man enjoying a luxurious life, ignoring his debts, even monetizing his presidential audiences; his wife Mama Ngina benefited extensively from presidential largesse, and was at times embroiled – along with her children – in corruption scandals.[69] Since the 1970s, the range of his family's economic activities has developed greatly. Its interests are spread across banking, real estate, mining, insurance, airlines, education, energy, dairy farming, transport, and telecommunications.[70] However, this degree of economic activity is not specific to Kenyatta's family, and exemplifies the importance of political and economic "dynasties" more or less closely related to the president.[71]

All top government officials occupied prominent functions in Kenyan business affairs.[72] Whether ministers had financial interests

---

[67] Hornsby, *Kenya*, 108; John Kamau, "How Former First Lady Lost a Huge Chunk of Land in Ruiru," *Daily Nation*, Sunday February 14, 2016. For details on irregular allocations of land during the Kenyatta regime see *Report of the Commission of Inquiry into the Illegal/Irregular Allocation of Public Land* and *Report of the Truth, Justice and Reconciliation Commission* (Truth Justice and Reconciliation Commission, 2013), 106, 222–298.

[68] John Kamau, "How Independence Era Leaders Laid Their Hands on Lands of Quitting Whites," *Daily Nation*, November 9, 2009; "Top Officials Bypassed Mzee to Acquire Land at the Coast," *Daily Nation*, November 12, 2009; Laban Wanambisi, "We Own 30,000 Acres in Taveta – Uhuru," *Capital News*, February 25, 2013; Nzioka and Namunane, "Political Families Own Half of Private Wealth."

[69] Ibid., 263–264, 312–313.

[70] Nzioka and Namunane, "Political Families Own Half of Private Wealth"; "Mama Ngina Listed Top Investor at Kenya Power with 2.2 Million Shares," *Business Daily*, May 20, 2013; Juma, "Kenyatta Business Empire Goes into Expansion Drive."

[71] Hornsby, *Kenya*, 314–316, 323, 403, 665, 674.

[72] A comprehensive picture of their positions is provided by the Christian Council of Kenya's economic and industrial survey of the 1960s: *Who Controls Industry in Kenya?*

in companies, or simply sat on boards of directors, they played an influential role in many prominent industries of the country after independence.[73] To mention but a few examples, James Gichuru, finance and defense minister in Kenyatta's government, was once director of Kenya Power (listed third of the biggest and richest Kenyan twenty-six public companies in the 1960s) and in which Mama Ngina remained a substantial individual investor.[74] Mbiyu Koinange, minister of state and Kenyatta's brother-in-law, owned large land estates (which later inflamed divisions among their inheritors) and was one of the directors of the Naivasha-based Pan-African Produce and Development Company Ltd., the Magadi Soda Company, and owned significant shares in other leading firms, such as the Theita Group, Commercial Development Corporation.[75] Similarly, his younger brother and former provincial commissioner Charles Koinange owned vast tea and coffee farms as well as rental houses.[76] Duncan Ndgewa, appointed governor of the Central Bank of Kenya in 1967, was also chairman of the National Bank of Kenya, the Agricultural Finance Corporation (which supplemented the Land Bank in providing loans for citizens with loose assets to buy land), and the Kenyan Pipeline Company, and owned the First Chartered Securities company and Unga Group (ninth biggest and richest public company in the 1960s).[77] Attorney general Charles Njonjo was director of CfC Stanbic Holdings, and chief executive of CMC Holdings, a car business closely working with the government, and in which both Bruce McKenzie and (former permanent secretary in the Office of the President) Jeremiah Kiereini owned shares as well.[78] Other prominent members of

---

[73] Leys highlights the postcolonial government's strategy to africanize equity shares in profitable enterprises remaining under the purportedly safe control of foreign actors. See Leys, *Underdevelopment in Kenya*, 128–135.

[74] *Who Controls Industry in Kenya?*, 133; "Mama Ngina Listed Top Investor at Kenya Power with 2.2 Million Shares."

[75] "The Sh10bn Empire Koinange Built," *Daily Nation*, July 6, 2013; Wambugu, "Thirty-Two Years on, Koinange Family Fights over Estate as Brokers Profit"; *Who Controls Industry in Kenya?*, 41, 50.

[76] R. Munguti, "Ex-PC's Kin Battle for SH5bn Estate," *Daily Nation*, January 10, 2015.

[77] "Uhuru Appointments Are Proof That Political Dynasties Alive and Well," *Daily Nation*, May 2, 2015.

[78] Mwaura Kimani, "Is It the End of the Affair for Kenya's Oligarchs?" *Daily Nation*, November 12, 2011; Paul Juma, "Kiereini Cleared for Boardroom Return," *Daily Nation*, August 22, 2013 and Victor Juma "Moi-Era Political Elite Exits Top CfC Stanbic Shareholders Roll," *Business Daily*, January 30, 2014.

Kenyatta's government occupied just as prominent economic positions. Men such as the enigmatic Humphrey Slade, a white lawyer fond of golf, and inaugural speaker in the national assembly from 1963 to 1970, and John Michuki, treasurer in the Kenyatta government, were both listed among the "top fifty" company directors, with respectively sixteen and ten directorships held in the country between 1966 to 1968.[79] Michuki was one of Ndegwa's successors at the Central Bank of Kenya, while it should be noted that both men were members of the joint board for the Land Bank and the Agricultural Finance Corporation.[80]

In fine, the definition of Kenyatta's family cannot be detached from the roots of Kenyatta's state-building: they are consubstantial. The closest definition of his family is that of familial and political alliances forged into an ethnic background. Neither the biological connection, ethnic affinities, political functions, nor economic influence suffice to define who and what the Kenyatta family is, for whoever is best deemed to protect the political, economic, and financial assets of the family will be included. Hence, the Kalenjin Daniel arap Moi was chosen by Kenyatta as a successor, with the support of only a fragment of Kenyatta's political family, namely attorney general Charles Njonjo. It is barely surprising that forty year later, Moi remained a powerful supporter of Kenyatta's son, Uhuru, when the later ran for and won the presidency.[81]

---

[79] *Who Controls Industry in Kenya?*, 145–146.   [80] Ibid., 170, 191–192.
[81] Lynch, "Courting the Kalenjin."

Conclusion

Writing the history of Jomo Kenyatta's presidency, it was particularly difficult to disentangle the history of a politician from that of a newly created institution: the presidency. The inherently discreet and distant nature of Kenyatta's presidential style, together with the scattered and incomplete nature of the available sources, only partially explains this difficulty. A more thorough explanation highlights the unprecedented connection between the sudden emergence of a politician and the unexpected formation of the presidency. Contingency played a central role in Kenyatta's political career and significantly shaped the nature of his presidential rule. Soon after he was released from jail, it became clear that Kenyatta had virtually no political resources with which to command political loyalties, other than the popularity he owed to his ambiguous past. The independence negotiations further exposed his shallow political anchoring, as Kenyatta refrained from committing himself personally to any of the debates. In the end, the presidency was tailor-made to turn his political isolation into a political system.

The Twin Birth of President and Presidency

Nothing prepared Kenyatta to become president. He never imagined state authority as an inclusive authority for all. This lack of nationalist perspective was inherent in his Kikuyu ethics, although it was certainly reinforced by the colonial legacy, which prevented the formation of nationalist parties and thus legitimized political tribalism. Colonization not only froze tribal politics, but also altered their internal tribal logics, causing substantial rifts within the Kikuyu tribe in particular. Kenyatta was very much aware of the contradictions caused by colonization, and the difficulty he would have to reconcile Kikuyu tribal history with a changing political and social order. Rather than expanding his political rhetoric toward greater inclusiveness, however, he chose to reduce it to the smallest possible social entity, the family.

The family, I argue, became the foundation of both his political imagination and his politics, as he built his political network around his Kiambu family. Far from being reduced to a failed nationalist leader, I have shown that exploration of Kenyatta's political imagination highlights a central aspect of his leadership: his constant care for family politics and his mistrust for any nationalist ambitions he saw as betraying his tribal origins.[1]

His rise to power left him virtually without political resources when it came to imposing his leadership over a divided, and even hostile, elite. No politician who campaigned for his release from jail expected that he would dominate the political scene and side-line their own political ambitions. His political career was revived through the myth of the father of the nation, which his comrades had created, and wrongly thought they could manipulate and control. In fact, the inexorable success of the narrative of the father of the nation revealed the pervasiveness of internal divisions more than it altered political alliances. Although the nationalist elite was small, it faced the difficult task of appealing to divided and heterogeneous political entities: the Mau Mau fighters, the loyalist Kikuyu, other ethnic tribes, the white settlers, and the British – thus hindering claims to national authority and preventing alternative patterns of decolonization from emerging. The narrative of the father of the nation took root so rapidly precisely because Kenyatta had unique symbolic capital: the complexities of Mau Mau history – caught up between the secrecy of oathing, the traumatic repression during the Emergency, and the silencing of resilient fighters after independence – enabled him to be both the "owner" of the Mau Mau, when, to the Kenyan elite, he was clearly not. His well-calculated silence when visited by delegations while he was still in restriction, or when speaking publicly shortly before independence, showed that he was very much aware that he ought to use this singular yet fragile asset sparingly.

---

[1] Kenyatta's long-time opposition to the KANU radicals, and in particular to the Kikuyu Bildad Kaggia must be understood as a Kikuyu internal issue rather than a struggle between two universal ideologies, socialism *versus* capitalism. Similarly, Kenyatta's rhetorical attacks against the KANU radicals were all framed in Kikuyu terms, whether he criticized Kaggia for his lack of self-achievement or denounced Odinga's KPU on the grounds that its leaders took no part in the struggle for independence along the Mau Mau movement! See Kenyatta, Speech on Kenyatta Day, October 20, 1967, *Suffering without Bitterness*, 343–344.

Kenyatta's later political rise had a profound impact on the construction of presidential rule in independent Kenya. He became the "sole spokesman" of a nationalist elite he could not trust, and yet he alone could unite. Far from resolving political divisions, his political ascent laid the groundwork for the creation of a political system absorbing divisions and dissensions. In a way, the president emerged before the presidency itself, forcing presidential rule onto the negotiation table. The negotiations on the decolonization of land institutions prepared the way for a centralized government, before the arguments over federalism or centralization were settled among the Kenyan elite. The British fear of a security breakdown considerably influenced the creation of centralized institutions for land transfer, and did play a role in favoring Kenyatta as a political leader. In doing so, their interests converged with KANU's. Nevertheless, the British took little interest in the negotiations over a presidential republic. Records of the independence negotiations reveal that KADU leaders did not foresee this question, while Kenyatta remained uncompromising. Their final and almost inevitable convergence with KANU's plans for a presidential constitution, which *de facto* annihilated any claims to regionalism, testifies to the novelty of presidentialism as a system of government, which had been well prepared by the establishment of new land institutions.

The hasty negotiations on presidentialism left Kenyatta with not only a new, but also a large and vague set of prerogatives. He had no experience with, and even less control over, other state institutions – either over the party or the legislative council, or even, after independence, parliament. This lack of institutional resources further limited his ability to control a territory that was politically, socially, and ethnically divided. Kenyatta's popularity depended on his ability to satisfy diverging expectations: those of the landless and squatters who demanded free redistribution of land, among them the former Mau Mau fighters, and those of the white settlers and British authorities, whose support for the government was bound to the willing buyer–willing seller principle of land buying. The Ministry of Land thus emerged as a powerful institution to cut short any subversive land claim. Besides, the fact that Kenyatta did not choose someone estranged from the Mau Mau movement as the minister for lands – that is, Jackson Angaine – also highlights the centrality of the Mau Mau struggle in the construction of the postcolonial state, reaffirming the view that Kenya was not just a postcolonial state, but a postwar country.[2]

Kenyatta had little choice but to keep his political authority insulated from potential challengers. This strategy was reinforced by the fact that he lacked any vision of national development that could have fostered more political unity. He chose to continue colonial land politics so as to maintain the stable political order from which he had benefited. The colonial legacy should not overshadow the agency of the independent government, however. Central to this agency was the appropriation and politicized redistribution of land resources. On the one hand, land buying was used to appease political dissents, to the great frustration of British officials who saw their funds misused for politicking. On the other hand, perpetuating colonial politics reduced the political influence of the landless, squatters, resilient Mau Mau fighters or even "radical" or populists politicians, who remained dependent on the goodwill of the central government. This phenomenon was best illustrated by the Kenyan writer Ngugi wa Thiongo in his historical novel *Petals of Blood,* which retraced the silent lives of landless and Mau Mau fighters in a remote, deserted village. In the midst of a drought, the village organizes a delegation to meet their MP in the capital, but will only succeed in being given some *harambee* "developmental" projects opening the way for big men to grab yet more of their land.[3] Subaltern studies argued that a history of elites necessarily silences the voices "from below," but did not fully explore the mechanisms that underpin such a system. In fact, this silence must be read in light of the president's political imagination, and must be contextualized politically, as it appears that Kenyatta's ignorance of the technicalities of the land issue, together with his disinterest in the squatters, fitted best his desire to remain politically unexposed: a strategy he had employed since being released from jail.

Although Kenyatta did delegate regional powers to the provincial administration (or to the Ministry of Lands), the main beneficiaries of his distant rule were not necessarily the PCs, as the literature has tended to emphasize, but rather cabinet ministers, who took significant advantage of the loopholes in Kenyatta's presidential rule, especially after 1965. By then, the fragile alliance of convenience set up between

---

[2] Branch, *Defeating Mau Mau, Creating Kenya,* 180.
[3] Ngugi wa Thiong'o, *Petals of Blood* (London: Penguins Books, 2002).

Kenyatta and his main contenders, the Luo Oginga Odinga and Tom Mboya, was beginning to crack. Kenyatta's fragile health revived the question of the presidential succession that haunted the political elite since independence. The government's merciless repression against any form of opposition and dissent culminated with the murder of Tom Mboya in 1969. It was also accompanied by an increased politicization of land accumulation organized by cabinet ministers, which revealed the latter's ability to establish and control a propertied dynasty in the top spheres of power. In the 1970s, Kenyatta further distanced himself from the hustle of politics. In fact, a much greater transformation was under way. The struggle for Kenyatta's succession, coupled with the general political developments, shows that presidential rule was becoming increasingly authoritarian and increasingly distant from important decision-making – the latter being left to influential ministers. The lack of sources dealing with cabinet ministers, and the scattered information as to their relationship to the "Old Man," their personal connections, or conflicts point to a significant shortcoming in our current understanding of presidential rule. These latter remained, however, literally untraceable.

All in all, this book described the twin birth of a president and the presidency. Such an interpretation goes beyond analyses that link the history of the postcolonial African state to the personality of the leader. Personality does matter – I showed that Kenyatta's political imagination certainly influenced his presidential style. Nevertheless, the independence negotiations revealed a political vacuum that, far from opening-up creative political opportunities, was obstructed by political divisions tearing apart the national elite and significantly limited both Kenyatta's and his main contenders' political maneuvering. With Kenyatta's personality dominating the negotiation process, decolonization took an unexpected turn, as long-term debates about federalism and centralization were cut short and the question of presidential powers took center stage.

The establishment of the presidency institutionalized Kenyatta's political supremacy at the time of independence: it was a recent political construction, removed from the procedural aspects of day-to-day politics, and which transformed informal power relationships into strong yet only vaguely defined presidential powers. The quasi-limitless centralization of power granted to the presidency established an institutional imbalance that Kenyatta cultivated very carefully, sparsely meting out personal promises and favors. In this regard, the competition between parliament and civil administration shows how Kenyatta used tentacular informal powers to prevent both institutions from emancipating from presidential authority. This subtle imbalance may also explain why the landless and poor remained locked into Kafkaesque bureaucratic procedures, while Kenyatta remained politically unexposed.

Speaking of the twin birth of the president and the presidency again raises the question of the conceptualization of the African postcolonial state. The historical reconstruction of the origins and negotiations of presidential powers nuances the arguments placing the colonial legacy at the center of postcolonial African states.[4] The latter underestimate both the haste with which a presidential constitution was established and the unexpected character it would take on. Although it is indisputable that presidential rule was born out of the political divisions and weaknesses created by colonization, the presidential project was first and foremost the battleground of internal political struggles. Most importantly, presidential rule was a hazy constitutional principle at independence, whose most authoritarian and repressive characteristics only developed in its aftermath.

The sharp competition that opened up at independence forced the president to further cut off the presidency from territorial and institutional linkages to ensure his political survival. The imbalance of power between the presidency and other state institutions is not a side effect of the colonial legacy, but lies at the heart of the historical formation of the postcolonial Kenyan state. This assertion also challenges the theories that centralized African states are too small to control large territory, or that varying personalities of leaders explain different styles of presidential rules.[5] Such arguments do not provide a satisfying answer as to why presidential rule spread throughout the continent and has proved resilient to constitutional change.[6]

---

[4] For arguments emphasizing a colonial atavistic legacy, see Mamdani, *Citizen and Subject*; Young, *The Post-Colonial State in Africa*.

[5] Mamdani, *Citizen and Subjects*; Herbst, *States and Power in Africa*. See also Martin Murray, Atieno Odhiambu, and Chris Youé, "Debate and Commentary: Mamdani's Citizen and Subject," *Canadian Journal of African Studies* 34, no. 2 (2000): 375–412.

[6] A meaningful example can be found in the audit report on the 2010 Kenya constitution published in September 2016 by the auditor general-led team in charge of reviewing the constitution. The report blamed the resilience of an old

Far from trying to understand the theories and typologies of the many forms of African presidential rule, this book sought to question why such a system formed in the first place. A parallel might be established between Cooper's concept of the African "gatekeeper state" and what this book described as a "gatekeeper president."[7] Just like the gatekeeper state, which controls the threshold between world economy and territorial politics, the gatekeeper president acts as a boundary between the central government and the territory, using his direct control over state resources to reinforce his position. While presidential prerogatives are likely to expand as informal presidential powers pervade both institutional and civil organizations, the gatekeeper president remains vulnerable, for he is constantly surrounded by influential contenders potentially endangering his rule, and forcing him to retreat into ever greater isolation.

Kenyatta's Institutional Legacy

At first glance, and as the analysis of both his political imagination and accession to power tends to show, Kenyatta did not seem to have had any concrete intention to construct a political ideal that he would bequeath to the Kenyan nation. Unsurprisingly, then, his legacy is often perceived as a negative one, given the continuation of the so-called land issue, which took on ever more violent characteristics after the 2007 postelectoral violence, exposing the dirty underbelly of Kenyan politics.[8] Undoubtedly, his failure to achieve a more equal system of land distribution and ownership, together with his disinterest in land technicalities or the effective settlement of squatters, intensified the effects of a colonial policy that favored a landed bourgeoisie. Yet, the multiplicity of actors and interests involved stops us from attributing the perpetuation of this colonial legacy solely to Kenyatta's political legacy. We should emphasize, rather, the president's institutional

---

"institutional culture" that still ties state institution to the will of the Office of the President, significantly limiting the scope of the decentralization reforms, *Report of the Working Group on Socio-Economic Audit of the Constitution of Kenya, 2010*, September 2016, 91–107.

[7] Frederic Cooper, *Africa since 1940: The Past of the Present* (Cambridge: Cambridge University Press, 2002), 5–6.

[8] Karuti Kanyinga, "The Legacy of the White Highlands: Land Rights, Ethnicity and the Post-2007 Election Violence in Kenya," *Journal of Contemporary African Studies* 27, no. 3 (2009): 325–344.

legacy, which not only preserved the colonial architecture of such a system of land buying and redistribution, but passed it on to the hands of his successors. By expressing his preference for Daniel arap Moi as potential successor, Kenyatta not only chose a non-Kikuyu, but, more importantly, an isolated political player, like himself ten years earlier. Far from preparing the ground for tribal inclusion in the top sphere of government, Kenyatta's choices led the presidency to prevail over a divided elite, to compensate weak institutional ties by presidential favors, and to preserve parochial family interests.[9]

In fact, the tribal inclusiveness of the Kenyan state mirrored the mutual dependency that tied the president to the government members, and still does. The increasing size and number of ministries since independence shows less how inclusive the state is than the degree of pressure on the president to accommodate divisions at the top. Significantly, the number of cabinet ministers increased from fifteen after independence to forty-two under the presidency of Mwai Kibaki between 2008 and 2013; already before his death in 1978, Kenyatta's cabinet had been increased to twenty.[10] Another example is the formal strengthening of parliamentary powers over the years, which has not challenged the informal powers of the presidency: a similarity Kenya shares with many other African countries.[11] Neither has the gradual strengthening of regional powers, which culminated with the 2013 decentralized constitution, undermined presidential authority, despite forcing the government to negotiate and compromise with the regional authorities.[12]

Nevertheless, the continuing insulation of presidential authority warrants further investigation, especially to explain why so few outsiders are able to compete for presidency. The Kenyan state has indeed remained a family state: the three presidents who succeeded Kenyatta came from the same political and even biological family, as does the current president Uhuru Kenyatta, Jomo's son. As Charton and Fouéré

---

[9] I thank Nicholas Cheeseman for the useful discussion we had on this issue and his interesting insights.
[10] E. Omari, "Presidents Took Advantage of Legal Gap to Increase Ministries," *Daily Nation*, April 23, 2013.
[11] P. Chaisty, N. Cheeseman, and T. Power, "Rethinking the 'Presidentialism Debate': Conceptualizing Coalitional Politics in Cross-Regional Perspective," *Democratisation* 21, no. 1 (2014): 1–23.
[12] Cheeseman, Lynch, and Willis, "Decentralisation in Kenya," 28, 31.

explained, the connection to the "father of the nation" has become a powerful political resource, and the parallels made between Uhuru Kenyatta's trial at the International Criminal Court between 2011 and 2016 and that of his father by the colonizers in 1952–1953 further prove the point.[13] Yet, the reproduction of family ties and political inheritance remain unclear processes. It is still impossible to know, for lack of sources and testimonies, to what extent Mama Ngina, Jomo's wife and Uhuru's mother, may have influenced both presidents' politics, whereas Daniel arap Moi's influential role in supporting Uhuru Kenyatta has been well studied. The latter also allied with a Kalenjin politician, William Ruto, to strengthen his presidency.[14]

This lack points to the limits of the interpretations that depict the African state as "personalized," failing to acknowledge why, how and when personalization has become a system of rule. Further comparative research into the independence negotiations could show why a personalized form of presidentialism spread so quickly, and almost homogeneously among African postcolonial states. The question is all the more pressing given that postcolonial leaders have had very different styles of rule. Kenyatta's politics differed radically, for example, from those of the Senegalese Leopold Sédar Senghor or the Tanzanian Julius Nyerere, who both conceptualized a much more direct form of leadership, and attempted to give concrete shape to their political ideas, as well as to their presidential legacies.[15] Yet, all three built strong presidential states. Arguments framed in terms of personal ambition for power should give way to a more thorough investigation of why and how the independence negotiations turned out to be negotiations of presidential powers. Neither do socialist paradigms or development doctrines, whose shallow ideological bases I showed in

---

[13] Obuya Bagaka, "Striking Similarities between Uhuru Kenyatta's Trial at the Hague and Jomo Kenyatta's Kapenguria Case," *Daily Nation*, September 28, 2014.

[14] Lynch, "Electing the 'Alliance of the Accused'."

[15] On Senghor, see Vaillant, *Black, French, and African*; Souleymane Bachir Diagne, *African Art as Philosophy: Senghor, Bergson and the Idea of Negritude* (London: Seagull Books, 2011); Gary Wilder, *Freedom Time: Negritude, Decolonisation, and the Future of the World* (Durham, NC: Duke University Press, 2015). On Nyerere, see Paul Bjerk, *Building a Peaceful Nation: Julius Nyerere and the Establishment of Sovereignty in Tanzania, 1960–1964* (Rochester, NY: University of Rochester Press, 2015).

the sixth chapter, suffice to explain the construction of a strong state. The colonial legacy does not suffice as an explanation for such a transition either, as it obscures the political divisions which, although inherited from colonization, did not dissolve at independence but became part and parcel of the making of the presidential state.

Sources

The British National Archives, Kew (BNA)

Records of the Foreign and Commonwealth Office and predecessors (FCO)
- East Africa Departments, Registered Files: FCO 31/3; FCO 31/32; FCO 31/33; FCO 31/206; FCO 31/209; FCO 31/356; FCO 31/593; FCO 31/596; FCO 31/597; FCO 31/851; FCO 31/1191; FCO 31/1197; FCO 31/1496; FCO 31/1497; FCO 31/1707; FCO 31/1883; FCO 31/1885; FCO 31/1886; FCO 31/2019; FCO 31/2020; FCO 31/2120; FCO 31/2121; FCO 31/2314; FCO 31/2321; FCO 31/2322.
- Migrated Archives: FCO 141/1895; FCO 141/6364; FCO 141/6764; FCO 141/6766; FCO 141/6767; FCO 141/6768; FCO 141/6769; FCO 141/6772; FCO 141/6918; FCO 141/6919; FCO 141/6923; FCO 141/6924; FCO 141/18960; FCO 141/18963; FCO 141/18985; FCO 141/19010.

Records of the Colonial Office, Commonwealth and Foreign and Commonwealth Offices, Empire Marketing Board, and related bodies (CO)
- Colonial Office: East Africa: Original Correspondence: CO 822/1247; CO 822/1909; CO 822/1910; CO 822/1911; CO 822/1912; CO 822/3117.

Records of the Cabinet Office (CAB)
  CAB 21/4772; CAB 128/35/61; CAB 129/106/14; CAB 133/215; CAB 133/216; CAB 195/23/21.

Records of the Dominion Office (DO)
- East and General Africa: Registered Files: DO 168/45; DO 168/48; DO 168/49.
- East Africa Departments: Registered Files, East Africa: DO 213/37; DO 213/65; DO 213/66; DO 213/69; DO 213/159; DO 213/161; DO 213/204; DO 213/294.

- East Africa Economic Department and Development Policy and East and West Africa Economic Department: Registered Files, East Africa Economic: DO 214/39; DO 214/40; DO 214/46; DO 214/53; DO 214/104; DO 214/105; DO 214/106; DO 214/107.
- High Commission and Consular Archives, Kenya: Registered Files: DO 226/11; DO 226/13; DO 226/15.

Records of the Prime Minister's Office (PREM)
PREM 2179.

Durham University Library, Archives, and Special Collections

Malcom MacDonald Papers. Reproduced by kind permission of the Trustees of the Malcolm MacDonald Papers and of the University of Durham.

Kenya National Archives, Nairobi (KNA)

District Commissioner Machakos (DC/MKS)
DC/MKS/10B/13/1.
District Commissioner Maralal (DC/MRL)
DC/MRL/1/6/9.
District Commissioner Meru (DC/MRU)
DC/MRU/1/4/5; DC/MRU/1/12/1, DC/MRU/1/15/1.
Provincial Commissioner, Nakuru (PC/NKU)
PC/NKU/13/20.
Provincial Commissioner, Central Province (VQ)
VQ/11/7; VQ/14/86; VQ/16/80; VQ/16/81; VQ/16/94; VQ/16/95.
Murumbi Africana Collection (MAC/KEN)
MAC/KEN/38/4; MAC/KEN/38/5; MAC/KEN/38/8; MAC/KEN/69/1; MAC/KEN/70/3; MAC/KEN/70/4; MAC/KEN/72/4.
Governors' House (KA.1 and AZG1)
KA.1/11/73; KA.1/11/173; AZG1.3.20.
Ministry of Land and Settlement
- (BN): BN/81/8; BN/81/24; BN/81/31; BN/81/87; BN/81/89; BN/81/161; BN/81/162; BN/81/164; BN/82/1; BN/84/7; BN/87/26; BN/96/2; BN/97/3.
- (AVS): AVS/3/5; AVS/15/41.

Eastern Province (BB)
    BB/1/148; BB/1/149; BB/1/158; BB/1/247; BB/11/36; BB/12/48;
        BB/12/49; BB/49/49; BB/49/59; BB/59/49; BB/82/21; BB/88/20.
Coast Province
    (CA): CA/10/3/2; CA/10/3/3; CA/39/1; CA/39/3.
    (CQ): CQ/9/16; CQ/9/30; CQ/20/30.
Office of the President (KA)
    KA/2/21; KA/4/9; KA/4/11; KA/5/25; KA/6/10.
Ministry of Finance (ACW)
    ACW/27/76; ACW/76/27.
Attorney General (AAC)
    AAC/1/51; AAC/3/6.
Library
    K.354.6762002; K2008-216/526-926762.
Kenya Hansards (1962–1965)

National Council of Churches of Kenya, Limuru (NCCK)

African church leaders, general correspondence (1961–1962)
    LIM/1/1/260.

National British Library, London.

Newspapers
    The Times (1961–1964); *East African Standard* (1964); *Daily Nation* (1962–1969).

Interviews

Gitu wa Kahengeri, September 28, 2015, Nairobi.
Hon. Thimangu-Kaunyangi, October 21 and November 5, 2015, Kenjai (Meru).
Hon. John Kerimi, October 19 and November 4, 2015, Makutano (Meru).
John Nottingham, May 16, 2014, Nairobi.
Maina Macharia, May 5 and 15, 2014, Nairobi.
Peter Kamau Gacho, May 5, 2014, Nairobi.
Kiburu Marete, November 5, 2015, Makutano (Meru).
M'Murungi M'Kobia, November 6, 2015, Makutano (Meru).

Reverend Stephan Mûgambî, October 12 and 23, 2015, Nairobi.
Hon. Joseph Muturia, October 21, Laare (Meru).
Hon. Jacob Mwongo, October 22, 2015, Tigania (Meru).
Hon. Julius M'Mworia, October 24, 2015, Nairobi.
Hon. Lawi Nguwito, October 22, 2015, Tigania (Meru).
Grouped interview with Cypriam M'Mutiga M'Aritho, Simon Mtoruru John, Ciahampiu M'Munyi, Ciokirichiu M'Mutime, Ciorukunga M'Kithumai, Paulina Mwamunju M'Ndewa, Mgiliki M'Mumya, Mukoiti M'Mukindia, October 22, 2015, Muthara (Meru).

Bibliography

Ajulu, Rok. "Kenya: One Step Forward, Three Steps Back: The Succession Dilemma." *Review of African Political Economy* 28, no. 88 (2001): 197–212.

——. "Politicised Ethnicity, Competitive Politics and Conflict in Kenya: A Historical Perspective." *African Studies* 61, no. 2 (2002): 251–268.

Anderson, David. "Le Déclin et la Chute de la Kanu." *Politique Africaine*, no. 90 (2003): 37–55.

——. "Burying the Bones of the Past." *History Today* 55, no. 2 (2005). www.historytoday.com/archive/burying-bones-past. Accessed May 31, 2016.

——. "Mau Mau in the High Court and the 'Lost' British Empire Archives: Colonial Conspiracy or Bureaucratic Bungle?" *The Journal of Imperial and Commonwealth History* 39, no. 5 (2011): 699–716.

Anderson, David M. "'Yours in Struggle for *Majimbo*': Nationalism and the Party Politics of Decolonisation in Kenya, 1955–64." *Journal of Contemporary History* 40, no. 3 (2005): 547–564.

Angelo, Anaïs. "Virtues for All, State for No One? Jomo Kenyatta's Postcolonial Political Imagination." In *African Thoughts on Colonial and Neo-Colonial Worlds: Facets of an Intellectual History of Africa*, edited by Arno Sonderegger, 67–86. Berlin: Neofelis, 2015.

——. "Jomo Kenyatta and the Repression of the 'Last' Mau Mau Leaders, 1961–65." *Journal of Eastern African Studies* 11, no. 3 (2017): 442–459. www.tandfonline.com/doi/abs/10.1080/17531055.2017.1354521.

Anyang' Nyong'o, Peter. "Succession et Héritage Politiques: Le Président, l'État et le Capital après la Mort de Jomo Kenyatta." *Politique Africaine* 1, no. 3 (1981): 7–25.

Arnold, Guy. *Kenyatta and the Politics of Kenya*. Nairobi: Transafrican Publishers, 1974.

Aseka, Eric Masinde. *Ronald Ngala*. Nairobi: East African Educational Publishers, 1993.

Atieno-Odhiambo, Elisha S. "The Production of History in Kenya: The Mau Mau Debate." *Canadian Journal of African Studies* 25, no. 2 (1991): 300–307.

"Kula Raha: Gendered Discourses and the Contours of Leisure in Nairobi, 1946–63." *Azania: Archaeological Research in Africa* 36–37, no. 1 (2001): 254–264.

"Hegemonic Enterprises and Instrumentalities of Survival: Ethnicity and Democracy in Kenya." *African Studies* 61, no. 2 (2002): 223–249.

Atieno-Odhiambo, Elisha S., and John Lonsdale, eds. *Mau Mau & Nationhood: Arms, Authority & Narration*. Oxford: James Currey, 2003.

Atlani-Duault, Laëtitia, and Jean-Pierre Dozon. "Colonisation, Développement, Aide Humanitaire: Pour une Anthropologie de l'Aide Internationale." *Ethnologie française* 41, no. 3 (2011): 393–403.

Attwood, William. *The Reds and the Blacks: A Personal Adventure*. New York: Harper & Row, 1967.

Babou, C. A. "Decolonisation or National Liberation: Debating the End of British Colonial Rule in Africa." *The Annals of the American Academy of Political and Social Science* 632, no. 1 (2010): 41–54.

Bachir Diagne, Souleymane. *African Art as Philosophy: Senghor, Bergson and the Idea of Negritude*. London: Seagull Books, 2011.

Barkan, Joel D. "Legislators, Electors and Political Linkage." In *Politics and Public Policy in Kenya and Tanzania*, edited by Joel D. Barkan and John J. Okumu, 64–92. New York: Praeger, 1979.

Barkan, Joel D., and Frank W. Holmquist, "Peasant–State Relations and the Social Base of Self-Help in Kenya." *World Politics* 41, no. 3 (1989): 359–380.

Barkan, Joel D., and Michael Chege. "Decentralising the State: District Focus and the Politics of Reallocation in Kenya." *The Journal of Modern African Studies* 27, no. 3 (1989): 431–453.

Barnett, Don, and Karari Njama. *Mau Mau from Within: Autobiography and Analysis of Kenya's Peasant Revolt*. New York: Monthly Review Press, 1966.

Bayart, Jean-François. "L'Afrique dans le Monde: Une Histoire d'Extraversion." *Critique Internationale* 5, no. 5 (1999): 97–120.

Bayart, Jean-François, and Romain Bertrand. "De Quel 'Legs Colonial' Parle-T-On?" *Esprit* 12 (2006): 134–160.

Beckman, Björn. "Imperialism and Capitalist Transformation: Critique of a Kenyan Debate." *Review of African Political Economy* 7, no. 19 (1980): 48–62.

Bell, Duncan. *Reordering the World: Essays on Liberalism and Empire*. Princeton, NJ: Princeton University Press, 2016.

Bennett, George, and Carl G. Rosberg. *The Kenyatta Election: Kenya 1960–61*. Oxford: Oxford University Press, 1961.

Berman, Bruce. *Control and Crisis in Colonial Kenya: The Dialectic of Domination*. Nairobi: East African Publishers, 1990.

"Ethnography as Politics, Politics as Ethnography: Kenyatta, Malinowski, and the Making of *Facing Mount Kenya*." *Canadian Journal of African Studies* 30, no. 3 (1996): 313–344.

"Ethnic Territory, Land Tenure and Citizenship in Africa: The Politics of Devolution in Ghana and Kenya." In *Territorial Pluralism: Managing Difference in Multinational States*, edited by John McGarry and Richard Simeon, 240–264. Vancouver: University of British Columbia Press, 2015.

Berman, Bruce, Eyoh Dickson, and Will Kymlicka, eds. *Ethnicity & Democracy in Africa*. Oxford: James Currey, 2004.

Berman, Bruce J., and John M. Lonsdale. "Louis Leakey's Mau Mau: A Study in the Politics of Knowledge." *History and Anthropology* 5, no. 2 (1991): 143–204.

Unhappy Valley: Conflict in Kenya & Africa. Oxford: James Currey, 1992.

"The Labors of *Muigwithania*: Jomo Kenyatta as Author, 1928–45." *Research in African Literatures* 29, no. 1 (1998): 16–42.

"Custom, Modernity, and the Search for Kihooto: Kenyatta, Malinowski, and the Making of *Facing Mount Kenya*." In *Anthropology, European Imperialism and the Ordering of Africa*, edited by Robert J. Gordon and Helen Tilley, 173–198. Manchester: Manchester University Press, 2007.

Bernardi, Bernardo. *The Mugwe: A Blessing Prophet: A Study of a Religious and Public Dignitary of the Meru of Kenya*. Nairobi: Gideon S. Were Press Ltd., 1959.

"Old Kikuyu Religion Igongona and Mambura: Sacrifice and Sex: Re-Reading Kenyatta's Ethnography." *Africa: Rivista Trimestrale Di Studi E Documentazione dell'Istituto Italiano per l'Africa E l'Oriente* 48, no. 2 (1993): 167–183.

Bertrand, Romain. "Locating the 'Family-State': The Forgotten Legacy of Javanese Theories of the Public Domain (17th–20th c.)." In *Patrimonial Capitalism and Empire (Political Power and Social Theory, Volume 28)*, edited by Mounira M. Charrad and Julia Adams, 241–265. Bingley: Emerald Group Publishing Limited, 2015.

Bienen, Henry. *Kenya: The Politics of Participation and Control*. Princeton, NJ: Princeton University Press, 1974.

Bjerk, Paul. *Building a Peaceful Nation: Julius Nyerere and the Establishment of Sovereignty in Tanzania, 1960–1964*. Rochester, NY: University of Rochester Press, 2015.

Blacker, John. "The Demography of Mau Mau: Fertility and Mortality in Kenya in the 1950s: A Demographer's Viewpoint." *African Affairs* 106, no. 423 (2007): 205–227.

Boone, Catherine. "Land Conflict and Distributive Politics in Kenya." *African Studies Review* 55, no. 1 (2012): 75–103.
  Property and Political Order in Africa: Land Rights and the Structure of Politics. Cambridge: Cambridge University Press, 2014.
  "Land Tenure Regimes and State Structure in Rural Africa: Implications for Forms of Resistance to Large-Scale Land Acquisitions by Outsiders." *Journal of Contemporary African Studies* 33, no. 2 (2015): 171–190.
Bourmaud, Daniel. "Élections et Autoritarisme. La Crise de la Régulation Politique au Kenya." *Revue Française de Science Politique* 35, no. 2 (1985): 206–235.
  Histoire Politique du Kenya: Etat et Pouvoir Local. Paris: Karthala, 1988.
Branch, Daniel. "Loyalists, Mau Mau, and Elections: The First Triumph of the System, 1957–58." *Africa Today* 53, no. 2 (2006): 27–50.
  Defeating Mau Mau, Creating Kenya: Counterinsurgency, Civil War and Decolonisation. Cambridge: Cambridge University Press: 2009.
  "The Search for the Remains of Dedan Kimathi: The Politics of Death and Memorialisation in Post-Colonial Kenya." *Past and Present* 206, no. 5 (2010): 301–320.
  Kenya: Between Hope and Despair, 1963–2011. New Haven, CT: Yale University Press: 2011.
  "Violence, Decolonisation and the Cold War in Kenya's North-Eastern Province, 1963–1978." *Journal of Eastern African Studies* 8, no. 4 (2014): 642–657.
Branch, Daniel, and Nicholas Cheeseman. "The Politics of Control in Kenya: Understanding the Bureaucratic-Executive State, 1952–78." *Review of African Political Economy* 33, no. 107 (2006): 11–31.
  "Democratisation, Sequencing, and State Failure in Africa: Lessons from Kenya." *African Affairs* 108, no. 430 (2009): 1–26.
Bratton, Michael, and Mwangi S. Kimenyi. "Voting in Kenya: Putting Ethnicity in Perspective." *Journal of Eastern African Studies* 2, no. 2 (2008): 272–289.
Buijtenhuijs, Robert. *Mau Mau Twenty Years After: The Myth and the Survivors*. The Hague: Mouton and Co., 1973.
Burton, Andrew, and Michael Jennings. "The Emperor's New Clothes? Continuities in Governance in Late Colonial and Early Colonial Postcolonial East Africa." *International Journal of East African Histories* 40, no. 1 (2007): 1–26.
Cagnolo, Fr. C. *The Agĩkũyũ: Their Customs, Traditions and Folklore*. Nairobi: Wisdom Graphic Place, 2006.
Césaire, Aimé. *Les Armes Miraculeuses*. Paris: NRF Gallimard, 1946.

Chaisty, P., N. Cheeseman, and T. Power. "Rethinking the 'Presidentialism Debate': Conceptualizing Coalitional Politics in Cross-Regional Perspective." *Democratisation* 21, no. 1 (2014): 1–23.

Charton, Hélène. "La Genèse Ambiguë de l'Elite Kenyane. Origines, Formations et Intégration de 1945 à l'Indépendance." Ph.D. diss., Université Paris 7, 2002.

Cheeseman, Nic, Gabrielle Lynch, and Justin Willis. "Decentralisation in Kenya: The Governance of Governors." *The Journal of Modern African Studies* 54, no. 1 (2016): 1–35.

Cheeseman, Nicholas. "The Rise and Fall of Civil-Authoritarianism in Africa: Patronage, Participation, and Political Parties in Kenya and Zambia." Ph.D. diss., University of Oxford, 2007.

Chege, Michael. "Introducing Race as a Variable into the Political Economy of Kenya Debate: An Incendiary Idea." *African Affairs* 97, no. 387 (1998): 209–230.

Clough, Marshal S. *Fighting Two Sides: Kenyan Chiefs and Politicians, 1918–1940*. Niwot: University Press of Colorado, 1990.

Mau Mau Memoirs: History, Memory, and Politics. Boulder, CO: L. Rienner Publishers, 1998.

Cocks, Paul. "The Rhetoric of Science and the Critique of Imperialism in British Social Anthropology, c. 1870–1940." *History and Anthropology* 9, no. 1 (1995): 93–119.

"The King and I: Bronislaw Malinowski, King Sobhuza II of Swaziland and the Vision of Culture Change in Africa." *History of the Human Sciences* 13, no. 4 (2000): 25–47.

Coldham, Simon. "Land Control in Kenya." *Journal of African Law* 22, no. 1 (1978): 63–77.

"The Effect of Registration of Title Upon Customary Land Rights in Kenya." *Journal of African Law* 22, no. 2 (1978): 91–111.

"Land-Tenure Reform in Kenya: The Limits of Law." *The Journal of Modern African Studies* 17, no. 4 (1979): 615–627.

Connan, Dominique. "La Décolonisation des Clubs Kényans: Sociabilité Exclusive et Constitution Morale des Elites Africaines dans le Kenya Contemporain." Ph.D. diss., Paris 1, 2014.

"Race for Distinction: A Social History of Private Members' Clubs in Colonial Kenya." Ph.D. diss., European University Institute, 2015.

Connan, Dominique, and Johanna Siméant. "John Lonsdale, le Nationalisme, l'Ethnicité et l'Economie Morale: Parcours d'un Pionnier de l'Histoire Africaine." *Genèses* 2, no. 83 (2011): 133–154.

Connelly, Matthew. *A Diplomatic Revolution: Algeria's Fight for Independence and the Origins of the Post-Cold War Era*. Oxford: Oxford University Press, 2002.

Coombes, Annie E. "Monumental Histories: Commemorating Mau Mau with the Statue of Dedan Kimathi." *African Studies* 70, no. 2 (2011): 202–223.
Cooper, Frederick. "Conflict and Connection: Rethinking Colonial African History." *The American Historical Review* 99, no. 5 (1994): 1516–1545.
  Africa since 1940: The Past of the Present. Cambridge: Cambridge University Press, 2002.
  "Development, Modernisation, and the Social Sciences in the Era of Decolonisation: The Examples of British and French Africa." *Revue d'Histoire des Sciences Humaines* 10, no. 1 (2004): 9–38.
  Citizenship between Empire and Nation: Remaking France and French Africa, 1945–1960. Princeton, NJ: Princeton University Press, 2014.
Corfield, Frank D. *The Origins and Growth of Mau Mau: A Historical Survey*. London: Her Majesty's Stationery Office, 1960.
Cottrell, Jill, and Yash Ghai. "Constitution Making and Democratisation in Kenya (2000–2005)." *Democratisation* 14, no. 1 (2007): 1–25.
Darwin, J. "What Was the Late Colonial State." *Itinerario* 22, nos. 3–4 (1999): 73–82.
Dauch, Gene. "Kenya: J. M. Kariuki ou l'Éthique Nationale du Capitalisme." *Politique Africaine* 2, no. 8 (1982): 21–43.
Dauch, Gene, and Denis Martin. *L'Héritage de Kenyatta: La Transition Politique au Kenya, 1975–1982*. Paris: L'Harmattan, 1985.
Delf, George. *Jomo Kenyatta: Towards Truth about the Light of Kenya*. London: Gollancz, 1961.
Dimier, Véronique. "Enjeux Institutionnels Autour d'une Science Politique des Colonies en France et en Grande-Bretagne, 1930–1950." *Genèses* 37, no. 1 (1999): 70–92.
Droz, Yvan. *Migrations Kikuyus: des Pratiques Sociales à l'Imaginaire*. Paris: Editions MSH, 1999.
  "L'Ethos du Mûramati Kikuyu: Schème Migratoire, Différenciation Sociale et Individualisation au Kenya." *Anthropos* 95, no. 1 (2000): 87–98.
Duara, Prasenjit, ed. *Decolonisation: Perspectives from Now and Then*. London: Routledge, 2003.
Dunning, Thad. "Conditioning the Effects of Aid: Cold War Politics, Donor Credibility, and Democracy in Africa." *International Organization* 58, no. 2 (2004): 409–423.
Elkins, Caroline. *Britain's Gulag: The Brutal End of Empire in Kenya*. London: The Bodley Head, 2014.
  "Looking Beyond Mau Mau: Archiving Violence in the Era of Decolonisation." *The American Historical Review* 120, no. 3 (2015): 852–868.

Ensminger, Jean. "Changing Property Rights: Reconciling Formal and Informal Rights to Land in Africa." In *The Frontiers of the New Institutional Economics*, edited by John N. Drobak and John V. W. Nye, 165–196. San Diego, CA: Academic Press, 1997.

Fouéré, Marie-Aude. "Julius Nyerere, *Ujamaa*, and Political Morality in Contemporary Tanzania." *African Studies Review* 57, no. 1 (2014): 1–24.

Frederiksen, Bodil F. "Jomo Kenyatta, Marie Bonaparte and Bronislaw Malinowski on Clitoridectomy and Female Sexuality." *History Workshop Journal* 65, no. 1 (2008): 23–48.

Furedi, Frank. *The Mau Mau War in Perspective*. London: James Currey, 1989.

Galaty, John G. "'The Land Is Yours': Social and Economic Factors in the Privatisation, Sub-Division and Sale of Maasai Ranches." *Nomadic Peoples*, no. 30 (1992): 26–40.

Galaty, John G., and Munei Ole Kimpei. "Maasai Land, Law and Dispossession." *Cultural Survival Quarterly* 22, no. 4 (1998). https://culturalsurvival.org/publications/cultural-survival-quarterly/maasai-land-law-and-dispossession. Accessed August 26, 2019.

Gavaghan, Terence. *Of Lions and Dung Beetles*. Ilfracombe: Arthur H. Stockwell, 1999.

Gertzel, Cherry J. "The Provincial Administration in Kenya." *Journal of Commonwealth & Comparative Politics* 4, no. 3 (1966): 201–215.

The Politics of Independent Kenya, 1963–8. London: Heinemann, 1970.

Ghai, Yash Pal, and J. P. W. B. McAuslan. *Public Law and Political Change in Kenya: A Study of the Legal Framework of Government from Colonial Times to the Present*. London: Oxford University Press, 1970.

Gikandi, Simon. "Pan-Africanism and Cosmopolitanism: The Case of Jomo Kenyatta." *English Studies in Africa* 43, no. 1 (2000): 3–27.

Githuku, Nicholas K. *Mau Mau Crucible of War: Statehood, National Identity, and Politics of Postcolonial Kenya*. London: Lexington Books, 2015.

Godfrey, E. Martin, and Gideon-Cyrus Makau Mutiso. "The Political Economy of Self-Help: Kenya's '*Harambee*' Institutes of Technology." *Canadian Journal of African Studies* 8, no. 1 (1974): 109–133.

Goldsworthy, David. *Tom Mboya: The Man Kenya Wanted to Forget*. London: Heinemann, 1982.

Good, Kenneth. "Kenyatta and the Organisation of KANU." *Canadian Journal of African Studies* 2, no. 2 (1968): 115–136.

Goody, Jack. *The Expansive Moment: The Rise of Social Anthropology in Britain and Africa 1918–1970*. Cambridge: Cambridge University Press, 1995.

Grignon, François. "Le Politicien Entrepreneur En Son Terroir: Paul Ngei à Kangundo (Kenya) 1945–1990." Ph.D. diss., University of Bordeaux, 1997.

Hakes, Jay Edward. "The Parliamentary Party of the Kenya African National Union: Cleavage and Cohesion in the Ruling Party of a New Nation." Ph.D. diss, Duke University, 1970.
Hanhimäki, Jussi M., and Odd Arne Westad, eds. *The Cold War: A History in Documents and Eyewitness Accounts*. Oxford: Oxford University Press, 2003.
Harbeson, John W. "Land Reforms and Politics in Kenya, 1954–70." *The Journal of Modern African Studies* 9, no. 2 (1971): 231–251.
  Nation-Building in Kenya: The Role of Land Reform. Evanston, IL: Northwestern University Press, 1973.
Haugerud, Angelique. "Land Tenure and Agrarian Change in Kenya." *Africa* 59, no. 1 (1989): 61–90.
  The Culture of Politics in Modern Kenya. Cambridge: Cambridge University Press, 1997.
Hazlewood, Arthur. *The Economy of Kenya: The Kenyatta Era*. New York: Oxford University Press, 1980.
Herbst, Jeffrey. *States and Power in Africa: Comparative Lessons in Authority and Control*. Princeton, NJ: Princeton University Press, 2000.
"Héros Nationaux et Pères de la Nation en Afrique," Special Issue Edited by Marie-Aude Fouéré and Hélène Charton." *Vingtième Siècle. Revue d'Histoire* 118, no. 2 (2013).
Himbara, David. *Kenyan Capitalists, the State, and Development*. London: L. Rienner Publishers, 1994.
Hobsbawm, Eric, and Terance O. Ranger. *The Invention of Tradition*. Cambridge: Cambridge University Press, 1992.
Holding, E. Mary. "Some Preliminary Notes on Meru Age-Grades." *Man* 42 (1942): 58–65.
Holmquist, Frank. "Self-Help: The State and Peasant Leverage in Kenya." *Africa* 54, no. 3 (1984): 72–91.
Holtham, Gerald, and Arthur Hazlewood. *Aid and Inequality in Kenya: British Development Assistance to Kenya*. London: Routledge, 1976.
Hornsby, Charles. *Kenya: A History since Independence*. London: I. B. Tauris, 2013.
Howell, John. "An Analysis of Kenyan Foreign Policy." *The Journal of Modern African Studies* 6, no. 1 (1968): 29–48.
Hughes, Lotte. "Malice in Maasailand: The Historical Roots of Current Political Struggles." *African Affairs* 104, no. 415 (2005): 207–224.
  "Mining the Maasai Reserve: The Story of Magadi." *Journal of Eastern African Studies* 2, no. 1 (2008): 134–164.
  "Les Racines Historiques des Conflits Socio-Politiques en Pays Maasai, Kenya." In *Politique de La Terre et de l'Appartenance. Droits Fonciers*

et Citoyenneté Dans Les Sociétés Du Sud, edited by Jean-Pierre Jacob and Pierre-Yves Le Meur, 279–317. Paris: Karthala, 2010.

"'Truth Be Told': Some Problems with Historical Revisionism in Kenya." *African Studies* 70, no. 2 (2011), 182–201.

Hunter, Emma. *Political Thought and the Public Sphere in Tanzania: Freedom, Democracy, and Citizenship in the Era of Decolonisation*. New York: Cambridge University Press, 2015.

"Languages of Freedom in Decolonising Africa." *Transactions of the Royal Historical Society* 27 (2017): 253–269.

Hydén, Göran. *African Politics in Comparative Perspective*. Cambridge: Cambridge University Press, 2012.

Hydén, Göran, Robert Jackson, and John Okumu. *Development Administration: The Kenyan Experience*. Nairobi: Oxford University Press, 1970.

Iliffe, John. *The Emergence of African Capitalism: The Anstey Memorial Lectures in the University of Kent at Canterbury 10–13 May 1982*. London: Macmillan, 1983.

Jackson, R. T. "Problems of Tourist Industry Development on the Kenyan Coast." *Geography* 58, no. 1 (1973): 62–65.

Jackson, Robert H. Jr., and Carl G. Rosberg. *Personal Rule in Black Africa: Prince, Autocrat, Prophet, Tyrant*. Berkeley: University of California Press, 1982.

Jalal, Ayesha. *The Sole Spokesman: Jinnah, the Muslim League and the Demand for Pakistan*. Cambridge: Cambridge University Press, 1994.

James, Leslie. *George Padmore and Decolonisation from Below: Pan-Africanism, the Cold War, and the End of Empire*. New York: Palgrave Macmillan, 2014.

Jones, Carey. *The Anatomy of Uhuru. An Essay on Kenya's Independence*. Manchester: Manchester University Press, 1966.

Jones, Carey, and Norman Stewart. "The Decolonisation of the White Highlands of Kenya." *Geographical Journal* 131, no. 2 (1965): 186–201.

Josse-Durand, Chloé. "Le 'Temps des Musées': Bâtir les Mémoires Locales, Donner Corps au Récit National. L'Hybridation de l'Institution Muséale au Prisme des Appropriations Contemporaines du Passé au Kenya et en Ethiopie." Ph.D. diss., University of Bordeaux, 2016.

Kabiri, Ngeta. "Ethnic Diversity and Development in Kenya: Limitations of Ethnicity as a Category of Analysis." *Commonwealth & Comparative Politics* 52, no. 4 (2014): 513–534.

Kaggia, Bildad. *Roots of Freedom, 1921–1963: The Autobiography of Bildad Kaggia*. Nairobi: East African Publishing House, 1975.

Kaggia, Bildad M., W. de Leeuw, and M. Kaggia. *The Struggle for Freedom and Justice*. Nairobi: Transafrica Press, 2012.

Kamunchuluh, Samuel J. T. "The Meru Participation in Mau Mau." *Kenya Historical Review* 3, no. 2 (1975): 193–216.

Kanogo, Tabitha. *Squatters and the Roots of Mau Mau (1905–1963)*. London: James Currey, 1987.

Kantai, Parselelo. "In the Grip of the Vampire State: Maasai Land Struggles in Kenyan Politics." *Journal of Eastern African Studies* 1, no. 1 (2007): 107–122.

Kanyinga, Karuti. *Re-Distribution from Above: The Politics of Land Rights and Squatting in Coastal Kenya*. Uppsala: Nordic Africa Institute, 2000.

"Land Redistribution in Kenya." In *Agricultural Land Redistribution: Toward Greater Consensus*, edited by Hans P. Binswanger-Mkhize, Camille Bourguignon, and Rogier J. Eugenius van den Brink. Washington, DC: The International Bank for Reconstruction and Development, 2009.

"The Legacy of the White Highlands: Land Rights, Ethnicity and the Post-2007 Election Violence in Kenya." *Journal of Contemporary African Studies* 27, no. 3 (2009): 325–344.

Kaplinsky, Rafael. "Capitalist Accumulation in the Periphery: The Kenyan Case Re-examined." *Review of African Political Economy* 7, no. 17 (1980): 83–105.

Kareithi, Peter J. M. "Multinational Corporations and Foreign Owned Media in Developing Countries." *Crime, Law and Social Change* 16, no. 2 (1991): 199–212.

Karimi, Joseph, and Philip Ochieng. *The Kenyatta Succession*. Nairobi: Transafrica Press, 1980.

Kariuki, James. "'Paramoia': Anatomy of a Dictatorship in Kenya." *Journal of Contemporary African Studies* 14, no. 1 (1996): 69–86.

Karume, Njenga. *Beyond Expectations: From Charcoal to Gold: An Autobiography*. Nairobi: Kenway Publications, 2009.

Kelemen, Paul. "The British Labor Party and the Economics of Decolonisation: The Debate over Kenya." *Journal of Colonialism and Colonial History* 8, no. 3 (2007): 1–33.

Kenyatta, Jomo. *My People of Gikuyu and the Life of Chief Wangombe*. London: Lutterworth Press, 1942.

Kenya: The Land of Conflict. London: Panaf Service Limited, 1945.

Facing Mount Kenya. New York: Vintage Books, 1965.

Suffering without Bitterness: The Founding of the Kenya Nation. Nairobi: East African Publishing House, 1968.

Kershaw, Greet. "Mau Mau from Below: Fieldwork and Experience, 1955–57 and 1962." *Canadian Journal of African Studies* 25, no. 2 (1991): 274–297.

Mau Mau from Below. Oxford: James Currey, 1997.

Khapoya, Vincent B. "The Politics of Succession in Africa: Kenya after Kenyatta." *Africa Today* 26, no. 3 (1979): 7–20.

Kiereini, Jeremiah Gitau. *A Daunting Journey*. Nairobi, Kenway Publications, 2014.

Kimani, Kamau, and John Pickard. "Recent Trends and Implications of Group Ranch Sub-Division and Fragmentation in Kajiado District, Kenya." *The Geographical Journal* 164, no. 2 (1998): 202–213.

Kinyatti, Maina wa. *Mau Mau: A Revolution Betrayed*. Jamaica, NY: Mau Mau Research Center, 1991.

History of Resistance in Kenya (1884–2002). Nairobi: Mau Mau Research Center, 2008.

Kipkorir, Benjamin E. "The Alliance High School and the Origins of the Kenya African Elite 1926–1962." Ph.D. diss., University of Cambridge, 1969.

Kirk-Green, Anthony H. "His Eternity, His Eccentricity, or His Exemplarity? A Further Contribution to the Study of HE the African Head of State." *African Affairs* 90, no. 359 (1991): 163–187.

Kitching, Gavin. "Politics, Method and Evidence in the 'Kenya Debate'." In *Contradictions of Accumulation in Africa*, edited by Henry Bernstein and Bonnie K. Campbell, 115–151. Beverly Hills, CA: Sage Publications, 1984.

Klaus, K. and Mitchell, M. I. "Land Grievances and the Mobilisation of Electoral Violence Evidence from Côte d'Ivoire and Kenya." *Journal of Peace Research* 52, no. 2 (2015): 622–635.

Klopp, Jacqueline M. "Electoral Despotism in Kenya: Land, Patronage and Resistance in the Multi-Party Context." Ph.D. diss., McGill University, 2001.

"Can Moral Ethnicity Trump Political Tribalism? The Struggle for Land and Nation in Kenya." *African Studies* 61, no. 2 (2002): 269–294.

Klose, Fabian. *Human Rights in the Shadow of Colonial Violence: The Wars of Independence in Kenya and Algeria*. Philadelphia: University of Pennsylvania Press, 2013.

Knauss, Peter. "From Devil to Father Figure: The Transformation of Jomo Kenyatta by Kenya Whites." *The Journal of Modern African Studies* 9, no. 1 (1971): 131–137.

Knighton, Ben. "Going for Cai at Gatundu: Reversion to a Kikuyu Ethnic Past or Building a Kenyan National Future." In *Our Turn to Eat:*

Politics in Kenya Since, edited by Daniel Branch, Nic Cheeseman, and Leigh Gardner, 107–128. Berlin: Lit Verlag, 2010.
Koinange, Mbiyu. "Jomo Colleague in the Struggle for Freedom and Independence." In *Struggle to Release Jomo and His Colleagues*, edited by Ambu H. Patel, 21–22. Nairobi: Kenya New Publishers, 1963.
Kuper, Adam. *Anthropology and Anthropologists: The Modern British School*. London: Routledge, 1996.
Kyle, Keith. *The Politics of the Independence of Kenya*. New York: Palgrave Macmillan, 1999.
Lamb, Geoff. *Peasant Politics: Conflict and Development in Murang'a*. New York: St. Martin Press, 1974.
Langdon, Steven W. *Multinational Corporations in the Political Economy of Kenya*. London: Macmillan, 1981.
Lemarchand, René. "Political Clientelism and Ethnicity in Tropical Africa: Competing Solidarities in Nation-Building." *The American Political Science Review* 66, no.1 (1972): 68–90.
Leo, Christopher. "The Failure of the 'Progressive Farmer' in Kenya's Million-Acre Settlement Scheme." *The Journal of Modern African Studies* 16, no. 4 (1978): 619–638.
"Who Benefited from the Million-Acre Scheme? Toward a Class Analysis of Kenya's Transition to Independence." *Canadian Journal of African Studies* 15, no. 2 (1981): 201–222.
Land and Class in Kenya. Toronto: University of Toronto Press, 1984.
Leonard, David K. *African Successes: Four Public Managers of Kenyan Rural Development*. Berkeley: University of California Press, 1991.
Leys, Colin. *Underdevelopment in Kenya*. London: Heinemann, 1975.
"Capital Accumulation, Class Formation and Dependency: The Significance of the Kenyan Case." *Socialist Register* 15, no. 15 (1978): 241–266.
Lonsdale, John M. "La Pensée Politique Kikuyu et les Idéologies du Mouvement Mau-Mau," *Cahiers d'Études Africaines* 27, nos. 107/108 (1987): 329–357.
"The Prayers of Waiyaki: Political Uses of the Kikuyu Past." In *Revealing Prophets: Prophecy in Eastern African History*, edited by David M Anderson and Douglas Hamilton Johnson, 240–291. London: James Currey, 1995.
"'Listen While I Read': The Orality of Christian Literacy in the Young Kenyatta's Making of the Kikuyu." In *Ethnicity in Africa: Roots, Meanings & Implications*, edited by Louise de la Gorgendiere, Kenneth King, and Sarah Vaughan, 17–53. Edinburgh: University of Edinburgh Centre of African Studies, 1996.

"Moral Ethnicity, Ethnic Nationalism and Political Tribalism: The Case of the Kikuyu." In *Staat und Gesellschaft in Afrika*, edited by Peter Meyns, 93–106. Hamburg: Lit, 1996.

"KAU's Cultures: Imaginations of Community and Constructions of Leadership in Kenya after the Second World War." *Journal of African Cultural Studies* 13, no. 1 (2000): 107–124.

"Town Life in Colonial Kenya." *Azania: Archaeological Research in Africa* 36–37, no. 1 (2001): 206–222.

"Contest of Time: Kikuyu Historiography, Old and New." In *A Place in the World: New Local Historiographies from Africa and South Asia*, edited by Axel Harneit-Sievers, 201–254. London: Brill, 2002.

"Jomo Kenyatta, God & the Modern World." In *African Modernities: Entangled Meanings in Current Debate*, edited by Peter Probst, Heike Schmidt, and Jan-Georg Deutsch, 31–66. Oxford: James Currey, 2002.

"Les Procès de Jomo Kenyatta. Destruction et Construction d'un Nationaliste Africain." *Politix* 17, no. 66 (2004): 163–197.

"Ornamental Constitutionalism in Africa: Kenyatta and the Two Queens." *The Journal of Imperial and Commonwealth History* 34, no. 1 (2006): 87–103.

"Soil, Work, Civilisation and Citizenship in Kenya." *Journal of Eastern African Studies* 2, no. 2(2008): 305–314.

"Henry Muoria, Public Moralist." In *Writing for Kenya: The Life and Works of Henry Muoria*, edited by Wangari Muoria-Sal, Bodil F. Frederiksen, John M. Lonsdale, and Derek R. Peterson, 3–58. Leiden: Brill, 2009.

Lynch, Gabrielle. "Negotiating Ethnicity: Identity Politics in Contemporary Kenya." *Review of African Political Economy* 33, no. 107 (2006): 49–65.

"The Fruits of Perception: 'Ethnic Politics' and the Case of Kenya's Constitutional Referendum." *African Studies* 65, no. 2 (2006): 233–270.

"Courting the Kalenjin: The Failure of Dynasticism and the Strength of the ODM Wave in Kenya's Rift Valley Province." *African Affairs* 107, no. 429 (2008): 541–568.

"Moi: The Making of an African 'Big-Man'." *Journal of Eastern African Studies* 2, no. 1 (2008): 18–43.

"Electing the 'Alliance of the Accused': The Success of the Jubilee Alliance in Kenya's Rift Valley." *Journal of Eastern African Studies* 8, no. 1 (2014): 93–114.

"What's in a Name? The Politics of Naming Ethnic Groups in Kenya's Cherangany Hills." *Journal of Eastern African Studies* 10, no. 1 (2016): 208–227.

Macharia, Rawson. *The Truth about the Trial of Jomo Kenyatta*. Nairobi: Longman Kenya, 1991.

Maekawa, Ichiro. "Neo-Colonialism Reconsidered: A Case Study of East Africa in the 1960s and 1970s." *The Journal of Imperial and Commonwealth History* 43, no. 2 (2015): 317–341.

Mahner, Jurg. "The Outsider and the Insider in Tigania Meru." *Africa* 45, no. 4 (1975): 400–409.

Makinda, Samuel M. "From Quiet Diplomacy to Cold War Politics: Kenya's Foreign Policy." *Third World Quarterly* 5, no. 2 (1983): 300–319.

Maloba, Wunyabari O. *Mau Mau and Kenya: An Analysis of a Peasant Revolt*. Bloomington: Indiana University Press, 1998.

The Anatomy of Neocolonialism in Kenya: British Imperialism and Kenyatta (1963–1978). Cham: Palgrave Macmillan, 2017.

Kenyatta and Britain: An Account of Political Transformation, 1929–1963. Cham: Palgrave Macmillan, 2018.

Mamdani, Mahmood. *Citizen and Subject: Contemporary Africa and the Legacy of Late Colonialism*. Princeton, NJ: Princeton University Press, 1996.

di Matteo, Francesca. "The Fora of Public Action in Kenya: From the Origins of the National Land Policy to Its Politicisation." *Mambo!* 12, no. 4 (2014).

Maupeu, Hervé. "Kikuyu Capitalistes. Réflexions sur un Cliché Kenyan." *Outre-Terre* 2, no. 11 (2005): 493–506.

Maxon, Robert M. *East Africa: An Introductory History*. Morgantown: West Virginia University Press, 2009.

Kenya's Independence Constitution: Constitution-Making and End of Empire. Madison, NJ: Fairleigh Dickinson University Press, 2011.

Maxon, Robert M., and Thomas P. Ofcansky, eds. *Historical Dictionary of Kenya*. Plymouth: Rowman & Litlefield, 2014.

Mazrui, Ali A. "The Monarchical Tendency in African Political Culture." *The British Journal of Sociology* 18 (1967): 231–250.

Mbembe, Achille. *On the Postcolony*. Berkeley: University of California Press, 2001.

Mbithi, Philip M., and Rasmus Rasmusson. *Self Reliance in Kenya: The Case of Harambee*. Uppsala: The Scandinavian Institute of African Studies, 1977.

Mboya, Tom. *Freedom and After*. Nairobi: East African Publishers, 1986.

McClellan, Woodford. "Africans and Black Americans in the Comintern Schools, 1925–1934." *The International Journal of African Historical Studies* 26, no. 2 (1993): 371–390.

McMahon, Robert J., ed. *The Cold War in the Third World*. Oxford: Oxford University Press, 2013.

Médard, Claire. "Territoires de l'Ethnicité: Encadrement, Revendications et Conflits Territoriaux au Kenya." Ph.D. diss., Paris 1, 1999.

Médard, Jean-François. "Charles Njonjo: Portrait d'un 'Big Man' au Kenya." In *L'État Contemporain en Afrique*, edited by Emmanuel Terray, 49–87. Paris: L'Harmattan, 1987.

États d'Afrique Noire. Formations, Mécanismes et Crises. Paris: Karthala, 1991.

Meisler, Stanley. "Tribal Politics Harass Kenya." *Foreign Affairs* 49, no. 1 (1970): 111–121.

Morton, Andrew. *Moi: The Making of an African Statesman.* London: Michael O'Mara, 1998.

Moses, A. Dirk. "Das Römische Gespräch in a New Key: Hannah Arendt, Genocide, and the Defense of Republican Civilization." *The Journal of Modern History* 85, no. 4 (2013): 867–913.

Moskowitz, Kara. "'Are You Planting Trees or Are You Planting People?' Squatter Resistance and International Development in the Making of a Kenyan Postcolonial Political Order (c. 1963–78)." *Journal of African History* 56, no. 1 (2015): 99–118.

Mueller, Susanne D. "Political Parties in Kenya, Patterns of Opposition and Dissent 1919–1969." Ph.D. diss., Princeton University, 1979.

"Government and Opposition in Kenya, 1966–9." *The Journal of Modern African Studies* 22, no. 3 (1984): 399–427.

Mûgambî Mwithimbû, Reverend S. A. "Njûrî Ncheke: An Instrument of Peace and Conflict Resolution." In *Culture in Peace and Conflict Resolution within Communities of Central Kenya*, edited by Njuguna Gĩchere, S. A. Mûgambî Mwithimbû, and Shin-ichiro Ishida. Nairobi: National Museum of Kenya, 2014).

Muriuki, Godfrey. *A History of the Kikuyu 1500–1900.* Oxford: Oxford Univeristy Press, 1974.

Murray, Martin, Atieno Odhiambo, and Chris Youé. "Debate and Commentary: Mamdani's Citizen and Subject." *Canadian Journal of African Studies* 34, no. 2 (2000): 375–412.

Murray-Brown, Jeremy. *Kenyatta.* London: George Allen & Unwin Ltd., 1972.

Murumbi, Joseph, and Anne Thurston. *A Path Not Taken: The Story of Joseph Murumbi.* Nairobi: The Murumbi Trust, 2015.

Musila, Grace A. *Death Retold in Truth and Rumour: Kenya, Britain and the Julie Ward Murder.* Woddbridge: James Currey, 2015.

Mwangi, Esther. "The Footprints of History: Path Dependence in the Transformation of Property Rights in Kenya's Maasailand." *Journal of Institutional Economics* 2, no. 2 (2006): 157–180.

"The Puzzle of Group Ranch Subdivision in Kenya's Maasailand." *Development and Change* 38, no. 5 (2007): 889–910.

Naim, Asher. "Perspectives – Jomo Kenyatta and Israel." *Jewish Political Studies Review* 17, nos. 3–4 (2005): 75–80.

Natsoulas, Theodore. "The Politicisation of the Ban on Female Circumcision and the Rise of the Independent School Movement in Kenya, the KCA, the Missions and Government, 1929–1932." *Journal of Asian and African Studies* 33, no. 2 (1998): 137–158.

Ndegwa, Duncan. *Walking in Kenyatta Struggles: My Story*. Nairobi: Kenya Leadership Institute, 2011.

Nellis, J. R. "Is the Kenyan Bureaucracy Developmental? Political Considerations in Development Administration." *African Studies Review* 14, no. 3 (1971): 389–401.

The Ethnic Composition of Leading Kenyan Government Positions. Research Report no. 84. Uppsala: The Scandinavian Institute of African Studies, 1974.

Ng'ethe, Njuguna. *Harambee and Development Participation in Kenya*. Ottawa: Carleton University, 1979.

Ngau, Peter M. "Tensions in Empowerment: The Experience of the 'Harambee' (Self-Help) Movement in Kenya." *Economic Development and Cultural Change* 35, no. 3 (1987): 523–538.

Njonjo, Charles. "Recent Constitutional Changes in Kenya." *East African Law Journal* 1, no. 2 (1965): 98–107.

Nkrumah, Kwame. *Consciencism: Philosophy and Ideology for Decolonisation and Development with Particular Reference to African Revolution*. London: Heinemann, 1964.

Nugent, Paul. *Africa since Independence: A Comparative History*. Basingstoke: Palgrave Macmillan, 2004.

Nyangena, Kenneth O. "Jomo Kenyatta: An Epitome of Indigenous Pan-Africanism, Nationalism and Intellectual Production in Kenya." *African Journal of International Affairs* 6, nos. 1–2 (2003): 1–18.

Nyangira, Nicholas. "Ethnicity, Class and Politics in Kenya." In *The Political Economy of Kenya*, edited by Michael G. Schatzberg, 15–29. New York: Praeger Publishers, 1987.

Nye, Joseph. *Pan-Africanism and East African Integration*. Cambridge, MA: Harvard University Press, 1965.

Ocobock, Paul. *An Uncertain Age: The Politics of Manhood in Kenya*. Athens: Ohio University Press, 2017.

Odinga, Oginga. *Not Yet Uhuru*. Nairobi: East African Publishers, 1995.

Ododa, Harry. "Continuity and Change in Kenya's Foreign Policy from the Kenyatta to the Moi Government." *Journal of African Studies* 13, no. 2 (1986): 47–57.

Ogot, Bethwell Allan. *Historical Dictionary of Kenya*. London: The Scarecrow Press, Inc., 1981.

Ogot, Bethwell Allan, and William Robert Ochieng'. *Decolonisation & Independence in Kenya: 1940–93*. Athens: Ohio University Press, 1995.

Okoth-Ogendo, H. W. O. "The Politics of Constitutional Change in Kenya since Independence, 1963–69." *African Affairs* 71, no. 282 (1972): 9–34.

"Some Thoughts on Kenya's Foreign Policy." *The African Review* 3, no. 2 (1973): 263–290.

Omolo, Kenneth. "Political Ethnicity in the Democratisation Process in Kenya." *African Studies* 61, no. 2 (2002): 209–221.

Onoma, Ato Kwamena. "The Contradictory Potential of Institutions the Rise and Decline of Land Documentation." In *Explaining Institutional Change: Ambiguity, Agency, and Power*, edited by James Mahoney and Kathleen Thelen, 63–93. Cambridge: Cambridge University Press, 2009.

The Politics of Property Rights Institution in Africa. Cambridge: Cambridge University Press, 2010.

Osborne, Myles. "'The Rooting Out of Mau Mau from the Minds of the Kikuyu Is a Formidable Task': Propaganda and the Mau Mau War." *Journal of African History* 56, no. 1 (2015): 77–97.

Oucho, John O. *Undercurrents of Ethnic Conflicts in Kenya*. Leiden: Brill, 2002.

Overton, John. "The Origins of the Kikuyu Land Problem: Land Alienation and Land Use in Kiambu, 1895–1920." *African Studies Review* 31, no. 2 (1988): 112–122.

Parsons, Timothy. "The Lanet Incident, 2–25 January 1964: Military Unrest and National Amnesia in Kenya." *The International Journal of African Historical Studies* 40, no. 1 (2007): 51–70.

"Being Kikuyu in Meru: Challenging the Tribal Geography of Colonial Kenya." *Journal of African History* 53, no. 1 (2012): 65–86.

Pearce, R. "The Colonial Office and Planned Decolonisation." *African Affairs* 83, no. 330 (1984): 77–93.

Peatrik, Anne-Marie. "Un Système Composite: l'Organisation d'Age et de Génération des Kikuyu Précoloniaux." *Journal des Africanistes* 64, no. 1 (1994): 3–36.

La Vie à Pas Contés. Génération, Age et Société dans les Hautes Terres du Kenya (Meru Tigania – Igembe) (Nanterre: Société d'Ethnologie, 1999).

"Le Singulier Destin de *Facing Mount Kenya. The Tribal Life of the Gikuyu* (1938) de Jomo Kenyatta. Une Contribution à l'Anthropologie des Savoirs." *L'Homme* 4, no. 212 (2014): 71–108

Percox, David A. "Circumstances Short of Global War: British Defence, Colonial Internal Security, and Decolonisation in Kenya, 1945–65." Ph.D. diss., University of Nottingham, 2001.

"Internal Security and Decolonisation in Kenya, 1956–63." *The Journal of Imperial and Commonwealth History* 29, no. 1 (2001): 92–116.

Britain, Kenya and the Cold War: Imperial Defence, Colonial Security and Decolonisation. London: I. B. Tauris, 2004.

Péron, Xavier. *Occidentalisation des Maasaï du Kenya: Privatisation Foncière et Destructuration Sociale chez les Maassaï du Kenya,* two vols. Paris: L'Harmattan, 1995.

Peterson, Derek R. "Gambling with God: Rethinking Religion in Colonial Central Kenya." In *The Invention of Religion: Rethinking Belief in Politics and History,* edited by Derek Peterson and Darren Walhof. New Brunswick, NJ: Rutgers University Press, 2002.

Creative Writing: Translation, Bookkeeping, and the Work of Imagination in Colonial Kenya. Portsmouth, NH: Heinemann, 2004.

"'Be Like Firm Soldiers to Develop the Country': Political Imagination and the Geography of Gikuyuland." *International Journal of African Historical Studies* 37, no. 1 (2004): 71–101.

Plender, Richard. "The Exodus of Asians from East and Central Africa Some Comparative and International Law Aspects." *The American Journal of Comparative Law* 19, no. 2 (1971): 287–324.

Prestholdt, Jeremy. "Politics of the Soil: Separatism, Autochtony and Decolonisation at the Kenyan Coast." *The Journal of African History* 55, no. 2 (2014): 249–270.

Ranger, Terence. "From Humanism to the Science of Man: Colonialism in Africa and the Understanding of Alien Societies." *Transactions of the Royal Historical Society (Fifth Series)* 26 (1976): 115–141.

Rathbone, Richard. "Review: *Racial Bargaining in Independent Kenya: A Study of Minorities and Decolonisation*: By Donald Rothchild." *International Affairs* 50, no. 4 (1974): 665–666.

Report of the Commission of Inquiry into the Illegal/Irregular Allocation of Public Land. Nairobi: Commission of Inquiry into the Illegal/Irregular Allocation of Public Land, 2004.

Report of the Truth, Justice, and Reconciliation Commission. Nairobi: Truth, Justice, and Reconciliation Commission, 2013.

Republic of Kenya. *African Socialism and Its Application to Planning in Kenya.* Nairobi, 1965.

Robertson, Claire C. *Trouble Showed the Way: Women, Men, and Trade in the Nairobi Area, 1890–1990.* Bloomington: Indiana University Press, 1997.

Rosberg, Carl G. and John C. Nottingham. *The Myth of "Mau Mau": Nationalism in Kenya.* New York: Praeger, 1966.

Rothchild, Donald. "Kenya's Africanisation Program: Priorities of Development and Equity." *American Political Science Review* 64, no. 3 (1970): 737–753.

"Changing Racial Stratifications and Bargaining Styles: The Kenya Experience." *Canadian Journal of African Studies* 7, no. 3 (1973): 419–432.

Racial Bargaining in Independent Kenya: A Study of Minorities and Decolonisation. London: Oxford University Press, 1973.

Rutten, Marinus M. E. M. *Selling Wealth to Buy Poverty: The Process of the Individualisation of Landownership among the Maasai Pastoralists of Kajiado District, Kenya, 1890–1990.* Saarbrücken: Verlag breitenbach Publishers, 1992.

"The Kenya 1997 General Elections in Maasailand: Of 'Sons' and 'Puppets' and How KANU Defeated Itself." In *Out for the Count: The 1997 General Elections and Prospects for Democracy in Kenya*, edited by Marinus M. E. M. Rutten, Ali Mazrui, and François Grignon, 405–440. Kampala: Fountain Publishers, 2001.

Sanger, Clyde, and John Nottingham. "The Kenya General Election of 1963." *The Journal of Modern African Studies* 2, no. 1 (1964): 1–40.

Senghor, Léopold Sédar. *Liberté 4: Socialisme et Planification.* Paris: Seuil, 1983.

Shachtman, Tom. *Airlift to America: How Barack Obama Sr., John F. Kennedy, Tom Mboya and 800 East African Students Changed Their World and Ours.* New York: MacMillan, 2009.

Shipway, Martin. "Colonial Politics Before the Flood: Challenging the State, Imagining the Nation." In *Decolonisation and Its Impact: A Comparative Approach to the End of the Colonial Empires*, edited by Martin Shipway, 35–60. Malden, MA: Blackwell, 2008.

Slater, Montagu. *The Trial of Jomo Kenyatta.* London: Secker & Warburg, 1955.

Sorrenson, Maurice P. K. *Origins of European Settlement in Kenya.* London: Oxford University Press, 1968.

Spear, Thomas, and Richard Waller, eds. *Being Maasai: Ethnicity and Identity in East Africa.* London: James Currey, 1993.

Spencer, John. *KAU: The Kenya African Union*, first edition. London: Kegan Paul International, 1985.

Steeves, Jeffrey. "Beyond Democratic Consolidation in Kenya: Ethnicity, Leadership and 'Unbounded Politics'." *African Identities* 4, no. 2 (2006): 195–211.

Stren, Richard. "Factional Politics and Central Control in Mombasa, 1960–1969." *Canadian Journal of African Studies* 4, no. 1 (1970): 33–56.

Swainson, Nicola. *The Development of Corporate Capitalism in Kenya, 1918–77.* London: Heinemann, 1980.

Tamarkin, Mordechai. "The Roots of Political Stability in Kenya." *African Affairs* 77, no. 308 (1978): 297–320.

"From Kenyatta to Moi: The Anatomy of a Peaceful Transition of Power." *Africa Today* 26, no. 3 (1979): 21–37.

"Recent Developments in Kenyan Politics: The Fall of Charles Njonjo." *Journal of Contemporary African Studies* 3, nos. 1–2 (1983): 59–77.

Tatiah, Irungu, and Nyagah Trust, Jeremiah. *Jeremiah Nyagah: Sowing the Mustard*. Seattle: Rizzan Media, 2013.

Thiong'o, Ngugi wa. *Petals of Blood*. London: Penguins Books, 2002.

Thomas, Barbara P. "Development through *Harambee*: Who Wins and Who Loses? Rural Self-Help Projects in Kenya." *World Development* 15, no. 4 (1987): 463–481.

Thomas, Donald B., and Nugent, Paul J. "Walter Martin, 'Friends Visit Jomo Kenyatta at Maralal'." *Quaker History* 99, no. 1 (2010): 32–46.

Thomas, Lynn M. "*Ngaitana* (I Will Circumcise Myself)": The Gender and Generational Politics of the 1956 Ban on Clitoridectomy in Meru, Kenya." *Gender and History* 8, no. 3 (1996): 338–363.

"Imperial Concerns and 'Women's Affairs': State Efforts to Regulate Clitoridectomy and Eradicate Abortion in Meru, Kenya, c. 1910–1950." *The Journal of African History* 39, no. 1 (1998): 121–145.

Politics of the Womb: Women, Reproduction, and the State in Kenya. Berkeley: University of California Press, 2003.

Throup, David W. *Economic and Social Origins of Mau Mau, 1945–1953*. London: James Currey, 1987.

"The Construction and Destruction of the Kenyatta State." In *The Political Economy of Kenya*, edited by Michael G. Schatzberg, 33–74. Portsmouth: Praeger Publishers, 1987.

Tidwell, Alan C., and Zellen, Barry Scott. *Land, Indigenous Peoples and Conflict*. London: Routledge, 2015.

Tignor, Robert L. *Colonial Transformation of Kenya: The Kamba, Kikuyu, and Maasai from 1900–1939*. Princeton, NJ: Princeton University Press, 2015.

Tilley, Helen L., and Robert J. Gordon, eds. *Ordering Africa*. Manchester: Manchester University Press, 2007.

Tischler, J. "Cementing Uneven Development: The Central African Federation and the Kariba Dam Scheme." *Journal of Southern African Studies* 40, no. 5 (2014): 1047–1064.

Vaillant, Janet G. *Black, French, and African: A Life of Léopold Sédar Senghor*. Cambridge, MA: Harvard University Press, 1990.

Vassanji, M. G. *The In-Between World of Vikram Lall*. New York: Vintage, 2005.

Walton, Calder. *Empire of Secrets: British Intelligence, the Cold War and the Twilight of Empire*. London: Harper Press, 2013.

Wasserman, Gary. "Continuity and Counter-Insurgency: The Role of Land Reform in Decolonizing Kenya, 1962–70." *Canadian Journal of African Studies* 7, no. 1 (1973): 133–148.

Politics of Decolonisation: Kenya Europeans and the Land Issue. Cambridge: Cambridge University Press, 1976.

Watkins, Elizabeth. *Jomo's Jailor: Grand Warrior of Kenya: The Life of Leslie Whitehouse*. Watlington: Britwell Books, 1996.

Who Controls Industry in Kenya? Report of a Working Party. Nairobi: East African Publishing House, 1968.

Widner, Jennifer A. *The Rise of a Party-State in Kenya: From "Harambee!" to "Nyayo!"* Berkeley: University of California Press, 1992.

Wilder, Gary. *Freedom Time: Negritude, Decolonisation, and the Future of the World*. Durham, NC: Duke University Press, 2015.

Willis, Justin, and George Gona. "Tradition, Tribe, and State in Kenya: The Mijikenda Union, 1945–1980." *Comparative Studies in Society and History* 55, no. 2 (2013): 448–473.

Worcester, Kent. *C. L. R. James: A Political Biography*. Albany: State University of New York Press, 1996.

Wrong, Michaela. *It's Our Turn to Eat: The Story of a Kenyan Whistle Blower*. London: Fourth Estate, 2009.

Young, Crawford. *The African Colonial State in Comparative Perspective*. New Haven, CT: Yale University Press, 1994.

The Post-Colonial State in Africa: Fifty Years of Independence, 1960–2010. Madison: The University of Wisconsin Press, 2012.

Newspapers Articles

"African's 40 Richest: #26 Uhuru Kenyatta." *Forbes*. www.forbes.com/lists/2011/89/africa-billionaires-11_Uhuru-Kenyatta_FO2Q.html. Accessed March 13, 2019.

Bagaka, Obuya. "Striking Similarities between Uhuru Kenyatta's Trial at the Hague and Jomo Kenyatta's Kapenguria Case." *Daily Nation*, September 28, 2014. www.nation.co.ke/oped/Opinion/Uhuru-Kenyatta-Jomo-Kenyatta-The-Hague-Kapenguria/-/440808/2467776/-/9vlj79z/-/index.html. Accessed May 15, 2016.

Biko, Jackson. "I Miss the Power to Do Good, Former AG Njonjo Says." *Daily Nation*, May 22, 2015. www.nation.co.ke/lifestyle/I-miss-the-power-to-do-good/-/1190/2725274/-/crwbxs/-/index.html. Accessed April 5, 2016.

Cobain, Ian, and Richard Norton-Taylor. "Sins of Colonialists Lay Concealed for Decades in Secret Archive." *The Guardian*, April 18, 2012.

Bibliography

www.theguardian.com/uk/2012/apr/18/sins-colonialists-concealed-secret-archive. Accessed February 4, 2016.

Juma, Paul. "Kiereini Cleared for Boardroom Return." *Daily Nation*, August 22, 2013. www.nation.co.ke/business/news/Kiereini+cleared+for+boardroom+return/-/1006/1964230/-/d1sic/-/index.html. Accessed April 5, 2016.

Juma, Victor. "Kenyatta Business Empire Goes into Expansion Drive." *Business Daily*, November 11, 2013. www.businessdailyafrica.com/Corporate-News/Kenyatta-business-empire-goes-into-expansion-drive/-/539550/2069704/-/g4fwge/-/index.html. Accessed April 5, 2016.

"Moi-Era Political Elite Exits Top CfC Stanbic Shareholders Roll." *Business Daily*, January 30, 2014. www.businessdailyafrica.com/Moi-era-political-elite-transfer-Sh4-billion-CfC-Stanbic-shares/-/539552/2165810/-/r5f84s/-/index.html. Accessed April 6, 2016.

Kagwanja, Peter. "Generational Change of Guard and the Odinga Dynasty." *Daily Nation*, October 25, 2014. www.nation.co.ke/oped/Opinion/Raila-Odinga-Dynasty-Politics-Nyanza/-/440808/2499252/-/21j64xz/-/index.html. Accessed May 24, 2016.

Kahura, Dauti. "Who Is Who in the Exclusive Big Land Owners' Register." *East African Standard*, October 3, 2004. https://web.archive.org/web/20140227111355/www.marsgroupkenya.org/blog/2008/02/04/who-owns-Kenya/. Accessed April 14, 2014.

Kaikai, Linus. "When Kenyatta and Jaramogi Were Caught Up in Cold War Intrigues." *Daily Nation*, December 14, 2013. www.nation.co.ke/news/politics/When-Kenyatta-and-Jaramogi–were-caught-up-in-Cold-War-intrigues/-/1064/2112244/-/dehpkdz/-/index.html. Accessed February 4, 2016.

Kamau, John. "How Tom Mboya Used Rawson Macharia." *Daily Nation*, December 18, 2008. www.nation.co.ke/oped/Opinion/-/440808/503980/-/41loor/-/index.html. Accessed December 17, 2015.

"How Independence Era Leaders Laid Their Hands on Lands of Quitting Whites." *Daily Nation*, November 9, 2009. www.nation.co.ke/News/-/1056/684064/-/uon487/-/index.html. Accessed April 5, 2016.

"How Kenyatta Government Flouted Loan Deal So That Big Names Could Get Land." *Daily Nation*, November 11, 2009. www.nation.co.ke/News/-/1056/685210/-/uontyq/-/index.html. Accessed February 4, 2016.

"Top Officials Bypassed Mzee to Acquire Land at the Coast." *Daily Nation*, November 12, 2009. www.nation.co.ke/news/-/1056/685756/-/4chhdiz/-/index.html. Accessed April 5, 2016.

"How Mahihu Got Kenyatta to Sign Away Beach Plots." *Business Daily*, November 19, 2009. www.businessdailyafrica.com/Corporate-News/-/539550/685660/-/15s7yj1/-/index.html. Accessed April 5, 2016.

"Coup Haste That Saw Lumumba Institute Collapse." *Daily Nation*, March 13, 2010. www.nation.co.ke/news/politics/Coup-haste-that-saw-Lumumba-Institute-collapse-/-/1064/879104/-/rwun43/-/index.html. Accessed January 10, 2016.

"How Former First Lady Lost a Huge Chunk of Land in Ruiru." *Daily Nation*, Sunday February 14, 2016. www.nation.co.ke/oped/Opinion/How-former-first-lady-lost-a-huge-chunk-of-land-in-Ruiru/-/440808/3075646/-/p7rhtuz/-/index.html. Accessed April 5, 2016.

"Jomo's Foreign Minister Dr Munyua Waiyaki Dies at 91." *Daily Nation*, April 26, 2017. www.nation.co.ke/news/Jomo-s-foreign-minister-Dr-Waiyaki-dies-/1056-3903938-86x4gx/index.html. Accessed January 5, 2019.

"Kenyatta Party Threatened by Tribal Rivalries." *The Times*, January 3, 1963.

Kimani, Mwaura. "Is It the End of the Affair for Kenya's Oligarchs?" *Daily Nation*, November 12, 2011. www.nation.co.ke/News/Is+this+the+end+of+the+affair+for+Kenyas+oligarchs/-/1056/1272122/-/1358b1h/-/index.html. Accessed April 6, 2016.

Kwama, Kenneth. "Mama Ngina Listed Top Investor at Kenya Power with 2.2 Million Shares." *Business Daily*, May 20, 2013. www.businessdailyafrica.com/Corporate-News/Kenya-Power-puts-Mama-Ngina-on-top-shareholders-list/-/539550/1857144/-/a58fcl/-/index.html. Accessed April 5, 2016.

"When 'Ghosts' Haunted Kenya's First President Mzee Jomo Kenyatta out of State House." *The Standard*, July 12, 2013. www.standardmedia.co.ke/article/2000088164/when-ghosts-haunted-kenya-s-first-president-mzee-jomo-kenyatta-out-of-state-house. Accessed May 19, 2016.

"Jackson Angaine Dominated Politics in Eastern Province for over Five Decades." *The Standard*, November 15, 2013. www.standardmedia.co.ke/article/2000097705/jackson-angaine-dominated-politics-in-eastern-province-for-over-five-decades. Accessed May 19, 2016.

Muchui, David. "Land Shortage Hits Town as Individuals Grab 200 Plots." *Daily Nation*, February 24, 2015. www.nation.co.ke/counties/Land-shortage-hits-town-as-individuals-grab-200-plots/-/1107872/2634448/-/153kkia/-/index.html. Accessed December 16, 2015.

Mungati, R. "Ex-PC's Kin Battle for SH5bn Estate." *Daily Nation*, January 10, 2015. www.nation.co.ke/news/Ex-PC-kin-battle-for-Sh5bn-estate/-/1056/2585192/-/o4s9di/-/index.html. Accessed April 5, 2016.

Mutembei, Phares. "CS Charity Ngilu Urges Meru Residents to Avoid Court during Land Disputes." *The Standard*, November 30, 2014. www.standardmedia.co.ke/article/2000143050/cs-charity-ngilu-urges-meru-residents-to-avoid-court-during-land-disputes. Accessed December 16, 2015.

Mwaura, Peter. "Koinange's Death Marks the End of a Dynasty That Reigned in Kiambu." *Daily Nation*, September 7, 2012. www.nation.co.ke/oped/

Opinion/-/440808/1499610/-/lmkb7bz/-/index.html. Accessed May 24, 2016.
Namwaya, Otsieno. "Who Owns Kenya?" *East African Standard*, October 1, 2004. https://web.archive.org/web/20140227111355/www.marsgroup kenya.org/blog/2008/02/04/who-owns-Kenya/. Accessed April 14, 2014.
"Nyambene Residents Desperate for Land Titles." *Daily Nation*, August 25, 2015. www.nation.co.ke/oped/Letters/Nyambene-residents–desperate- for-land-titles/-/440806/2846254/-/format/xhtml/-/q3mr34/-/index.html. Accessed December 16, 2015.
Nzioka, Patrick, and Bernard Namunane. "Political Families Own Half of Private Wealth." *Daily Nation*, February 20, 2014. http://mobile.nation .co.ke/news/Kenyans-Wealth-Families-Politicians/-/1950946/2215578/-/ format/xhtml/-/krwmhtz/-/index.html. Accessed April 5, 2016.
Omari, Emman. "When They Were Kings: How Kiambu's Power Men Ruled." *Daily Nation*, June 15, 2011. www.nation.co.ke/counties/ When-they-were-kings-How-Kiambu-power-men-ruled-/-/1107872/118 1458/-/jobdxmz/-/index.html. Accessed February 6, 2015.
"Presidents Took Advantage of Legal Gap to Increase Ministries." *Daily Nation*, April 23, 2013. www.nation.co.ke/oped/opinion/Ministries-Cab inet/440808-1756650-10s7plxz/index.html. Accessed August 6, 2019.
"The Day the President Died." The Weekly Review, September 1, 1978.
"The Sh10bn Empire Koinange Built." *Daily Nation*, July 6, 2013. www.nation.co.ke/news/politics/The-Sh10bn-empire-Koinange-built/-/ 1064/1907266/-/10eyu9cz/-/index.html. Accessed April 6, 2016.
"Uhuru Appointments Are Proof That Political Dynasties Alive and Well." *Daily Nation*, May 2, 2015. www.nation.co.ke/news/politics/Uhuru- appointments-are-proof-that-political-dynasties-alive/-/1064/2704546/-/ lep0m7/-/index.html. Accessed April 5, 2016.
Wambugu, Benson. "Thirty-Two Years On, Koinange Family Fights over Estate as Brokers Profit." *Daily Nation*, July 6, 2016. www.nation.co.ke/News/politics/Family-fights-as-lawyers-make-a-kill/-/ 1064/1907272/-/c30mekz/-/index.html. Accessed April 5, 2016.
Wanambisi, Laban. "We Own 30,000 Acres in Taveta – Uhuru." *Capital News*, February 25, 2013. www.capitalfm.co.ke/news/2013/02/we- own-30000-acres-in-taveta-uhuru/. Accessed April 5, 2016.

Websites

www.africaresearchinstitute.org

Films

"End of Empire." Granada Television.

Index

Angaine, Jackson H., 33, 109, 138, 142–158, 168, 172, 176–178, 185–195, 203–205, 214, 217, 226–232, 237, 246, 256, 268
Arwings-Kodhek, Clement, 107, 207

Baimungi, Field Marshal, 24, 33, 142, 144, 147, 159–174, 202
Banda, Hastings Kamuzu, 71, 121
Boit, P. K., 191
Brockett, Neil, 189–190

Catling, R. C., 160
Chadwick, Jonathan, 110
China, General, 13, 143, 159
Chotara, Kariuki, 74
Chui, General, 144, 168–173, 200, 202

Gachati, Peter, 184, 191
Gaciatta, Abraham, 174, 204
Garner, Sir Saville, 188
Gavaghan, Terence J. F., 177
Gecaga, Udi, 262
Gichoya, K. N., 117
Gichuru, James, 10, 30, 60, 78–79, 81, 91–94, 105–110, 136, 138, 186–189, 194, 197, 226, 230, 238, 242, 246, 256, 264
Gituma, Jenaru, 174
Griffith-Jones, Eric, 103

Hanyotu, James, 261
Hinga, Bernard, 261
Hinga, Waiyaki wa, 159

Josiah, S. O., 211

Kaggia, Bildad, 1, 12, 56, 99, 109, 131, 133, 166, 172–174, 195–196, 198, 200–203, 215, 229, 246
Kahengeri, Gitu wa, 176
Kariithi, Godfrey K., 215, 238, 261
Kariuki, J. M., 24, 99, 109, 131–133, 182, 246, 248, 250, 255–258
Kariuki, Jesse, 159, 191
Karumba, Kungu, 12
Keen, John, 232
Kenyatta, Jane, 59, 262
Kenyatta, Jomo, 11–14
  and Africanization of land ownership, 33, 131, 179, 187, 235
  "Back to the Land" speech, 181
  and Coast land, 231–240
  and conception of decolonization, 64–65
  and conception of the family, 56–62
  and disempowered regionalism, 30, 33, 209, 249
  and early years, 3–15
  and *Facing Mount Kenya*, 8–9, 13, 38, 42–43, 45, 47–48, 51, 54, 57, 59, 113, 156, 181, 224
  and family, 246, 253–254, 258, 261–265
  and Gatundu house, 37, 87–88, 90, 158–159, 167, 206, 247, 263
  and GEMA, 248, 250–251
  and *harambee*, 17, 269
  and KADU, 78–90, 110, 115–126, 134–137, 139, 232, 243, 256, 268
  and KANU, 22, 32, 35, 79–81, 84–85, 87–94, 98–99, 107–111, 116, 120, 130, 155, 159, 191, 198, 201, 206–208, 210, 212, 227, 234, 242, 251, 253, 255, 258, 262, 268
  and Kenyatta campaign, 31, 66–67, 70, 74, 76, 82, 90, 92–94, 143

and Kenyatta succession, 34, 111, 138, 219, 222, 240–241, 245–246, 248, 250–253, 259–260, 270
and Kiambu, 4, 10, 39, 59–62, 98, 141, 159, 246, 250, 262, 267
and Kikuyu thought, 42, 45
and Kikuyu tribe, 57, 61, 156, 172, 266
and land consolidation, 89, 182, 184–186, 225
and the landless, 6, 23–24, 26, 28, 31, 37, 87, 96–97, 105, 108, 129–132, 141, 156, 172, 174, 176, 178–180, 182–183, 186, 195, 199–201, 213–218, 232, 251, 268–271
and legacy, 272–275
and Maasailand, 231–240
and Maralal conference, 85–86
and Mau Mau bodyguards, 175–176
and Mau Mau movement, 1–2, 22–24, 74–79, 84, 96, 100, 173, 267–268
and Mau Mau oathing, 12
and Mau Mau resilience, 24, 36, 108, 129, 142–146, 158–170, 202, 269
and Mombasa state house, 261
and Nairobi state house, 56
and nationalism, 11–13, 51, 76, 108, 113
and Office of the President, 30–31, 33, 36, 170, 173, 177, 199, 202, 207–212, 217, 278
and Pan-Africanism, 46
and parliamentary powers, 41, 46, 49, 67, 74, 88, 108, 116–119, 123, 128, 134–137, 139, 145, 179–180, 201, 205, 207, 215, 227, 242–245, 251, 255–259, 268, 271, 273
and political imagination, 33, 38, 41, 45–46, 63, 213, 267, 269–270, 272
and politicization of land affairs, 33, 102, 180, 189, 198, 212, 219, 222–231, 270
and presidential powers, 32, 115–116, 128–129, 135, 139, 179, 218, 221, 239, 257, 270–272, 274
and prime minister, 107–108, 116–117, 120, 123, 130, 135, 155, 159, 165–166
and provincial administration, 27–30, 33, 93, 177, 180, 191, 207–210, 212, 269
and self-help, 17, 53–55, 217
and the squatters. *See* landless
and tribalism, 48–49, 58, 64, 87, 112, 178, 246, 248, 266
Kenyatta, Mama Ngina, 59, 238, 252, 260, 263–264, 274
Kenyatta, Margaret, 59, 261–262
Kenyatta, Muhoho, 60
Kenyatta, Peter Magana, 59, 260
Kenyatta, Peter Muigai, 59, 260, 262
Kenyatta, Uhuru Muigai, 60, 262, 265, 273
Kiano, Julius, 68, 75–76, 91, 109, 138, 186, 238, 246, 256
Kibaki, Mwai, 175, 207, 246, 256, 261, 273
Kiereini, Jeremiah Gitau, 177, 264
Kimathi, General Dedan, 144
Kimunai, A., 191
Kiprotich, C., 171
Koinange, Charles, 264
Koinange, Peter Mbiyu, 10, 76, 109, 261
Koinange, Senior Chief, 59
Koitie, J. K. arap, 108
Konchellah, John ole, 232
Kubai, Fred, 1, 12, 74, 166
Kubu Kubu, General, 166

Lamare, Stanley, 174
Lennox-Boyd, Alan, 72
Linyiru, M'Iminuki, 1

M'Kithumai, Ciorukunga, 160, 162
M'Kobia, M'Murungi, 169
M'Mûraa, Chief, 153
M'Mworia, Julius, 152
MacDonald, Malcom, 46, 109, 116, 119–124, 126–127, 130, 137–138, 195–196, 226
Macharia, Rawson, 72
MacLeod, Ian, 78
Mahihu, Eliud, 170, 173–174, 191, 202–205, 210, 238, 261
Maina, K. M., 191
Makasembo, D. O., 73
Malinowski, Bronisław, 8, 50, 53

Mate, Bernard, 68, 148, 152–153, 204
Mathenge, Isaiah, 176, 238, 254
Mboya, Tom, 24, 34, 68, 72–73, 76, 79–82, 88, 91–92, 94, 99, 107–110, 120–121, 134–138, 158, 186, 193–194, 198, 207, 222, 226, 236, 239, 241–248, 250, 270
Mburu, James, 163–164, 167–168, 191, 211
McKenzie, Bruce, 102–107, 110, 127, 130, 132, 138, 186, 188, 193–197, 215, 227, 230, 245, 264
Michuki, John, 265
Moi, Daniel arap, 68, 117, 123–124, 135–136, 138, 186, 205, 242, 245–247, 251–252, 255–256, 260–261, 265, 273–274
Mucemi, L. Ngatia, 191
Mûgambî, Reverend Stephan, 152
Muimi, James, 68
Muliro, Masinde, 68, 124, 135
Mungai, Njoroge, 30, 60, 79, 109, 138, 166, 169, 216, 238, 242, 245–246, 252, 256, 260, 262
Munyi, Kamwithi, 204
Murgor, William, 123, 145
Murumbi, Joseph, 16, 36, 70, 73, 108, 124, 126, 138, 207, 222, 236, 242, 246
Muthama, Nyokabi, 60
Muthamia, Julius, 174, 202, 204–205
Mwangi, R., 191
Mwariama, Field Marshal, 1–2, 144, 159–168
Mwendwa, Eliud, 109

Natu, Koi ole, 91
Ndegwa, Duncan, 23, 170, 174–175, 177, 230–231, 239, 265
Ngala, Ronald, 68, 78, 92, 101, 117, 119, 121, 134–135, 137, 198, 207, 232, 235–236, 242
Ngei, Paul, 12, 74, 87, 98–99, 107, 109, 124, 138, 166, 173–174, 246
Njonjo, Charles, 29–30, 60, 161, 195, 209, 211, 226, 229–230, 238–239, 243–246, 250, 255–258, 264–265
Njonjo, Chief Josiah, 60
Nkrumah, Kwame, 16, 71, 213, 239

Nyachae, Simeon, 211–212
Nyagah, Jeremiah, 68, 109, 157, 256
Nyambati Nyamweya, S. Nyambati, 191
Nyamweya, J., 118
Nyerere, Julius, 16, 50, 120, 274

O'Loughlin, J. A., 184, 229
Obote, Milton, 120
Odinga, Oginga, 66–70, 73–74, 76, 78, 80, 82, 88, 92–93, 99, 107, 109–110, 120, 124, 131, 136, 138, 158, 174, 189, 198, 201–207, 240–244, 246, 248, 255, 270
Omanga, A. S., 190
Oneko, Achieng, 12, 137, 166, 196
Owino, Daniel, 191

Pearson, Commander, 175
Pinto, Pio da Gama, 24, 201

Renison, Sir Patrick Muir, 74–78, 80, 82, 97–98, 105
Rotich, W. K., 136

Sagini, Lawrence, 190
Sandys, Duncan, 121, 124, 126–127, 134, 137
Senghor, Léopold Sédar, 16, 93, 213, 223, 274
Seroney, Jean-Marie, 123, 256–259
Shikuyah, Peter, 190
Shimechero, Z. B., 217
Singh, Chanan, 109
Slade, Humphrey, 265
Soi, A., 191
Stephan Mugambi, Reverend Stephan, 146

Thimangu-Kaunyangi, K. M., 204
Thung'u, Arthur Wanyoike, 175, 258
Tipis, Justus ole, 68, 117, 124, 232
Toweett, Taaitta arap, 68, 123
Turnbull, Richard, 130

Waiyaki, Munyua, 158, 261
Walters, P. E., 163
Wambui-Pratt, Christine, 60
Wariithi, Henri C., 118
Wilson, F. R., 151

African Studies Series

1 *City Politics: A Study of Leopoldville, 1962–63*, J. S. La Fontaine
2 *Studies in Rural Capitalism in West Africa*, Polly Hill
3 *Land Policy in Buganda*, Henry W. West
4 *The Nigerian Military: A Sociological Analysis of Authority and Revolt, 1960–67*, Robin Luckham
5 *The Ghanaian Factory Worker: Industrial Man in Africa*, Margaret Peil
6 *Labour in the South African Gold Mines*, Francis Wilson
7 *The Price of Liberty: Personality and Politics in Colonial Nigeria*, Kenneth W. J. Post and George D. Jenkins
8 *Subsistence to Commercial Farming in Present-Day Buganda: An Economic and Anthropological Survey*, Audrey I. Richards, Fort Sturrock, and Jean M. Fortt (eds),
9 *Dependence and Opportunity: Political Change in Ahafo*, John Dunn and A. F. Robertson
10 *African Railwaymen: Solidarity and Opposition in an East African Labour Force*, R. D. Grillo
11 *Islam and Tribal Art in West Africa*, René A. Bravmann,
12 *Modern and Traditional Elites in the Politics of Lagos*, P. D. Cole
13 *Asante in the Nineteenth Century: The Structure and Evaluation of a Political Order*, Ivor Wilks
14 *Culture, Tradition and Society in the West African Novel*, Emmanuel Obiechina
15 *Saints and Politicians*, Donal B. Cruise O'Brien
16 *The Lions of Dagbon: Political Change in Northern Ghana*, Martin Staniland
17 *Politics of Decolonization: Kenya Europeans and the Land Issue 1960–1965*, Gary B. Wasserman
18 *Muslim Brotherhoods in the Nineteenth-Century Africa*, B. G. Martin
19 *Warfare in the Sokoto Caliphate: Historical and Sociological Perspectives*, Joseph P. Smaldone
20 *Liberia and Sierra Leone: An Essay in Comparative Politics*, Christopher Clapham
21 *Adam Kok's Griquas: A Study in the Development of Stratification in South Africa*, Robert Ross
22 *Class, Power and Ideology in Ghana: The Railwaymen of Sekondi*, Richard Jeffries
23 *West African States: Failure and Promise*, John Dunn (ed)
24 *Afrikaaners of the Kalahari: White Minority in a Black State*, Margo Russell and Martin Russell

25 *A Modern History of Tanganyika*, John Iliffe
26 *A History of African Christianity 1950–1975*, Adrian Hastings
27 *Slaves, Peasants and Capitalists in Southern Angola, 1840–1926*, W. G. Clarence-Smith
28 *The Hidden Hippopotamus: Reappraised in African History: The Early Colonial Experience in Western Zambia*, GywnPrins
29 *Families Divided: The Impact of Migrant Labour in Lesotho*, Colin Murray
30 *Slavery, Colonialism and Economic Growth in Dahomey, 1640–1960*, Patrick Manning
31 *Kings, Commoners and Concessionaries: The Evolution of Dissolution of the Nineteenth-Century Swazi State*, Philip Bonner
32 *Oral Poetry and Somali Nationalism: The Case of Sayid Mahammad 'Abdille Hasan*, Said S. Samatar
33 *The Political Economy of Pondoland 1860–1930*, William Beinart
34 *Volkskapitalisme: Class, Capitals and Ideology in the Development of Afrikaner Nationalism, 1934–1948*, Dan O'Meara
35 *The Settler Economies: Studies in the Economic History of Kenya and Rhodesia 1900–1963*, Paul Mosely
36 *Transformations in Slavery: A History of Slavery in Africa,1st edition*, Paul Lovejoy
37 *Amilcar Cabral: Revolutionary Leadership and People's War*, Patrick Chabal
38 *Essays on the Political Economy of Rural Africa*, Robert H. Bates
39 *Ijeshas and Nigerians: The Incorporation of a Yoruba Kingdom, 1890s-1970s*, J. D. Y. Peel
40 *Black People and the South African War, 1899–1902*, Peter Warwick
41 *A History of Niger 1850–1960*, Finn Fuglestad
42 *Industrialisation and Trade Union Organization in South Africa, 1924–1955*, Stephen Ellis
43 *The Rising of the Red Shawls: A Revolt in Madagascar 1895–1899*, Stephen Ellis
44 *Slavery in Dutch South Africa*, Nigel Worden
45 *Law, Custom and Social Order: The Colonial Experience in Malawi and Zambia*, Martin Chanock
46 *Salt of the Desert Sun: A History of Salt Production and Trade in the Central Sudan*, Paul E. Lovejoy
47 *Marrying Well: Marriage, Status and Social Change among the Educated Elite in Colonial Lagos*, Kristin Mann
48 *Language and Colonial Power: The Appropriation of Swahili in the Former Belgian Congo, 1880–1938*, Johannes Fabian
49 *The Shell Money of the Slave Trade*, Jan Hogendorn and Marion Johnson

50 *Political Domination in Africa*, Patrick Chabal
51 *The Southern Marches of Imperial Ethiopia: Essays in History and Social Anthropology*, Donald Donham and Wendy James
52 *Islam and Urban Labor in Northern Nigeria: The Making of a Muslim Working Class*, Paul M. Lubeck
53 *Horn and Crescent: Cultural Change and Traditional Islam on the East African Coast, 800–1900*, Randall L. Pouwels
54 *Capital and Labour on the Kimberley Diamond Fields, 1871–1890*, Robert Vicat Turrell
55 *National and Class Conflict in the Horn of Africa*, John Markakis
56 *Democracy and Prebendal Politics in Nigeria: The Rise and Fall of the Second Republic*, Richard A. Joseph
57 *Entrepreneurs and Parasites: The Struggle for Indigenous Capitalism in Zaire*, Janet MacGaffey
58 *The African Poor: A History*, John Iliffe
59 *Palm Oil and Protest: An Economic History of the Ngwa Region, South-Eastern Nigeria, 1800–1980*, Susan M. Martin
60 *France and Islam in West Africa, 1860–1960*, Christopher Harrison
61 *Transformation and Continuity in Revolutionary Ethiopia*, Christopher Clapham
62 *Prelude to the Mahdiyya: Peasants and Traders in the Shendi Region, 1821–1885*, Anders Bjorkelo
63 *Wa and the Wala: Islam and Polity in Northwestern Ghana*, Ivor Wilks
64 *H.C. Bankole-Bright and Politics in Colonial Sierra Leone, 1919–1958*, Akintola Wyse
65 *Contemporary West African States*, Donal Cruise O'Brien, John Dunn, and Richard Rathbone (eds)
66 *The Oromo of Ethiopia: A History, 1570–1860*, Mohammed Hassen
67 *Slavery and African Life: Occidental, Oriental, and African Slave Trades*, Patrick Manning
68 *Abraham Esau's War: A Black South African War in the Cape, 1899–1902*, Bill Nasson
69 *The Politics of Harmony: Land Dispute Strategies in Swaziland*, Laurel L. Rose
70 *Zimbabwe's Guerrilla War: Peasant Voices*, Norma J. Kriger
71 *Ethiopia: Power and Protest: Peasant Revolts in the Twentieth-Century*, Gebru Tareke
72 *White Supremacy and Black Resistance in Pre-Industrial South Africa: The Making of the Colonial Order in the Eastern Cape, 1770–1865*, Clifton C. Crais
73 *The Elusive Granary: Herder, Farmer, and State in Northern Kenya*, Peter D. Little

74 *The Kanyok of Zaire: An Institutional and Ideological History to 1895*, John C. Yoder
75 *Pragmatism in the Age of Jihad: The Precolonial State of Bundu*, Michael A. Gomez
76 *Slow Death for Slavery: The Course of Abolition in Northern Nigeria, 1897–1936*, Paul E. Lovejoy and Jan S. Hogendorn
77 *West African Slavery and Atlantic Commerce: The Senegal River Valley, 1700–1860*, James F. Searing
78 *A South African Kingdom: The Pursuit of Security in the Nineteenth-Century Lesotho*, Elizabeth A. Elredge
79 *State and Society in Pre-colonial Asante*, T. C. McCaskie
80 *Islamic Society and State Power in Senegal: Disciples and Citizens in Fatick*, Leonardo A. Villalon
81 *Ethnic Pride and Racial Prejudice in Victorian Cape Town: Group Identity and Social Practice*, Vivian Bickford-Smith
82 *The Eritrean Struggle for Independence: Domination, Resistance and Nationalism, 1941–1993*, RuthIyob
83 *Corruption and State Politics in Sierra Leone*, William Reno
84 *The Culture of Politics in Modern Kenya*, Angelique Haugerud
85 *Africans: The History of a Continent, 1st edition*, John Iliffe
86 *From Slave Trade to "Legitimate" Commerce: The Commercial Transition in Nineteenth-Century West Africa*, Robin Law (ed)
87 *Leisure and Society in Colonial Brazzaville*, Phyllis Martin
88 *Kingship and State: The Buganda Dynasty*, Christopher Wrigley
89 *Decolonialization and African Life: The Labour Question in French and British Africa*, Frederick Cooper
90 *Misreading the African Landscape: Society and Ecology in an African Forest-Savannah Mosaic*, James Fairhead, and Melissa Leach
91 *Peasant Revolution in Ethiopia: The Tigray People's Liberation Front, 1975–1991*, John Young
92 *Senegambia and the Atlantic Slave Trade*, Boubacar Barry
93 *Commerce and Economic Change in West Africa: The Oil Trade in the Nineteenth Century*, Martin Lynn
94 *Slavery and French Colonial Rule in West Africa: Senegal, Guinea and Mali*, Martin A. Klein
95 *East African Doctors: A History of the Modern Profession*, John Iliffe
96 *Middlemen of the Cameroons Rivers: The Duala and Their Hinterland, c.1600–1960*, Ralph Derrick, Ralph A. Austen, and Jonathan Derrick
97 *Masters and Servants on the Cape Eastern Frontier, 1760–1803*, Susan Newton-King

98 *Status and Respectability in the Cape Colony, 1750–1870: A Tragedy of Manners*, Robert Ross
99 *Slaves, Freedmen and Indentured Laborers in Colonial Mauritius*, Richard B. Allen
100 *Transformations in Slavery: A History of Slavery in Africa*, 2nd edition, Paul E. Lovejoy
101 *The Peasant Cotton Revolution in West Africa: Cote d'Ivoire, 1880–1995*, Thomas E. Basset
102 *Re-imagining Rwanda: Conflict, Survival and Disinformation in the Late Twentieth Century*, Johan Pottier
103 *The Politics of Evil: Magic, State Power and the Political Imagination in South Africa*, Clifton Crais
104 *Transforming Mozambique: The Politics of Privatization, 1975–2000*, M.Anne Pitcher
105 *Guerrilla Veterans in Post-War Zimbabwe: Symbolic and Violent Politics, 1980–1987*, Norma J. Kriger
106 *An Economic History of Imperial Madagascar, 1750–1895: The Rise and Fall of an Island Empire*, Gwyn Campbell
107 *Honour in African History*, John Iliffe
108 *Africans: A History of a Continent*, 2nd edition, John Iliffe
109 *Guns, Race, and Power in Colonial South Africa*, William Kelleher Storey
110 *Islam and Social Change in French West Africa: History of an Emancipatory Community*, Sean Hanretta
111 *Defeating Mau Mau, Creating Kenya: Counterinsurgency, Civil War and Decolonization*, Daniel Branch
112 *Christianity and Genocide in Rwanda*, Timothy Longman
113 *From Africa to Brazil: Culture, Identity, and an African Slave Trade, 1600–1830*, Walter Hawthorne
114 *Africa in the Time of Cholera: A History of Pandemics from 1817 to the Present*, Myron Echenberg
115 *A History of Race in Muslim West Africa, 1600–1960*, Bruce S. Hall
116 *Witchcraft and Colonial Rule in Kenya, 1900–1955*, Katherine Luongo
117 *Transformations in Slavery: A History of Slavery in Africa*, 3rd edition, Paul E. Lovejoy
118 *The Rise of the Trans-Atlantic Slave Trade in Western Africa, 1300–1589*, Toby Green
119 *Party Politics and Economic Reform in Africa's Democracies*, M. Anne Pitcher
120 *Smugglers and Saints of the Sahara: Regional Connectivity in the Twentieth Century*, Judith Scheele

121 *Cross-Cultural Exchange in the Atlantic World: Angola and Brazil during the Era of the Slave Trade*, Roquinaldo Ferreira
122 *Ethnic Patriotism and the East African Revival*, Derek Peterson
123 *Black Morocco: A History of Slavery and Islam*, Chouki El Hamel
124 *An African Slaving Port and the Atlantic World: Benguela and Its Hinterland*, Mariana Candido
125 *Making Citizens in Africa: Ethnicity, Gender, and National Identity in Ethiopia*, Lahra Smith
126 *Slavery and Emancipation in Islamic East Africa: From Honor to Respectability*, Elisabeth McMahon
127 *A History of African Motherhood: The Case of Uganda, 700–1900*, Rhiannon Stephens
128 *The Borders of Race in Colonial South Africa: The Kat River Settlement, 1829–1856*, Robert Ross
129 *From Empires to NGOs in the West African Sahel: The Road to Nongovernmentality*, Gregory Mann
130 *Dictators and Democracy in African Development: The Political Economy of Good Governance in Nigeria*, A. Carl LeVan
131 *Water, Civilization and Power in Sudan: The Political Economy of Military-Islamist State Building*, Harry Verhoeven
132 *The Fruits of Freedom in British Togoland: Literacy, Politics and Nationalism, 1914–2014*, Kate Skinner
133 *Political Thought and the Public Sphere in Tanzania: Freedom, Democracy and Citizenship in the Era of Decolonization*, Emma Hunter
134 *Political Identity and Conflict in Central Angola, 1975–2002*, Justin Pearce
135 *From Slavery to Aid: Politics, Labour, and Ecology in the Nigerian Sahel, 1800–2000*, Benedetta Rossi
136 *National Liberation in Postcolonial Southern Africa: A Historical Ethnography of SWAPO's Exile Camps*, Christian A. Williams
137 *Africans: A History of a Continent*, 3rd edition, John Iliffe
138 *Colonial Buganda and the End of Empire: Political Thought and Historical Imagination in Africa*, Jonathon L. Earle
139 *The Struggle over State Power in Zimbabwe: Law and Politics since 1950*, George Karekwaivanane
140 *Transforming Sudan: Decolonisation, Economic Development and State Formation*, Alden Young
141 *Colonizing Consent: Rape and Governance in South Africa's Eastern Cape*, Elizabeth Thornberry
142 *The Value of Disorder: Autonomy, Prosperity and Plunder in the Chadian Sahara*, Julien Brachet and Judith Scheele

143 *The Politics of Poverty: Policy-Making and Development in Rural Tanzania*, Felicitas Becker
144 *Boundaries, Communities, and State-Making in West Africa: The Centrality of the Margins*, Paul Nugent
145 *Politics and Violence in Burundi: The Language of Truth in an Emerging State*, Aidan Russell
146 *Power and the Presidency in Kenya: The Jomo Kenyatta Years*, Anaïs Angelo